DILKE

Discover books by Roy Jenkins published by
Bloomsbury Reader at
www.bloomsbury.com/RoyJenkins

Baldwin
Dilke
European Diary, 1977–1981
Mr. Balfour's Poodle
Portraits & Miniatures
Truman

DILKE
A Victorian Tragedy

ROY JENKINS

BLOOMSBURY READER

LONDON · NEW DELHI · NEW YORK · SYDNEY

This edition published in 2012 by Bloomsbury Reader

Bloomsbury Reader is a division of Bloomsbury Publishing Plc,

50 Bedford Square, London WC1B 3DP

First published 1958 by Collins as *Sir Charles Dilke: A Victorian Tragedy*

ISBN: 978 1 4482 0049 8
eISBN: 978 1 4482 0181 5

Visit www.bloomsburyreader.com to find out more about our authors and their books
You will find extracts, author interviews, author events and you can sign up for
newsletters to be the first to hear about our latest releases and special offers

Contents

Preface

My principal source of information has been the Dilke Papers in the British Museum. They were placed there by Miss Gertrude Tuckwell in 1938. She was the niece of the second Lady Dilke and the literary executrix of Sir Charles. She had used the papers to complete the standard biography of Dilke which had been begun by Stephen Gwynn, Irish Nationalist M.P., and which was published in 1917. This amply-proportioned two-volume work is still invaluable to any study of Dilke, even though it eschews the divorce case and makes most ruthless use of Dilke's own writings, omitting, altering and even interpolating without any indication of what has been done.

Moreover, Miss Tuckwell clearly exercised her own censorship over the papers. Dilke himself was addicted to laceration (see p. 279 *infra*.), but it seems clear that much which he left intact was subsequently excised by Miss Tuckwell. In addition she stipulated in the terms of her bequest to the Museum that Dilke's papers dealing with the case should not be available for inspection until 1950 had passed and the death of Mrs. Crawford had occurred. Later she made the terms still more strict. When both these qualifications had been fulfilled Mr. Harold Macmillan was to pronounce whether the papers could be seen. The Prime Minister (then Foreign Secretary) discharged this duty in the autumn of 1955 and freed the papers; in addition he gave to the Museum a box of papers which Miss Tuckwell had placed in his custody before her death. The hitherto reserved volume and the papers which were made available by Mr. Macmillan provide the bulk of the new information which I have used in the chapters on the case.

References are given in most cases to the volume and folio number of the document quoted. This practice has, however, been made more difficult by the decision of the Manuscript Department of the Museum to re-arrange the Dilke Papers between the time of my working on them and the publication of this book. As a result all references have had to be changed; and as some of the new volumes are still without folio numbers these folio numbers have in some cases been omitted. In chapters 13 and 14 the quotations to which no references are given are from the transcript of evidence taken at the second trial.

The list of those to whom I am indebted is long. Mr. Mark Bonham Garter, who suggested the subject to me; Mr. P. M. Williams, Fellow of Nuffield College, Oxford; Mr. Harry Pitt, Fellow of Worcester College, Oxford; Mr. J. E. S. Simon, Q.C.; Mr. W. H. Hughes; Mr. Geoffrey Roberts; Mr. Anthony Barnes; Lady Waverley (the daughter of J. E. C. Bodley); Miss Violet Markham; Mr. Christopher Dilke; Mr. Eustace Roskill, Q.C.; the late Mr. Harry K. Hudson (who was Dilke's private secretary from 1887 and who died only a few months ago); Mr. Francis Bywater; Lord Beaverbrook; Sir Frederick Whyte; and my successive secretaries, Mrs. P. C. Williams and Miss Julia Gill. To all these and to others whom I have not mentioned, I am very grateful.

London, June, 1958   ROY JENKINS

Preface to Revised Edition

Since this book was first published in 1958 the events and the characters with which it deals have formed the basis of a novel (*The Tangled Web*, by Betty Askwith, published in 1960), a television court drama (*The Dilke Case*, produced by Granada in 1960) and a highly successful stage play (*The Right Honourable Gentleman*, by Michael Dyne, first presented at Her Majesty's theatre in 1964). The first and third of these offered new, imaginative solutions to the Dilke riddle. But they uncovered no new facts. So an element of mystery still persists. This new edition does not claim to dispel it. Like the first edition, it leaves the reader, in the last resort, having to choose between a balance of probabilities. But it does offer a little new information about Cardinal Manning's attitude to the case, as well as a new surmise about the nature of Dilke's relationship with Mrs. Crawford. These changes occur in chapter 16. Otherwise, apart from adjustments to the description in chapter 15 of Rosebery's relationship to the case, the book is substantially the same.

ROY JENKINS

London, January, 1965

Introduction

Sir Charles Dilke died in 1911. Although he was then twenty-five years past the zenith of his career his name was still a great one. But in the years that have since gone by his fame has crumbled rapidly. There are few to-day to whom he is more than a rather shadowy Victorian politician who became involved in a half-forgotten scandal.

This decline has perhaps been inevitable, for his fame has had no base of solid attainment to which to anchor itself. He did not rise above the lower ranks of the Cabinet and there are no memorable measures which are popularly associated with his name. His career, broken as it was by the great scandal of the Crawford divorce case, was almost entirely an affair of promise and influence on others rather than of achievement. Had the case not occurred and shattered his life the story might have been very different. He was very near to high office and great power when the blow fell. If, as he himself insisted and as the evidence now available makes likely, he was the victim not of his own actions but of an elaborate conspiracy, his case was unique in recent British history. Few men of wealth and influence have found themselves hopelessly imprisoned in a net of entirely fabricated accusations. More, no doubt, have looked likely candidates for the premiership without in fact achieving that office. But no one, other than Dilke, has got within striking distance of 10 Downing Street and then been politically annihilated by a woman's false accusations.

In these circumstances the unravelling of the case, which dominated Dilke's own mind for more than a third of his life, inevitably becomes a major part of the interest of recounting his life and occupies a correspondingly large section of the book. But it would be a great mistake to see Dilke as a not very significant politican who achieved fame through his involvement in a divorce case. On the contrary, had the case never occurred, his name would to-day almost certainly be better known.

Moreover, the course of politics might have been markedly different. The discussion of political 'might-have-beens' is never the most useful historical pursuit, and the year 1886, when Dilke's influence could have been most decisive, is so full of events which might easily have gone otherwise that too much significance cannot be attributed to any single difference. Nevertheless, there is obviously a strong possibility that, had Dilke retained his full influence over Chamberlain the Liberal split might have involved only a Whig, and not a radical, secession from Gladstone. It was not that Dilke was notably less imperialist, more favourable to the Irish or more dazzled by Gladstone than Chamberlain. But he had an instinctive and deep-seated loyalty to the left which the latter entirely lacked; and his character was less ruthless and more compromising.

Had Dilke's influence prevailed many events might therefore have unfolded themselves differently. The twenty years of Tory hegemony which began in 1886 might have been avoided, the Irish question might have been settled much earlier, and, with this out of the way, a more radical Liberal party might have turned, in the 'nineties, to a massive programme of social reform. The effect on the emergence of the Labour party (which attracted much of Dilke's sympathy in his later years) might clearly have been considerable. The Crawford divorce case must therefore be recorded not only as a personal disaster for Dilke, but also as a major political event.

Chapter One

A Determined Preparation

Charles Wentworth Dilke was born at 76, Sloane Street, on September 4th, 1843. He was the first child of the marriage of his father, also called Charles Wentworth Dilke, with Mary Chatfield, the daughter of an Indian Army captain. Mary Dilke, almost certainly unhappy in her marriage, was to bear one more child, Ashton Dilke, born in 1850, before she fell into a decline which led to her death in 1853. Her influence on her son Charles was not great. She left him with a low church devoutness, but he was to grow out of this by the age of twenty. More important, perhaps, was her firm desire to entrust his upbringing to her father-in-law rather than to her husband. "But moral discipline your grandfather will teach you,"[1] she wrote to Charles a short time before her death.

It was not that Wentworth Dilke, as the father was known, was a dissolute man. In his early life he was admittedly idle, and did no work until his marriage at the age of thirty. This habit he apparently acquired in Florence, where, after leaving Westminster

1

School, he had been sent to live with the British Consul, Baron Kirkup. It persisted throughout his time at Cambridge and his first years as a young man in London. During this period, in the words of his son, "he was principally known to his friends for never missing a night at the Opera." After his marriage, however, he manifested a wide range of practical energies. Through his connection with the Royal Horticultural Society he founded two specialised but profitable periodicals—the *Gardeners' Chronicle** and the *Agricultural Gazette*—and added to his already comfortable means. He was an active member of the Society of Arts, and the experience which he gained through the organisation by the Society of a national exhibition of "art manufactures" led him to be one of the first to put forward the idea of the Great Exhibition of 1851. With three other members of the Society, Wentworth Dilke waited upon Prince Albert in 1849. At this meeting it was decided to proceed with the plans for the Exhibition. Six months later Wentworth Dilke was appointed one of an executive committee of four, and took a large share of the administrative responsibility for the whole enterprise.

When the Exhibition showed itself a great success, Wentworth Dilke was accorded his full share of the credit. He became—and remained—a close associate of the Prince Consort and a man who had the full approval of the Queen. He was offered, but declined, a knighthood. He achieved some international repute, and was showered with presents and minor decorations by foreign sovereigns. He established himself as a great man in the

---

* Joseph Paxton, formerly the Duke of Devonshire's gardener at Chatsworth and later the deviser of the Crystal Palace, was one of his collaborators in this enterprise.

field of exhibitions; and as exhibitions were very much the fashion of the age this gave him an occasional occupation of importance for the rest of his life. He was British Commissioner at the New York Industrial Exhibition of 1853, at the Paris Exhibition of 1855, and at a number of smaller displays. He was one of the five royal commissioners for the London Exhibition of 1862, and when he died of influenza at St. Petersburg in 1868 the occasion of his visit was to represent England at a Horticultural Exhibition. In the meantime he had been made a baronet in 1862—by the personal act of the Queen—and had sat in the House of Commons for three years as the Liberal member for Wallingford.

The aspect which he presented to the world was that of a highly successful man. He had a wide range of acquaintance—English and foreign, political, scientific and literary—and a comfortable fortune. He had established his family at 76, Sloane Street, on the border of Belgravia and Chelsea, a lease of which he had taken immediately after his marriage, and he rented Alice Holt, a small country property near Farnham.

His achievement was marred only by his unimportance within his own family. He was in no way indifferent to family ties. He encouraged the filling up of his house in London with his wife's relations. Her grandmother, her mother and her unmarried cousin all came to live there in 1840 (the last two surviving and remaining in Sloane Street until the 'eighties). Thirteen years later his own father gave up his house in Lower Grosvenor Place, made over his property to his son, and joined the Sloane Street establishment for the rest of his life. Wentworth Dilke could surround himself with dependent relations, but he could not make himself pivotal to the household which was thus created, and he could not win the respect of his elder son.

Of this latter fact there can be no doubt. Much later in his life Charles Dilke could look back and feel that his father had perhaps been harshly treated by himself and by others. "He was a man of great heart and of considerable brainpower," he was to write in 1890, "but brain-power wasted and heart misunderstood."[2] But at the time, in the 'fifties and the early 'sixties, he was consistently disparaging of his father. He could feel no real respect even for Wentworth Dilke's work for the Great Exhibition. "Father was concerned with matters in themselves interesting," he wrote, "but his part in them was one of detail, and his share in the planning and direction of the '51,' for instance, large as it was, is not a share an account of which would be of more interest than would a reprint of the minutes of the executive committee."[3] ". . . he was entirely without literary power," was another of Charles Dilke's severe judgments. At another time he noted with mild contempt that his father was jealously resentful of his own growing influence over his younger brother. And he wrote letters of patronising advice during the Wallingford campaign such as a father can rarely have received from a twenty-one-year-old son: "You must set to work. . . . You must get up the last debates. . . . You must make up your mind what to do as to Church Rates, and not budge an inch!"[4] So the instructions flowed from the pen of Charles Dilke. And he summed up his disparagement of his father, and his preference for his grandfather, in a comparison that was as cool as it was sweeping. ". . . my father was in every way a man of less real distinction than his father," he wrote, "although much better known by the public on account of the retiring nature of my grandfather."[5]

This grandfather, Mr. Dilke as he can best be called for purposes of differentiation from his son and grandson, was unquestionably the dominating influence on Charles Dilke's boyhood. He had been born in 1789, the son of yet another Charles Wentworth Dilke, who was a clerk in the Admiralty, but who came of a cadet branch of a landed family of some note, the Dilkes of Maxstoke Castle in Warwickshire. Mr. Dilke was also appointed to an Admiralty clerkship, but he did not retain it for his whole working life. His interests were literary and his talents were not negligible. From 1815 onwards he was contributing frequently to the *Quarterly* and other reviews. He was a close friend of Keats, and he had intimate associations, extending over a long period, with Charles Lamb and Thomas Hood.

In 1830 he resigned from the Admiralty and turned all his energies to letters. In the words of his grandson, "he brought the but-just-born yet nevertheless dying *Athenaeum* . . . and restored its fortunes and his own." For the first sixteen years of his proprietorship he acted in effect as editor and chief contributor, in addition to being principal shareholder. During this period he gave the paper a unique reputation for the detachment and impartiality of its literary criticism. Most comparable journals were in the hands of one publisher or another, and reflected this attachment in their literary columns. But the *Athenaeum* remained austerely independent; and Mr. Dilke fortified its reputation for incorruptibility by the extreme—and perhaps slightly priggish—course of withdrawing entirely from general society. This was "to avoid making literary acquaintances which might either prove annoying to him, or be supposed to compromise the independence of his journal."[6]

After 1846 Mr. Dilke's supervision of the *Athenaeum* became less detailed and his social life less restricted. He continued his publishing activities, however. For three years, working in close association with Charles Dickens, he acted as manager of the radical and recently established, *Daily News*. Despite his favourite description of himself as an "antiquary," his political views were fully in accord with those of the paper, but this was not enough to make his work here as successful as it had been with the *Athenaeum*. It was left to a later manager to establish the *Daily News* on a secure financial basis. With weekly papers, however, Mr. Dilke continued to show a surer touch. In 1849 he helped to found *Notes and Queries*, and thereafter contributed frequently to this successful literary journal which later passed into the full ownership of his grandson.

After he left the *Daily News* Mr. Dilke's interests were increasingly engrossed by the upbringing of this grandson, Charles Dilke. The death in 1850 of his own wife, a Yorkshire farmer's daughter whom he had married forty years before when he was only eighteen and she even younger, that of his daughter-in-law in 1853, and his abandonment of his own house in the same latter year, all helped to concentrate his attention in this direction. This concentration was further assisted by the fact that Charles Dilke never went to school. He was not judged to be strong enough. "My health at that time (1856)," he was to write later, "was not supposed to be sufficiently strong to enable me even to attend a day-school, and still less to go to a public school, but there was nothing the matter with me except a nervous turn of mind, over-excitable and over-strained by the slightest circumstance. This lasted until I was eighteen, when it suddenly disappeared, and left me strong and well."[7]

Charles Dilke did not entirely escape formal education, however. At the age of ten, immediately after his mother's death, he began lessons in classics and mathematics with a Chelsea curate. Three years later he became half-attached to a Kensington day-school, doing the work which was set without regularly attending the school. In addition his grandfather

6

sought to fill some of the gaps which were left by this tuition. But all this did not add up to the pattern of instruction which he would have received, still less to the way of life he would have experienced, had he been sent to school in the normal way. In the first place his ill-health led not merely to his being kept away from school, but to the discouragement of intellectual applica- tion. "I was a nervous, and, therefore, in some things a backward child," he wrote, "because my nervousness led to my being forbidden for some years to read and work, as I was given to read and work too much, and during this long period of forced leisure I was set to music and drawing, with the result that I took none of the ordinary boy's interest in politics. . . ."[8] The music lessons, which continued for fourteen years, constituted no useful training. He abandoned them on going to Cambridge, where, because of their proximity to the Fellows' Combination Room, he was allowed to keep no piano in his rooms, and retained barely the normal, untutored man's capacity for musical appreciation. Drawing he abandoned almost equally quickly, but in this case there was no revulsion of feeling. Throughout his life he retained and developed a carefully culti- vated taste for pictures.

Charles Dilke's training was further untypical in that, behind his rather sketchy formal education, he was given a background of cultural experience and knowledge of the world such as few children have experienced. At the age of ten he began regular play-going. His earliest theatrical recollection was Rachel, who ceased to perform in the early 'fifties. She aroused his great enthusiasm and he was later to remember her as being far supe- rior to Bernhardt; Charles Kean, Madame Vestris and her husband Charles James Mathews also excited his admiration. By his middle 'teens, Charles Dilke was familiar with the

7

performances of all the actors and actresses of note in both Paris and London; and before he was nineteen his passion for the theatre had burnt itself out, exhausted by over-indulgence. In later life he rarely went to a play, and, even when he did, was most unlikely to stay for the whole performance.

He travelled widely for a child of his period, both in England and in France. With his grandfather he visited every English cathedral, both university towns, and a wide range of other monuments. In the autumn of 1854 he paid his first French visit, also with his grandfather. But it was in the summer of the following year, when he was eleven years old, that his close association with France began. Wentworth Dilke, as one of the English Commissioners to the French International Exhibition, took his family to live in Paris for four months. It was a glittering year, in many ways the apogee of the Empire, and was marked not only by the Exhibition, but by the visit of Queen Victoria, and by superb military displays. Charles Dilke was not a retiring child. He was present at the great balls—that given by Walewski, the son of the first Emperor, at the Quai d'Orsay, that of Flahaut, the father of Morny, at the *Légion d'Honneur*, and that at the Hôtel de Ville for the Emperor and Empress and Queen Victoria. He heard Lablache in his last great part at the Opéra, and saw Rachel for the last time at the Théâtre Français. He was present at the military reviews and at the entry and departure of the Queen. The entry, he thought, was the finest display of troops which he ever witnessed. In the evenings he used to go regularly to the Place Vendôme to hear the combined tattoo of the Guards, and this remained his most vivid and persistent memory of the visit: "Every regiment was represented, and the drummers were a wonderful show in their different brilliant uniforms—Chasseurs of the Garde, Dragoons, Lancers,

Voltigeurs, and many more. In the midst was the gigantic sergeant-major waiting, with baton uplifted, for the clock to strike. At the first stroke he gave the signal with a twirl and a drop of his baton, and the long thundering roll began, taken up all round the great square."[9]

For part of the visit Mr. Dilke was present in Paris with his son's family, and during this period Charles Dilke became familiar not only with the splendours of the Second Empire but also with the aspects and antiquities of the pre-Haussmann city, soon to be so greatly changed. The impact of the whole visit upon Charles Dilke can hardly be exaggerated. He became strongly Francophile, and remained so, in matters of culture and way of life, if not always in those of politics and diplomacy, until his death. He began to know the language well—thereafter he and his brother Ashton regularly spoke and wrote to each other in French—and frequent and prolonged visits to France were henceforth an important part of his life.

Whether in England or in France, Charles Dilke had unusual opportunities of getting to know people of note, and also perhaps an unusual talent for doing so. Towards the end of his life he was able dogmatically and confidently to state: "I have known everyone worth knowing from 1850 until my death." The '51 Exhibition was effectively the beginning of his knowledge of the famous. "I was in the Exhibition every day," he wrote, "and made acquaintance there through Father with the Iron Duke, of whom I remember only that, small as I was, I thought him very small."[10] Later that summer Charles Dilke's mother was to write: "The Queen came and talked to me and Charley at the building on Friday"; and her son subsequently noted against this: "This was the occasion of which the Queen, twenty years afterwards, said that she remembered having stroked my head, and that she supposed she must have rubbed the hairs the wrong way."[11]

From about the same period are Charles Dilke's memories "of the bright eyes of little Louis Blanc, of Milner-Gibson's pleasant smile, of Bowring's silver locks, of Thackeray's tall stooping figure, of Dickens' goatee, of Paxton's white hat, of Barry Cornwall and his wife, of Robert Stephenson the engineer to whom I wanted to be bound apprentice, of Browning (then known as 'Mrs. Browning's husband'), of Joseph Cooke (another engineer), of Cubitt the builder (one of the promoters of the Exhibition), of John Forster the historian, of the Red-graves, and of that greater painter, John Martin."[12] With Thackeray, Charles Dilke's acquaintance was to prove productive, for it is recorded that a year or two later the novelist came upon the boy lying in the grass of the garden at Gore House in South Kensington and reading *The Three Musketeers*, borrowed the book from him, and as a direct consequence wrote one of *The Roundabout Papers*.

By the end of the 'fifties Charles Dilke had also built up a large French acquaintanceship, although there, at this time, it was the fringes of the Imperial family, rather than the men of solid Victorian achievement, literary, commercial or scientific, who frequented 76, Sloane Street, which most impressed him. Parts of the summers of both 1859 and 1860 he spent with his family in Normandy.

"At Havre," he wrote, "I got to know King Jerome, father to 'Plon-Plon,' and father-in-law to my friend Princess Clothilde, and was duly interested in this last of the brothers of Napoleon. The ex-King of Westphalia was a wicked old gentleman; but he did not let a boy find this out, and he

10

was courteous and talkative. . . . He used to walk in the garden with me, finding me a good listener. The old Queen of Sweden[†] was still alive, and he told me how . . . (she) had thrown Bonaparte over for him, and then had thrown him over for Bernadotte. He also described riding through Paris with Bonaparte on the day of Brumaire."[13]

At Trouville in 1860 Charles Dilke came to know the Duc de Morny and "hopelessly lost my heart to his lovely young Troubetsky wife, afterwards Duchess of Sesto"—"a fact of which she was probably unaware," he added. At the end of that year he set out for the first time on his own to Paris, and after being blocked by snow at Amiens, arrived safely, and paid calls upon his acquaintances. In England in 1862 the Exhibition of that year gave him an opportunity to meet Palmerston, whom he found "still bright and lively in walk and talk and . . . extremely kind in his manner to me," and from whom he received an invitation to one of Lady Palmerston's Saturday evening parties at Cambridge House, which was duly accepted.

In the autumn of 1862 Charles Dilke went up to Cambridge. He was matriculated as a member of Trinity Hall, his father's college. It was (and is) a medium-sized college with a strong legal connection. It had been founded in the fourteenth century by a bishop who had been so alarmed by the ravages of the Black Death that he thought it necessary to make provision against a possible shortage of lawyers. In Wentworth Dilke's day it had been a college of little distinction, but by the time of his son's

---

† Désirée Clary, who had married Jean-Baptiste Bernadotte, afterwards Charles XIV, in 1798.

entry its academic standards had considerably improved; and its rowing reputation stood extremely high.

In part it owed both these attributes to Leslie Stephen, a typical if not altogether attractive Cambridge nineteenth-century figure. Stephen had been elected to a Trinity Hall fellowship in 1854, and had been ordained in the following year so that he might retrospectively qualify for the office. Of a figure so characteristic of his age it is hardly necessary to say that no sooner had he become a priest than he began to torment himself with religious doubt. By the time of Charles Dilke's arrival in Cambridge he was already deeply influenced by Darwinism and profoundly shocked by the levity of Bishop Wilberforce's famous jest against Huxley in the Oxford debate.[‡] But the force of Stephen's reaction against his cloth was as little compared with his determination not to appear before the world as a sensitive intellectual. Perhaps because he had been remorsely bullied as a day-boy at Eton, he developed an almost pathetic desire to be liked by the rowing men of his college and thought of as an acceptable figure in a world of hearty, masculine good fellowship. He was a poor oar as an undergraduate, but he later made himself into one of the great rowing coaches of the century; and he further expiated the sin of his own lack of prowess by writing the college boating song. He thought a

---

[‡] "Accustomed to manipulate ecclesiastical machinery, the Great Diocesan (Wilberforce), a genial and often attractive prelate, fell into the trap which awaits men of good humour who become politicians—he made a joke at the wrong moment. When he asked Huxley which of his grandparents claimed descent from an ape, the earnestness of Clapham passed in an instant into the hands of his adversaries; his levity made Belief an issue of moral rectitude." (Noel Annan, *Leslie Stephen*, pp. 166–7.)

thirty-mile walk the most agreeable way of passing a quiet Sunday afternoon, and he was known on occasion to walk from Cambridge to London during the day, attend a dinner in the evening, and walk back during the night. It was natural that, later in his life, he should become a leading exponent of that great English, Victorian, upper-middle class sport of alpine climbing.

Stephen, despite his growing agnosticism, has been described by one of his biographers as the true founder of muscular Christianity. He was also a strong formative influence in a Cambridge intellectual tradition which has extended to the present day. He believed in plain living and hard work. He had a high respect for the discipline of the mathematical tripos and the habit of cool, detached enquiry, founded upon intensive application, to which it led. He was as distrustful of enthusiasm in affairs of the intellect as he was respectful towards its exhibi-tion on the tow-path.[§] He disliked obscurity and ambiguity of expression, and thought of them as inevitable results of specu-lative generalisation. Let a man stick to his last, write or talk only about those subjects to which he had applied himself (without attempting to weave them all into a single metaphysic), and it could all be done in good, calm, clear, Cambridge English. Stephen was almost perfectly suited to the Cambridge tripos system of the day, under which a man reading for honours

---

[§] He was also distrustful of emotional enthusiasm, at least towards the other sex. His first wife was Minnie Thackeray, younger daughter of the novelist, and on the day on which he became engaged to her he "lunched (by himself) at the Oxford and Cambridge Club, thought over the whole affair in a philosophic spirit and (then) went to 16, Onslow Gardens." (Noel Annan, *op. cit.* p. 62.)

was toned up like an athlete and won his awards by a combination of staying power during the long period of preliminary work and speed in the examination room. He was well placed in the first class list himself and he subsequently helped a growing number of Trinity Hall men to similar positions.

The other dominant influence in the Trinity Hall of Charles Dilke's day was Henry Fawcett, the son of a Salisbury shopkeeper, who had been blinded in a shooting accident at the age of twenty-five and who was soon to be elected Liberal member of Parliament for Brighton. Later he became Postmaster-General in the second Gladstone Government. Fawcett was a similar if by no means an identical influence to Stephen. His blindness meant that he could not be equally athletic, but he was in many ways an even more extreme example of the Cambridge habit of mind. He believed in a severe stoicism and regarded all expressions of emotion as unmasculine and un-English. He saw the mathematical tripos as the most perfect and complete intellectual training to which a man could be subjected, and had little patience with those whose minds were not attuned to it. He shared Stephen's radicalism and he shared also a certain insularity which went with it. Stephen only knew one foreigner well in the course of his life, and that was his alpine guide. Fawcett visited Paris for six weeks at the age of twenty-four, but formed such an unfavourable view of the characteristics of the French that he never returned.

There could, therefore, hardly have been a sharper contrast between the Trinity Hall atmosphere into which Charles Dilke was immersed in the autumn of 1862 and the life which he had glimpsed as a boy. But there is no evidence that, as might perhaps have been expected, he rebelled against Cambridge, and particularly his own little corner of it, as being austere, provincial and dull. He was certainly capable of bursts of uncompromising nonconformity. Thus, in the same year that he went up to Cambridge he decided that shooting, of which he had done a great deal since the age of fourteen, and to which his father's country estate near Farnham was largely devoted, was an undesirable pastime. This was in spite of, or perhaps because of, his father's increasing absorption in the sport. But Charles Dilke's mind was clearly made up. He would have no more of it. Equally he would drink no wine during his time at Cambridge, although in later life he was to become a connoisseur of note.[1] In the case of shooting a humanitarian objection was a mild contributory cause, but in the case of drink moral objections played no part. It was simply that Dilke liked to decide what he thought best for himself and to present the result to the world with an unyielding self-confidence.

He was by no means unyielding to the Trinity Hall influence, however. In some ways, despite his francophilia and his nervous sensibility, he was already well-suited to it. He was a great walker—in 1861 he had covered the distance from London to

---

[1] Charles Dilke alternated almost as abruptly and curiously in his attitude towards alcohol as in his religious beliefs—although there was no connection between the two. When he came down from Cambridge he ceased to abstain and became a normal drinker. But from 1874 to 1885, a period covering the zenith of his career, he was a complete teetotaller. In 1885 he again began to drink alcohol. Of the swing of his religious beliefs he wrote as follows: "In the course of 1863 I ceased my attendance upon Holy Communion, and fell into a sceptical frame of mind which lasted for several years, was modified in 1874, and came to an end in 1875. . . . From 1885 to 1888 the Holy Sacrament was a profound blessing to me, but in 1905 I ceased again to find any help in forms." (D.P. 43930, 134).

Brighton in a single day in order to attend a Volunteer Review—
and he was by nature a very hard worker, more attracted by facts
than by generalisations, and deeply imbued with the competitive
spirit. He took to rowing with an immediate and successful
enthusiasm which persisted for nearly forty years. And although
he claimed to have been abnormally uninterested in politics as a
boy and never to have formed an opinion until the outbreak of
the American Civil War, he was soon active—and loquacious—
in the Cambridge Union Society. These three activities—the
tripos, the river and the Union—were the core of Dilke's life at
Cambridge; and he took them all a little too seriously.

So far as his work was concerned he was subjected to
constant pressure from home. Not only Mr. Dilke, until he
died in the summer of 1864, but Sir Wentworth Dilke, too,
despite his own extreme idleness at a similar stage in life, were
constantly urging him on to still greater academic efforts.
Concern that he should not overstrain his health seemed
completely to have disappeared. Thus within a fortnight of his
arrival in Cambridge he was writing defensively (and a little
pompously) to his father:

> "I am very sorry to see by your letter of this morning
> that you have taken it into your head that I am not reading
> hard. I can assure you, on the contrary, that I read harder
> than any freshman except Osborn, who takes no exercise
> whatever; and that I have made the rowing men very
> dissatisfied by reading all day three days a week. On the
> other three, I never read less than six hours besides four
> hours of lectures and papers. I have not missed reading a
> single evening yet, since I have been here. . . ."[14]

Certainly this account of Charles Dilke's undergraduate days left more room for doubt about his sense than his assiduity. Nevertheless, Mr. Dilke at least, who as befitted a friend of Keats and Lamb was by far the least athletic of the three generations, remained constantly afraid that his grandson would be diverted by the pleasures of rowing from the rigours of mathematics. Charles Dilke often had to reassure him that this was not the case. He soon accumulated a substantial basis of achievement on which to do so. At the end of his first year he won a college mathematical scholarship, but he then deserted the subject, not for the river but for the law. This change brought with it the beginning of an intensely concentrated personal rivalry with George Shee, an Irishman whose father was later to be the first Roman Catholic since the time of the Stuarts to sit on the English Bench.

Dilke was warned by his tutor when he gave up mathematics that if he took to the law he would have Shee, a dangerous adversary who started with the advantage of some knowledge of the subject, in his year. He returned an aggressive answer: "I said I should read with Shee; and make him understand that I was intended by Nature to beat him."[15] Later, watching Shee with intense concern, he had occasional bursts of worry. "Shee has been sitting up till ominously late hours for some nights past. His father came up last night and left again to-night, but I fear he did not make his son waste much time."[16] The worry proved misplaced. Dilke triumphed over Shee and other lesser contenders at almost every stage. In 1864 he won the college annual English Essay prize with a piece on Sir Robert Walpole and in the following year he was again successful, this time with an essay on the theory of government. At the end of his second year at Trinity Hall (and his first year reading law) he gained the college law prize, and at the end of the following year he was announced Senior Legalist, the highest University distinction open to a law student. He achieved his academic results not by effortless bursts of imaginative thought, but by the continuous, painstaking accumulation of knowledge—and this remained his approach throughout his life. He thought that the surest way to be wise about a subject was to know as much about and around it as possible.**†† There were clearly limitations to such an attitude, but the Cambridge examination system did not recognise them, and he emerged from Trinity Hall (in 1866, for he stayed up for two terms after taking his degree, reading moral science and presiding over the Cambridge Union) as a man of high academic distinction and self-confident ability.

On the river he was little less successful. When he first arrived in Cambridge Dilke knew nothing about rowing. But it offered exactly the sort of purposive, vigorous, comparatively non-time-wasting athleticism which he wanted. He was inducted into the sport by D. F. Steavenson, a Trinity Hall freshman from Northumberland, who in later years was to serve him with an almost canine fidelity. By the summer term of his first year Dilke

---

** Thus when working for his second prize essay, the subject which was Pope's Couplet

> "For forms of Government let fools contest
>   Whate'er is best administered is best"

he spent long hours in the Reading Room of the British Museum endeavouring to familiarise himself with all the writers on political utopias and ideal commonwealths.

18

was rowing No. 4 in the Trinity Hall first boat, and in the same season he took part in a notably fast Grand Challenge heat at Henley. In the following year, when Dilke rowed No. 3, Trinity Hall went head of the river on the second night and stayed there for the rest of the week. He wrote to his father (who on this subject was a more sympathetic audience than his grandfather), dating his letter "the ever-memorable May 12th, 1864," and described how the "whole of the crew and Stephen were chaired and carried round the court."[17] Four years later the boat in which they had rowed was cut up and distributed amongst the crew which had performed these feats. Dilke piously kept his piece hanging against the wall of his study in Sloane Street until the end of his life.

In his third year Dilke was promoted to the position of stroke, but the boat, under his leadership, did not do so well as in the previous year. On the second night it was bumped by Third Trinity, a strikingly good crew containing five University oars. Trinity Hall had only one—Steavenson—although Dilke himself, both in this year and in 1866, had been offered his "blue" and the place of No. 7. "I declined on the score of constitution," he wrote. "I was strong, but afraid of the rowing in training over the long course, although perfectly able to stand up to the short course work of Cambridge or of Henley." Later he added: "I believe that I was unduly frightened by my doctor, and that I might have rowed."[18]

The Union, the third of Charles Dilke's principal Cambridge activities, had its premises in a former Wesleyan chapel in Green Street. They were clearly unsatisfactory, the more so as a few years earlier the Oxford Union, already a more distinguished nursery of politicians and ecclesiastics, had erected its own elaborate gothic structure. A building fund had been in existence in

19

Cambridge since 1857, but it had produced no physical result.[‡‡] Nor did it do so until Dilke had risen to a high place in the Union hierarchy. This he did quite quickly, being elected to the Library and Standing Committees in his first year, and becoming Vice-President for the second term of his second year. At this stage serious negotiations to bring the fund to fruition and to set the builders to work were undertaken. Dilke was the leading figure in these negotiations. He was re-elected to the Vice-Presidency and then, in October, 1864, was elected unopposed to the Presidency. In the following academic year he was re-elected to the office, a most unusual event, and came back to Cambridge for two terms of a fourth year largely in order to fill it. By this time the work was almost complete, but Dilke nominated his successor—Lord Edmond Fitzmaurice[§§]—in order to guard against anything going wrong with the final stages.

This was undoubtedly Dilke's distinctive contribution to Cambridge politics. He made a great number of speeches in the Union. He advocated a Greek republic. He advanced with a wealth of illustration the value of the metric system. He upheld

---

[‡‡] This fact combined with a motion on the American Civil War enabled G. O. Trevelyan, later to be a Cabinet colleague, to produce at the first debate which Dilke attended a remark which has all the characteristics of a typical Union joke, whether at Oxford or at Cambridge, whether of this century or the last. Trevelyan was a supporter of the South. "Can the North restore the Union?" he asked. "Never, sir; they have no building fund." Charles Dilke, however wrote to his grandfather that the speech was "mere flash, but very witty."

[§§] 1846–1935. Second son of the fourth Marquess of Lansdowne. Unlike his elder brother he remained faithful to the Liberal party, and was a lifelong friend of Dilke's.

the Federal cause in America. He denounced Mr. Lowe's views on the franchise. He supported, to the surprise of many of his political friends, the foreign policy of Lord Palmerston, and he was firmly ranged on the Prussian side in her dispute with Denmark over Schleswig-Holstein.¶ Indeed he foreshadowed most of his later political attitudes. He was a thoroughgoing radical, but without the slightest tinge of pacifism or Little Englandism. He respected strength, whether military or political, and there was little place for either sentiment or romanticism in his politics. And the possibility of practical achievement always exercised a strong fascination for him. Despite his disparaging references to the pedestrian nature of his father's work for the Great Exhibition, his own role in Cambridge politics bore more than a slight resemblance to this work. He would not have been remembered for his wit, his oratory, or the unusual penetration of his political judgments; but he was the man who got the new Union built.***

In the summer of 1864 Mr. Dilke died at Alice Holt. Charles Dilke had hurried from Cambridge to his bedside, but despite affecting scenes of farewell, he was later to write: "I did not greatly feel my grandfather's death at the moment," although he went on to add that "the sense of loss has been greater with every year that followed."[19] The immediate effect of Mr. Dilke's death, however, was emotionally somewhat to reorientate his grandson,

---

¶ At this stage Dilke carried his admiration for Bismarck, never to be wholly absent from his mind, to the extent of putting up a photograph of him in his rooms.

*** His voice was also decisive in determining the form which the new building took. His choice as architect—Waterhouse—was selected against Gilbert Scott and Digby Wyatt, whose claims were also canvassed.

and, in Charles Dilke's own words, to bring him "too close" to H. D. Warr, a fellow-undergraduate at Trinity Hall. Warr was a clergyman's son and a classical exhibitioner. He later became a barrister of no great note, and was appointed on Dilke's recommendation the secretary of the Royal Commission on City Companies in 1880. He was a sententious young man, who wrote long, rather pompous letters to Dilke, and maintained a curious love-hate attitude towards him for several years to come. In 1868, for instance, he contributed to the *Pall Mall Gazette* the only really waspish review of Dilke's first published book which was to appear in any journal. Even in 1864 he was already strongly critical of Dilke, despite being one of his closest friends, and wrapped up in his turgid letters there were some grains of good sense and some judgments of penetration.

"Yours being vastly the wider range of knowledge," he wrote, "our being frequently alone would put a great burden of conversation upon you and would tax my powers of feigning attention in a formidable degree. . . . Your ponderous and extensive studies have in some degree, especially as they began early in your life and have been continued with an unremitted devotion, tainted your general ways. A manner of analysing books perpetually and amassing information upon all subjects is not good. At least it appears to me a pity that you have got into such a groove of application to study, because it has led you to a formal mapping out of your time and a sort of pipeclay and cross-belt habit, in consequence of which you set about being greater friends with me after a fashion which, though I loved you deeply all the while for your soft fondness for me, seemed almost businesslike.[20]

22

Dilke used subsequently to assert that Warr and Henry Fawcett between them cured him at this time of his priggishness. In part this may have been so. In middle life he certainly developed a lighter touch than he had in his Cambridge days; but some of the characteristics referred to in Warr's letter remained with him throughout. He was always addicted to the amassing of information and he was always a little businesslike in his approach to emotional relationships.

These criticisms, however, even if heeded, did little to impair Dilke's self-confidence. Things were going very well for him. His Cambridge career had been a great success, and the two additional terms for which he remained in residence after completing his tripos formed an agreeable postscript. He lived as a fellow-commoner (dining at the high table) and nominally reading moral science. But, apart from supervising the completion of the Union building, his interests were increasingly outside the University. He was doing some regular weekly journalism, mainly book reviewing, for his grandfather's paper, the *Athenaeum*. He sketched out a plan for an ambitious history of radicalism which was to begin with the pre-Christian thinkers, and he spent a lot of time in London reading for the work in the British Museum. He had become a member of the Reform Club, and was looking with increasing certainty towards a career in radical politics. He had made his début as a public speaker during his father's by-election at Wallingford at the beginning of 1865. But when he finally left Cambridge, more than a year later, he was still only twenty-two. Even for so highly ambitious and talented a young man there was no immediate hurry to find a seat in the House of Commons. First he was anxious to do some serious travel. His mind turned towards Russia, a country in which he had long been and was to remain deeply interested; but he later decided that a journey to North America, with a possible extension to Australia, would provide at least equivalent natural excitements, with more useful material for his work on radicalism and his interest in ideal commonwealths. Early in June, 1866, he sailed from Liverpool, without companions. The ship was the S.S. *Saratoga*, and the immediate destination was Norfolk, Virginia.

Chapter Two

A Greater Britain

The America in which Dilke arrived was only fourteen months free of the Civil War. In Chesapeake Bay and up the James River, the *Saratoga* had to thread her way through the wrecks of vessels of both the South and the North. Richmond, which he visited immediately after Norfolk, could only be approached through a maze of rebel forts and earthworks, and when reached, its streets and bars were full of the demobilised and unoccupied troops of the Confederate army, still toasting Jefferson Davis—"the caged eagle"—and complaining bitterly that they had been let down by the weakness of regiments from Mississippi or Alabama.

Even away from such a centre of memories of the conflict as the former Confederate capital, the aftermath of the war lay heavily upon the pattern of life. Washington, of which Dilke's first view was the glint of the sun on the dome of the Capitol as he steamed up the Potomac in the early morning of a fierce July day, was still the city in which Lincoln had just been shot and into which the rebel forces had so nearly advanced. New York was still the city and the state which had done least to help the Federal Government. Boston, on the other hand, was still the spiritual centre of the Northern cause. But the support which it gave was not only spiritual. "Of the men who sat beneath Longfellow, and Agassiz, and Emerson," Dilke noted, "whole battalions went forth to war."[1]

It was a strangely remote America in many other ways. The population was thirty-five million and immigrants were pouring in at an enormous rate. The Irish were already predominant in New York and Boston, and the Germans had arrived in Philadelphia, but the Italians were yet to come. Large cities, particularly in the Mississippi basin, were still subject to the most frightful waves of disease. "I was unfortunately driven from Cincinnati by the violence of the cholera,"[2] Dilke wrote on August 17th. There were eighty to ninety deaths in a day. Later in the same month he was to strike still worse conditions at St. Louis, where a population of 180,000 "much diminished by flight," were suffering losses at the rate of two hundred a day, and convicted murderers were offered free pardons if they would help bury the dead.

The transcontinental railway line, although advancing rapidly from both ends, was still five years in time and more than 1,500 miles in distance away from completion. Between the middle of Kansas and the Californian slopes of the Sierra Nevada travel had still to be undertaken by mail-coach or in some more primitive wagon. Across the plains the journey was made dangerous by the Indians, and in the mountains and on the great plateau they were replaced by almost equivalent natural hazards. On the Pacific coast, San Francisco, already several times damaged by fire and earthquake in its twenty years of existence, had just emerged from lynch law enforced by a committee of vigilance to some form of settled government.

This was the United States in which Dilke spent the summer and early autumn months of 1866. He began in a less controlled mood than was his habit, and sought, in Virginia, to express his emotions in a long, autobiographical poem, which he later described as "a feeble mutation of *Childe Harold.*" This poem was intended to express his sense of loss at the death of his grandfather and to explain his special relationship to the old man. This he did principally in terms of the early death of his mother, to which fact also he attributed certain weaknesses of his nature, such as "the fatal gift of facile tears." The poem was not a success. Dilke had no gift for writing verse, and soon after an opening stanza in which he referred to himself at Cambridge as "a youth of nineteen springs, a hearty rosy laughing English lad," he wisely abandoned his task. He persisted for some time, however, in the belief that, while travelling, he could do serious work on his history of radicalism. But this, in turn, was soon given up too. For the remainder of the trip he settled down to a less diligent pattern of life than had been his habit at Cambridge. He took in the scenes around him, he experienced physical danger for the first time, he commented on what he saw, and he recorded his impressions in a series of long letters home, either to his brother or his father.

Charles Dilke's comments were always made within a framework of certain firm beliefs. He was a radical and instinctively favourable not only to the most complete democracy but also to experiment in governmental institutions. He believed in women's rights, and he was as delighted with Kansas for having introduced female suffrage as he was censorious of the Mormons in Utah. He also believed in the virtue of hard work, and was opposed to slavery far more because it made the whites think labour degrading than because it oppressed the blacks. He had a horror of "soft" climates and of the easy, purposeless living to which he thought they gave rise. The banana, the most typical product of such a climate, he regarded with particular horror, and constructed a whole theory of social decline out of its prevalence in some of the Southern states.

> "The terrible results of the plentiful possession of this tree," he wrote, "are seen in Ceylon, at Panama, in the coastlands of Mexico, at Auckland in New Zealand. . . . (It) will make nothing; you can eat it raw or fried, and that is all; you can eat it every day of your life without becoming tired of its taste; without suffering in your health, you can live on it exclusively. In the banana groves of Florida and Louisiana there lurk much trouble and danger to the American free States."[3]

Combined with these other views, or prejudices, Dilke had a great pride of race. He believed implicitly that the English were the best stock in the world, and that the spread of their power and influence could hardly fail to be generally beneficial. This belief sometimes made him ruthless in his attitude to "lesser breeds." He had no doubt that it was right to sweep the Red Indians off the plains as quickly as possible. He could write with pride that "the Anglo-Saxon is the only extirpating race on earth."[4] And he could sum up his American impressions in the following paragraph, at once arrogant and radical:

> "The first thing which strikes the Englishman just landed in New York is the apparent latinization of the English in

America; but before he leaves the country, he comes to see that this is at most a local fact, and that the true moral of America is the vigour of the English race—the defeat of the cheaper by the dearer peoples, the victory of the man whose food costs four shillings a day over the man whose food costs fourpence. Excluding the Atlantic cities, the English in America are absorbing the Germans and the Celts, destroying the Red Indians, and checking the advance of the Chinese."[5]

Despite these views, Dilke could not have been counted a straightforward imperialist, even if the word had held much meaning in the 'sixties. He was too distrustful of existing English institutions of government, from the Queen to the oligarchic Parliament, for that to be possible. It was the influence of the race rather than of London which he wished to extend. Thus, in Canada, which he visited briefly before proceeding west, he immediately took an extreme position against the maintenance of the British connection. Its severance, he thought, would greatly improve relations between England and the United States, and the result would be well worth the price, Dilke, indeed, was as naturally disposed to be pro-American as it is possible to imagine. To find English energy and to hear the English language without the English Queen or other archaic paraphernalia was for him an exhilarating experience. ". . . America offers the English race the moral directorship of the globe," he wrote, "by ruling mankind through Saxon institutions and the English tongue. Through America, England is speaking to the world."[6]

Even when American institutions did not fit into his framework of beliefs, Dilke was still capable of being a good observer.

Here his talent for amassing facts became useful. It carried with it a desire to understand how things worked and how different men defended their different beliefs. Whether confronted by polygamy in Salt Lake City or the mentality of slavery in Richmond, he did not carry his disapproval to the extent of being uninterested in that with which he could not agree. His own views were always firmly implied, but they did not lead him into incomprehension; and he was quickly developing a sharp edge of comment which had been lacking in his writings at Cambridge.

It was notably exercised upon the city of New York, which he thought corrupt, vulgar and, except for its striking physical beauty, generally undesirable. New York drawing-rooms, he was prepared to concede, might already be the most exclusive in the world, but this was no sign of grace, for those who were kept out included the most eminent and the most intellectually distinguished, while those who did the keeping out were marked by none of that special merit which alone could make aristocracy tolerable. The expatriate New Yorkers aroused his especial contempt:

"Many American men and women, who have too little nobility of soul to be patriots, and too little understanding to see that theirs is already, in many points, the master country of the globe, come to you, and bewail the fate that has caused them to be born citizens of a republic, and dwellers in a country where men call vices by their names. The least educated of their countrymen, the only grossly vulgar class that America brings forth, they fly to Europe 'to escape democracy,' and pass their lives in Paris, Pau, or Nice, living libels on the

30

country they are supposed to represent."[7]

Boston he greatly preferred, on account both of its moral tone and of its intellectual quality.

". . . I met there," he wrote, "a group of men undoubtedly, on the whole, the most distinguished then collected at any city in the world. At one party of nine people, at Cambridge, I met Emerson, Agassiz, Longfellow, Wendell Holmes, Asa Gray, Lowell, Hosea Biglow, Dr. Collyer the Radical Unitarian, and Dr. Hedges the great preacher. It is hard to say by which of them I was the most charmed. Emerson, Longfellow, Asa Gray, and Wendell Holmes seemed to me equal in the perfection of their courtesy, the grace of their manner, and the interest of their conversation, while Hedges and Collyer were full of an intellectual energy which was new to me, and which had a powerful effect on my work of the time."[8]

Unfortunately it subsequently appeared that, in matters of moral tone at least, Dilke did not make so favourable an impression upon President Lowell as that which the President's colleagues, and to a lesser extent the President himself, made upon Dilke.

Harvard evoked from Dilke the curiously premature comment that it showed an air of classic repose which was lacking in the English universities. Cambridge, Massachusetts, he thought much more conducive to quiet study than the intolerable noise of Oxford High Street. But he found New England academic life sadly lacking in a proper respect for athleticism, and rowing assigned a place far below that which it deserved. This he saw as one facet of an excessive regard for brains as opposed to brawn, and, in consequence, of a generally declining standard of health, which he believed to be a feature of New England and to some extent of America as a whole. "The women show even greater signs of weakness than the men," he added, "and the high undulating tones which are affectation in the French are natural to the ladies of America; little can be expected of women whose only exercise is excessive dancing in overheated rooms."[9] Part of the trouble he was prepared to attribute to the fact that the Americans as a people were prospectors of virgin land. The turning of untilled soil he believed to be one of the unhealthiest occupations in the world. The first beams of sunlight upon hitherto untouched mould were apt to release harmful, malarious gases.

After New England and his short visit to Canada, Dilke moved about the Middle West until, in late August, he went to St. Louis to meet Hepworth Dixon, who had just arrived from England. Dixon was at that time forty-five years of age and the editor of the Dilke family journal, the *Athenæum*. He had come out in order to travel across the great plains with Dilke and to penetrate as far into the mountains as Salt Lake City. This was a more vital point in his itinerary than in Dilke's, for he was particularly concerned to study the position of women in American society, and the Mormons offered important even if peripheral evidence. By the beginning of the following year—1867—Dixon had published in London a two-volume account of his travels.[*] This was a tolerably shrewd and interesting account of what he had seen, but it was hardly a book of outstanding quality. Nevertheless it was a great success, and ran into five editions during its first year of

---

[*] New America.

publication. It was in the hands of the public long before Dilke himself could publish anything, before he had returned to England indeed, and it is doubtful whether he regarded a warm dedication as an adequate recompense for this jumping of the gun. In 1869 he dismissed Dixon from the editorship of the *Athenæum*, citing as a reason that the latter wrote books without leave. But in 1866 this trouble was all in the future. Dilke and Dixon found each other agreeable enough travelling companions under very difficult circumstances, although Dilke thought that Dixon's insistence on changing his shirt once a fortnight betrayed an excessive rigidity of mind.

From St. Louis they went, mostly by rail, to Atchison on the Kansas bank of the Missouri, which they believed to be the starting-point of the overland mail to Salt Lake City and San Francisco. On arrival they were told that, by a sudden decision of Congress, this route, the Platte route, had been abandoned in favour of the shorter but more hazardous Smoky Hill route. They therefore moved south to Leavenworth, the new starting-point. While waiting in this Kansas town Dilke wrote two important letters. In the first he told his father of his intention, conceived but not announced before he left home, to extend his journey to Australia and to make a complete circle of the globe before returning home. In the second, with more than a touch of the old priggishness, he gave his brother Ashton a great deal of advice on his Cambridge career, and in the course of doing so announced his own plans for the longer-term future. "My aim in life," Charles Dilke wrote, "is to be of the greatest use I can to the world at large, not because that is my duty, but because that is the course which will make my life happiest—i.e. my motives are *selfish*—in the *wide* and unusual sense of that word. I believe that, on account of my temperament and education, I can be most useful as a statesman, and as a writer. I have therefore educated myself with a view to getting such power as to make me able at all events to teach men my views, whether or not they follow them."[†][10]

On August 28th Dilke and Dixon left Leavenworth. The journey across the plains took place first in an old Concord coach and then in a light prairie wagon, with no doors and very bad springs. Their only companions were the driver and forty-two unsealed bags of United States mail. The former was an inadequate substitute for the impressive mounted guard which they were promised would join them at Junction City, but which never arrived. The latter made the interior of the coach still more uncomfortable than it would otherwise have been. For the opportunity of travelling in such circumstances they were charged the enormous fare of 500 dollars a head, from Leavenworth to Salt Lake City. It was a high price to pay, as they both observed, for the privilege of guarding the mail.

The first major stage of the journey, to Denver, took just over four days and nights. During this stage they were subjected to the constant danger of Indian attack. The Platte route to the north and the Santa Fé route to the south had both been accepted, but the use of this central Smoky Hill route was still bitterly contested by the Cheyennes. It ran through excellent buffalo country, and the Indians rightly thought that the coaches

---

[†] In the Gwynn and Tuckwell life of Dilke this letter is quoted in full, and the authors then add: "'What a prig he was' is scrawled across the page, as Charles Dilke's judgment on himself, when later the letter fell into his hands," The comment might have been reasonable, but it is doubtful if it was ever made. The original of the letter, amongst the Dilke papers in the British Museum, is free both of annotation and of any marks of erasure.

would be merely the forerunners of a railway. In the event Dilke and Dixon saw nothing of marauding tribes, but several of the posts at which they stopped were to be wiped out within a few weeks. Despite the teeming animal, bird and reptile life of the plains, food was a great problem. They got no full meal between breakfast on their first morning out and their arrival in Denver. Occasional rather inadequate helpings of prairie dog were the best that they could do. Great herds of buffalo, each about three hundred strong, were in sight most of the time, but their hides could not be pierced with ordinary rifles.

Once in Denver, Dilke's health and spirits recovered rapidly under the influence of the mountain air and "the heaven-blessed climate," as he expressed it. He was soon in a sufficiently buoyant mood to assure the Governor of Colorado, who pressed him to settle in Denver with the offer to name a mountain peak after him, that this was not enough. "I told him that unless he would carry a constitutional amendment allowing a foreign-born subject to be President of the United States, he would not receive my services,"[11] he wrote.

From Denver to Salt Lake City the journey took five days. Here, after interviews with Brigham Young and other appropriate investigations into Mormonism, Dixon and Dilke separated. The former made his way back to the East Coast and to England. The latter pushed on to the Californian gold-workings and eventually to San Francisco. He began by reducing himself to a state of desperate tiredness with another sleepless five days and nights stage across Nevada to Virginia City. "The brain seemed divided into two parts," he wrote, "thinking independently, and one side putting questions while the other answered them; but this time there was also a sort of half insanity, a not altogether disagreeable wandering of the mind, a replacing of the actual

35

by an imagined ideal scene."[12] Later, however, the going was much easier. First, between Virginia City and Carson City, he struck a reasonable road, with grades and bridges. Then, from Placerville to Sacramento, he was able to take a train for the first time for 1,800 miles. Finally he steamed down the Sacramento River to reach San Francisco Bay and the Pacific. California, he decided rather surprisingly, was "too British to be typically American."

From San Francisco he continued to follow "England round the world." By November he was in New Zealand, by the end of December in Sydney, and by April in Calcutta. He remained a vigorous traveller and a keen observer, but his descriptions, his judgments and his comments lost something of the sharpness and spirit they had possessed in North America. Perhaps he was growing tired of being away, perhaps the scenes he now saw would at any time have been less interesting to his eyes. Whatever the reason, his writings lost something of their earlier verve. There were occasional familiar Dilke touches, however. In New Zealand he saw in the gradual replacement of the native fly by the imported English fly a parallel with the relative performances of the indigenous and immigrant races. In Victoria and South Australia he accumulated a great deal of detailed and useful information on the working of the secret ballot and the machinery of registration. In the Ganges Valley he expatiated on the ill-health of the British in the sub-continent, and decided that most of it was due to a combination of carelessness and over-indulgence. "If a man wears a flannel belt and thick clothes when he travels by night, and drinks hot tea," he concluded, "he need not fear India."[13]

He returned from Bombay by way of Egypt—where he thought he saw French influence overseas at its worst—and Italy.

In June, 1867, he was back in London. He had been away a full year. His general summing-up was that the future belonged in an unrealised degree to the Anglo-Saxon race. "No possible series of events," he wrote, "can prevent the English race itself in 1970 numbering 300 millions of beings—of one national character and one tongue. Italy, Spain, France, Russia become pigmies by the side of such a people."[14]

Immediately upon his return, Dilke set to work to construct out of the letters which he had written home a book of travel reminiscences and political judgments. The work took him a year, being a good deal interrupted by ill-health. He had been infected with malaria in Ceylon,‡ and this led to a long period of weak appetite and delirious sleeplessness at night. Finally, in the summer of 1868, he developed typhoid, but by that time the book was already in the press, and the only permanent result was that, in consequence of the proofs being corrected by his father, the first edition contained what Charles Dilke regarded as a gross crop of errors. Dilke had signed an agreement with Macmillans in March, 1868, under the terms of which they were to print a first impression of 1,500 copies, and the author was to receive an advance of £200 and no less than 200 free copies. The terms were highly favourable to a young man of twenty-four, publishing his first book, but they were more than justified by the success which was achieved. *Greater Britain*, the title chosen by Dilke to sum up not only his itinerary but a large part of his political philosophy, was extremely well received by the Press. It quickly ran through four editions in

---

‡ References to having "lunched off horrible oysters in the mangrove swamps of the Kaluzanga river" suggest that he was lucky not to have contracted worse diseases.

England, and remained a widely read book for nearly fifty years. In America it sold even more copies, but as the editions were pirated this brought no financial benefit to Dilke. A truncated version was translated and published in Russia.

The book gave Dilke not only a considerable politico-literary reputation, but also a wide range of new contacts. Perhaps the 200 free copies helped here, for throughout the winter months of 1868–9 a steady stream of letters of thanks and commendation poured into 76, Sloane Street. The most important came from J. S. Mill, then at Avignon. On February 9th, 1869, Mill, who had never met Dilke, wrote in the following terms:

"It is long since any book connected with practical politics has been published on which I build such high hopes of the future usefulness and distinction of the writer, shewing, as it does, that he not only possesses a most unusual amount of real knowledge on many of the principal questions of the future, but a mind strongly predisposed to what are (at least in my opinion) the most advanced and enlightened views of them."[15]

This letter, which went on to make some criticism, including the point that the author attributed far too exclusive an influence upon national character to race and climate, was the beginning, for Dilke, of a most valuable and formative relationship. As soon as Mill returned to England he invited Dilke to dine at Blackheath. On Easter Day, 1869, the meeting took place. Thereafter the acquaintance rapidly developed into a close friendship, with Dilke happily accepting the role of disciple. In May of the same year Mill secured Dilke's election to the Political Economy Club, his candidature prevailing over that of such distinguished if heterogeneous rivals as Shaw Lefevre, Louis Mallet, Monckton Milnes and John Morley. At that time Mill was endeavouring to lead the club away from the rigidly individualist doctrine which it had been taught by Ricardo, Malthus, and his own father and towards his own, recently developed, semi-socialist views. He was strongly opposed by Henry Fawcett. Dilke, however, had little difficulty in deciding to support his new master rather than his old teacher. "I gradually deserted Fawcett," he wrote, "and, more and more influenced by Mill's later views, finally came to march even in front of Mill in our advance."[16]

For the remaining four years of Mill's life, Dilke was constantly in touch with him. When Mill was at Blackheath there were frequent meetings. When he was at Avignon there was regular correspondence, with Mill pouring out advice to Dilke on the widest possible range of subjects. Women's suffrage, the position of trades unions, land reform, colonial policy, and opposition to the Cowper-Temple approach to denominational teaching in schools were all issues on which Mill wrote to his disciple, and on which Dilke saw almost completely eye to eye with his master. Even on foreign policy there was substantial agreement, Mill being little more attracted by a peace-at-any-price approach than was Dilke. "If Gladstone had been a great man," he wrote about the Franco-Prussian conflict on September 30th, 1870, "this war would never have broken out; for he would have nobly taken upon himself the responsibility of declaring that the English navy should actively aid whichever of the two powers was attacked by the other. This would have been a beginning of the international police we are calling for."[17]

Dilke, both in his speeches and in his private writings, always used Mill's name with a respect that was little short of reverence. Discussing the payment of members of Parliament at a public meeting, he expressed a preference for the plan of payment by the constituency put forward by "Mr. Mill, the great leader of political thinkers." Considering his own attitude towards the trades unionist, George Odger,[§] he settled the matter by noting that Odger was "a man of whom the highest opinion was entertained by Mr. Mill." When Mill died, in May, 1873, it was a severe loss to Dilke. Throughout his life he retained his respect for Mill's memory, and was always eager to rush to the defence of the latter's reputation. He took a curious pride in the fact that 76, Sloane Street was the last house at which Mill dined out, and derived a less curious satisfaction from the completion in the last few weeks of the sitter's life of the portrait of Mill by G. F. Watts, which Dilke had commissioned and which at present hangs in the Westminster City Hall.

Some part of the notice which was attracted by *Greater Britain* may have been due to the fact that its publication coincided, within a week or so, with Dilke's election to the House of Commons. In November, 1867, while in the middle of his work on the book, he had been adopted as a Liberal candidate for the two-member parliamentary borough of Chelsea. This was a new constituency, created under the Reform Act of that year, with the enormous electorate, for those days, of 30,000. Its size enabled Dilke to announce proudly, if a little rhetorically, at his opening meeting, that he "would willingly wait any time rather than enter the House of Commons a member for some small trumpery constituency." The Chelsea division contained Dilke's family house in Sloane Street and the whole of the present metropolitan borough, but it contained a great deal else as well.

[§] A large part of whose expenses at the Stafford by-election of 1869 were paid by Dilke.

It covered the prosperous residential districts of South Kensington and Notting Hill, as well as the more working-class areas of Fulham, Hammersmith and Kensal Green.

Despite his temporary ill-health and the competing claims of his work on *Greater Britain*, Dilke was a vigorous campaigner. He spoke all over his constituency, and he never skimped his speeches. He believed that the electorate should hear his views "not upon any one subject or upon any two subjects or any three, but as nearly as might be upon all." The platform upon which he stood might be described as one of moderate radicalism. He was in favour of the ballot and of removing election petitions from the House of Commons to the Courts of Law. He wanted triennial parliaments and the payment of members. He believed that the onus of proof must be on those who wished to exclude anyone from the suffrage, but he also put forward the balancing view that he saw sufficient proof at that time for the temporary exclusion of certain classes. On Ireland, he advocated church disestablishment, land reform, and a wide measure of parliamentary reform. Then, when "we have done our duty . . . we may well call upon the Irish to do theirs." He disassociated himself from the violence of the Fenian approach. Army reform, including the abolition of flogging, of the purchase of commissions, and of the office of an independent commander-in-chief, was also prominent in his programme.

Dilke later indicated that his true position at this time was well to the left of his platform. "I tried to be moderate, in order to please my father, and not to lose the general Liberal vote," he wrote; "and my speeches were more timid than were my opinions."[18] Despite these efforts Sir Wentworth Dilke was disturbed, and wrote a letter of remonstration within a month of the commencement of his son's candidature. The reply which he received was uncompromising.

"For my own part," Charles Dilke's letter ran, "though I should immensely like to be in Parliament, still I should feel terribly hampered there if I went in as anything except a Radical. Now I have spoken against Fenianism in spite of my immense sympathy for it. Radicalism is too much a thing of nature with me to throw it off by any effort of mine. If you think it a waste of money for me to contest Chelsea, I will cheerfully throw the thing up and turn to any pursuit you please."[19]

The offer to abandon his candidature was not perhaps to be taken too seriously (it is certainly difficult to imagine Charles Dilke cheerfully turning to any other career nominated by his parent), but it served its purpose. Little more complaint was heard from Wentworth Dilke, who paid the election expenses of his radical son with a good deal more cheerfulness than his son would have obeyed his instructions.

The dissolution came in the autumn of 1868, and polling in Chelsea was on November 18th. The other Liberal candidate was Sir Henry Hoare, who had already been in the House of Commons for a short time as member for Windsor, and whose views at that stage of his life were almost as radical as those of Dilke. There were two Conservatives in the field, C. F. Freake, a Kensington contractor, who had built the Cromwell Road, and W. H. Russell, who had achieved fame as the correspondent of *The Times* in the Crimea. The result was a decisive victory for the Liberals, and a personal triumph for Dilke, who polled nearly 200 votes more than the much older and politically more experienced Hoare. The figures were:

Dilke	.. ..	7,374
Hoare	.. ..	7,183
Russell	.. ..	4,177
Freake	.. ..	3,929

Dilke's moderation had apparently been more successful in conciliating the general Liberal vote than in reassuring his father. Indeed it could be claimed that his own feigned moderation was more successful in winning votes than was his father's genuine moderation, for at the same election Wentworth Dilke lost his seat at Wallingford. Despite his son's opinions and the often strained relations between them, Wentworth Dilke was probably well enough satisfied with the exchange. He knew his own political limitations, and, as was shown by his work on the proofs of *Greater Britain*, he was eagerly ambitious for his son. Within three months of his election, in July, 1865, he had written to Charles Dilke: "We will talk about the H(ouse) of C(ommons). I fear I cannot make a hit there—you could, after a little maturity comes on you, and that will come whether you like it or not."[20] His attitude in 1868 was probably well summed up by a note which Lord Granville, who knew the family well, wrote to him immediately after the results were known. Granville wrote to Wentworth Dilke "to condole with you and to congratulate you. I suspect," he added, "that the cause of the latter gives you more pleasure than the cause of the former gives you regret. How very well your son seems to have done!"[21] At this election Mill, also, lost the seat at Westminster which he too had held since 1865.

Neither of these defeats did much to mar Charles Dilke's sense of triumph and opportunity—Mill, of course, he had not met at this stage. He was still only twenty-five. He had added a world tour to his Cambridge achievements. He had published a most successful book. He had been elected with gratifyingly large support for a constituency of note. His name was known; his presence was in demand; and his future seemed assured. With all this to contemplate he set off for a brief visit to Paris and Toulon, the latter the centre of an area which he now saw for the first time and with which he was later to be closely associated. By December 10th he was back in London for the meeting of Parliament and the swearing-in of members.

Chapter Three

Member for Chelsea

The General Election of 1868 not only brought Charles Dilke into the House of Commons; it also produced the only clear-cut party majority since 1841 and made Gladstone Prime Minister for the first time. The Liberals had 112 seats more than their opponents, and a still greater preponderance in the country. They polled more than one and a half million votes, the Conservatives less than a million. Gladstone's personal triumph was less marked than that of his party. He was defeated in South-west Lancashire, his seat in the previous Parliament, but he had also been nominated for Greenwich, where he was elected, in Dilke's words, "as junior colleague to a gin distiller." Undeterred by these setbacks, he received the Queen's intimation that he was to form a Government with the statement, "My mission is to pacify Ireland," and returned briefly to the tree-felling upon which he had been engaged when interrupted. Of the Cabinet which he subsequently formed, Lord Morley tells us, he always spoke as "one of the best instruments for government that ever were constructed."[1] Lord Clarendon, against the opposition of the Queen, was Foreign Secretary, Robert Lowe Chancellor of the Exchequer, Lord Granville Colonial Secretary, and the Duke of Argyll Indian Secretary. John Bright entered the Cabinet for the first time as President of the Board of Trade, and W. E. Forster, who did not come into the Cabinet itself until two years later, was Vice-President of the Council, in charge of education.

This Government commanded less admiration from Dilke than from its chief. "The Cabinet is somewhat behind the party, which is bad," the former wrote on December 10th, adding laconically, "Too many peers."[2] Even the party, however, was not greatly to Dilke's liking. He noted with approval that it had shed most of its "Adullamites," but thought it equally bereft of radicals. At first, indeed, either through arrogance or pessimism, he believed himself to be the only member to whom this label could be applied. It soon became clear that he was wrong in this view, and he worked during the parliament in shifting alliance and varying degrees of closeness with Harcourt, Fawcett, G. O. Trevelyan and Lord Edmond Fitzmaurice, as well as with a group of nonconformist provincial radicals which included Peter Rylands from Warrington, Llewellyn Dillwyn from Swansea, Henry Richard from Merthyr Tydfil, George Anderson from Glasgow, George Dixon from Birmingham and Peter Taylor from Leicester. The members of this group saw eye to eye with Dilke on most home policy questions, but in foreign affairs they were "peace-at-any-price" men of the Bright school, and as such had little in common with him. Furthermore, they were socially and personally much less close to Dilke than were the Cambridge radicals, Harcourt, Trevelyan and Fitzmaurice, and, a little more doubtfully, Fawcett.

Trevelyan, who was at this time Civil Lord of the Admiralty, recorded long afterwards his recollections of his early friendship with Dilke.

"I was a very young Minister," he wrote in 1911, "worked hard all day by Mr. Childers, a very strict but very friendly taskmaster, and never, according to the Treasury Bench discipline of those heroic times, allowed to be absent from the House for a single moment. I used to come to the House unlunched and desperately hungry; and I got my dinner at four o'clock in an empty dining-room. Afternoon after afternoon, Charles Dilke used to come and sit with me; and a greater delight than his company, young to the young, I can hardly describe. But it does not need description . . . for never did anyone's talk alter less as time went on."[3]

Harcourt, who was then new to the House of Commons and not in the Government, although possessing a considerable outside reputation, was Dilke's closest associate at the time. Brilliant in phrase, tempestuous in character, patrician in manner,* and radical in view, his make-up was nicely calculated to appeal strongly to the young member for Chelsea.

Dilke, in his early days in the House, had little social contact either with the Tories or with the Whigs on his own side. This was despite the view, which he expressed half seriously a few

---

* A few years later Dilke noted that a meeting had been "sufficiently interesting to keep Harcourt and a Duke standing for three hours—putting Harcourt first because he was the more august."

years later, that "in politics one always personally prefers one's opponents to one's friends."[4] But he was fascinated by Disraeli (who attracted him far more than did Gladstone), and he had the highest respect for Gathorne Hardy, whom he considered the most genuinely eloquent Englishman to whom he ever listened, and whose services he thought were not fully used by the Conservative party.

From his first days in the House, Dilke was a most regular attender in the Chamber; and this regularity quickly became a habit which never left him throughout his parliamentary career. In an age when members were far more willing to listen to the speeches of others than is the case to-day, he was noted for his almost unfailing attention to all aspects of the business of the House. He sat below the gangway, on the front bench on the Government side, and he soon acquired a proprietary right to the corner seat—a position separated from the official Government front bench above the gangway by the shortest physical distance but by a rather wider political gap. From this seat he first addressed the House on March 9th, 1869. The subject he chose was a typically complicated one. Harcourt had moved to appoint a Select Committee to enquire into the system of registration of electors in parliamentary boroughs, and Dilke spoke in support of this motion, drawing in great detail on his French and Australian observations. As a maiden speech it was a ponderous effort, and could not possibly have been considered an oratorical triumph. But it showed the House that he had a capacity for mastering a subject, and he soon attained more fame through the heterodoxy of his opinions than even the most flamboyant rhetoric would have brought him.

Within a month or so of his first speech he was sharply at odds with the Liberal Government, which he found excessively timid, on an election expenses bill, on a move to disenfranchise a corrupt borough, on university tests, on competitive entry to the civil service, and on the navy estimates. On the first four points he was strongly radical, but on the last he supported a technical criticism put forward by the former Conservative First Lord of the Admiralty. These displays of independence brought remonstrances both from the Chief Whip, George Glyn, and from Sir Wentworth Dilke. He was disinclined to listen to either. "I don't mean to let either you or Glyn frighten me into supporting the Government when I think they are wrong," he wrote to his father in April, "but I vote with them when I am at all doubtful. I voted with them against Groves on 1/2 d. postage which was a very tight fit for my conscience."[5]

This was one of the last letters he wrote to his father. Sir Wentworth Dilke was at that time on a tour of northern Europe with his younger son. He reached St. Petersburg, where he was to be English Commissioner at a Horticultural Exhibition, but almost as soon as he got there he was attacked by what was described as a "deadly form of Russian influenza." Charles Dilke was summoned from London by telegram and set out immediately for Russia. Before he could complete the long train journey across Europe, his father was dead. In St. Petersburg he could do no more than arrange for the transportation of the body back to England, and make some useful Russian contacts which he was to follow up in a series of seven return visits in the following three years.[†]

[†] He made an extended visit in the autumn of 1869, accompanied by his brother, and penetrated as far as Siberia in the east and Astrakhan in the south. A year later, he was again there for several months, and on this

In the course of his twenty-sixth year, therefore, Charles Dilke not only became a member of Parliament, but also succeeded to his father's baronetcy and to a large part of his family fortune. Wentworth Dilke divided his property into two unequal parts, two-thirds going with the tide to his elder son, and one-third to his younger son. Three years later Charles Dilke was to alter this arrangement by voluntarily making over a sixth of the total to Ashton Dilke and thus placing himself and his brother upon an equal footing. In the subsequent decade Ashton Dilke, largely as a result of successful newspaper proprietorship, became a very much richer man than his brother. But Charles Dilke was never badly off. He did not, of course, have the income of a great landed magnate or a famous financier, but for a member of the top ranks of the upper-middle class, pursuing throughout most of his life no gainful occupation, he was extremely well placed. In 1870 his unearned income was £8,000. By 1872, when the new arrangement with Ashton Dilke had been made, it had fallen to £7,000, and by 1880, owing to the "depression of trade," it had fallen further to £5,700. In this last year, however, it was supplemented by an official salary for part of the year which amounted to £980. He saved little, as indeed, with a capital of £100,000 at his disposal, he had small need to do, but in most years he lived within his income. 1872, the year of his first marriage, when he

occasion he spent more time in St. Petersburg and Moscow. His intention was to publish a book on Russia which would be to some extent a companion volume to *Greater Britain*. But he never fulfilled this intention. Curiously, Hepworth Dixon, his companion and literary rival in America, was in the field again, and produced in 1870 exactly such a companion volume—*Free Russia*—to his own American book. This may have had something to do with Dilke's change of plan.

spent £9,330, was an exception, but 1880, with total outgoings of £5,050, was a more typical year.

About half of Dilke's income came from journalistic properties with which his grandfather had been concerned. In 1880, which was a bad year, these provided £2,845—£1,900 from the *Athenæum*, £620 from the *Gardener's Chronicle*, and £325 from *Notes and Queries*. Of the remainder, nearly £1,800 came from dividends and interest on various Stock Exchange securities, £700 from house and other property in London, and the remaining £1,150 from miscellaneous sources, including one or two small family trusts. *Greater Britain*, twelve years after publication, produced a royalty of £8 12s.

Despite this comparative affluence to which he succeeded, Charles Dilke did not respond to his inheritance by any immediate increase in his scale of living. On the contrary, one of his first actions was to dispose of Alice Holt—"a mere shooting place"— and of Hawkley, another Hampshire property which his father had acquired. 76, Sloane Street, on the other hand, now became Charles Dilke's own home, and remained so until the end of his life. Mrs. Chatfield, his grandmother, continued to run the house, as she had done in his father's lifetime, and her niece, Miss Folkard, and Ashton Dilke, when he was not at Cambridge or abroad, continued to live there.

Dilke's activities in English politics were reduced neither by the death of his father nor by the rearrangement of affairs and the Russian visits to which this gave rise. During 1869, his first session in Parliament, he succeeded, with Jacob Bright, in restoring to women ratepayers the right to vote in municipal elections which they had lost in 1835. He also took the lead in securing the abolition of hanging, drawing and quartering in New Zealand. At the end of that year, he worked hard for Odger, who was supported also by Fitzmaurice and Fawcett, at the Southwark by-election. Odger stood as a radical working man's candidate against an official Whig, and the result of the contest was to hand to the Tories what was normally a safe Liberal seat. Another result was to strengthen Dilke's sense of isolation from the main body of his party, and to turn his thoughts increasingly towards some sort of independent radical organisation.‡

During the session of 1870 Dilke was again active in the cause of women's suffrage, and succeeded, once more in association with Jacob Bright, in obtaining a Second Reading for a measure providing for this. The bill died in Committee, but it was the only time until 1897 that the House of Commons pronounced in favour of the principle. In this year, too, Dilke became chairman of the Commons Preservation Society, which fought a largely successful campaign, both inside and outside Parliament, to stop the enclosure of open spaces—a process which had been going on fast for the previous quarter of a century. "We saved Wisley Common and Epping Forest," Dilke noted. Another office which Dilke took on at the same time was

---

‡ Even after Southwark, however, an attempt was made by the leadership to pull Dilke back into closer communion with the Liberal party. Gladstone, who never understood Dilke well and who at this time regarded him with more suspicion than respect, made a rather typically half-hearted attempt to entice him away from his militant radicalism. He asked him to second the Address to the Crown at the opening of the session of 1870, adding to the letter some rather belated words of congratulation on *Greater Britain*. Dilke accepted, appeared in the traditional court dress, and made a trite little speech entirely devoted to foreign affairs and the cloudless prospect which he saw before Europe. This done, he returned with unabated enthusiasm to his attacks on the Government on the home front.

that of secretary of the newly-formed Radical Club. The club was to have forty members, half of them in the House and half outside. Mill was the leading member, and others of note were John Morley, Leslie Stephen, Frank Hill (the editor of the *Daily News*), and Henry Sidgwick. It never attained quite the influence which was anticipated by its founders.

By far the most important issue in home politics during these years was the education controversy. English popular education was appallingly inadequate. In Birmingham, which was to become the centre of a great agitation, less than half the children received any schooling at all, and that given to most of the remainder was irregular in time and indifferent in quality. In the rest of the country the position was little better. Such schools as existed were voluntary and denominational. The demand for a large measure of educational reform was greatly reinforced by the franchise reform of 1867. There were obvious political as well as commercial dangers in allowing the urban working class, now given the vote, to remain so largely illiterate. When the Liberal Government came into office, a number of its members and most of its supporters believed that one of its most pressing tasks was to introduce a national system of elementary education. And at least one powerful group amongst these supporters—the nonconformist middle-class element—insisted that the national system should be universal, compulsory and non-sectarian. Such religious instruction as continued in the schools should be confined to simple bible-teaching. This was the basis on which, at the beginning of 1869, the National Education League was set up, with George Dixon, one of the members for Birmingham, as chairman, Jesse Collings as secretary, and Joseph Chamberlain as vice-chairman.

Chamberlain, seven years Dilke's senior, was then thirty-three years of age. He was a successful business man, with no political experience—he did not become a member of the Birmingham City Council until later that year—but with a pulsating, ruthless energy, and a clear if sometimes narrow sense of political purpose. He was by no means an uncultivated man. Indeed, for one of his background at the time he was very much the reverse. He spoke French well, he was widely read, and he was always willing to be interested in new subjects, from painting to wine, of which he had previously known little. But the pursuit of ideas and the acquisition of knowledge were completely subordinated, with him, to the achievement of results. He wanted power, although he was indifferent to place, and he was contemptuous of speculation that did not lead to action.

From the first he was the effective leader of the Education League; and he made it, in the words of his biographer, "the most powerful engine of agitation since the Anti-Corn Law League."[6] But it was not powerful enough to make the Government produce the sort of bill which it wanted. The Prime Minister was about as far from his nonconformist support-ers on the education issue as it is possible to imagine. Like many highly-educated classicists, he was never very interested in the subject, and least of all was he interested during the period of preparation of the Bill when his mind was wrapped in the Irish land question to the exclusion of almost all else. In so far as he did think about the matter his thoughts were those of a High Anglican who attached first importance to the proper teaching of the catechism. From this it followed naturally, as he was later laconically to tell a Hawarden audience, that he thought "volun-tary schools the best."

The member of the Cabinet most directly concerned with

the issue was Lord de Grey, the Lord President. Although a man of firm Liberal views on most subjects, de Grey was soon to become a convert to Roman Catholicism, and was no better from the nonconformist point of view than Gladstone himself. The third minister involved was W. E. Forster, who had charge of the bill in the House of Commons. Forster, who shared with the Queen alone the great Victorian distinction of having a railway terminus[§] named after him, seemed more promising to the Education League. He was a Quaker by upbringing, and he had been excluded from that communion on the ground that he had married a sister of Matthew Arnold. He had spent twenty years of his life preaching the need for State action to remedy the deficiencies of English education, and he sat for Bradford, which had a strong radical tradition. But Forster was a complicated man. Despite his Quaker background and his marriage with Dr. Arnold's daughter, his favourite recreation was card-playing and his favourite companion in this pursuit was the Duchess of Manchester. He developed a close sympathy for the Anglican church and a desire to preserve what was good in the existing order—which meant building a national education system around the framework of the voluntary schools. In addition he was a stubborn, irascible man, with a great capacity for defying his constituents or anyone else who disagreed with him.

The bill which Forster introduced into the House of Commons on February 17th, 1870, in a speech of high distinction, and which he was later to defend with unfailing tenacity, was a major blow to the nonconformists and the radicals. The existing

---

§ Forster Square Station, Bradford

voluntary schools were to be the pivot of the new system. Indeed the denominations were to be given a year's grace in which to fill up gaps before any public elementary school should be established; and even in these public elementary schools any religious instruction which the newly-established local School Boards thought proper might be provided. The National Education League responded to the challenge by launching a new campaign and by organising a great deputation, nearly 500 strong, including forty-six members of Parliament, which waited upon Gladstone, de Grey and Forster at 10, Downing Street, on the afternoon of Wednesday, March 9th. There were two principal spokesmen of the deputation. The first was Chamberlain, still very new to national politics; and the second was Dilke, who had more political sophistication and more experience, but less years and, perhaps, less natural authority on the issue.

Dilke's position in the controversy was somewhat different from Chamberlain's. He was not a nonconformist provincial manufacturer. He was a metropolitan *rentier*, whose religious views when they existed were Anglican, but who was passing through a period of temporary scepticism. As such he was not particularly attracted by the "bible-teaching" approach of the National Education League. Nevertheless he was a radical, suspicious of Gladstone, impatient of the established English tradition, and horrified by the relative educational backwardness of his country. He was therefore more than willing to accept the chairmanship of the London branch of Chamberlain's League and to take a prominent part in the deputation to the Prime Minister. But he was essentially a secularist and not a protestant in his approach to the question of religion in schools. Later in the year he was the only Liberal member of Parliament who voted against the Cowper-Temple amendment, which was accepted by the Government as its main concession to nonconformist pressure and which provided that, in the Board schools, a simple undenominational religion should be taught. This compromise, in Dilke's view, did injustice to important classes in the community—notably the Roman Catholics and the non-believers—while the religion which it would introduce would be only "of the driest and baldest kind, and such as would be hardly worthy of the name." In this view he was supported by Mill but by hardly anyone else. The London branch of the League was not with him, and he resigned the chairmanship. Chamberlain, still a practising Unitarian at this time, believed that secularism would be a hopelessly disruptive platform on which to stand. And Harcourt, who was working in partial alliance with the League, agreed with Chamberlain from the very different premise of a loose, Whiggish attachment to the Church of England, to which religious body he usually referred in patronising, Erastian terms as the "parliamentary church." "Now as a politician (not as a philosopher)," he wrote to Dilke, "I am quite satisfied that neither in the House of Commons nor in the country can we beat Denominationalism by Secularism."[7]

Thereafter Dilke pursued a course to some extent independent of his nonconformist allies. But it was not one which brought him any closer to the Government. Throughout the committee stage of the bill, during the summer of 1870, when Gladstone was constantly dependent on Conservative votes to maintain his majority,¶ Dilke voted rather more frequently

---

¶ On one occasion fewer than a hundred liberal back-benchers voted with the Prime Minister. One hundred and thirty-two went into the lobby against him; and a similar number ostentatiously abstained.

against the Treasury Bench than with it. His varying support was not without results, for he was able to secure two significant changes in the Bill. The first provided that the new School Boards should be directly elected by the ratepayers instead of being committees of the Boards of Vestries, as had originally been proposed; and the second that these elections should be by ballot.

Much the most important result of the education contro-versy for Dilke was that it made Chamberlain known to him. They may have met briefly in 1869, but their first encounter of note was on the occasion of the Downing Street deputation in March, 1870. It would be an exaggeration to say that this meeting marked the beginning of a tumultuous friendship. Chamberlain never took quickly to new acquaintances, and on personal grounds he greatly preferred John Morley to Dilke throughout most of the 'seventies. This was at least partly due to a certain social and political jealousy of Dilke, with his seat in the House of Commons, his literary reputation, and his wide range of international contacts. With a young journalist from Blackburn, even if of a character as prickly as John Morley's, Chamberlain thought he knew more where he was. But both he and Dilke were quick to perceive that they could each be of use to the other. Dilke's usefulness to Chamberlain was perhaps the more obvious. He could introduce the Birmingham City Councillor to the London political world, and teach him much about the working of parliamentary poli-tics. Chamberlain, for his part, could offer Dilke a close contact with the provincial radical movement. The Chelsea radical organisation was strong, and Dilke could later claim with some justification that he had developed an effective caucus there before the Birmingham Election Association was thought of,

58

and before Schnadhorst had emerged from his draper's shop. But Chelsea was far less typical of English radicalism than was Chamberlain's nonconformist Birmingham. If Dilke was to be a national radical leader with some sort of organisation behind him, and not merely a young parliamentary gadfly, perhaps sowing a few political oats like Harcourt, perhaps preparing to develop into a House of Commons eccentric like Labouchere, the Chamberlain connection was essential to him. The National Education League, as Chamberlain himself was soon to see, was erected on too narrow a platform to be a fully effective political movement, but it offered greater possibilities than the radical Eleusis Club in Chelsea or the Commons Preservation Society.

It was on a basis of mutual political advantage that the Dilke-Chamberlain relationship began, even though it was later to develop, certainly on Dilke's side and probably on Chamberlain's too, into a warm and genuine personal friendship. The first letter in a long and intensive series was written by Dilke from Sloane Street on October 27th, 1870, and was typically brief:

My dear Sir,
What day (except a Wednesday) could you dine with me? I should be very glad to see you sometimes in London and could offer you a bed for a few nights whenever you are coming up.

Yours truly,
Charles W. Dilke.[8]

The invitation was accepted, and was followed by many more. The terms of the letters became a little more intimate. "My dear Sir" was replaced by "My dear Chamberlain," "Yours truly" by "Yours ever" and "Charles W. Dilke" by "Ch. W. D."; and the replies which came from Birmingham progressed in step. All the political letters, on both sides, were hard, sinewy communications, plunging straight into their subject. On social subjects Chamberlain, in the early days, was sometimes a little less assured and direct.

> "If so I hope you will stay with me," he wrote in the autumn of 1872, discussing a possible visit by Dilke to Birmingham; "and if you would bring Lady Dilke with you (Dilke had then been seven months married), to see one of the ugliest towns in England, my wife would be delighted to make her acquaintance. . . . We have room and can easily accommodate Lady Dilke's maid, if she would like to have her with her—and perhaps it would be better as my wife has no lady's maid."[9]

Difficulties as to ladies' maids, the ugliness of Birmingham and other similar points were triumphantly surmounted, however; correspondence, mutual visiting and general intercourse became steadily more frequent and more relaxed.

Before the end of the session of 1870, on July 19th, France declared war against Prussia. Dilke hated the Second Empire and was full of vague feelings of nordic solidarity with the Germans. "Our true alliance," he had told his Chelsea electors in 1868, "is not with the Latin peoples, but with men who speak our tongue, with our brothers in America, and with our kinsmen in Germany and Scandinavia."[10] At first, therefore, he wished for a Prussian victory, and was one of the few who believed it likely. But the war aroused his curiosity more strongly than his sympathy. It was the first major campaign in Western Europe for 55 years, and he was determined to see what he could of it.

Four days after the declaration he left London by train for Paris, travelled on to Strasbourg on the same night, and paid brief visits to the fortifications at Metz and the Imperial Guard at Nancy before returning to England in the following week. Immediately on his return he arranged with two other members of Parliament, Auberon Herbert, whom he described as "politically the bravest, although not politically the strongest, man of our time," and Winter-botham, who was later under-secretary at the Home Office before dying young, that they should all three attach themselves in an ambulance capacity to the army of the Crown Prince of Prussia. A few days later they caught up with the headquarters at Sulz, near Stüttgart, and were duly enrolled as Prussian Knights of St. John. Throughout the first three weeks of August they advanced with the invading Prussian troops. Dilke witnessed the battles of Worth, Phalsbourg, Mars-la-Tour and Gravelotte; and was able, many years later, to silence an interrupting Tory colonel in a House of Commons debate on the army estimates with the retort: "I have been on more battlefields than the honourable and gallant member has ever seen."

The atmosphere, even on the Prussian side, was strangely informal. Dilke's party were very short of food at times, but kept themselves going by such expedients as buying part of the King of Prussia's luncheon from an innkeeper at Pont-à-Mousson. While they were eating this purchase they were interrupted by General Sir Henry Havelock, who had been brought out to see the fighting by the Prussian military attaché in London and was "in hiding," being apparently absent without leave from the Horse Guards. Another Englishman Dilke encountered was the town commandant of Wissembourg, of whom he at first wrote as "a most accomplished man. . . . an English volunteer, who lives in London when at home," but whom he later discovered to be a lunatic, who had assumed the office of commandant under no authority other than his own, but who held it unchallenged for several weeks.

Despite these engaging signs of Prussian disorganisation, Dilke's sympathies were soon changing. "Winterbotham continued to be very German," he wrote, "but Herbert and I began to wish to desert when we saw how overbearing success had made the Prussians and how determined they were to push their successes to a point at which France would have been made impotent in Europe. . . ."[11] In these circumstances Dilke was glad of the opportunity to go back to Heidelberg in charge of an ambulance train of wounded French officers, and thus to escape from the battle area. As soon as he reached Heidelberg, which took him several days because the signalling system on the French side of the frontier had broken down, he freed himself from his engagement and made his way back to London by Switzerland and Paris.

On the evening on which he reached home the capture of the Emperor at Sedan was announced in the evening papers. In consequence Dilke decided to return to Paris immediately. He was there, having given the first news of Sedan to an incredulous crowd in front of the railway station at Calais, in time for the change of régime.

> "On the morning of the 4th September," he wrote later, "my birthday and that of the French Republic, I was standing in Paris with Labouchere . . . in front of the Grand Hotel upon the Boulevard in an attitude of expectation. We had not long to wait. A battalion of fat National Guards from the centre of Paris, shopkeepers all, marched firmly

past, quietly grunting 'L'abdication! L'abdica-tion!' They were soon followed by a battalion from the outskirts marching faster, and gaining on them to the cry of 'Pas d'abdication! La déchéance! La déchéance!' It was a sunny cloudless day. The bridge leading to the Corps Législatif was guarded by a double line of mounted Gardes de Paris, but there were few troops to be seen, and were indeed but very few in Paris. . . . Labouchere kept on making speeches to the crowd in various characters: sometimes as a Marseillais, sometimes as an Alsatian, sometimes as an American, sometimes as an English sympathiser; I in terror all the while lest the same listeners should catch him playing two different parts and should take us for Prussian spies. We kept watching the faces of the cavalry to see whether they were likely to fire or charge, but at last the men began one by one to sheath their swords and to cry 'Vive la République!' and the captain in command at last cried 'Vive la République!' too and withdrew his men, letting the crowd swarm across the bridge. So fell the Second Empire, and I wished that my grandfather had lived to see the day of the doom of the man he hated."[12]

Dilke watched the leaders go into the Chamber for a short discussion and then emerge to chalk up on one of the columns the names of the members of the Provisional Government. ". . . I drew the moral," he wrote, "on a day of revolution always have a bit of chalk." He then went with the crowd to the flower-bedecked statue of Strasbourg—where Labouchere made yet another speech—and was afterwards swept through the imperial apartments in the Tuileries, seizing on the way a piece of one of the broken eagles. In the evening he dined with Lord Lyons in "such a costume as had never till then been seen at dinner at the Embassy." For another twelve days he remained in Paris, inspecting the fortifications, watching the bedraggled French troops prepare for the defence of the city, and seeing something of such political leaders as Louis Blanc, Jules Favre and Blanqui. The investment of the city was complete by September 15th, and on the following day Dilke, taking one of the last trains from the Gare de Lyon, left for Geneva. He then made his way through Lyons and up to Tours, where he saw the Army of the Loire, and collected some "despatches" from the Ambassador, which included the correspondence of Mme. de Pourtalès and the Princesse de Metternich, before leaving for Rouen, Calais and England. "What a sad farce the whole thing was," he commented rather condescendingly on the Empire whose fall he had witnessed, "but how seriously Europe took it at the time!"[13]

During most of the autumn and early winter Dilke was in Russia, but the fascination of the conflict in France remained strong for him. Almost as soon as he was back in England he set off across the Channel again in order to see something of the January campaign in the north of France. He was present at Bapaume and at Longwy, and at Lille he heard Gambetta, whom he did not then know, make one of his great speeches. "It was the finest oratorical display to which I ever listened," he wrote, "though I have heard Castelar, Bright, Gladstone, the Prime Minister Lord Derby, Gathorne Hardy, and Father Félix (the great Jesuit preacher) often, at their very best."[14] Food was short at this time, but Dilke used to make frequent day trips by the packet to Dover in order to stock up. As soon as the siege of Paris was raised, on January 29th, he went in armed with large quantities of condensed milk, and made presents to his friends.

Seven weeks later the Commune was proclaimed in Paris,

and fighting broke out between the National Guard battalions of the capital and the troops of the Provisional Government, which had transferred its headquarters to Versailles. Dilke was in London at the time, rather heavily involved with political disputes arising out of the Russian abrogation of the Black Sea Treaty, but he left for Paris within a fortnight, accompanied on this occasion by his brother, and arrived outside the Hôtel de Ville, where the Central Committee was in session, early on the morning of April 3rd. He had obtained an appointment as *Daily News* correspondent, which was largely honorary, but which allowed him to obtain passes and move about more easily. On the next day he and his brother went to Issy and spent the day sitting under a cemetery wall while a battle went on around them.

> "Here we sat in safety while the bullets sang in swarms through the trees over our heads, while the forts cannon-aded the heights, and the heights bombarded the forts, and while the federal regiments of the National Guard tried in vain to carry once more the line of hills which they had carried on the previous day, but had of their own accord at night abandoned, having no commissariat. They used in fact to go home to dinner. Indeed many would in the morning take an omnibus to the battlefield, and fight, and take the omnibus back home again to dine and sleep. . . ."[15]

On the day after that Ashton Dilke went again to see the fighting, this time at Neuilly, while Charles Dilke left Paris early by the Porte Montrouge and walked by Bourg la Reine and Châtenay to Versailles. There he had an interview with the Duc de Broglie, who was then Foreign Minister under Thiers, but by whom Dilke was unimpressed, finding him "a silly cunning person." "It afterwards became the fashion," he added, "as a part of that Conservative tradition which makes eagles of all Whigs and Tories, to declare that this vain and pompous person was a statesman."[16] After Versailles, Dilke went on to St. Germain, where he sat at luncheon watching the guns of Mont Valérien firing on Paris, and then drove to the Prussian head-quarters at St. Denis and on to Pantin. Then, "after a long parley the Belleville-Villette drawbridge was lowered for me, and I was admitted to Paris, having been almost all round it in the two days."

Dilke's sympathies were not clearly on the side of the Commune. He found that many of its supporters did not know what they were fighting about, and he thought that some of its actions, notably the massacre of hostages in the last days, were both criminal and useless. But he was by no means as inclined to dismiss its cause out of hand as were most foreign observers, nor to excuse all the acts of its opponents.

"On the 7th my brother and I were all but killed by a shell from Mont Valérien," a typical comment ran, "which suddenly burst, we not having heard it, close to us in a garden at the corner of the Place de l'étoile and the Avenue d'Urich (now the Avenue Foch), as the Avenue de l'Impératrice had at this time been named. . . . During the 7th and 8th a senseless bombardment of a peaceable part of Paris waxed warm, and continued for some days uselessly to destroy the houses of the best supporters of the Conservative Assembly, without harming the Federalists, who did not even cross the quarter. . . . The Commune had a broad back, and that back was made to bear the responsibility of the destruction."[17]

After a few more days of this Dilke returned to London for the post-Easter reassembly of the House of Commons. But he was back again in Paris on May 25th for the last agony of the Commune and the destruction by fire of large parts of the city. When he left finally several days later he was accompanied by his old opponent at Chelsea, W. H. Russell of *The Times*, and had seen as much of the war and its aftermath as almost anyone except for this redoubtable military correspondent. The pro-Prussian feeling with which he had begun had completely disappeared. The collapse of the Empire had removed the only obstacle to his natural feelings of affinity for France. Henceforward he was to be one of the most Francophile of Englishmen, assuming an almost proprietary interest in the fortunes of the Republic whose birth he had witnessed.

Chapter Four

An English Republican

Dilke's interest in republicanism was not confined to France. As a matter of general theory he had believed from his Cambridge days or earlier that a republic was the best form of government for any advanced country. "My grandfather was a conservative republican in old age," he wrote, "a radical republican in youth, but a republican through life, and . . . my young ideas were my grandfather's ideas."[1] Nor was his theoretical preference tempered by any excessive respect for the person of the Queen; despite, or perhaps because of, his father's close association with the Prince Consort and the Court, he regarded her as at best an expensive nuisance and at worst a strong reactionary force. But it was tempered, during most of his career, by the conviction that constitutional monarchy was firmly established in England, and that, this being so, attempts to uproot it were likely to be both unsuccessful and politically disadvantageous. To the extent that the monarchy was constitutional such attempts were also less necessary, of course. "To think and even to say that monarchy in Western Europe is a somewhat cumbersome fiction is not to declare oneself ready to fight against it on a barricade,"[2] he wrote; and this attitude of quiet detachment was that which he normally adopted towards the Throne.

During 1871, however, the roots of the English monarchy seemed a little less firm than usual. The Queen, in her tenth year of widowhood, remained almost totally withdrawn from public gaze and ceremonial duty. Much the greater part of her time was passed in her private residences at Osborne and Balmoral. She visited Windsor occasionally, but Buckingham Palace was untenanted from the beginning of a year to the end. She took no part in the entertainment of foreign visitors, and expended no substantial portion of the vast income she received from public funds upon the performance of State duties. "There is only one great capital in Europe where the Sovereign is unrepresented," one of the Queen's own equerries wrote to Gladstone, "and that capital is London."[3] The Prime Minister was not disposed to quarrel with this view, for he had tried three times during his premiership, on each occasion without success, to persuade the Queen to open or prorogue Parliament. But to the Parliament which she would not open she was constantly applying for marriage or coming-of-age grants to her sons or daughters.

The Prince of Wales did little to sustain the monarchy. Since his marriage in 1863 he had escaped from strict parental control and had become the leader of a section of London society. But he was allowed to perform no public duties, and his most notable public appearance had been in the witness-box, as a co-respondent, although one against whom no case was sustained, in the Mordaunt divorce suit of 1870. "To speak in rude and general terms," Gladstone wrote to Granville at the end of that year, "the Queen is invisible, and the Prince of Wales is not respected."[4]

In the following year, 1871, a great rash of republican clubs sprang up in the large towns and in some of the smaller ones too. More than fifty were established. Chamberlain became a member of one at Birmingham, and Fawcett founded one at Cambridge. Dilke took no part in this particular movement, and he also held aloof from a republican demonstration, largely under trades union auspices, which took place in Hyde Park in April. He sympathised warmly, however, with an anonymous pamphlet, written in fact by his friend G. O. Trevelyan and entitled *What does she do with it?* which appeared at about the same time. This was an attack on the Queen for her parsimony and her alleged hoarding of money. It achieved a large circulation.

In the same spirit Dilke opposed the two applications for Royal grants which came before the House of Commons during that session. The first was for a dowry of £30,000 for Princess Louise upon the occasion of her marriage with the Marquess of Lorne. Peter Taylor, the member for Leicester, took the lead in resisting this, and he was supported in the division lobby only by Dilke and Fawcett. The second was for an annual allowance of £15,000 to Prince Arthur, later Duke of Connaught, and aroused wider opposition. Fifty-three members voted for a reduction, and eleven for no allowance at all.

Encouraged to some extent by this vote and by the other manifestations of feeling (although certainly not to the extent of believing that the country was seething with republicanism and that he had merely to place himself at the head of the movement to achieve immediate success), Dilke decided to widen the front. He was engaged during the autumn of 1871 to make a series of speeches in the big provincial centres advocating a redistribution of seats. At the first of these meetings, in Manchester, he kept narrowly to his subject. But at the second, in Newcastle-upon-Tyne on November 6th, he led himself through the question of Princess Louise's dowry to a broader discussion of the monarchy. He saw it as a centre of waste, corruption and inefficiency in the national life. He began with an attack upon its privileged troops. The Foot Guards he excepted, but the Life Guards and the Royal Horse Guards he pilloried as being markedly less efficient than the ordinary cavalry of the line. He proceeded to list some of the fantastic sinecures, many of them carrying heavy salaries, which still existed around the Court. In the nature of these appointments and in the way in which they were made he saw the corrupting influence of the monarchy.

"To return for a moment to the consideration of the cost with which I began this speech," he said, "I have shown that it is enormous, and that the expenditure is chiefly not waste but mischief. . . . In the Army, we have a Royal Duke, not necessarily the fittest man, at the head of it by right of birth, and the Prince of Wales, who would never be allowed a command in time of war, put to head the Cavalry Division in the Autumn Manœuvres, thus robbing working officers of the position and of the training they had a title to expect."[5]

It does not sound very inflammatory material for a Tyne-side audience, but *The Times*, which reported the meeting as being largely composed of the working class, said that there was "great enthusiasm."

In his peroration Dilke was at once cautious and tendentious:

"It is said that some day a commonwealth will be our

government. Now, history and experience show that you cannot have a republic unless you possess at the same time the republican virtues. But you answer: Have we not public spirit? Have we not the practice of self-government? Are we not gaining general education? Well, if you can show me a fair chance that a republic here will be free from the political corruption which hangs about the monarchy, I say, for my part—and I believe that the middle classes in general will say—let it come."[6]

The speech provoked no immediate storm. It was not even reported in London until three days later, when *The Times* gave its readers in the same issue a one-and-a-half column account of what Dilke had said and a first leader strongly attacking his views. The leader was written in terms that were both venomous and magisterial. It quoted Dilke's peroration and commented: "Now we pass over the presumption which emboldens Sir Charles Dilke to speak in the name of the middle classes, and forbear to enquire how far he may be himself indebted to Royal favours. Looking only at the language as it is reported, and remembering that it comes from a member of the legislature, we cannot but recognise it as a recklessness bordering on criminality." After going on to discuss Dilke's detailed allegations of waste and nepotism, and suggesting in a more level tone that these might be proper points for the House of Commons, it announced severely: "But even these are not fair and legitimate points, and many others touched by Sir Charles are eminently improper points, to be handled, and that with little candour or delicacy, before an assembly of working men."[7] This leader attracted plenty of notice and from then on the comment was voluminous. Newspaper reaction was summarised by the

London correspondent of the *New York Tribune.** After remarking that Dilke's speech surpassed every other event of the day in popular interest, she wrote: "The *Standard* is in hysterics ... The *Saturday Review* condemns the speech in an article which would be called bitter in any other paper. The *Spectator*, which allows nobody to be radical without its express permission and after its own manner, attacks Sir Charles Dilke with ferocity."[8]

Verbal comment was if anything more severe. The wife of the Master of Trinity Hall, Mrs. Geldart, said that she had nursed her father on his death-bed, witnessed the dying agony of two sisters and the last moments of a beloved brother, but that she had never experienced any blow like that occasioned by Sir Charles's speech. Other comment from Cambridge acquaintances ranged from horror at the thought that the commentator might be called upon to row in the same boat as Dilke to the clear view that he ought to be shot. Lord Chelsea, perhaps feeling that his title gave him a personal responsibility for Dilke's utterances, regretted in a speech at Bath that the days of duelling were over. Chamberlain, almost alone, wrote a letter of firm support. "I am glad to see," he said, "that you have roused the Philistine indignation of *The Times* by your speech at Newcastle, which, as well as that at Manchester, I have read with interest and agreement. The Republic must come, and at the rate at which we are moving, it will come in our generation."[9]

No sooner had Dilke made his Newcastle speech than the Prince of Wales fell seriously ill. He was infected with typhoid fever while staying with Lord Londesborough near Scarborough. Lord Chesterfield and the Prince's groom, who were both present at Londesborough Lodge, were also attacked, and both

---

* Miss Kate Field, see *infra.* p. 81.

succumbed to the disease. The Prince became ill at Sandringham on November 9th, and on November 23rd the nature of his illness was made public. He became gradually worse until December 14th, the tenth anniversary of his father's death from the same disease. During the last week almost all private and public hope had been abandoned, but on the morning of the anniversary a sudden improvement set in, and a week later all danger was pronounced past. The youth of the sufferer, the long-drawn out nature of the illness, and the dramatic repetition and then reversal of the death-bed experience of the Prince Consort all served to concentrate public sympathy upon the monarchy to a remarkable extent. During the six weeks in which he lay ill at Sandringham the Prince accomplished more for the popularity of his house than during the whole of his previous thirty years of life. Republicanism immediately became unattractive. "What a sell for Dilke this illness has been,"[10] Lord Henry Lennox wrote to Disraeli.

The position was made more difficult by the fact that Dilke's speaking programme continued throughout the autumh. At each stage of the Prince's illness, he was due to expound his views in some provincial town. He was not always made very welcome, either by the audience, or, on occasion, by the sponsors of the meeting themselves. But he continued with his scheduled appearances. The first, after Newcastle, was at Bristol on November 20th. The chairman of the meeting was a brother of John Henry Newman, Professor F. W. Newman, who because of his habit of not reading the newspapers was apparently quite unaware of any special animosity against Dilke, and totally unprepared for trouble. Dilke commented that "the Cardinal himself could not have been more out of place than this feeble philosopher, who however tried to do his duty."[11] The meeting ended in uproar, a large part of the noise coming not from Tories, but from anti-Dilke Liberals.

Three days later, on the evening of the public announcement of the nature of the Prince's illness, Dilke was at Leeds. Here he had a much better reception, and was able to re-argu some of his Newcastle case. He withdrew little, although he denied using discourteous words about the Queen herself. He concluded with a slight re-statement of his position:

"To say these things is not to condemn the monarchy, because they are no necessary part of the monarchy, although the opposite idea—that of promotion by merit alone and of the non-recognition of any claims founded upon birth—is commonly accepted as republican. I care not whether you call it republican or whether you do not, but I say that it is the only principle upon which, if we are to keep our place among the nations, we can for the future act."[12]

Leeds was followed by an equally easy meeting at Middlesbrough, but Bolton, on November 30th, was the most difficult of the series. The meeting had been organised by the local Liberal Association, but this body, under the lead of J. K. Cross, later under-secretary for India, withdrew its support at the last moment, and the chairman also refused to appear. Perhaps encouraged by these defections, the opposition decided completely to wreck this meeting—and they succeeded. "There was a fearful riot," Dilke wrote, "at which a man was killed and a great number of persons injured by iron nuts and bars being thrown through the windows by the Tory roughs outside the hall."[13] It was believed by some that Dilke himself was in danger of his life. George Harwood, who was present at the meeting and who was later Liberal member for Bolton, described the scene many years afterwards:

> "The crowd was very thick and very fierce," he wrote, "having declared that Sir Charles should not get away alive; but when the excitement was hottest, Sir Charles came out of the main door and stood quietly in sight of all, then struck a match and lit his cigar, and walked unguarded and unaccompanied through the thickest part of the crowd. His cool courage took everyone's breath away, so not a sound was uttered."[14]

Dilke, however, denied the story, saying that "there was a large force of police in the street when I lighted (*sic*) my cigar and the mob could only howl."[15] After the meeting eight of those who had started the riot were brought to trial. The principal defence put forward on their behalf was that Dilke's opinions were so unpopular that his presence alone constituted an intolerable incitement. This was apparently accepted by the jury, who acquitted them all.

After Bolton, Dilke went to Birmingham. He spoke to a full Town Hall at the beginning of the week of greatest anxiety about the Prince's health. The meeting was a noisy one, according to Chamberlain's biographer, with the "monarchists" throwing cayenne pepper about the hall.[16] But according to Dilke the opposition was dealt with in a typically ruthless Chamberlain way. ". . . (he) had the whole borough police force present or in reserve," Dilke wrote, "and had every interrupter (and there were several hundred) carried out singly by two policemen, with a Conservative Chief of Police to direct them; after which I delivered an extremely humdrum speech to a very dull assembly."[17] The Birmingham Town Hall was then a safer place for radical politicians than it was to be when Chamberlain became an imperialist.

An excess of zeal on the part of the Birmingham police force was not required, however, to make Dilke deliver a dull speech. The excitement which his meetings aroused owed everything to his opinions and nothing to his oratory.

". . . given the fact that my speaking was always monotonous," he was later rather engagingly to write, "and that at this time I was trying specially to make speeches which no one could call empty noise, and was therefore specially and peculiarly heavy, there was something amusing to lovers of contrast in that between the stormy heartiness of my reception at most of these meetings, and the ineffably dry orations which I delivered to them between cheers of joy when I rose and cheers of relief when I sat down."[18]

During the early months of 1872 Dilke did not continue his platform campaign. The Prince of Wales's recovery was followed, on February 27th, by a national thanksgiving service in St. Paul's, to which both the Queen and the Prince drove in procession, through scenes of great enthusiasm.[†] The tide was running strongly the other way, and Dilke was troubled by rumours that

---

[†] Dilke, no doubt in common with all other members of Parliament, was sent two tickets for this ceremony, and a report afterwards circulated that he had used them, when he had much better have stayed away. But Dilke denied this, and the tickets, clearly marked "not used," are still to be seen amongst his papers.

an official Liberal was to be put into the field against him in Chelsea,‡ and by social ostracism. The first danger he took sufficiently seriously to discuss with Chamberlain the possibility of a move—Cardiff and Dewsbury being suggested as alternative constituencies. Social ostracism he certainly did not like, and, for a short period, it was so intense that, except for G. O. Trevelyan and Lord Edmond Fitzmaurice, he had no friends in London and lived in almost complete isolation.

Nevertheless, although Dilke was by now fully aware that a continuation of the agitation was politically pointless, he felt that he could not drop the subject until he had repeated in the House of Commons the arguments which had provoked so sharp a reaction outside. He sought to provide an occasion for this by moving to set up a Select Committee to enquire into the Civil List, but a day could not be obtained for such a motion until March 19th. Even then, George Dixon had something of a prior claim to be the mover, for he had given notice in the previous session that he wished to bring forward a similar proposal. In the event, however, he was only too anxious to leave the matter to Dilke. "Of course," he added, according to Dilke's report, "I shall go into the lobby with you if you divide the House"; "but . . . he did nothing of the kind," Dilke commented bitterly. "Neither did George Trevelyan,"[19] he added. Nor did

---

‡ Labouchere wrote to tell Dilke that he had heard that Lord Enfield, the son of the Earl of Strafford and a junior Minister, was proposing to stand for Chelsea as a "moderate Liberal." Dilke's reply was not particularly moderate: "1. If Lord Enfield resigns his office and does this—then I run a Tory against him. 2. If he keeps office he dare not oppose a Liberal. If he did we should run a radical against every moderate Liberal m the country." (D.P. 43892, 133.)

Fawcett, who even spoke against Dilke during the debate, nor Cowen, who had been chairman of the Newcastle meeting, nor Fitzmaurice. Auberon Herbert seconded the motion and acted with Dilke as a teller, while the lobby was composed only of Sir Wilfrid Lawson, the temperance reformer—"the wit of the public platforms, but a dismal man enough in private," as Dilke described him—and George Anderson, one of the Glasgow members.

Dilke stood up in a crowded House and was received with a loud and prolonged hostile demonstration. One Conservative member attempted to get the Speaker to refuse him a hearing on the ground that he had violated his oath of allegiance. When the noise died down, Dilke delivered a speech which was long, dull, and painstakingly factual. Towards the end members were trooping out of the chamber and amongst the few who remained conversation was so general that the speaker could scarcely be heard. ". . . my want of vivacity," Dilke noted, "tended to prevent the interruptions which had been organised. . . . This was exactly what I wished and intended. . . ."[20] Gladstone followed, and delivered a full-scale, declamatory attack upon Dilke. He had the House behind him, but the unequalness of the battle gave him no desire to cut it short. "He simply tried to trample upon Dilke," Lawson wrote. After the Prime Minister, Auberon Herbert insisted on speaking, and did so in terms which were much more provocative and much less soporific than Dilke's. Not merely at the beginning, but throughout his speech, the House was in an uproar. In the middle strangers were spied by Lord George Hamilton, and the Press having been removed, the noise became still worse. When he concluded the division was taken, and Dilke was beaten by 276 votes to 2.

Honour being thus satisfied, Dilke could abandon a campaign

which had brought him national fame (or notoriety) but which had rapidly become a political embarrassment to him. His summing-up, written many years later, was that "at Newcastle I made references to this subject (Court expenditure) which were accurate, though possibly unwise."[21] He never changed his basic beliefs about the Civil List or about monarchy in general, and even when he became a Minister he was pedantically careful not to vote for proposals against which he had committed himself a decade earlier. But he never again attempted to take the issue to the public. He realised that to link the fortunes of British radicalism with those of British republicanism would be to deliver a damaging and unnecessary blow to the former cause.

Although Dilke's republicanism temporarily cost him many acquaintances, it restored to him the friendship of a near neighbour in Sloane Street, Miss Katherine Sheil, and precipitated his marriage with her. Miss Sheil was an orphan, a year older than Dilke, who lived with a Miss Courtenay, a family friend of the Dilkes. Her father, a captain in the 89th Foot, had died young. Her mother came of an old, well-connected Devonshire family and left her property in that county which brought her about £1000 a year. Dilke, writing in 1895, described his reconciliation with her in somewhat curious terms:

"I had seen a good deal of Miss Sheil in 1869 at Lady Heathcote-Amory's, but we had quarrelled, as she generally managed to quarrel with her friends from her violent temper and unwillingness, in spite of the possession of strong opinions upon many points, to brook contradiction. For a long time we avoided one another, and I was only forgiven when the attacks on me in November, 1871, and the Bolton riot led to an expression of sympathy on her part, a sympathy which she had been far from having shown on previous occasions when it had been less needed, but might also have been pleasant."[22]

On January 30th, 1872, the wedding took place. The ceremony was at Holy Trinity, Sloane Street, Dilke's parish church. Only three persons besides the participants were present— Dilke's grandmother, his great-uncle from Chichester, and a stranger—and only four others, Trevelyan, Fitzmaurice, Ashton Dilke and Miss Sheil's maid, knew that it was to happen. "I walked home with my great-uncle," Dilke recorded, "after seeing my grandmother into her new home, which was next the church, while Katie, who had her brougham waiting, drove to Miss Courtenay's and told her, and then to the station where we met."[23]

Miss Courtenay did not allow failure to inform her beforehand to prejudice her against the arrangement. "A very suitable marriage," she commented. "You are neither of you in love with one another, but you will get on admirably together." "Miss Courtenay was, perhaps, at this time not far wrong," Dilke reflected evenly. "I had a profound respect for Miss Sheil's talent and a high admiration of her charm and beauty; and I think she had more liking than love for me."[24]

Elsewhere in the same document, written long after her death, he supplied more details of her talents and beauty as well as of some of her other qualities:

". . . her extreme attractiveness of appearance, her singing, and her wonderful power of mimicry had given her a considerable position in society. On the other hand people were afraid of her . . . and she was known to have a violent temper. She was accused by her many enemies of laziness (but this only because very doubtful health caused her to lie down a good deal), of pride, of violence, and of mercilessness in ridicule. On the other hand (*sic*) with her exquisite prettiness of appearance, with her perfect taste in dress, and with her extraordinary powers of conversation, hers was a marked figure in every room. She did not go out very much on account of her health, which had been largely owing to a disappointment in love of which I knew. Her great talent and extraordinary powers of sarcasm made her the terror of the ordinary 'dancing idiot,' and her love affair had been with a man old enough to be her father, a very handsome man of great distinction, who was either married or believed to be by some; a fact which caused others to interfere and stop a half-engagement. Some used to speak of Katie as exquisitely lovely. She had features which would ruin most reputations for beauty—a large mouth, small eyes, and a turned-up nose. Her eyes, however, which had the blue-white so seldom seen, were, in spite of their smallness, perhaps her greatest attraction. Her voice was perfect. Her greatest beauties, however, were her arched hand, her neck, the pose and shape of her head, and her tiny ears. . . . She insisted on marrying me without settlements as far as personalty was concerned, and with only a curious kind of settlement as to her Devonshire estates, intended to facilitate their sale, upon which we were resolved and which took place at once. Her lawyer, to his horror, knew nothing of the marriage until he received a note from her on the day on which it took place. She was extravagant, and spent her capital as income—chiefly on horses and dress."[25]

This difficult, distinguished woman was also a singer of some note—"the favourite pupil of Delsarte"—and a croquet player of match standard. The latter talent Dilke shared with her, and they used frequently to drive down to Wimbledon to play on the All England lawns there, as well as spending long weeks at the Granville Hotel, Ramsgate, which commended itself by the unusual possession of a ground so well drained that play was possible even in the wettest weather. It was there that they travelled when they met at Victoria Station after their clandestine wedding. Any more extended marriage journey was made temporarily impossible, both by Dilke's conviction that he must first face his critics in the House of Commons, and by his unwillingness to go abroad again while, as he believed had been the case on the occasion of a visit at the end of 1871, he was likely to be watched by the French police. They suspected him, falsely in fact, of assisting in the smuggling out of ex-Communards. Eventually, at the instigation of Louis Blanc, Dilke received a written assurance from Casimir-Périer, later to be President of the Republic, but at the time writing on behalf of his father, the Minister of the Interior, that there would be no more surveillance.

By Easter both of the obstacles had been removed, and the Dilkes were able to leave for an extended visit to Paris. Here they "attended sittings of the Assembly at Versailles, drove over the battlefields, dined with the Louis Blancs to meet Louis's brother, Charles Blanc, the critic and great master of style . . . met, at the Franquevilles, Henri de Pène and Robert Mitchell, the Conservative journalists; and saw *Mignon*, Katie's favourite opera, and *Rabagas*."[26] Incomparably more important than all this, the visit marked the beginning of the close friendship between Dilke and Gambetta. They had met briefly the previous

December, but it was during this Easter honeymoon that they got to know each other well. Whether arranging for the transportation of his father's body from St. Petersburg or taking his wife on a *voyage de noces*, Dilke was never too occupied to make new contacts.

Dilke was playing with the idea of writing a history of European politics in the nineteenth century, and was particularly concerned to enquire closely into the origins of the Franco-Prussian War. Much of his time in Paris was devoted to interviews in connection with the work. One of them was with Gambetta. Dilke had invited him to "breakfast," as he always called it when in Paris, although both in time and composition the meal was much more the equivalent of luncheon. Gambetta came, and stayed the whole day, talking throughout with immense vitality. He and Dilke were both equally delighted with each other. Thereafter, whenever Dilke was in Paris, they spent much of the time together. Long "breakfasts" at the Café Anglais formed the regular background to their friendship. Sometimes they were alone; sometimes Gambetta produced one or two of those now rather shadowy figures of the early days of the Third Republic, men with names like a Paris street guide, Edgar Quinet or Denfert-Rochereau; and sometimes Dilke introduced Englishmen—Harcourt, Lord Randolph Churchill, and John Morley were amongst them—who were anxious to meet the great French orator.

Gambetta's attraction for Dilke was partly political. Anyone who was French, republican, and a great world figure would have been three-quarters of the way to arousing his admiration. "My friendship with Gambetta," he wrote, "perhaps meant to me something more than the friendship of the man. Round him gathered all that was best and most hopeful in the state of the

84

young republic. He, more than any other individual, had both destroyed the Empire and made the new France; and to some extent the measure of my liking for the man was my hatred of those that he had replaced."[27] At the same time there was a degree of genuinely strong personal attraction, and Dilke could describe Gambetta, with perhaps a little exaggeration, as "for a long time . . . my most intimate friend."

Back in England, Dilke settled down to a somewhat quieter political life than he had lived immediately before his marriage. He continued to be discontented with the Government, to act as secretary of the Radical Club, and to discuss in correspondence with Chamberlain the most violent measures for bringing Gladstone to heel. But neither in the House of Commons nor in the country did he speak much. His attitude was well summed up in a letter which he wrote on May 1st, 1873, to Miss Kate Field, a young American journalist whom he described as "a slightly outrageous person," but who was nonetheless one of his closest friends during this period. "I am going to keep quiet until the general election as the best means of retaining my *present* seat," he wrote. "If I should be turned out—look out for squalls— as I should then stand on an extreme platform for every vacancy in the North."[28]

This temporary political withdrawal, combined with a gradual lessening of the ostracism of the winter of 1871–2, enabled the Dilkes to build up a more active social life. Dilke claimed that they did not go out much, partly because they were so wrapped up in each other and partly because of Katie's ill-health, but said that they gave two dinners a week at 76, Sloane Street, and "saw a good many people in this way." They saw most of Miss Field, and after her of William Harcourt. Henry James (the politician, not the novelist) was also an habitué of the house, as were Robert

Browning, Kinglake the historian, and Monckton Milnes (by that time Lord Houghton). Among frequent foreign guests were Moret, the Spanish Minister in London, and Gavard, at that time at the French Embassy; among those who came less frequently were Ricciotti Garibaldi, the son of a more famous father, Mark Twain, the dancer Taglioni, who in her old age had become "the stupidest and most respectable of old dames," and the tragédienne Ristori, then the Marchesa del Grillo. Stanley, the explorer, came on one occasion, but he struck Dilke as "brutal, bumptious, and untruthful," and was presumably not asked again. The dinners were mostly for twelve people, and the menus were long rather than exciting.[§] During the first year of the married establishment at Sloane Street, 262 different people received and accepted invitations to dinner.

On at least one occasion the Dilkes offered a much more elaborate entertainment. For a sum of 12,000 francs (about £500) they engaged Brasseur, a famous comedy actor of the Théâtre du Palais Royal, to come to London with two other players and

---

[§] That for August 4th, 1872, provides an adequate example:

PREMIER SERVICE	SECOND SERVICE
Potages	*Rôtis*
Consommé	Filet de Boeuf aux racines
Poissons	Poulet aux cressons
Truite Sauce Hollandaise	*Entremets*
Entrées	Compôte
Cotelettes de Pigeon	Fruit à la condé
Pieds d'Agneau billerie	
Ortolans sur Canapé	
Relevés	
Gelée de Poisson	

give six performances at 76, Sloane Street. For each evening from June 2nd to June 7th, 1873, more than fifty invitations were sent out.

Nor was it by any means entirely the case that Dilke never went out. He began at this time to visit Strawberry Hill, the house of Lady Waldegrave and of her fourth husband, Chichester Fortescue, then President of the Board of Trade; and he often dined with Harcourt and other political friends and acquaintances. But his great period of social activity did not come until the spring and summer of 1874. Then, in the sharpest possible contrast to the position two and a half years earlier, he was invited everywhere in London. This arose directly out of the publication of his second book.

In September, 1873, Lady Dilke had been delivered of a still-born son, and had been seriously ill as a result. As soon as she was well enough to travel her husband took her to Monaco, where they remained until after Christmas. While there Dilke wrote a short, satirical novel entitled *The Fall of Prince Florestan.* In twelve thousand words he recounted the story of a Cambridge undergraduate who succeeded unexpectedly to the throne of the Principality of Monaco, who there attempted to put into practice the liberal ideas he had learned in England, and who, in consequence of an unpopular collision with the Church, came to an early downfall. The beginning contained some agreeable satire on Cambridge life and English politics; the middle part made the most of the ludicrous aspects, less well known then to the English-speaking public than they are to-day, of a tiny court resting in theory upon the full panoply of feudal privilege, but in fact upon the enterprise of M. Blanc, the manager of the casino; and at the end a moral was drawn, although not too portentously, and addressed to the author's French friends. "No system of government can be permanent," he wrote, "which has for its opponents all the women in the country, and for supporters only half the men; and any party will have for opponents all the women which couples the religious question with the political and the social, and raises the flag of materialism. Women are not likely to abandon the idea of a compensation in the next world for the usage which too many of them meet with in this."[29] The whole thing was written with a delicate touch, and still makes easy and agreeable reading.

The novel was published anonymously on March 16th, 1874. Dilke had at first tried to conceal his identity from his publisher, Daniel Macmillan, but this attempt foundered when Macmillan objected, on the ground that he must protect the interests of the author of *Greater Britain*, to some jokes at Dilke's own expense which, by a rather elaborate stratagem, had been included in *Prince Florestan*. "As a republican," one passage ran, "I had a cordial aversion for Sir Charles Dilke, a clever writer, but an awfully dull speaker, who imagines that his *forte* is public speaking, and who, having been brought up in a set of strong prejudices, positively makes a merit of never having got over them."[30] Macmillan was then let into the secret, and a highly complex memorandum of Dilke's wishes and intentions was drawn up and accepted by the publisher. The first edition was to be strictly anonymous and "Mr. Macmillan's secrecy as a man of honour" was "to be relied upon to this end." If, however, "the work is, as it most likely will be, a success," the author undertook to make known his name on the appearance of the second edition, Dilke was to receive no payment for the first edition, but as a substitute he stipulated that the book should enjoy both expensive binding and extensive advertising. There should be full-page advertisements in the *Pall Mall Gazette*, the *Saturday Review*, and the *Academy*.

He was also to receive fifty presentation copies, which were to be carefully packed, addressed to Mr. Robert Allnert, not marked on the outside, and delivered to No. 6 sitting-room on the ground floor of the Grosvenor Hotel at Victoria Station. It was all very elaborate. Provision was also made for Macmillan to bring out an edition in French. "If not seized in France the work would have a large sale there," Dilke stated, "and if seized there would sell in Belgium."[31]

Dilke was right in predicting the success of the book. Within two days of publication it had been reviewed in five London dailies, and a spate of notices continued for some time. It became the fashionable success of the moment, and was the more talked about because of the mystery surrounding its authorship. The wildest guesses were made at this, but Dilke's name was mentioned as a possible object of the satire rather than as its author. The editor of the *Pall Mall Gazette* was convinced that Matthew Arnold was the author, while others confidently attributed the book to pens ranging from Benjamin Jowett's to a Cambridge undergraduate's. Frederic Harrison was alone in making a correct guess, and wrote urging Dilke to "make the joke better" by revealing his identity. It had always been Dilke's intention to make such a revelation, and he required little urging, even although Macmillan was at this stage suggesting to him that it would be better to maintain the incognito. It was broken by Lady Dilke, on arrival at a party, causing herself to be announced as "Princess Florestan."

What were Dilke's motives in writing the book and in presenting it to the public in the manner described? In part, no doubt, as his official biographers suggested,[32] he found it a convenient way of explaining to his acquaintances, as he had failed to do by more direct methods, that he could combine a theoretical preference for republicanism with a belief that it was unwise to attempt to upset even the most absurd government if it suited the people who lived under it. In part, also, he wished to present himself to the London social world in a more attractive light. He was widely thought of as a dull extremist. This was not a very engaging combination, and anything which was known to come from his pen would have started with a strong prejudice against it. If he wrote anonymously he would still this prejudice; if he wrote a light-hearted satire he might achieve a new reputation for the unknown author; and if the book were a success he could reveal his identity and exchange something of this reputation for his own. This is how matters in fact worked out, and it may well be that this was how he had planned them. Certainly he was delighted with the changed social atmosphere which followed the revelation of his identity. From a position of semi-ostracism he passed quickly to being the much sought-after, fashionable success of the moment. There were a few, however, who stood out against the stream, and in noting two attacks on his views which appeared several months after the general change, Dilke added the revealing comment: "Everything that was needed to set me right with cultivated people had not been done at once by *Prince Florestan* . . ."[33] But a great deal had been done, and Dilke was very pleased that it was so.

While *Florestan* was in the press, Dilke had triumphantly survived an ordeal the prospect of which had worried him for some time. On January 24th, Gladstone promised the abolition of the income tax and announced a sudden dissolution of Parliament. The country was less impressed by the promise than by the evident exhaustion of the Liberal Government, and the Conservatives were returned with a clear majority of more than fifty. Ten Liberal seats were lost in London, but Dilke's was not amongst them. He was again at the head of the poll, and in at least one sense it was still more of a personal triumph than in 1868; the second seat was taken by a Conservative, Gordon, and Sir Henry Hoare was defeated.

Dilke's election tactics were to free himself, so far as possible, of the twin handicaps of republicanism on the one hand and of the record of the Liberal administration on the other. A few days before the announcement of the dissolution he had followed the practice of the age for those who wished to explain away embarrassing actions or statements by writing a letter for publication to one of his Chelsea supporters. This constituent had indicated his support by asking the most convenient questions.

"You ask me whether you are not justified in saying that I have always declined to take part in a republican agitation," Dilke wrote. "That is so. I have repeatedly declined to do so; I have declined to attend republican meetings and I have abstained from subscribing to republican funds. I also refused to join the Republican Club formed at Cambridge University, though I am far from wishing to cast a slur on those Liberal politicians—Professor Fawcett and others—who did join it. The view I took was that I had no right to make use of my position as a member of the House of Commons, gained largely by the votes of those who are not even theoretical republicans, to push on an English republican movement. On the other hand, when denounced in a Conservative paper as a 'republican' as though that were a term of abuse, I felt bound as an honest man to say that I was one. But I am not a 'republican member' or a 'republican candidate' any more than Mr. Gordon is a monarchical candidate, because there is neither Republican party nor Monarchical party in the English Parliament. I said at Glasgow two years ago: 'The majority of the people of Great Britain believe that the reforms they desire are compatible with the monarchic form of government,' and this I believe now as then."

Dilke then referred to the suggestions that in his Newcastle speech he had made a personal attack upon the Queen.

"Opinion has become so much calmer upon this point," he added, "that all will believe me when I say that nothing was further from my mind than to impute blame to Her Majesty, that I never for a moment thought my words to be so under-stood, that I am heartily sorry that they were so understood, and that the very fact that they were shows that they were wrong."[34]

He could not go much further than that.

On the second issue Dilke made it clear that, with the intro-duction of the Education Bill of 1870, he had ceased to be a "steady supporter" of the Government. He instanced the Trades Union Act of 1871,[¶] and the Irish Peace Preservation Act of 1873 as other measures which had helped to separate him from official Liberal opinion. He asked for the continued support of the electors of Chelsea, not in order that the Gladstone

---

¶ It was in fact the associated Criminal Law Amendment Act which aroused Dilke's hostility. This Act re-emphasised the provisions of an Act of 1825 which made peaceful picketing illegal. In 1875 the new Conservative Government replaced it with a measure much more favourable to the trades unions.

Government might be sustained in office, but in order that he might continue, as an individual, to put forward a radical point of view in the House of Commons. Paradoxically, however, the tenure which he gained on this highly personal platform in 1874 he used markedly less independently than the tenure which, in 1868, he had secured by means which were far more conformist. As a very young politician, Dilke, in his first Parliament, had learnt a number of important lessons. One was that influence was not to be equated with notoriety. Another was the need to concentrate his fire upon essential objectives. He was not again to be diverted from more important radical purposes by matching his strength against the British monarchy, an institution which, even at one of its weakest moments, had shown surprisingly rock-like characteristics.

Chapter Five

The Birmingham Alliance

D ilke was not for long able to enjoy the calm contemplation of either the more assured political future or the new social reputation which the early part of 1874 had brought him. His wife was again pregnant and again ill. As her pregnancy advanced, her own and Dilke's sense of foreboding increased. Indeed Dilke was later to decide that their last fully happy time together had been in Paris at Christmas, 1873, when "Gambetta's brightness was answered by our own," and that "throughout this pregnancy Katie expected death." Until the beginning of August, however, they continued to lead as normal a social life as had ever been possible for Lady Dilke. Their last dinner party at 76, Sloane Street was on August 9th. After that Harcourt dined informally on two occasions and another friend on one. They were the last people outside the family to see Lady Dilke. On September 18th a son was born. Two days later she died.

Dilke later wrote a strange and harrowing account both of the death-bed scene and of his subsequent actions:

"The (first) night over, she seemed to me to recover fast. The next night she slept five hours. The next day she slept almost continuously, and each time she woke I gave her water, and she talked and listened. She asked to see the child, and saw it, although without a smile . . . all day she did not smile. I did not know the danger; but by the books on the subject that I afterwards read I found that from the expression on the face I ought to have expected death, and also that we could have done nothing to avert it. At seven in the evening she woke delirious but knowing me, and cried 'I am going to die.' I kissed her and she went quietly to sleep again. I sent off again to the doctor, but when he came he was able to do nothing. At nine in the evening she woke again, the doctor standing by her side with me; she threw up her arms and fell back dead.

"I was unable to realise what had happened. I sat in my room quietly writing a kind of certificate for which the frightened doctor asked me, to say that to me he seemed to have done his duty. I then went back to her room, kissed her, said farewell for ever to her old Scotch maid, 'Mrs.' Watson, and walked down the street quietly to my grand-mother's, and there told her what had happened, and asked her to lie down by my side on her bed for a few hours, and we lay there side by side holding hands. I then asked her to do everything, calling in only my brother, and told her what should be done, and begged her to return to take charge of my house and of the child. At daylight she went to the house, where she again lived until her death, and I went to Victoria Station, and, having shaved off my beard to prevent myself from being recognised and spoken to by any friend, went to Paris and there took careful steps not to be found. I took rooms in the Rue de l'Arcade; and only after some weeks rooms in my own name at the Grand Hotel, and for about a month I think I did not see a letter. I worked steadily at historical work; but I have little recollection of the time (except by looking at the notebooks which contain the work I did), and even within a few months afterwards was unable to recall it. For all practical purposes I was mad."[1]

In this way Dilke passed the last days of September and almost the whole of October. Not only did he not see a letter, but he did not write one either. All the readjustments in Sloane Street had to be carried through without his presence or instructions.* Ashton Dilke carried out the rather complicated funeral wishes of his sister-in-law, which involved transporting her body to Dresden, and there arranging for its burning. Mrs. Chatfield not merely arranged for the baptism of the child, but did it herself, in what Dilke described as "a form used by lay members of the Church in case of necessity." At least the choice of names presented her with no difficulty; the child became the fifth Charles Wentworth Dilke.

At the end of October Dilke began to write from Paris to

---

* Dilke had behaved in a somewhat similar way after the death of his father in 1869. In September of that year, when there was still much to be settled he was writing to Mrs. Chatfield from Kazan, apologising for running away and leaving so much in her hands, and adding "but I could not have stood any business after the great fatigues and anxieties of the last few months." (D.P., 43902,283.)

friends in England. But he said little except that he did not feel able to return. Then, at about the same time, he was recognised in the street by Gambetta—"my beard having partly grown again"—and from then onwards Dilke saw him constantly, and was brought back by him into normal human intercourse. Later, while attributing some of the credit for his recovery to Ashton Dilke and to Harcourt, he gave the clear judgment that it was Gambetta who "saved" him. The task was not an easy one. At the beginning of November he still felt incapable of taking any further part in politics and was determined to resign his seat. The only activity he was willing to contemplate was an extensive and prolonged journey into Africa. He had not only become a teetotaller (which he was to remain for eleven years), but also an extreme vegetarian with the strongest possible views on the killing of animals (which was to be only a passing phase), and what he himself described as a "primitive Christian." He carried on a very strange correspondence about the existence of the human soul with Frances Power Cobbe, the author of a little book entitled *Hopes of the Human Heart*, and he again indulged his extremely limited talent for writing poetry.

By the middle of the month there was a distinct improvement. He replied to a resolution of sympathy from his constituents, and while he mentioned the possibility that he might not take his seat throughout the session of 1875, he did not threaten resignation. He took to reading Balzac and Mme. de Staël instead of Miss Cobbe, and he contemplated a less extended African tour. "From this time forward I got rapidly better as far as nervousness at meeting people went," he wrote, adding cautiously "although for many months I was completely changed and out of my proper self, and not really responsible for what I wrote or said or did."[2]

He left for North Africa in December. He made an excursion southwards into the desert from Algeria and then returned to Paris during the last week in January, 1875; within a few days he travelled on to London. His intention had been to go straight to Harcourt's house in Stratford Place, then a bachelor establishment, for Harcourt did not marry his second wife until the following year and his son by his first wife was at Eton. Here Harcourt had suggested rather heartily to Dilke that "we will live together as if in college rooms," and Dilke had fallen in with the plan, but for the moment it could not be.

"On reaching London . . ." Dilke wrote, "I had to go first to my own house, for I was sickening with disease, and had indeed a curious very slight attack of smallpox, which passed off, however, in about two days, but I had to be isolated for another week. When I became what the doctors called well I moved to Harcourt's; but my hand still shook, and I had contracted a bad habit of counting the beating of my heart, and I was so weak of mind that the slightest act of kindness made me cry. To my grandmother and brother I wrote to ask them to let me go on living with Harcourt for the present, not because I preferred him to them, but because I could not live in my own house, and should have a better chance of sleep if I returned elsewhere at night from the House of Commons."[3]

The arrangement was a success and lasted until the Easter holidays. Then Dilke wrote in the following terms:

Dear Harcourt:

I don't mean to come back here after Easter. I am quite well enough to go home now. But I shall never forget all your goodness to me. I fear I must have bored you at times tho' of course you are good enough to say the reverse. But while I do not on many days get gloomy—I do get nervously excited which is worse. Still I am going to get all right again. Once more thank you for all your tender kindness.

Ever yours,

Charles W. D.

I write this because I can't say anything without breaking down.[4]

Dilke was undoubtedly grateful to Harcourt at this time. In another letter to him he wrote: "How little credit you get for your heart! How few people know you have one!" But he was always a little cynical about him, and his typical reaction to the mention of his name, then as for many years to come, was to recall some anecdote, usually affectionate but often mildly ridiculous, about Harcourt's behaviour. And their friendship did not for long retain the intensity of this period. Whether because of the advent of the second Lady Harcourt, of whom Dilke wrote that she "was too remarkable a linguist to be clever in other ways," or for other reasons, they were no longer intimate when they served together in a Cabinet; and when the second great crisis of Dilke's life arrived there was no question of his receiving from Harcourt the support which had been given in the first.

So far as his health and even his spirits were concerned, Dilke was probably better by Easter than he admitted in his letter of thanks to Harcourt. In February he had renewed an old friendship which had lapsed for over ten years, but which was henceforth to be the dominant influence in his life; and in the same month he had begun, despite all his protestations, a session of Parliament which he was to describe many years later as his "most successful." The friendship was with Emilia Pattison, formerly Emilia Strong. She was the daughter of an officer in the service of East India Company and was three years older than Dilke. He had known her in 1859 when they were both members of a curious institution called the South Kensington Trap-Bat Club, and had then found her attractive and accomplished, but bigoted in the intensity of her High Church belief. Two years later she had married Mark Pattison, the Rector of Lincoln College, Oxford, and a highly contro-versial figure in mid-Victorian university life. Pattison was nearly thirty years older than his wife. He was stubborn, self-pitying, harsh in his judgments of himself and others, and ungracious in manner; and by the 'seventies his health was poor.[†] Even without the difference in age, he would have been far from easy as a husband, and there is no doubt that Mrs. Pattison was unhappy in her marriage, and regretted, both for

---

[†] A college rhyme of the period gave an unattractive but perhaps not inac-curate picture of Pattison:

> "And now the Rector goes,
> With a dew drops at his nose,
> And his skinny hands in loose black gloves enveloped;
> Irresistably, fear
> Suggesting the idea
> Of a discontened lizard with a cold."

(Quoted in V.H.H. Green's Oxford Common Room, p. 265.)

her own sake and her husband's, that it had ever taken place.‡ She consoled herself by creating the only *salon* in Oxford (there was little competition in the days before 1871 when heads of houses were alone allowed to marry), by establishing herself as an art critic of note, especially of French eighteenth-century work (of which she was later to publish a four-volume history), and by philosophical meditation. This last activity led her away from Tractarianism and, for a short time, into a Positivist position.§ But in 1875 she was again a "believer" and influenced Dilke in this direction, teaching him to accept "the words of Christ received in Gospel as contrasted with the Pauline tradition of the Epistles." She was a remarkable woman, both in talent and appearance. Her command of French was such that she wrote one of her books in that language, and she spoke fluently three other foreign tongues.

---

‡ In 1876 she wrote to Pattison from Nice stating with brutal frankness that she felt a strong physical distaste for him. "I cannot forget," she said, "that from the first I expressed the strongest aversion to that side of the common life; during 73–4 this became almost insufferable—for I tried to conceal it hoping that it might settle itself." (Green, *op. cit.* p. 309.) The characters of Edward Casaubon and Dorothea Brooke in *Middlemarch* are generally considered to be closely based on Mark Pattison and his wife. They were both well known to George Eliot.

§ In the abandonment of Tractarianism at least she followed in the steps of her husband. As a young don he had been a disciple of Newman, but he afterwards reacted sharply against the whole spirit of the Oxford Movement. "I once and only once," he wrote, "got so low by fostering a morbid state of conscience as to go to confession to Dr. Pusey. Years afterwards it came to my knowledge that Pusey had told a fact about myself, which he got from me on that occasion, to a friend of his, who used it to annoy me." (Pattison: *Memoirs*, p. 189.)

She carried on voluminous correspondence with some of the most distinguished European scholars of her age. And she matched her interest in French painters of the *Grand Siècle* with an equally intense concern for the conditions of women's labour in England and the beginnings of female trades union organisation. A revealing glimpse of her appearance was given by her devoted niece, Miss Tuckwell. "Some touches seemed subtly to differentiate her dress from the prevailing fashion," the latter wrote, "and to make it the expression of a personality which belonged to a century more dignified, more leisured, and less superficial, than our own."[5]

For many years after her marriage Mrs. Pattison came to London only rarely, and lost almost all contact with Dilke. In 1875 she was convalescent from a crippling attack of rheumatism, which for many months had kept her arms strapped to her sides, and had involved the construction of a special machine to turn the pages of the books she read. Part of this convalescence she spent staying at the Gower Street house of Sir Charles Newton, Keeper of Greek and Roman Antiquities at the British Museum. During this visit Dilke called upon her, and there then began a friendship which was to lead eventually to their marriage ten years later. More immediately it led to a correspondence which within four years was to involve the interchange of letters at least three times a week, and sometimes once a day. Dilke poured out all his political information to Mrs. Pattison and asked her advice about every difficult decision which he had to take.[¶]

His parliamentary successes of the year came after Easter.

[¶] "She is now wholly unsympathetic—reserving all her interest for the other man and his affairs," Pattison wrote about his wife after six years of this

The main event before Easter was the election of a new Liberal leader to replace Gladstone, who had retired with an ill grace after expressing his conviction that political activity was not "the best method of spending the closing years of (his) life"; and Dilke took no part in this. He did not attend the Reform Club meeting on February 3rd. This resulted in the unanimous election of Lord Harrington, even though the issue had previously been in considerable doubt, with many of Dilke's former associates, such as Fawcett, Trevelyan and Mundella, working hard to advance the claims of W. E. Forster. Harcourt, however, under whose roof Dilke was living at the time, was equally vehemently in favour of Harrington; and Chamberlain and the Birmingham Nonconformists carried dislike of the author of the Education Act of 1870 to the extent of swallowing their natural suspicion of Hartington's indolent, patrician whiggery. The pulls upon Dilke's loyalty would therefore have been by no means all in one direction, and he may not have been sorry to have escaped participation in a dispute of which no possible outcome would have aroused his enthusiasm. In the last speech which he delivered before his wife's death (on September 8th), he had referred in disparaging terms to Forster as having "been returned by Tory votes at Bradford, than which nothing is more weakening to a Liberal politician." Dilke never liked Hartington's politics, but he had, and retained, the highest personal respect for him— "Hartington is a man, but on the wrong side," he was to write five years later. Because of this, and of his intimacy with Harcourt, he was probably not dissatisfied with the way the issue was resolved.

---

correspondence. (Green, *op. cit.* p. 311.) But it must be said that he was by this time anxious to see as little of her as possible.

His own activities concerned the promotion of three parliamentary resolutions and one bill. The first resolution, which was carried, provided for the setting up of a committee to enquire into the working of the Ballot Act. Dilke had believed from the outset that secrecy was vitiated by the system of numbering the voting papers which was (and still is) in force. "A dull speech on a dull subject," was his comment on his own performance, but he secured his immediate object. The second related to the need for a redistribution of seats, never a popular subject with the House of Commons, and less so than usual at a time when more than 400 members sat for constituencies whose existence could not be justified by their size. Dilke did not succeed in carrying this resolution, but he got the whole Liberal party to commit itself to his support.

The third resolution drew attention to the abuses of unreformed borough corporations, which were such an inherently funny subject that even Dilke's treatment of them kept the House in almost continuous laughter. He was answered by Lord Randolph Churchill, whom he had come to know well a few weeks previously when he had taken him to "breakfast" with Gambetta, and who, Dilke thought, was funnier than he himself had been, although not so respectful of the truth.

"One of the Corporations which I had attacked was that of Woodstock," he wrote, "and Randolph Churchill brought the Prince of Wales down to the House to hear his defence of his constituency. I had said in my speech that the Mayor of Woodstock had been lately fined by his own Bench, he being a publican, for breaking the law in a house the property of the Corporation, and that he had said on that occasion in public court, after hearing the evidence of the police: "I have always had a high respect for the police, but in future I shall have none." Randolph Churchill, answering me, said that I had slightly mistaken the Mayor's words, and that what he had really said was: "I have always had a high respect for the police, but in future I shall have *more*." After the debate was over, Randolph came up to me outside, and said: "I was terrified lest you should have heard anything to-day, but I see you have not." I said: "What?" He said: "He was fined again yesterday."[6]

Dilke's bill was an Allotments Extension Bill, which had originally been drawn up for Mill and which sought to provide for the letting to cottagers of lands held for the benefit of the poor. Here again Dilke did not succeed in carrying the House, but committed the Liberal party. "(They) were all four great successes, and so spoken of in all the papers," he wrote of his parliamentary enterprises of the year.

During the summer of 1875 Dilke published *Papers of a Critic*, a two-volume collection of the essays and articles of his grandfather, introduced by a 30,000-word memoir which he had written in France the previous autumn. This work, naturally enough, created no great stir, although Disraeli, to whom Dilke had sent a copy, pronounced it "very refreshing."

The session over, Dilke made another trip around the world. He visited Miss Field in New York, and then went to Japan, China, Java and Singapore. He was back in London by January, 1876, and he published an account of his travels in the Far East in a series of magazine articles which were later to be appended, somewhat incongruously, as additional chapters to subsequent editions of *Greater Britain*.

The session of 1876 was a comparatively uneventful one for

Dilke. There were no great parliamentary controversies of which he was the centre, and the election of Chamberlain to the House of Commons, in June, was more important to him than anything which occurred within the walls of the chamber itself. Chamberlain had wanted to come into Parliament for some time. At the general election of 1874 he had stood unsuccessfully for Sheffield, and he had subsequently considered the possibility of being adopted for Norwich or Northampton. He was torn between his desire to complete his identification with Birmingham by becoming one of its members and his conviction that it was useless to enter the House of Commons after the age of forty. By the margin of a few weeks he was able to attain both his objectives. At the beginning of 1876, George Dixon, the chairman of the Education League and the senior of the three members for the town, indicated that he might be contemplating retirement. Thereafter Chamberlain and his supporters gave him no respite. Dixon was soon regretting that he had ever raised the issue. He was sufficiently attached to the House of Commons to come back later for another seat, but he was not allowed to change his mind about Birmingham. At the end of May he announced that he was applying for the Chiltern Hundreds. Chamberlain had lost Dixon's friendship,[**] but he got his seat. He was returned unopposed on June 17th, but was prevented from appearing in the House of Commons for several weeks by a sharp, first attack of gout—a malady which, he

---

[**] In 1878 Dixon reminded the country that they must not believe that "Chamberlain is Birmingham or Birmingham Chamberlain." Chamberlain responded with a typical truculence by announcing that "Birmingham must choose between Dixon and me," but the quarrel subsided without being put to the test. (Garvin, *Life of Joseph Chamberlain*, Vol. I, p. 225.)

thought, should be "reserved by a just providence for Tories exclusively," but which in fact claimed not only himself but also Dilke and Morley as victims. By mid-July he had recovered, and on the 13th of the month, exactly five days after his fortieth birthday, he was introduced into the House of Commons by John Bright and Joseph Cowen, the radical member for Newcastle.

Dilke, although not asked to be one of Chamberlain's sponsors on this occasion,[††] immediately set about his introduction to London political and social life. The new member for Birmingham did not acquire a London house until four years later, when he became a Minister, and, particularly at first, he passed many of his nights under Dilke's roof. Almost as frequently as they could be absent from the House of Commons, there were dinner parties in Sloane Street designed to introduce Chamberlain to Dilke's friends. Chamberlain was a willing guest at almost all their gatherings. Once, when Dilke had suggested they should dine together at the Political Economy Club, Chamberlain had written protesting that he was "not interested in the gay science or its professors"; but in general he was happy to be presented to

---

[††] Bright was an obvious choice as a parliamentary sponsor, but Cowen a good deal less so. Although he had succeeded his Whig father in the representation of Newcastle he affected a style of dress—"like a workman, with a black comforter round his neck, and the only wide-awake hat at that time known in the House of Commons"—which can hardly have commended him to the meticulous and elegant Chamberlain. Furthermore, according to Dilke, he spoke with an almost incomprehensible Tyneside burr. But he was regarded as a considerable force in radical politics at the time. Within a year, however, the strength of his anti-Russian views had driven him into a position of virtual support for Disraeli's foreign policy, and hence of isolation from his former associates.

all whom Dilke suggested—artists, writers, diplomats, soldiers or politicians. Nor were Dilke's activities with Chamberlain confined to the evenings. He constantly took him to art galleries and wrote in February, 1877: "We had now the habit, whenever he came to stay with me . . . of going to the picture exhibitions."[7] A month later he even took him to the Boat Race—"at an unearthly hour in the morning for his lazy habits."

At the end of Dilke's most intensive period of Chamberlain dinners, in the first weeks of the session of 1877, the latter was summoned to Marlborough House to dine with the Prince of Wales. Dilke, who at that time did not know the Prince, although he was later to become one of his intimate acquaintances, wrote rather doubtfully: "I call this nobbling my party." The "party" to which Dilke was referring and to which, he hastened to add, he did not normally apply the possessive pronoun, was composed of six members. Apart from Chamberlain and Dilke himself, there were Dillwyn, the member for Swansea, "who looked like a Methodist parson and shot like an angel," Cowen of Newcastle, Thomas Burt, the miner who sat for Morpeth, and Edmund Gray, the Nationalist owner of the Dublin *Freemen's Journal*. These six held an eve-of-the-session dinner party at 76, Sloane Street in 1877, but "the dinner . . . which assembled democratically without dressing in order to suit Burt's habits, was not graced by that copy of the Queen's Speech which is sent by the Government to the leaders of the regular opposition. Chamberlain and I," Dilke added, "dressed after dinner and went off to Lady Granville's to the regular Liberal Party Assembly where the Queen's Speech was shown to us by Hartington."[8]

This small group quickly began to disintegrate. Cowen became too friendly to the foreign policy of the Government, and Burt was dropped because "he never originated anything and was of no utility." Gray presented a rather different problem. His chief sin appeared to be that he got drunk at Dilke's house, left with Chamberlain's hat, and took it to Rome with him on the following morning—an inverted act of cardinal-making to which Chamberlain reacted most unfavourably. Dillwyn remained both faithful and acceptable, and the party became one of three—"two leaders and a follower—and Dillwyn acknowledged Chamberlain and myself as equal leaders."

The exiguousness of this group did not greatly worry Dilke. He found his relations with his official leaders much smoother in this parliament than in the previous one, and he became more interested in being a force, although a firmly radical one, within the Liberal party as a whole, than in the leadership of an isolated faction. In May of 1876 he had become chairman of the Elections Committee of the Liberal Central Association, an office which he was to hold until 1880, and which gave him an influence upon the choice of candidates and a considerable position within the party machine. Then there was his personal respect for Lord Hartington, much stronger up to this point than any favourable feeling which had ever been aroused in him by Mr. Gladstone's personality. On October 16th, 1876, he had gone so far as to write to Harcourt:

"I, as you know, think Hartington the best man for us—the Radicals—because he is quite fearless, always goes with us when he thinks it safe for the party, and generally judges rightly—or takes the soundest advice on this point. In fact, I don't think he's ever made a mistake at all—as yet; but Chamberlain seems, by a sort of quasi-hereditary Birmingham position, to look at him as Bright used to look at Palmerston."[9]

The major foreign policy issue of the parliament—the revival of the Eastern Question, which began with the Bulgarian massacres of May, 1876, and subsided only after the Congress of Berlin in the summer of 1878—served further to remove Dilke from an extremist position. It was not so much that he came to agree with his leaders, which indeed would have been difficult in a period when they were so little inclined to agree with each other, as that he fell out of sympathy with his normal radical allies. From the "peace-at-any-price" men he was quickly separated, as was inevitable in almost any foreign policy dispute, but he also became detached from Chamberlain, who, he thought, went too far in support of Gladstone's agitation.

This agitation began with the sale within three weeks of 200,000 copies of Gladstone's hastily written and emotionally charged pamphlet, *The Bulgarian Horrors and the Question of the East*. Dilke had little liking for it. He did not go as far as Beaconsfield, who said that Gladstone was worse than any Bulgarian horror, but he told Harcourt: "If Gladstone goes on much longer, I shall turn Turk." He did not deny the evils of Turkish rule, but he believed those of Russian rule to be if anything worse.

> "Were the choice between Russia at Constantinople and Turkey at Constantinople," he told a meeting of his constituents at the beginning of 1878, "I should prefer the latter. The Turkish is in ordinary times a less stifling despotism than the Russian. . . . The Turks let any man go to church and read any book, the Russians do not, and in such a position of power as Constantinople I should prefer the Turk if, as I do not think, the choice lay only there."[10]

The third choice, at which Dilke hinted in this passage, lay, he believed, in a greater Greece. This was the result which he would have liked to see emerging from the crisis, and this was a policy which was to be associated with his name for the rest of his life, which was to make him in Athens one of the most prized of English philhellenes, and to cause the municipality there to name a street in his honour.[‡‡]

At first this approach led Dilke to support Hartington rather than Gladstone. Later, however, when Gladstone had tabled his four resolutions demanding the coercion of Turkey, which came up for debate in May, 1877, and threatened almost to destroy the Liberal party, Dilke felt that he must if necessary vote with Gladstone and against the titular leader of the opposition. The need to make this choice was in the event avoided, partly by Gladstone not pressing two of the resolutions, and partly by Hartington voting, with more loyalty than conviction, for the other two; but Dilke felt that, while open schism had been avoided, Gladstone had so mishandled the situation as to make himself look ridiculous. He therefore moved into a position, not of extreme, but of central isolation.

> "The new position of the Eastern Question," he wrote in the summer of 1877, "although it did not unite me with Mr. Gladstone, made a political breach between myself and Hartington. He fell more and more under the somewhat stupid influence of the surroundings of the Duchess of

---

[‡‡] Athens was the only municipality to accord him this honour. Dilke Street, Chelsea, is named not after Sir Charles, but after his father, who worked with Sir William Tite, similarly honoured, to arrange for the building of a part of the Embankment.

Manchester, and I, holding a position between the two wings of the party, found few with whom I myself agreed. Randolph Churchill, who upon this question was perhaps sincere, made advances towards me which led to joint action . . . in 1878. But in the autumn of '77 I was isolated, for Chamberlain went, although with moderation, into Mr. Gladstone's agitation."[11]

One reason for Dilke's isolation lay in the unusual combination of radicalism, realism and detailed information which always formed the basis of his foreign policy thinking. Another was that, unlike almost all the other radicals in the House, he was a metropolitan and not a provincial member. And there has rarely been a sharper split between the feeling of London on the one hand and that of Scotland and the provincial centres on the other than in these years of Beaconsfield ascendancy. Gladstone attained unprecedented popularity in the North, but was execrated in fashionable circles in the capital; and he exacerbated the split by the sharpness of his comments upon it. "Looking over all the great achievements that have made the last half century illustrious," he announced on one occasion, "not one of them would have been effected if the opinions of the West End of London had prevailed."[12] But it was not the opinion of the West End only which was hostile to Gladstone at this time. "On Sunday, March 10th (1878), in coming back from the Grosvenor Gallery," Dilke wrote, "I passed a great mob who were going to howl at Mr. Gladstone, at this time the ordinary Sunday afternoon diversion of the London rough."[13] On this and other occasions they howled sufficiently hard to wreck the windows of Gladstone's new house in Harley Street.

Dilke, therefore, had a certain obvious constituency interest in not appearing too resistant to Beaconsfield's determination to make the Russians disgorge part of their gains from the Turks; and the interest was the stronger because of his view that Chelsea was far from safe. But these considerations did not lead him to jump on the Government's jingo band wagon.

"There was a moment after the fall of Lord Derby (from the Foreign Office) when I became a supporter of the Government in their Eastern policy," Dilke wrote, "for they appeared to me to adopt my own, but it did not last long. . . . Speaking in the House on April 9th against the calling out of national reserves . . . . I repudiated the defence which had come from some on the Liberal side, of the conduct of Russia, and, looking upon the Government despatch as a vindication primarily of general European interests, and, in the second place, of Hellenic interests, against Russian violence and universal Slav dominion throughout the Levant, I separated myself from my party and praised the new Minister of Foreign Affairs. I was afterwards bitterly disappointed at finding the policy of the April circular abandoned by its authors in the Congress of Berlin."[14]

Even during this brief period of agreement with Lord Salisbury, Dilke spoke against the Government's action in calling out the reserves. He wanted pressure put upon Russia, but he wanted it done by conference rather than by force, and by Europe acting in concert rather than by England acting alone. Furthermore, he wanted the pressure directed not towards the maintenance of the integrity of the Turkish Empire but towards the full independence of the Balkan nationalities—it had been on this last point that he had co-operated, briefly and fruitlessly, with Lord Randolph Churchill in the early spring. These desires separated him sharply from Gladstone and most radicals but they separated him equally from the policy pursued by the Government both before and during the Congress of Berlin.

In these years of foreign policy dispute Dilke's political position became greatly strengthened. A period of rapidly shifting alliances within the Liberal party was almost inevitably helpful to one who had previously been a rather isolated and intransigent figure. Men who had hitherto assumed automatically that he would be against them began to bid for his support. He was no longer outside the range of combination; and he came increasingly to be consulted by his party chiefs. He assisted the process by a series of highly competent speeches in the House, and by occasional well-reported, well-informed, and independent addresses to his constituents.

Furthermore, in the session of 1878, he succeeded in carrying into law two important measures of electoral reform. The first was a Registration Bill, which although modest in its apparent impact, eventually effected a great addition to the number of voters on the lists. The second, an Hours of Polling Bill, made it much easier for those entitled to vote to do so. Hitherto, polling had closed at 4 p.m., a time by which it was quite impossible for many working-class voters to get to the booths. "Dilke's Act," as it was widely known, extended the hours until 8 p.m. At first it applied only to London, but was later extended to cover the whole country.

Not only did Dilke's political reputation grow rapidly, but he also had the agreeable experience of being frequently told that this was so. The most notable of his political admirers was Lord

Beaconsfield. Dilke never knew him well, and never indeed met him outside the House of Commons until a few weeks before his death in 1881; but he had a high respect for the successful adventure of the Prime Minister's career, and long retained as one of his most lively memories a picture of the latter leaving the House of Commons for the last time in August, 1876, "in a long white overcoat and dandified lavender kid gloves, leaning on his secretary's arm, and shaking hands with a good many people, none of whom knew that he was bidding farewell. . . ."[15] Beaconsfield, in turn, saw in Dilke the most effective politician of his generation. ". . . Mr. Disraeli stated it as his opinion," according to G. O. Trevelyan, "that Sir Charles Dilke was the most useful and influential member, among quite young men, that he had ever known."[16] Soon Beaconsfield went still further, and at the beginning of 1879 was responsible for a widely disseminated prophecy that Dilke was almost certain to be Prime Minister. Dilke heard of it from Chamberlain and from many others too. A year later he had become almost too well spoken of, by the newspapers at any rate, for his popularity, and was thought to have departed so far from his former intransigence that he wrote in the following terms to Mrs. Pattison:

"I guess rather than feel in interviews with different men that I have been so much talked of by the papers for the Cabinet, and so much has been said of my having been consulted last year a great deal—that there is intense personal jealousy of me on the part of Fawcett, Courtney, Cowen and others. It takes the form of an assumption which is very irritating, that I never say what I mean—unless it happens to be that which party interest requires. I think I can only control it by keeping a little in the

115

background this session."[17]

From 1876 onwards it was not only Dilke's political life which had gone well; he had also enjoyed himself in a more relaxed way and in a wider social circle than ever before. For a time the Waldegrave establishments became almost the centre of his life.

"I began this year (1876) to stay a great deal at Lady Waldegrave's," he wrote, "both at Dudbrook in Essex and at Strawberry Hill; and ultimately I had a room at Strawberry Hill to which I went backwards and forwards as I chose. The house was extremely pleasant, and so was Fortescue,[§§] and he passionately adored his wife, and was afterwards completely broken down and almost killed by her death. Fortescue was my friend. I never much liked An- in spite of her good nature, but she was an excellent hostess and the house was perfectly pleasant, and in a degree in which no other house of our time has been. The other house which was always named as 'the rival establishment,' Holland House, I also knew. Some of the same people went there—Abraham Hayward, commonly called the 'Viper,' and Charles Villiers, for example. But Lady Holland was

---

[§§] Chichester Fortescue, 1823–1898, created Lord Carlingford, 1874, Liberal politician (he had been Chief Secretary for Ireland and President of the Board of Trade in the first Gladstone Government) and fourth husband of Frances Braham (born 1821), the daughter of a great singer, who had married, previously and successively, John Waldegrave, his elder brother George, 7th Earl Waldegrave, and George Granville Harcourt, an uncle of Sir William.

disagreeable and bitter, and far from a good hostess, whereas Lady Waldegrave always made everybody feel at home. Those of whom I saw the most this year, in addition to the Strawberry Hill people (who were Harcourt, James, Ayrton, Villiers, Hayward, Dr. Smith the editor of the *Quarterly*, Henry Reeve the editor of the *Edinburgh*, the Comte de Paris and the Duc d'Aumale) were Lord Houghton and Mrs. Duncan Stewart."¶[18]

Despite his frequent visits to Strawberry Hill, Dilke always retained an element of reserve towards the charms of life at Horace Walpole's gothic mansion, as towards those of Frances Waldegrave herself. He listed first amongst its attractions his ability, when staying there, to walk down the road, take a train from Twickenham station to London, and escape from the chatter from morning until dinner-time. He was also a little cynical about the royal princes, mainly French and exiled, who frequently visited the place. He met there the Prince Imperial, usually remembered, perhaps on account of his early death, as a most sympathetic and agreeable youth, and wrote later of having "described him in my diary as having the manners and appearance of a tobacconist. Why tobacconist I do not know, although I remember his appearance, which was vulgar and his manners which were common, but at this distance of time I

¶ Mrs. Stewart's chief claim to a place in a biography of Dilke must rest upon her being the mother of Mrs. Rogerson, later Mrs. George Steevens, of whom more will be heard in subsequent chapters; but she also gave a luncheon party in 1876, which, according to Dilke, was "one of the most agreeable parties of clever people to which I ever went. . . at which I was the only man, the party chiefly consisting of old ladies. . ."

should be inclined to alter tobacconist into hairdresser." Lest it should be thought that he attached too much importance to manners and appearance, Dilke hastened to add that "his (the Prince Imperial's) father, who had not been brought up as a gentleman, was a gentleman in manners, although in character he was vile."[19]

The Orleanist princes pleased Dilke little better than the Bonapartes. After dining with the Duc de Chartres, again at Strawberry Hill, he wrote that he was "no better and no worse than the other princes of his house, all dull men, not excepting the Duc d'Aumale, who had, however, the reputation of being brilliant, and who . . . was interesting from his great memory of great men. They all grew deaf as they grew old . . ."[20] he added. Dilke was always a little patronising about those of royal blood. In 1879 there were two Crown Princes (those of Sweden and Baden) in London to whom he was introduced and of whom he noted: "Like all Kings and Princes, except the King of Greece, and in later days the Emperor William II, they seemed to me heavy men, bored by having to pretend to be thoughtful persons, and I found that difficulty in distinguishing them one from the other, which has always oppressed me in dealing with royal personages."[21]

Dilke's acquaintances during this period were by no means all heavy, anxious to be considered thoughtful, and difficult to distinguish from one another. Swinburne and Manning, for instance, were each in their different ways *sui generis*. The poet was brought into Dilke's life by Lord Houghton, and for a time became a frequent visitor to Sloane Street. "A wreck of glasses attests the presence of Swinburne," Dilke wrote of one visit in 1876. "He compared himself to Dante; repeatedly named himself with Shelley and Dante to the exclusion of all other poets; assured me that he was a great man only because he had been properly flogged at Eton . . . and finally informed me that two glasses of green Chartreuse were a perfect antidote to one of yellow, or two of yellow to one of green."[22] Some time after this visitation Swinburne wrote and sent to Dilke the following snatch of political verse:

> For the Greek will not fight, which is far from right
> And the Russian has all to gain
> Which I deeply regret should so happen—but yet
> 'Tis true, tho' it gives me pain
> And methinks it were vulgar to cheat a poor Bulgar
> With offers of help in vain."[23]

Dilke was greatly shocked by the quality of the poetry; but perhaps Swinburne did not take the Eastern Question as seriously as he himself did.

Dilke's acquaintance with the Cardinal Archbishop of Westminster had begun at the time of the death of Lady Dilke, when Manning had written a letter of sympathy. It did not ripen until 1878, however, when they met again at one of those frequent dinner parties which Manning thought it proper to attend, but at which he also thought it proper to touch neither food nor drink. After this occasion he asked Dilke to come and discuss Irish primary education with him, and by the following year a friendship had sprung up. The Cardinal's visits to 76, Sloane Street became almost as frequent as those of Dilke to Archbishop's House.

"I was amused by finding how much he cared for general gossip and even scandal," Dilke noted. "He insisted on

119

talking to me about Sarah Bernhardt, and Gambetta, and the Prince of Wales, and all sorts and conditions of people. He told me that if he was not Cardinal Archbishop he would stand for Westminster in the Radical interest. But, Radical though he be on social questions, he is a ferocious Jingo."[24]

Another more specifically political acquaintanceship of this period was with Parnell, who had entered Parliament in 1875 and was rapidly forcing himself into a position of leadership. Dilke and Chamberlain joined in inviting him to dinner, with a view both to securing his support against the Zulu war and to hammering out some sort of joint programme on Ireland, but "were able to make little of him." Dilke found him more useful as a consulting barber than as a political collaborator. "One of the grave questions upon which I consulted Parnell in the course of February (1878)," he wrote, "was suggested by my brother, who had objected to my becoming bald. Parnell had been going bald and had shaved his head with much success for his hair had grown again. . . ."[25] But Dilke did not in the event follow his example; perhaps he was frightened by the information, also imparted by Parnell, that in some cases the hair never grew again at all. Another of Dilke's memories of the Irish leader came from a Select Committee on House of Commons procedure, of which they were both members and before which Mr. Speaker Brand was examined as a witness. Parnell conducted a long cross-examination of the Speaker.

"Both of them were in a way able men," Dilke noted, "but both were extraordinarily slow of intellect—that is, slow in appreciating a point or catching a new idea—and Mr.

Brand. . . and Parnell used to face one another in inarticulate despair in the attempt to understand each the other's meaning. There were a good many fairly stupid men on the Committee, but there was not a single member of it who did not understand what Parnell meant by a question more quickly than could the Speaker, and not a man who could not understand what the Speaker meant by a reply more quickly than Parnell."[26]

Most of Dilke's dinner table acquaintances were more conversationally rewarding than Parnell, but not sufficiently so to induce a high view of English talk.

"In the best English political and literary society there is no conversation," he noted rather extremely. "Mr. Gladstone will talk with much charm about matters he does not understand, or books that he is not really competent to criticise; but his conversation has no merit to those who are acquainted with the subjects on which he speaks. Men like Lord Rosslyn, Lord Houghton, Lord Granville (before his deafness) had a pleasant wit and some cultivation, as had Bromley Davenport, Beresford Hope, and others, as well as Arthur Balfour, but none of these men were or are at a high level; and where you get the high level in England, as with Hastings, Duke of Bedford (the one who killed himself), Grant Duff, and some among their friends, you fall into priggism."[27]

It was much the same, Dilke was convinced, in Paris and St. Petersburg and probably in Berlin and Vienna too. Only in Rome, he rather surprisingly concluded, were things better.

There you had "conversation not priggish or academic, and yet consistently maintained at a high level." Dilke knew little Italian, and had passed hardly any time in Rome; but Mrs. Pattison had just spent a winter there.

Dilke went on to note two houses in which Gladstone talked particularly well: "In those two houses he was supreme; but if Coleridge or the Viper (Abraham Hayward) or Browning were present, who talked better than he did, and would not give way to him, he was less good."[28] A little later Dilke was struck by one of Gladstone's social peculiarities. The Duke of Cambridge, on arriving at a dinner party, gave Gladstone his left hand, saying that his right was too painful through gout. "Mr. Gladstone," Dilke wrote, "threw his arms up to the sky, as though he had just heard of the reception of Lord Beaconsfield in heaven, or of some other similar terrible news. His habit of play-acting in this fashion, in the interest of a supposed politeness, is a very odd one, giving a great air of unreality to everything he does; but of course it is a habit of long years."[29] Nevertheless Dilke's judgment of Gladstone became increasingly favourable during these years. He thought that, in contrast with Bright, who was seldom in earnest, Gladstone had real moral force, mainly because he always believed passionately in whatever he was speaking about at any particular moment. In 1879, characteristically mixing his praise with a sharp job of criticism, he wrote to Mrs. Pattison: "Gladstone is still a great power, and but for his Scotch toadyism to the aristocracy, which is a bad drawback, I could admire him with little reserve."[30]

Dilke's own dinner parties were frequent, with a great variety of guests, although after 1876 they were exclusively male. During that year—the first since the death of his wife in which he had entertained on any scale—he had tried holding parties

122

with ladies, but with only a grandmother to help him found the plan "so uncomfortable that I dropped it." At one stage it looked as though Dilke's sister-in-law might move into 76, Sloane Street with her husband and act as hostess, but eventually this came to nothing. Ashton Dilke, soon to be elected member of Parliament for Newcastle-upon-Tyne, had married Maye Smith in the spring of 1876. She was the eldest of six daughters of Thomas Eustace Smith, a prosperous but extravagant North of England shipbuilder, who was himself Liberal member for Tyne-mouth. Charles Dilke, who already knew the family and who was destined never to forget them, did not approve of the alliance.

> "In April there occurred the marriage of my brother," he rather mysteriously wrote, "which was a cause of considerable distress to me as he had been very good to me, and, on the other hand, there were circumstances (not connected with his wife or with himself) which made me unable to approve his marriage. As, however, he immediately quarrelled with these others, I contemplated for some months the possibility of asking him and his wife to come and live with me."[31]

The only hint at the circumstances in the Dilke papers for these years is in a letter which he wrote to Mrs. Pattison at the beginning of 1880. He was relating a conversation with Mrs. Grant Duff, and reported her as having said to him: ". . . and that set Ellen (Mrs. Eustace) Smith chattering, and you know—you know by your own case—what Ellen Smith's chatter is."[32]

Despite the absence of women from his parties, Dilke was far from moving in an exclusively male society. From Mrs.

123

Langtry to Miss Rhoda Broughton he met almost everyone. Of the former he wrote in 1877: "Persons had begun to rave at the beauty of Mrs. Langtry, whom I had known as an ugly child in Jersey and whom I had met in 1876 at Lord Houghton's before she had become a beauty and before anyone had noticed her"; and of the latter—"a very ignorant, very honest, good-hearted sort of woman, with loud, abrupt country-family sort of manners." A closer friendship was with Miss Alice de Rothschild, a daughter of Baron Lionel de Rothschild and a first cousin of Lady Rosebery. Dilke described her as "a clever and agreeable lady of whom I saw a great deal for several years" until they both began to be disturbed by a spate of congratulations on their approaching marriage. This, Dilke recorded, brought their acquaintance gradually to an end, to his great regret.

A few years later, in 1879, Dilke was writing to Mrs. Pattison, who was certainly herself an exception to his statement, that "the only woman with whom I am now on terms which can be called 'intimate' is our Lady Venetia."*** But this did not prevent his sending to Mrs. Pattison a whole series of very sharp comments upon others. Sometimes these comments were merely engagingly disrespectful, as when after meeting the Roseberys at dinner, he recorded the presence of "fat Hannah and her lord." At other times he was more severe and built up an impression of himself as a rather censorious individual. After a Sunday with

*** This was Dilke's somewhat mysterious method of referring to the wife of Mountstuart Grant Duff, then Liberal member for Elgin Burghs and later Governor of Madras. Her Christian name was Anna and she then had no title.

old Lady Russell (the widow of the Prime Minister) at Pembroke Lodge, which in 1879 replaced Strawberry Hill for him as a week-end rendezvous, he wrote of the presence of Miss Laffan,††† to whom he "did not quite take." "She is great fun," he added, "but she looks immodest. . . ." Later in that year he entered into a long discussion, again in a letter to Mrs. Pattison, of the morals of a Mrs. Ronalds. He drew a distinction between her and the Duchess of Manchester, whom "I believe for many years to have been faithful to L(or)d H(artingto)n and he to her," and ended by announcing firmly that Mrs. Ronalds ought to be cleared of the charges levelled against her "or else not received." Again in the next year he wrote: "At the State dinner last night Corti (Italian ambassador to the Porte), who is here for a few days . . . was the most interesting guest. But he is one of those clever, ugly, cynical men, who tho' interested in politics are more interested in the chatter of any and every woman, and so he rushes off to be chattered to."[33] The picture of Dilke trying vainly to get some detailed conversation about the intricacies of Near Eastern politics is a vivid one.

Another subject on which Dilke wrote to Mrs. Pattison, was his personal financial position. He was always rather neurotic about this, not out of meanness, but because of an ill-defined fear that some misfortune, perhaps political, perhaps personal, might befall him, which would make the possession of a liquid reserve highly desirable. He therefore began to hoard gold—and continued the practice for several years—depositing his reserves partly

---

††† Miss Laffan was a friend of the Rector of Lincoln. "I have a heap to tell you of *Dilke*—I can't write it," she wrote to him a few years later. (V. H. H. Green, *op. cit.* pp. 309–10.)

in England and partly in France. "I have saved very greatly on clothes and underclothes, and a little as yet on *everything* this year," he wrote in April, 1879. "I do not use nearly all I put down for 'self' (which includes luncheons and dinners at the House)—but at present I am hoarding it in cash to have a reserve."[34]

Apart from his neurosis there was little need for Dilke to economise. By the end of the 'seventies, in contrast with the position when his first wife had been alive, he was living within his income, even though this had fallen substantially. In 1880, for instance, he saved £1,650, quite apart from his "hoarding." But he was not living in a particularly modest way. He kept nine servants at 76, Sloane Street, including a coachman who was paid £70 a year and a stable lad who received £58. The butler's rate was £60 plus 3s. a week for beer money, and the footman's £28 plus 2s. 6d. for beer. The cook was paid £40 a year, the upper housemaid £24, and the under housemaid and the kitchenmaid each received £14. The ninth servant was a nurse for the child who was given, no wages as such, but who, in addition to her board, was clothed and given a small amount of pocket-money by Mrs. Chatfield.

A sample of how Dilke's other expenses ran is provided by the following schedule of payments for April, 1880:

The total, at £640, is somewhat larger than the monthly average for the year, but this is to be explained by a number of quarterly or half-yearly payments having fallen due.

Dilke's French visit was one of a regular series at this time. In the late summer of 1876 he had rented for four months La Sainte Campagne, a small Provençal property near Toulon. It was a small, grey-walled, eighteenth-century manor of a type more common amidst the poplars of the Ile de France than in the harsher landscape of die Midi. The situation was magnificent. The house stood high on the cliffs of Cap Brun, and its terrace commanded one of the best views on the whole coast. In the following year he bought the property, and for some time made a habit of spending several weeks there both at Christmas and Easter. One of his neighbours was Émile Ollivier, who fascinated Dilke because of his knowledge of the origins of the Franco-Prussian War; but for the most part Dilke's visits to Provence were periods of respite both from politics and from his normal social activities. He travelled alone, he rarely had guests in the house, and he lived a quiet and almost solitary life.[‡‡‡] But on his way to and from the South of France he usually spent a few days in Paris, staying at first in the Grand Hôtel, as he had done at the time of the Commune and after his wife's death, but later at the St., James et d'Albany in the Rue St. Honoré; and during these halts he plunged into a life as animated as that of La Sainte Campagne was quiet. Gambetta remained his closest French political friend, but there were many others as well.

During one of these visits to France—perhaps as early as 1874—Dilke was initiated into the art of fencing. He took to the sport immediately, although his style was somewhat boisterous, but for several years it provided him only with occasional holiday relaxation. During the autumn of 1878, however, he suffered unusually from want of exercise, and in the following February

---

[‡‡‡] There is, however, a local legend that his life there was not entirely solitary. The present owner of La Sainte Campagne writes: "Je me souviens toutefois que Mme, de Jonquières (an old lady now dead who knew Dilke well) racontait que c'était par amour d'une jeune beauté toulonnaise, et pour âtre près d'elle, que Sir Charles Dilke avait, durant plusieurs années, habité La Sainte Campagne."

he sought to repair his deficiency by instituting a daily period of fencing at 76, Sloane Street, At the back of the house on the ground floor the dining-room gave out through french windows on to a paved terrace, a few steps above the small garden which lay beyond. Here on the terrace, each morning during the parliamentary session, at least five and sometimes as many as eight or nine *escrimeurs* would assemble for an hour or more. They came at half past nine or ten o'clock and they left at about eleven. In addition to a fencing master, the regular participants included Sir Julian Pauncefote, later permanent under-secretary at the Foreign Office, Lord Desborough, and Baron d'Estournelles de Constant, later French Ambassador at The Hague but at that time a first secretary at Albert Gate. There were other more occasional visitors, amongst them any of the great French or Italian masters who happened to be in London. The clash of the foils and shouts of laughter from Dilke himself were recalled many years later as being familiar sounds in the neighbouring gardens.

His guests may have been earlier risers, but Dilke normally came straight from his bed to the fencing. When it was nearly over he would return to his room to bath and dress, before breakfasting alone, at about 11.15 a.m. This routine he maintained for nearly a decade, including the period when he was in office. He continued to fence, although not with equal regularity, for much longer. Even in the last decade of his life he kept an outfit at one of the best-known Paris fencing establishments, and used frequently to appear there. He was one of the first Englishmen to use the *épée*, and he acquired a considerable skill with this weapon, although he was less good with foils.

The first results of the new fencing régime at Sloane Street appeared to be excellent. Within six weeks Dilke secured by far the greatest parliamentary triumph that his career had known. When Parliament reassembled in February, 1879, the Zulu War had just begun. It was a conflict to which the Government, against the wishes of the Prime Minister and most of the Cabinet, had been committed by the impetuous local leadership of Sir Bartle Frere. And it had begun badly with defeat at Isandhlwana. Hartington was uncertain what line to take; Gladstone's eye was temporarily much more on Midlothian than on Westminster; and Dilke, who had a clear view that the war was as foolish as it was unjust, was able to take the lead. He was put up to reply to the statement with which Sir Stafford Northcote, as leader of the House, opened on the day of the re-assembly; and this led on to his tabling a motion which was certainly one of censure on Frere and might have been considered to be one upon the Government too. After some delay this came up for debate on March 27th and was the occasion of Dilke's triumph. "I write to you under the violent excitement of a splendid personal success," he informed Mrs. Pattison that night. "I had an extraordinary oratorical triumph, and received the congratulations of the leading men of both parties."[36]

Elsewhere he wrote rather more calmly of the speech:

"I spoke for two hours and a half, and kept the House full, without ever for an instant being in doubt as to the complete success of the speech; greatly cheered by my own side, without being once questioned or interrupted by the other. But the speech was far from being my best speech, although it was by far my greatest success. It was an easy speech to make—a mere Blue Book speech. The case from the papers was overwhelming. . . . While I was gratified by the success of the speech, I could not help feeling how completely these things are a matter of opportunity, inasmuch as I had made dozens of better speeches in the House, of which some had been wholly unsuccessful."[37]

The newspapers did not share all of Dilke's own reservations. There was general comment that he was the only successful young man that Parliament had produced in recent years; and the *Scotsman* said that no other speech had excited such general admiration since Gladstone's denunciation of the Treaty of Berlin in the previous summer. This suggestion that Dilke had attained great oratorical heights does not ring true, however. *Truth*, with a piece of Hiawathan verse,* caught much more accurately the note of keen, industrious efficiency which was the real characteristic of his speaking.

Another result of the Zulu debate was the offer to Dilke of a safe seat in Manchester, with the promise that his election expenses would be paid by the local committee. He was attracted by the offer, not least because he was expecting to be beaten at Chelsea. But he had given an undertaking to his supporters there that he would not move until this event actually occurred, which he did not attempt to evade.

Later in 1879 there was a sharp and public quarrel between Hartington and Chamberlain, which in Dilke's view substantially damaged Hartington's position and destroyed the possibility of his retaining the leadership. Dilke, who was not directly involved, supported Chamberlain, but with a little less enthusiasm than might have been anticipated. It was a House of Commons quarrel on the committee stage of the Army Bill. Chamberlain, who had surprisingly strong views against corporal punishment—he had been horrified a few weeks earlier to

130

discover that his son Austen had been beaten at Rugby—was trying to secure the abolition of flogging as a military punishment. Hartington was not opposed to this. Indeed, Henry James, whom Dilke described as the leader's "right-hand man," had encouraged the radicals to make as much as they could of the issue. But when the Government accused them of obstruction, Hartington, strolling casually into the House late on the night of July 7th, decided to throw his weight behind the Treasury bench. Chamberlain was deeply angered. "It is rather inconvenient that we should have so little of the presence of the noble Lord, lately the leader of the Opposition, but now the leader of a section only," he announced with frigid bitterness; and a quarrel began which could only be ended by an apology from Hartington. But this apology, which was forthcoming, could not put matters back where they had been before.

> "Never absent, always ready
>   To take up the burning question
>   Of the hour and make a motion:
>   Be it Cyprus, be it Zulu,
>   He can speak for hours about it
>   From his place below the gangway.
>   No Blue Book avails to fright him:
>   He's the stomach of an ostrich
>   For the hardest facts and figures,
>   And assimilates despatches
>   In the most surprising fashion."

"Later in the month," Dilke wrote, "the Whigs, or men above the gangway, showed great anger at the completeness of Hartington's surrender to us, which, indeed, meant more than the immediate conquest, for it involved the ultimate supersession of Hartington by Gladstone. Harcourt, James and Adam (the Chief Whip), in giving Chamberlain the victory, by insisting that Hartington should yield, were considering the constituencies, not the House. As regarded the House, the popularity of stamping upon us would have been great. There was strong Whig dislike of our activity, and strong radical personal hatred among ourselves. If Chamberlain were to have fought Hartington on any question on which he had not the Liberal constituencies with him, he would have got the worst of it; but then he was too wise to stir on any question on which he could not at least carry all the active elements of the party in large towns. The anti-Chamberlain set went to work to get up a banquet for Hartington, and were very cross with me when I told them that I was certain that the Whips would not let Hartington accept the banquet unless they obtained Chamberlain's signature to the requisition. It, of course, turned out as I expected. Some twenty men said they would not sign unless Chamberlain did so, and he was then begged to sign, and, when he did, at once deprived the manifestation of all significance. It was all rather small and mean, but when one went to the root of the matter, one saw that the whole difficulty sprang from the fact that the Whigs had now no principles."[38]

These events not only strengthened the position of Gladstone as against Hartington—a process which was carried further in the autumn by the tumultuous success of the former's first Midlothian campaign. They also gave a relative fillip to

Chamberlain as against Dilke. The latter still had much more of a general parliamentary reputation. His range of knowledge and of contacts was much wider. He was more consulted by his leaders, and he had behind him House of Commons triumphs such as Chamberlain had never then enjoyed. But it was Chamberlain who, as the spokesman of the radical caucuses throughout the Midlands and the North, had brought to heel the Whig leader of the Liberal party. His achievement was certainly not without significance.

Nevertheless, Dilke was not disposed to feel either jealous or dissatisfied with himself. He was rather less given to jealousy than most politicians, although when in 1880 he went so far as to tell Harcourt: "I believe I am the only English politician who is not jealous," the latter received the statement with understandable scepticism. "We all think that of ourselves," he replied.[39] Nor was Dilke ever inclined to self-dissatisfaction. But even if he had been, the winter of 1879–80 was not the time for it.

When the Liberals came back to power Dilke's place in the new administration seemed assured, and any strengthening of Chamberlain's position appeared likely, so long as they worked in combination, to improve rather than weaken his own. Nor was a change likely to be long delayed. The Beaconsfield Government was manifestly moving towards its end. The Prime Minister was ill and tired. The leadership in the Commons was ineffective. The diplomatic victories of 1878 were looking a little tarnished. There was a rising tide of economic discontent. And the innovation of a politician of Gladstone's stature stumping round the country was proving highly popular with the new electorate. There was some surprise when Beaconsfield decided to meet Parliament, for the Government's seventh session, at the beginning of February. It was not to be a long session. Encouraged by the false gleam of a chance Conservative victory at the Southwark by-election in the first week of March, the Prime Minister decided to go to the country. The dissolution was announced on March 8th, with most of the polls to be declared in the first week of April.

Chapter Six

The Dust without the Palm

On April 2nd Dilke was returned for Chelsea. He was top of the poll, but his new electoral partner, J. E. B. Firth, Q.C., was only a few hundred votes behind him; they both had comfortable leads over their Conservative opponents.* Dilke's fears about the safety of the seat had proved quite unfounded—at least in such a year of Liberal triumph as 1880. On April 5th, when Gladstone was elected for Midlothian, it was already clear that there was to be a big majority against the Government. When the results were complete they gave 349 seats to the Liberals, 243 to the Conservatives, and 60 to the Irish Nationalists. Mr. Gladstone returned to Hawarden, ruminating "on the great

---

* Dike	..	..	12,406
Firth	..	..	12,046
Lord Inverurie	..		9,666
W. J. Browne	..		9,488

135

hand of God, so evidently displayed."

Chamberlain, in Birmingham, ruminated on the great hand of the Caucus, which had also been in evidence and which he was determined to display. He wrote privately to Gladstone calling attention to the victories in the boroughs which had been achieved by the National Liberal machine, and publicly to *The Times* to stress the same point. And *The Times* responded by describing him as "the Carnot of the moment." Encouraged by the results and by this and similar tributes to his part in achieving them, Chamberlain raised his sights. Earlier in the year he had entertained Harcourt at Birmingham, had been beguiled by the latter's wit and flattery, and had been willing to contemplate the acceptance of what a Whig Government might be disposed to offer him. Now, after the first results, he thought that he might take his place, not as an individual, but as one of the leaders of a recognised wing of the party. In this spirit he wrote to Dilke on Sunday, April 4th, offering the conclusion between them of a firm political treaty. The letter is sufficiently important to be given in full:

Southbourne, Augustus Road,
Birmingham

My dear Dilke:

I find the same fault with your letters that the Scotch laird found with the Dictionary—"the stories are varra pretty but they are unco short!"

The time has come when we must have a full frank explanation. What I should like—what I hope for with you—is a thorough offensive and defensive alliance and in this case our position will be immensely strong. I am prepared to refuse all offices until and unless *both of us are satisfied*.

136

Can you accept this position with perfect satisfaction? If you think I am asking more than I can give I rely on your saying so—and in this case you may depend on my loyalty and friendship. I shall support your claims cordially and just as warmly as if I personally were interested. But my own feeling is that if you are stronger than I am in the House, my influence is greater than yours out of it—and, therefore, that, together, we are much more powerful than separated; - and that, in a short time—if not now—we may make our own terms.

To join a Government as subordinate members—to be silenced and to have no real influence on the policy—would be fatal to both of us. If we both remain outside, any Government will have to reckon with us and on the whole this would be the position which on many grounds I should prefer. I am ready to make all allowances for the difficulties in the way of giving to both of us the only kind of place which it would be worth our while to accept. If these are insuperable, I will give a hearty support to any Government which is thoroughly liberal in its measures; but I am not *going to* play the part of a radical minnow among Whig Tritons.

The victory which has just been won is the victory of the radicals—Gladstone and the Caucus have triumphed all along the line, and it is the strong, definite, decided policy which has commended itself and not the halting half-hearted arm-chair business. *The Times* sees this and said it yesterday—the country feels it—and we should be mad to efface ourselves and disappoint the expectations of our strongest supporters.

You will see that my proposed condition is—both of us to be satisfied.

As to what *ought to* satisfy us, if you agree to the principle, we will consult when the time comes, but my present impression is—all or nothing. *Tout arrive à qui sait attendre.* Write me fully your views and tell me whether and when you will pay me a visit.

Yours ever,

J. Chamberlain[1]

On the evening of the day on which this letter was written Dilke dined with Harcourt He found him still inclined to Hartington rather than Gladstone as Prime Minister, but otherwise in a cynically radical mood. "I found his ambition to be to worry out Lord Selborne with Radical measures to which he would be unable to assent, and then to succeed him as Lord Chancellor," Dilke noted. "He asked me what I should like," he added, "and I told him that I did not expect to be offered a great post, but that if there were any such chance the Navy was the only one that I should like."[2]

The next morning Dilke received Chamberlain's letter, and replied, on the same day, in the following terms:

My dear Chamberlain:

When I'm in London and you don't want to risk your letters being opened by Kennedy (Dilke's secretary)—you can write to the Reform Club. I generally go there each day. (I opened yours myself this morning.) I leave for Toulon on Wednesday night. I shall stay there for about a fortnight. I quite agree generally to the position that we should continue to work together and that each should see that the other is satisfied. My first enquiry when I hear anything will be—what about you? I also think that we are far more powerful together than separated and that we are in a position to make our own terms. I am convinced that the county franchise must be done at once and that makes it difficult for Lowe and Goschen to remain in. If Lord G(ranville) is Premier his personal affection will make him cling to Lowe, and if they keep Lowe—I don't see how they can offer the Cabinet at once to both of us. If Hartington is Premier—I don't see why they should not offer the Cabinet to *both* of us. The real difficulty will arise if they offer the Cabinet to one of us, and high office outside it with a promise of the first vacancy in it to the other. I call this a difficulty because I agree that neither of us would like to be responsible for a policy in which he had no voice. When a strong land Bill is brought in Lord Selborne must resign. The same difficulty stands in the way of Lord Derby and the Duke of Argyll, so it seems to me that they want us both, either now, or very soon. So much for the personal matter. For the political—I think we shall have no difficulties of principle in the first Session. They will only begin in November.

Ever yours,

Charles W. Dilke[3]

Garvin, Chamberlain's biographer, has summed up this letter as pouring water into Chamberlain's wine and amounting to a rejection of his offer. Dilke, Garvin believed, had been seduced by Harcourt's blandishments, set store by his own ability to move with ease "in what was still called the highest Whig society," and wished to try his hand at securing entry to the Cabinet without worrying too much about the provincial radical. Furthermore, in Garvin's view, Dilke's decision to go to his house near Toulon, and not to Birmingham, underlined his slight to Chamberlain.[4]

Dilke himself states clearly that he had a difference of opinion with Chamberlain at this stage. "In other words," he wrote later in a comment upon the correspondence, "Chamberlain's view was that we should insist on both being in the Cabinet. My own view was that we should insist on one being in the Cabinet, and the other having a place of influence, giving him the opportunity of frequent speech in the House of Commons. . . ."[5] But there was no necessary slight to Chamberlain in such a view; and Dilke's persistence in his plans to go to Toulon, whatever else it indicated, certainly showed no desire to exercise his entrée into "the highest Whig society" during the crucial period of speculation about the shape of the Cabinet.

Where Dilke's judgment was curiously at fault—and where Harcourt may well have been to blame—was in discounting the return of Gladstone to the lead. Admittedly the Queen was bitterly opposed to such an eventuality. On April 4th she had written to her private secretary that "she would sooner *abdicate* than send for or have anything to do with that *half-mad firebrand* who would soon ruin everything and be a *Dictator*." But the electorate had spoken equally clearly in Gladstone's favour; and in such a situation the constituencies were already more powerful than the sovereign. She conducted a strong rearguard action, but it was a battle against the inevitable. On April 22nd, the day after Lord Beaconsfield's unhurried resignation, she sent for Hartington and requested him to form a government. He at once suggested Gladstone, but the Queen forced him to attempt the task, at least to the extent of formally enquiring of Gladstone whether he would be prepared to accept a subordinate position. Gladstone replied that he would not, and when Hartington and Granville jointly took this intelligence back to the Queen (who added considerably to the inconvenience of these negotiations by remaining at Windsor), sweetening it with the suggestion that Gladstone would be unlikely to bear the strain of office for long, she accepted her defeat. The new Prime Minister kissed hands on April 24th, and immediately

140

demonstrated a view of his strength somewhat different from that of his colleagues by announcing that he intended to be his own Chancellor of the Exchequer.

Dilke remained at Toulon until April 22nd. While there he received a sulky letter from Chamberlain, written on April 19th.

"I am glad to see that all the Papers speak of you as a certainty for the Cabinet," this letter ran. "These reports are unauthentic, but they have a tendency to secure their own fulfilment. I feel that you may have a rather difficult question to decide, viz., whether you can safely take the *sole* representation of the radical element in the Government. If Fawcett is given office he may be a rather uncertain ally. For myself, I am absolutely indifferent to office and the only thing on which I am clear is that I will take no responsibility which does not carry with it some real power. Another point on which I have made up my mind is that I will not play second to Fawcett—or to any one of the same standing except yourself."[6]

In other words, if Dilke alone were to be offered the Cabinet, Chamberlain would prefer him to refuse, and, even if he accepted, was giving notice of a possibly independent and critical attitude towards the Government.

Dilke reached London on the evening of April 23rd and immediately saw Harcourt (a telegram from whom had summoned him home) and Frank Hill, the editor of the *Daily News*. From these two sources he gathered that the prospects were not as favourable as he had hoped. Gladstone, he was told, was strongly under the influence of Lord Wolverton, his former Chief Whip—"the evil counsellor of 1874" in Dilke's phrase—and was taking the view that his own position as a radical Prime Minister made a predominantly Whig Cabinet both necessary and acceptable. Furthermore, he was inclined to take his stand on what he called "Peel's rule" and allow no one into his Cabinet who had not previously served in subordinate office. This meant that the best for which Dilke could hope was the Financial Secretaryship to the Treasury or an under-secretaryship to a minister in the Lords, with Chamberlain in a roughly similar position. Harcourt, who had already been appointed Home Secretary, saw Dilke again on the following day and made him an informal offer—apparently on the Prime Minister's behalf—of the Financial Secretaryship. Later in the evening the offer was changed to that of the under-secretary-ship for the Colonies—the Secretary of State being Lord Kimberley. The first offer Dilke had not accepted; the second he indignantly refused. At thhis stage his mind, too, was moving towards a discontented independence, and he telegraphed to Birmingham to urge on Chamberlain the need for immediate consultation with a view to a joint refusal of office.

Chamberlain at first refused to come and telegraphed back to this effect. Dilke then wrote a slightly testy letter and sent it off to Birmingham by special messenger:

"I have your telegram refusing to come to-morrow," he wrote. "If I were not so tired after my journey I'd come down. You see you talk of consultation, but I can't consult you by telegram, and in Gladstone's stand and deliver kind of business there is no time for exchange of letters with Birmingham. My telegram of this evening was intended to mean that it was certain that Gladstone would not offer either of us the Cabinet, and to ask you whether it was clear that we ought to refuse all else. I dare not telegraph at length or openly as all telegrams get out to the other side. . . . Also I thought that when asked to take minor office, as you will be on Monday—you would probably have to come up and say no in more haste than if you came up to consult to-morrow. Harcourt urges that it is of special importance for *me* to take office to get over the Court hitch now and for ever—once and for all—but there are strong considerations the other way on that point which apply more to me than to you—but apply to both of us in some part."[7]

Chamberlain received this letter on the Sunday morning, and decided to come to London on the afternoon of the same day. Dilke met him at Euston Station and drove him to 76, Sloane Street. They spent the evening in consultation, Chamberlain taking the view that he stiffened Dilke to refuse office unless one of them were in the Cabinet, but Dilke recording that Chamberlain merely concurred in his own view to this effect. But there is no doubt that they were agreed. On the Monday morning Dilke stayed at home and received visits from Childers, Shaw Lefevre and Fawcett, and a letter asking him to call upon Mr. Gladstone at Lord Granville's house at 4 o'clock. Chamberlain, meanwhile, went to see Harcourt and informed him in rather truculent words of the minimum terms that would be acceptable to Dilke and himself, and of the consequences—the organisation of a "pure left" party—which would follow if the Prime Minister were to reject them. He also indicated, in the account of this interview which he wrote immediately afterwards to Jesse Collings, that he was accepting with some reluctance the possibility of being lower in the hierarchy than Dilke:

"Finally I said that, out of friendship for Dilke, I would if he were in the Cabinet take the Secretaryship of the Treasury—but, of course, an arrangement of this kind would not be so satisfactory as a frank recognition of the Radical wing with two at least in the Cabinet. . . . If Dilke is in the Cabinet," Chamberlain added to Collings, "I shall have the satisfaction of having helped most materially to place him there. I am still almost inclined to hope that we may all be out and independent."[8]

After luncheon Dilke went to Carlton House Terrace for his interview with the Prime Minister.

"When I got to Lord Granville's," he wrote, "I found Lord Granville, Lord Wolverton, and Mr. Gladstone in the room, and Mr. Gladstone at once offered me the Under-Secretaryship for Foreign Affairs. I asked who was to be in the Cabinet. I was told Mr. Gladstone, Lord Granville, Hartington, Harcourt and Lord Spencer. Further than this, they said, nothing was settled. I asked, 'What about Chamberlain?' Mr. Gladstone replied to the effect that Chamberlain was a very young member of the House who had never held office, and that it was impossible to put him straight into the Cabinet. I then said that this made it impossible that I should accept the Under-Secretaryship for Foreign Affairs, or any place. Mr. Gladstone said he would see whether anything could be done, but that he feared not . . . and I then left."[9]

The Prime Minister, however, discovered that something could be done. Dilke's refusal of junior office unless Chamberlain

144

were in the Cabinet was highly inconvenient for the Government. It was a difficulty which might have been overcome either by a better offer to Dilke himself or by accepting his terms with regard to Chamberlain. Against the former course was the consideration that Dilke was still highly objectionable to the Queen—a good deal more than was Chamberlain[†]; and this consideration was buttressed by the fact that it was Dilke who, in the view of both Gladstone and Granville, had been tiresomely irritating at that afternoon's interview. He had been irritating *about* Chamberlain, but that was not sufficient to spread the guilt evenly between them. When, therefore, John Bright, the only radical whom Gladstone regarded as thoroughly respectable, saw the Prime Minister later the same day and urged the solution of the difficulty by bringing his Birmingham colleague Chamberlain into the Cabinet, his advice was readily accepted. On the following morning—Tuesday, April 27th—Gladstone wrote to Chamberlain in characteristic terms and sent the letter by hand to 76, Sloane Street.

"I have made some progress since yesterday afternoon," he wrote, "and I may add that there is a small addition to my liberty of choice beyond what I had expected. Accordingly, looking as I seek to do all along to the selection of the fittest, I have real pleasure in proposing to you that you should allow me to submit your name to Her Majesty as President

---

[†] Frederic Harrison wrote to Dilke at this time: "It will take you a tremendous pull yet to force the poor old lady to let you kiss her hand. Harcourt, Fawcett, Chamberlain she might swallow without a wry face, but she will strain at you unless you are made absolutely inevitable and undeniable." (D. P. 439341 149.)

of the Board of Trade in the new Administration with a seat in the Cabinet to which you will be glad to know your friend and colleague Mr. Bright already belongs."[10]

The Prime Minister's messenger missed Chamberlain, but he found Dilke, to whom he communicated a summons tQ see Mr. Gladstone again at 1 o'clock that day. When this second interview took place the Prime Minister informed Dilke of his invitation to Chamberlain and again offered him the undersecretaryship at the Foreign Office. Dilke immediately accepted and went off to the Reform Club, where he met Chamberlain, still ignorant of Gladstone's letter, and informed him that the Board of Trade was at his disposal. Chamberlain left at once to see Gladstone, and heard of the offer from the Prime Minister's own lips. Then, he tells us, he became greatly worried against his elevation above Dilke, and offered to avoid the difficulty by himself becoming Financial Secretary to the Treasury, while Dilke remained at the Foreign Office. This offer, which it is difficult to believe was not a little rhetorical and which is in any event uncorroborated from any source other than Chamberlain's own writings, was refused by Gladstone. Chamberlain then accepted the Board of Trade; and, the difficulties with the radicals being thus temporarily removed, the completion of the Government was able to proceed quickly.‡

---

‡ Membership of the Cabinet was as follows:

Prime Minister and Chancellor of the Exchequer:	W. E. Gladstone
Lord Chancellor:	Lord Selborne
Lord President:	Earl Spencer
Lord Privy Seal:	Duke of Argyll
Home Secretary:	Sir Willam Harcourt

The Prime Minister's preference for Chamberlain over Dilke aroused widespread surprise and comment. Dilke's own files of incoming letters for the period are full of complaints that he had allowed himself to be most unfairly treated; and Chamberlain, looking back eleven years later upon these events, wrote:

> "As I expected, the announcement of this arrangement excited a good deal of discontent and ill-feeling. Dilke himself, although he must have been disappointed at not receiving the offer of a higher office, behaved admirably; but there were many other Radicals who thought that their claims were as good or better than any that I could put forward and were inclined to resent the quick promotion which I had, however unwillingly, secured."[11]

Most people believed, and continued to believe for many years, that Chamberlain had treated Dilke badly. J. L. Garvin set himself to refute this view, and did so with some success, although not sufficiently so to justify his innuendo that it was in fact Dilke who behaved badly to Chamberlain. No doubt both

---

Foreign Secretary:	Earl Granville
Colonial Secretary:	Earl of Kimberley
Secretary for War:	H. C. E. Childers
Secretary for India:	Marquess of Hartington
First Lord of the Admiralty:	Earl of Northbrook
President of the Board of Trade:	Joseph Chamberlain
President of the Local Government Board:	J. G. Dodson
Chief Secretary:	W. E. Forster
Chancellor of the Duchy of Lancaster	John Bright

men found it difficult to maintain a perfect balance between friendship and ambition; but the hard facts are that Dilke entered the period of negotiation well in the lead, that he emerged from it well in the rear, and that the decisive impetus to Chamberlain's advancement was given by his own ultimatum to Gladstone. Although this had not been his original intention, Dilke forced Chamberlain into the Cabinet over his own head; and no theory that he behaved with doubtful loyalty is compatible with this fact.

Furthermore, despite the temptations of jealousy, Dilke was far more emotionally involved in their friendship than was Chamberlain. Whatever may have been the position politically, personally Dilke needed Chamberlain more than Chamberlain needed Dilke. Dilke was ambitious and vain, but he was wholly lacking in Chamberlain's capacity for the ruthless subordination of personal emotions to political purposes. As a result he was far more liable to bursts of sudden, perhaps rather self-conscious generosity; and his attitude to Chamberlain was sometimes almost that of an anxious lover rather than a political ally.

> "I've not heard from you since the 18th (a letter written on the 16th)," he wrote on December 21st, 1882, "and had hoped to have heard from you this morning. I have not vexed you, have I, by anything I have done or left undone?" . . . "I *was* worried and cross until I saw you," he wrote again two days later. "You dispelled the clouds in a moment—I suppose it will not do for one politician to say to another—by your smile—but so it was."[12]

Dilke was sometimes capable of making more critical

judgments of Chamberlain. In a letter to Mrs. Pattison in October, 1881, he refers to "Chamberlain—with the unforgiving ferocity he displays when people don't do as he and I wish"[13]; and six months later he was complaining in his confidential diary: "I cannot always depend on Chamberlain to oppose foolish things in the Cabinet. At to-day's Cabinet Bright was the only Minister who opposed the prosecution of the *Freiheit*§ and Chamberlain positively supported it!"[14] Again, in November, 1882, Dilke's comment on a parliamentary situation was: "Chamberlain will of course have but one object—i.e. to damn Forster. He always cared more about damning Forster than about anything else at all."[15] But these are three isolated comments from private papers and letters covering a period of thirty months. On the whole, Dilke's judgments of Chamberlain were remarkably favourable—there was hardly a hint of jealousy and never a sneer at any aspect of Chamberlain's "provincialism," this despite or perhaps because of the fact that the latter insisted on regarding Dilke as his "*arbiter elegantarium*," who could advise him on his dealings with foreign royalties and similar difficult problems. In all Dilke was not

---

§ *Freiheit* was a German anarchist paper published in London. Dilke had no reason to be friendly towards it or its sponsors, as one of them—Maltman Barry—had recently announced that in 1877 Dilke had subscribed to the funds of the paper and the election expenses of revolutionary candidates in Germany. Dilke denied that this was so, although he thought that he might have given Barry a small sum of money for "some case of charity among his socialists." This incident caused him some embarrassment. Lord Randolph Churchill raised the matter in the House of Commons in terms sufficiently venomous to cause a breach between himself and Dilke which lasted for several years.

exaggerating when he wrote to Chamberlain in September, 1881: ". . . it is curious that in spite of what people believe about the jealousies of politicians you should be one of the two or three people in the world about whose life or death I should care enough for that care to be worth the name of affection."[16]

Chamberlain's replies were always a little less warm. However, he did go so far as to write in December, 1882:

"The fact is that you are by nature such a reserved fellow (a curious phrase to use in view of Dilke's letters) that all *demonstration* of affection is difficult, but you may believe me when I say that I feel it. . . . I suppose I am reserved myself—the great trouble we have both been through¶ has had a hardening effect in my case, and since then I have never worn my heart on my sleeve. But if I were in trouble I should come to you at once—and that is the best proof of friendship and confidence that I know of."[17]

Chamberlain gave some proof of his own friendship by taking Dilke's son, who was by no means an easy child, to live with his own children at Highbury. He remained there for more than two years until he went to school.

The new Government, to which Dilke and Chamberlain had been admitted after so much travail, was very much of a Whig affair. Gladstone compensated for his own incipient

---

¶ The loss of their wives in childbirth. In Chamberlain's case this occurred twice. His first wife, Harriet, died in 1863, when Austen was born; his second wife, Florence, in 1874.

150

radicalism—and also gave full play to his "Scottish toady-ism"—by giving six Cabinet posts (of a total of fourteen) to peers, five of whom were hereditary magnates, and a seventh to Hartington, who certainly counted as a nobleman despite the accident that he sat in the House of Commons. Still worse, Gladstone began his premiership on this occasion without any-clear sense of purpose. In 1868 he had announced that his mission was "to pacify Ireland." The Parliament of 1880 was to be dominated by Irish affairs to a far greater extent than that of 1868, but Gladstone had no conception of this when he took office. His policy was the negative one of undoing as quickly as possible the moral harm of "Beaconsfieldism." But in foreign affairs he found it difficult in practice not to accept the *status quo* in most fields—quite apart from the fact that he was soon bombarding Alexandria with an enthusiasm which Disraeli himself would have found it hard to surpass; and at home the fact that he was his own Chancellor of the Exchequer concentrated his mind upon the pettiest details of government expenditure in a most undesirable way. In Ireland he impro-vised rather than struck out along a consistent line of policy, and the result was a series of violent and confusing oscillations between conciliation and coercion.

In addition, the Parliament, which would in any event have been a bitter one, partly as a legacy of the Prime Minister's, own Midlothian campaign and partly as a result of the rise of "Parnellism," was bedevilled by the Bradlaugh controversy. Whether the militantly atheistic member for Northampton should be allowed to take the oath of allegiance or to affirm, whether he should be allowed to sit at all, whether the majority of the House of Commons should dictate to Northampton or to any other constituency whom it could or could not elect—these were all questions which racked the House for more than three years, which aroused some of its worst instincts, which frequently placed in a minority the Prime Minister, who despite his hatred of atheism was consistently liberal on the issue, and which acted as an open wound draining away much of the strength of the Government.

In these circumstances the Administration could not in any event have been a happy one in which to serve. It was made worse by internal dissension. All British Governments are coalitions, but this was a more rickety one than most, with the perforation between the Whigs and the Liberals always clearly apparent to all the world. Within three months one Whig magnate in junior office—the Marquess of Lansdowne—had resigned on the Irish land issue, and his defection was followed, still within the first year, by that of the Duke of Argyll. A year later the Chief Secretary, W. E. Forster, resigned as a protest against conciliation in Ireland, and three months after this John Bright resigned because of the forward policy in Egypt. In addition, Chamberlain and Dilke kept the Government in constant agitation by a series of threatened resignations. Gladstone's own practice under other Prime Ministers did not entitle him to much consideration in this respect, but even making full allowance for this, Chamberlain and Dilke behaved almost intolerably. "The only way in which I can get anything done is by threatening resignation," Dilke wrote on one occasion in 1882. "Lord Granville is so sick of these threats," he added, "that he tells me that nothing should be so sacred as the threat of resignation."[18]

Furthermore, Dilke was always prepared to threaten to go out whenever Chamberlain was restless. "Our relations are so close," he wrote to Lord Granville, "that I should resign with him if he were to resign because he thought Forster did not have his hair cut sufficiently often."[19]** Chamberlain, however, perhaps because he was more satisfied with his office, was not prepared to give quite such indiscriminate support to Dilke, and on two of the eight occasions between May, 1880, and July, 1882, when Dilke was threatening to go out, Chamberlain was not with him. These were both at the beginning of 1881, in January when Chamberlain was loath to go in opposition to a Coercion Bill for Ireland—"Chamberlain's position at this moment was that he personally did not believe in coercion, but that the feeling in the country was such that any Government would be forced to propose it, and he was not sufficiently clear that it was certain to fail to be bound as an honest man to necessarily oppose it,"[20] Dilke noted; and in March, when Dilke was insistent that the Government should give stronger support to Greek claims to frontier rectification against Turkey. On at least six other occasions, however, Dilke and Chamberlain were prepared to resign together: in support of an Irish Land Bill in July, 1880; against coercion without the Land Bill in November of the same year;

** A resignation on this account might not have been quite impossible. Chamberlain and Dilke were both highly critical of the tonsorial and sartorial deficiences of their colleagues. After Dilke had joined the Cabinet Chamberlain occupied himself at one meeting by writing and passing to Dilke the following note: "Someone ought to move the appointment of a hair-cutter to the Cabinet. It wd. not be a sinecure office. Look at the Chancellor, Harcourt, Ld. G. and Mr. G. for example—but really they are nearly all pretty bad." At another Cabinet Chamberlain wrote to Dilke: "Look at Dodson's boots! It is the Minister of Agriculture and not the Chancellor of the Duchy who is present to-day." (D.P. 43887, 149): (D.P. 43886,46.)

against an aggressive policy towards the Boers of the Transvaal in March, 1881; against the carrying on of diplomatic relations with the Vatican through the agency of a private gentleman— the Errington mission—in February, 1882; against a marriage annuity for the Duke of Albany in March, 1882; and in *favour* of resolute action against Arabi, the Egyptian nationalist leader, in July of that year. They did not always secure complete victories. "I suppose there'll be a compromise once more," Dilke wrote on one occasion, and this was indeed what usually happened. But the method by which compromises had to be exacted is a dismal indication of the atmosphere within the Government, even in its early days.

Dilke's mind, it is clear, ranged far beyond his departmental duties as under-secretary at the Foreign Office. He was auto-matically informed by Chamberlain of everything that passed in the Cabinet; and as he himself admitted:

> "I was rather given to interfering in the affairs of other offices, which is not as a rule a wise thing to do; but then it must be remembered that I was in the position of having to represent the interests and opinions of the men below the gangway, and that they used to come to Chamberlain and me in order to put pressure upon our colleagues through us, and that I was the person approached in all Indian, Colonial, naval and military questions, and Chamberlain in domestic ones."[21]

Sometimes Dilke's methods of exerting pressure were unusual for a member of a government. Thus, within two weeks of taking up his duties, having discovered that Forster's mind was moving rapidly in the direction of coercion, he used his henchman, Hill, the editor of the *Daily News*, to move against such a policy.

> "On the night of May 13th, between one and two o'clock
> in the morning," he wrote, "I did a thing which many will
> say I ought not to have done—namely, went down to a
> newspaper office to suggest an article against the policy of
> another member of the Government. Under the circum-
> stances, I think that I was justified. I was not a member of
> the Privy Council or of the Cabinet, and the interests of the
> party were at stake, as subsequent events well showed. . . .
> The result of it was that the *Daily News* had an article the
> next morning which smashed Forster's plan."[22]

Against this unorthodox conduct must be set the fact that other
members of the Government, including some in the Cabinet,
were using the Press most freely at this time. Chamberlain used
to pass a great deal of secret information to Escott of the
Standard, and Forster used both *The Times* and the *Leeds Mercury*
(of which Wemyss Reid, later his biographer, was editor) for his
own purposes. In addition, both Chamberlain and Dilke were
in almost daily touch with John Morley, who had just become
editor of the *Pall Mall Gazette*. "It would be worth silver and
gold and jewels," Morley wrote to Dilke as soon as the latter
had taken office, "if I could have ten minutes with you about
three times a week." And he added later, with a characteristic
Morley touch:

> "I should be very grateful if you would tell one of those
> brutal Cerberuses at the door of the House of Commons to
> let me pass to-morrow. If you have no time, never mind;
> but if it occurs to you it will save me quarter of an hour's

chafing and fuming at the indignities put upon the spiritual power by the d——d temporal."[23]

In the midst of these preoccupations, Dilke did, however, find some time for his work at the Foreign Office. Here his relations with Lord Granville, the Secretary of State, were of paramount importance. "Puss" Granville was an indolent but highly experienced Whig politician of great charm of manner who combined easy relations with the Queen and Court with a deep if occasionally rather tolerant loyalty to Mr. Gladstone. He had been an intimate friend of Dilke's father, but in spite of this (or perhaps because of it), Granville clearly disliked Charles Dilke at the time that the latter became his undersecretary. Dilke himself attributed the offer at one stage in the negotiations of the Colonial rather than the Foreign under-secretaryship to the fact that Granville would "like me in anybody's office but his." Later, after the interview at which he had been offered the Foreign Office post, Dilke recorded:

"Lord Granville made a disagreeable little speech in his most agreeable way as I went away, saying that he thought he had shown great forgetfulness of the past in being so pleased to have me in his office as his representative in the House of Commons; but for the life of me, I cannot remember what it was that had caused the coldness which seemed for some time before this to have existed between us, and there was no trace of it when we were in office together; although he may have been jealous of me—as people said."[24]

Relations between the two men improved once they were in

156

office together. There were occasional acerbities, usually beginning with an outburst of irritation from Dilke and ending with
an apology from the same source;[††] and their correspondence
suggests that they were never on terms of intimate friendship.
But Granville gained a high respect for Dilke's knowledge and
assiduity, and found him less difficult to work with than he had
anticipated. This may in part have been due to the Foreign
Secretary's decision, wise from his own point of view, to channel
off much of Dilke's assiduity into the detailed work of the
Commercial Department. Dilke accepted this special charge
with an expression of misgiving which goes some way to explain
Granville's anxiety that he should have it. "I should have
preferred to keep free of all departmental work in order to

[††] A fairly typical example is provided by the following letters: On February
12th, 1882, Dilke wrote a postcard to Granville: "Does anything occur to
you to be said in favour of the Garter Mission to Saxony, which appears to
have been a mere waste of public money? The one to Spain can be
defended, perhaps. I confess that it seems to me monstrous that the U.S.
for Foreign Affairs, who is not consulted on these missions, should be
expected to defend in the House such a one as that to Saxony, of which no
advantage to the country can, apparently, come." Granville protested
sharply, although good-humouredly, at the tone of this note and received
the following reply from Dilke, dated February 13th: "My dear Lord
Granville: I am very sorry the tone of my card was objectionable. I was
perhaps cross at the moment I wrote it, but as I was only cross with Dodson
that ought not to have made me seem cross with you. I will come over from
the office between one and two and if you are not in I will wait. It is not
given to everybody to have your unruffled calm, and Dodson is enough to
provoke a saint. But, seriously, I am very sorry indeed. I am writing in my
bath as I did not want to keep your messenger. Sincerely yours, Chas. W.
D." (D.P. 43880,72.)

attend to larger affairs of policy," he wrote.

This special responsibility kept him very busy, especially during the long negotiations for a new commercial treaty with France, which lasted in one form or another for nearly two years, which took Dilke to Paris for three or four months, and which concluded, as he had always expected would be the case, in failure. It also detached him from Granville, who was not much interested in the minutiae of commercial arrangements, but brought him close to Gladstone, who most certainly was. The Prime Minister was impressed by Dilke's work, was pleased to discover that his interest in the details of the tariff on printed calico squares or on ivory and pearl buttons was as great as his own, and wrote letters of warm commendation. Granville also wrote letters of commendation, but they were perhaps a little less warm. "Many thanks for your constant reports on the progress of the negotiations," he wrote on one occasion. "They are as interesting as the lists of the betting in the newspapers just before the Derby. I hope you win the race." [25]

Whatever Lord Granville may have wished, Dilke's work could not be confined to the Commercial Department. Except when the Prime Minister intervened, which was frequently, he was the spokesman of the Foreign Office in the House of Commons. This meant that he had to answer in the first instance all questions which were put down—Gladstone sometimes could not forbear from providing his own diffuse replies to supplementaries. These questions were not nearly as numerous as to-day, but there were usually several on two days a week, and Dilke's answers acquired a considerable reputation for succinct tact. His talent for satisfying the House without embarrassing the Government abroad was regarded as remarkable.

One of the most delicate subjects with which he had to deal

in this way related to the appointment of a new French Ambassador to London. Léon Say, whom Dilke regarded as "by far the best French Ambassador that we ever had," returned to Paris in June, 1880, to become President of the Senate. The French Government proposed the Marquis de Noailles, but, as Dilke wrote to Mrs. Pattison, "the Queen has been told that Mme. de Noailles before her marriage used to have four lovers, one for each season of the year, and that M. de N. was only the summer one." In consequence the Queen refused her *agrément* and that proposal had to be abandoned. The alternative suggested was M. Challemel-Lacour. He was not on the face of it much better, for he was accused both "of living with a washerwoman who posed as his grandmother" and of having shot a large number of monks when he was Prefect at Lyons in 1871. Dilke discounted these charges, saying, not fully reassuringly, that Challemel was "really only objectionable because he had the worst temper with which perhaps any human being was ever cursed." The Prince of Wales, however, who in Dilke's view suffered in his knowledge of French politics from believing everything which he read in the *Figaro*, protested violently against Challemel, and tried to persuade Dilke to intervene with Gambetta against the appointment.

An Irish member then put down a question in the House of Commons which specified all the charges against Challemel. Dilke refuted the allegations, but the member concerned— O'Donnell—was not satisfied and attempted to press the matter on the adjournment. This led to a procedural debate of several hours, to general disorder, and to Gladstone moving that O'Donnell be no longer heard. Dilke received a note from Gambetta—"Let me thank you from the bottom of my heart for the lofty manner in which you picked up the glove thrown down by that mad Irish clerical"—suggesting that he had been wise not to intervene on behalf of the Prince of Wales. The Prince's doubts he assuaged by telling him that Challemel was "not of the Clemenceau type"; but he was much surprised to discover that the Prince when he eventually met the new ambassador found him very agreeable.

During this period Dilke saw a great deal of the Prince of Wales and moved freely in what was known as the Marlborough House set. Their acquaintanceship began at a dinner party given by Lord Fife in March, 1880, just before the change of Government. "The Prince laid himself out to be pleasant, and talked to me nearly all the evening—chiefly about French politics and the Greek question," Dilke noted. Thereafter they met frequently—at Sandringham, at Marlborough House, at Chiswick, in Paris and at various English country houses. The Prince cultivated Dilke partly because of a genuine social affinity, partly because of a perverse desire to know those of whom his mother disapproved, and partly because, disliking Granville, he wished to maintain a Foreign Office contact. This last aspect of their relationship was of considerable value to an Heir Apparent, hungry for inside knowledge, who was ordinarily frozen out of all public business. "Throughout Dilke's official life," the Prince's official biographer has stated, ". . . the Prince privately derived from him a fuller knowledge than he enjoyed before of the inner processes of government."[26]

Not all of Dilke's endeavours to keep the Prince informed ended in success. In the spring of 1882 an arrangement was sought by which the latter might see copies of the secret Foreign Office telegrams (of which the secrecy was not such as to prevent their being seen by the private secretaries to all members of the Cabinet), but the Queen stamped upon the plan. The incident closed with a sharp exchange of letters between the private secretaries of the monarch and her son. "When the Prince of Wales desired me to write to you about the F.O. telegrams, etc.," Francis Knollys wrote, sending a copy to Dilke, "he was under the impression (an erroneous one it appears) that the Queen was anxious he should be behind the scenes of what was going on as much as possible, provided that this did not interfere with her own authority."[27]

There were other, less official, ways in which Dilke could provide information and contacts for the heir to the throne. Thus in 1882 he was summoned to travel down to Dover with the Prince for a brief inspection of the Channel Tunnel works and to bring with him a map (not of the works but of central Asia) for study and explanation in the saloon of the special train. In the preceding year, Dilke had undertaken a more delicate enterprise with the Prince and had arranged a "breakfast" at the shortly to be demolished *Moulin Rouge* restaurant in Paris for him to meet Gambetta. The occasion was apparently a success, and Knollys wrote in enthusiastic terms: "The Prince of Wales desires me to say how much he was interested by the breakfast which you were good enough to give to him yesterday and how well he thought it went off. H.R.H. would be much obliged if you would kindly let M. Gambetta know that it would give him great pleasure to possess his photograph. . . ."[28] Inscribed "*au plus aimable des princes*,– the photograph was duly delivered. Later the Prince arranged, on his own initiative, another luncheon with Gambetta.

Both because he had a taste for fashionable life as such, and because his popularity at Marlborough House provided something of a counter-balance to the ill-favour with which he was viewed at Windsor, Dilke was far from discouraging the Prince's attentions. But he allowed them neither to weaken his views about the Civil List nor to lead him towards an excessively favourable judgment of the Prince as an individual. "The Prince is, of course, in fact, a strong Conservative, and a still stronger Jingo, really agreeing in the Queen's politics, and wanting to take everything everywhere in the world . . ." he wrote of him. "He has more sense and more usage of the modern world than his mother . . . but less real brain power,"[29] he added. On another occasion he noted: "The only two subjects on which the Prince of Wales agrees with any Liberals are (1) Randolph Churchill (2) the government of London. But then, as I personally, though assaulted by Randolph, do not hate him—there remains only the government of London, which becomes well worn. He began it again last night at the Harcourts!"[30] Dilke was even capable of making a somewhat adverse comparison between the Prince and his mother. In 1883, after a visit to Windsor, he wrote to Mrs. Pattison: "The Queen's court is singularly dowdy by the side of the Prince of Wales's, but on the other hand, though the servants are shabby, the people about the Queen are more *uniformly* gentlemen and ladies than those about the Prince."[31] Nor did he always find that the Prince's guests compensated by the brilliance of their conversation for their doubtful respectability.

"Some of the parties to which the Prince of Wales virtually insisted that I should go were curious," he wrote; "the oddest of them a supper which he directed to be given on July 1st, 1881, for Sarah Bernhardt, at the wish of the Duc d'Aumale, and at which all the other ladies present were English ladies who had been invited at the distinct request of the Prince of Wales. It was one thing to get them to go,

162

and another thing to get them to talk when they were there; and the result was that, as they would not talk to Sarah Bernhardt and she would not talk to them, and as the Duc d'Aumale was deaf and disinclined to make conversation on his own account, nobody talked at all, and an absolute reign of the most dismal silence ensued. . ."[32]

All in all, indeed, the best thing that Dilke could find to say for the Prince was that, despite a somewhat discouraging reception at the time—"for he seems not to listen and to talk incessantly except when he is digesting"—it was often worth talking to him because he subsequently repeated, as his own remarks, what he had been told.

Another Liberal with whom the Prince was intimate, and whom Dilke, partly in consequence, came to know well, was Lord Rosebery. Rosebery in 1881 was a thirty-four-year-old Scottish earl who had been three years married to the principal Rothschild heiress of that generation. He had been Gladstone's host and sponsor in Midlothian, where he exercised great territorial influence, and he looked forward with some impatience to rapid political preferment. This impatience so impressed itself upon Dilke that, after a walk at Mentmore (the Roseberys' Buckinghamshire house) one Sunday afternoon in May, 1880, he "came to the conclusion that Rosebery was the most ambitious man I had ever met."[‡] But Gladstone, normally so ready to reward peers, was curiously unforth-coming towards Rosebery. He offered him junior office when the Government

<hr>

‡ Many years later Dilke wrote in the margin, alongside this opinion: "I have since known Winston Churchill." (D.P. 43934,198.)

was formed, but this was refused, from a mixture of motives. Just over a year later another offer was made and Rosebery came in as under-secretary at the Home Office, with a special responsibility for Scottish affairs. There was some feeling, and none participated in it more strongly than Rosebery and his wife, that Rosebery should be in the Cabinet, particularly in view of the resignation of Argyll. This led to growing bitterness and to frequent scenes, many of them noted by Dilke in his diary or in his letters to Mrs. Pattison, between Lady Rosebery and the Gladstones.

Dilke was inclined to think that Rosebery had been treated badly. In the last years of the Beaconsfield Administration and in the early days of the new Gladstone Government he and Chamberlain had thought Rosebery might be a useful radical ally in the Lords. But Rosebery grew bored with radicalism; his wife noted that by the early summer of 1881 his political relations with the "two Ministers of the Left" had cooled; and Dilke's comments upon his character became sharper. In May of 1883 he wrote: "At the State Ball Rose-brry broke out to me against Mr. G. He swears he will resign, giving health as his reason. He is not a gendeman, for he reproaches Mr. G. with the benefits he has conferred upon him, but he has been ill-used."[33] Within a week Rosebery did resign and remained out of the Government for nearly two years. Throughout the early years of the Parliament he and his wife hovered over Dilke's life, as discontented half-friends, constantly inviting him to visit them at their various houses.

At Dilke's own house the pattern of life underwent several changes during this period. In the summer of 1880 his private secretary, H. G. Kennedy, who had been ill for some time, finally left, and was replaced by a young Oxford graduate, J. E. C.

Bodley. Bodley, who was later to become both a distinguished writer on France and one of Cardinal Manning's closest friends, was a man of considerable intellect and wide social contacts. At first Dilke found him insufficiently serious. "Bodley is not beginning very well," he wrote to Mrs. Pattison. "Ought to be in bed by half past twelve—not sit up till five in the morning . . . to dance and flirt . . . Nothing on earth can get him up before 9–30."[34] Some time later the position had become still worse: "Bodley was not out of bed when I got back from the country at 10–15! "Dilke complained, and elsewhere he wrote despairingly: "*How* to get rid of Bodley?" These initial difficulties sorted themselves out, however, and from a little room at the turn of the staircase in 76, Sloane Street, Bodley played an important part in the remainder of Dilke's official life.

Another change came at the end of the same year when Dilke's grandmother, Mrs. Chatfield, and her niece, Miss Folkard, who had both lived in 76, Sloane Street since 1874, died within a few days of each other. Thereafter Dilke lived alone. But his house remained a centre of social activity. His dinner parties—exclusively male and consisting principally of politicians and diplomats, although with a sprinkling of literary and academic figures (one party was organised with especial care for the Rector of Lincoln)—continued with unabated frequency. From Saturday to Monday he was mostly away, sometimes at the houses of his friends and sometimes at riverside inns in order that he might scull or canoe upon the Thames. This last activity became of such importance that he began to think of building a riverside house to avoid "staying in the village pothouses." He kept his house near Toulon and was able during most years to pay two or three visits there; and in London the morning fencing continued.

There were some family difficulties. Ashton Dilke, who had suffered from tuberculosis for some years, entered a final decline in the autumn of 1882 and retired to North Africa. He died there in March, 1883. The Eustace Smith connection continued to give trouble. "Maye's sister, Helen, lost her third and youngest child a few days ago," Dilke informed Mrs. Pattison in March, 1882. "Yesterday she took a dose of poison and very nearly killed herself. Ashton tells me this, and also that it is not to be known. Maye (Ashton's wife) and Mrs. Donald Crawford[§§] are watching her day and night."[35] And a month earlier, on February 25th, Dilke had confided cryptically to his diary: "What is one to do when vile letters containing abominable charges are sent to all one's friends?"[36] But these were only clouds as big as a man's hand, appearing in a sky that was still otherwise clear and encouraging.

[§§] Mrs. Crawford (at this time aged eighteen) was a younger sister of Mrs. Ashton Dilke and Helen (Mrs. Robert Harrison). In the previous summer she had married Donald Crawford, a middle-aged Scottish lawyer, who had been a fellow of Lincoln College, Oxford, and was in consequence known to Mrs. Pattison.

Chapter Seven

A Laborious Promotion

Dilke Had accepted his subordinate office with a reasonably good grace, but one of his most urgent desires was to improve upon it, provided that this could be done without abandoning his political power or principles. His ambition was in no way tempered by an excessive admiration for his rivals.

"Suppose we force the Whigs out and become the next Whigs ourselves," he wrote to Mrs. Pattison in November, 1880, "whom (*sic*) are our men. Hartington is a man—but on the wrong side. Argyll is politically not a man, but a devil. Gladstone I thought an old man. Lord G. is old, and only about half of a man, tho' useful and ornamental. What remains? Chamberlain and (me)! Courtney is a radical devil to match that Whig devil. Fawcett is *a little* better than a windbag—but only a little better, and Mundella *no* better than a windbag. It seems to me that we shall be about as

167

badly off as France (I think Bryce may make a good third-rate man some day)."[1]

Nor was this the end of his strictures. "Imagine!" he was writing a few weeks later, "Harcourt who says one thing one moment and the exact opposite the next, and Lord North-brook who is just a nice idiotic bankers' clerk."[2] Occasionally, but not often, he could be a little less critical. Lord Spencer, the "red earl" from Northamptonshire (who was so-called on account of his beard not his politics), was a rather surprising exception whom Dilke designated as "one of my favourites." And there was always Chamberlain, to whom Dilke's loyalty was almost complete. "Regd. Brett (later Lord Esher, but at that time Hartington's private secretary) called just before the Cabinet to find out whether the offer of Chamberlain's place would tempt me to sell him"[3], Dilke noted contemptuously in December, 1880, when they were contemplating a joint resignation. "The Duchess of Manchester sent him," he added.

The next time that Dilke seemed near to promotion the prospect was more enticing but the result equally unrewarding. The winter of 1881–2 had been one of the most bitter in the history of Anglo-Irish relations. The Land Bill had become law by the autumn of 1881, but relations between Parnell and the chiefs of the Government were by then so embittered that there was no chance of its being allowed to work successfully. At Leeds in October Gladstone accused the Parnellites of preaching the doctrines of public plunder and warned them that "the resources of civilisation are not yet exhausted." Parnell replied by denouncing the Prime Minister as "this masquerading knight-errant, this pretending champion of the rights of every nation except those of the Irish nation." And the Prime Minister, on this occasion with the support of his whole Cabinet, responded by using the Coercion Act and putting Parnell into Kilmainham Jail. Dilke was a little doubtful, but Chamberlain was convinced that the working class in Birmingham did not like to see the law defied.

Parnell's arrest was but the beginning of the battle. The Land League immediately proclaimed a rent strike, and the Government could respond to this only by proscribing the organisation and sending its officers to join Parnell. Throughout the next six months the picture in Ireland was one of agrarian chaos and mounting violence, with a host of new secret societies and terrorist organisations springing up from month to month. By the spring both sides were prepared to try a new approach. Parnell, although not subjected to the full rigours of prison life, was weary of Kilmainham Jail. Personal and political factors joined to give him a new desire to be out. His child by Mrs. O'Shea had been born in February (and was to die in April). At the same time he wished to reassert his leadership over the various factions of Irish nationalism; he was worried not only by the extreme violence, but also by the independence of the new terrorist organisations. On the Government side it was obvious to almost the whole Cabinet that the policy of repression had proved sterile. The first move towards a better atmosphere was to allow Parnell a period of parole, ostensibly so that he might attend the funeral of a nephew in Paris, but also that he might go to Eltham and see his own child before her death.

He left Kilmainham on April 10th and returned there in accordance with his undertaking on April 24th. During his absence negotiations for an informal treaty had begun between Captain O'Shea and Chamberlain. The Captain, who was at that time moderate Nationalist member of Parliament for Clare, had a great hunger for office and a considerable complacency towards his wife's relations with Parnell; but he was also a willing go-between, and the negotiations proceeded well. On April 29th, O'Shea returned to London from a visit to Parnell at Kilmainham, bringing with him a letter which set out the heads of agreement. The Government was to introduce a bill to extend the benefits of the Land Act to tenants who were in arrears with their rent, and in return Parnell was to give his support to the Act, to discourage further illegality and to work generally with the Liberal party. The arrangement was accepted by the Cabinet, although not without dissension. Forster, the Chief Secretary, had been sullen throughout the negotiations, and he held Parnell's assurances to be vague and unsatisfactory. He was supported, almost to the end, by Selborne, the slow-witted Lord Chancellor; and by Lord Cowper, who had been Lord Lieutenant without a seat in the Cabinet and had left the Government a week earlier, nominally on grounds of ill-health, but in fact because he did not feel able to adjust himself to a new policy of conciliation. On May 2nd Forster resigned. On May 4th Parnell and his associates were released from Kilmainham.

Gladstone had already decided that Spencer should be the new Lord Lieutenant, but his being already in the Cabinet created a difficulty about the Chief Secretaryship. It was a firm tradition that only one of these two Irish ministers should be a member of the Cabinet. Dilke and Chamberlain allowed for this rule, but apparently assumed that Spencer would step down. They thought that the Chief Secretaryship was almost certain to be offered to one or other of themselves. Chamberlain had been (by and large) the principal challenger in the Cabinet of the policy which was being discarded; and Dilke was the man outside with the strongest claim to promotion. The arrangement he preferred was that Chamberlain should go to the Chief Secretary's Lodge and that he should succeed him at the Board of Trade. Rather curiously, Dilke in his diary attributed this preference to his own strong views in favour of Home Rule. It seems far more likely that he wished for this arrangement because the Irish problem never aroused his enthusiasm. ". . . *you* (and not I) are the man because you believe in success and I don't,"[4] he wrote to Chamberlain at this time. "The fact is that I never could see my way clearly on Ireland," Dilke wrote on another occasion. A somewhat pessimistic indifference was indeed his natural attitude to the problem. He was too much of a radical to put his faith in coercion or to wish to resist Home Rule; but he was too much of an English imperialist, believing in the superiority of his race, to have much liking for the Irish nation or sympathy with their problems.

At this stage, however, the issue did not present itself. No offer was made either to Chamberlain or Dilke.

"On May 3rd," Dilke wrote, "Chamberlain, who had decided to take the Irish Secretaryship if offered to him, was astonished at having received no offer. At 11–30 p.m. on the same day, the 3rd, I found that the appointment had been offered to and declined by Hartington; but the offer to, and acceptance by, his brother, Lord Frederick Cavendish, came as a complete surprise both to me and to Chamberlain."[5]

Cavendish, who had previously been Financial Secretary to the Treasury, accepted the office without the Cabinet. The eventuality which Dilke and Chamberlain had not considered therefore took place. "It will be seen that it had never occurred for a moment to either Chamberlain or myself," Dilke wrote, "that the Irish Secretaryship would be offered without a seat in the Cabinet; but we counted without remembering Mr. Gladstone's affection for Lord Spencer and Spencer's vanity."[6] By appointing Cavendish, Gladstone strengthened the Whig faction within the Government and gave a further indication of his view that radicals should be satisfied with their good fortune in having himself as Prime Minister. The only sop which he offered was that of interviewing Dilke on the evening of Friday, May 5th, and discussing with him, presumably with a view to an early promotion, his attitude to the Royal Grants. But on that evening there seemed no reason why a further vacancy should offer itself for some time to come.

On the following day Lord Frederick Cavendish was murdered. He was attacked, within a few hours of his arrival in Dublin, when walking with his permanent under-secretary in Phoenix Park. Dilke heard the news in London at a party of Lady Northbrook's.

"On the night of May 6th," he wrote, "the scene at the party at the Admiralty was most dramatic. Mrs. Gladstone[*] had come there from a dinner party at the Austrian Embassy, not knowing of the murder, while everybody else in the room knew. At last she was sent for suddenly to Downing Street to be told, and went away under the

[*] Lady Frederick Cavendish was her neice, and a great favourite both of her and of the Prime Minister.

172

impression that the Queen had been shot, for she was assured that it was very dreadful, but 'nothing about Mr. Gladstone.'"[7]

Next morning—a Sunday—Dilke received a visit from Parnell, accompanied by Justin McCarthy. He found Parnell "white and apparently terror-stricken" and attributed this to fear that the secret societies were running wild and would assassinate him next. Parnell's purpose in coming to see Dilke was apparently to discover what were the chances of a radical replacement for Cavendish—he went immediately afterwards to Chamberlain—and he received from Dilke the assurance that the events of the previous day would not make him refuse the Chief Secretaryship if it were offered. But Dilke would still have preferred Chamberlain to take that particular post, and indeed, on the following morning, he wrote to Chamberlain reiterating this view and offering, in rather extravagant terms, to give Chamberlain any help that he might need. "Still I would act or serve under you," Dilke wrote, "and if it were thought I could be of any use I would join you in Dublin on the day the House was up, and spend the whole autumn and winter with you as your chief private secretary. I could always have the work of my London post sent over in boxes."[8] One of the causes of Dilke's mood of obeisance was his sudden conviction that his own way might long be blocked. "On thinking matters over," he wrote again to Chamberlain on that same day, "I think the Queen's object is to keep me out of the Cabinet for her life, and in this I think she can succeed."[9]

At three o'clock that afternoon the body from which Dilke believed himself to be so permanently excluded assembled in 10, Downing Street. Across the road in the Foreign Office, Dilke sat in his room. The unusual procedure of the Cabinet, in session, trying to appoint a Chief Secretary was then followed. The first intimation which Dilke received was a message from Chamberlain saying: "Prepare for an offer."

"I was somewhat surprised at this," Dilke wrote, "because Chamberlain knew that I would not take it without the Cabinet, and that I would take it with the Cabinet, whereas his note seemed to imply a doubt. At four he came across himself, and the first difference that had ever occurred between us took place,[†] because, although he knew that I would not accept, he urged acceptance of the post without the Cabinet. He argued that it carried with it the Privy Council, that it established great personal claims upon the party, and that it afforded a means of getting over the difficulty with the Queen. I declined however without hesitation and with some anger. It was obvious that I could not consent to become 'a mere mouthpiece.' Mr. Gladstone and Lord Carlingford[‡] then sent back to say, personally from each of them, that I was to be present at the Cabinet at every discussion of Irish affairs; and I then asked: 'Why, then, should I not be in the Cabinet?' Carlingford came back to the Foreign Office again and again, and cried over it to me; and Lord Granville came in twice, and threatened me with loss of prestige by my refusal, by which I certainly felt that I had lost Mr. Gladstone's confidence. I was angry with

---

[†] This was not strictly true. See for example, page 137 *supra*.

[‡] Carlingford (formerly Chichester Fortescue) was an old friend of Dilke's. He had joined the Government as Lord Privy Seal in 1881.

Chamberlain at having placed me in this position.§ Had he acted on this occasion with the steadiness with which he acted on every other he would have told the Cabinet that the offer would be an insult; because he knew that this was my view. . . . Lord Granville came in finally, and said in his sweetest manner (which is a very disagreeable one) that he had vast experience, and had 'never known a man stand on his extreme rights and gain by it.' This I felt to be a monstrous perversion of the case. . . ."[10]

Despite these remonstrances Dilke persisted in his refusal, and on the following day G. O. Trevelyan, previously Financial Secretary to the Admiralty, was promoted over his head to the vacant office, accepting it without the Cabinet. Trevelyan undoubtedly counted as a radical (although his first duty was to introduce a new coercion bill), and this made Dilke's loss of seniority more marked than would have been the case had another Whig, like Cavendish, been elevated. Dilke was fully aware of the political risks involved in his refusal. "I have certainly lost Mr. G.'s confidence by my refusal," he wrote to

---

§ "And am still so 1903," Dilke later wrote in the margin; "and still 1906," he added by way of still greater emphasis. In 1890 he wrote to Chamberlain: "By the way they (Dilke's old political papers) reminded me of many things half forgotten, and I note that I never thought you wrong in any personal question except once—when you came from the Cabinet to my room at the F.O. to offer me from them the Chief Secretaryship without the Cabinet, after we had decided together that it was impossible to take it. I know, however, that two things weighed with you in giving me the chance of reconsideration: the difficulty about the Queen, and the fear of my being accused of personal cowardice in declining. But it was wrong . . ." (D.P. 43936, 106.)

Mrs. Pattison, "which now makes it certain that I shall not rise above my present place as long as he lasts. . . . I fear they'll all be cold with me and think me a very conceited fellow."[11]

He also feared that the public might believe he had been influenced by personal cowardice, although he subsequently considered this view to have gained no currency. But he was certain that his decision was right, and once taken, it was greatly fortified by his stubbornness and pride. The clearest expression of his motive is conveyed in a letter to Grant Duff.[¶]

"I should have had to defend any policy that Spencer chose to adopt, without having a voice in it," he wrote. "Acceptance would not have been only a personal mistake; it would have been a political blunder. Outside the Cabinet I should not have had the public confidence, and rightly so, because I could not have had a strong hand. I should have inherited accumulated blunders, and I was under no kind of obligation to do so, for I have never touched the Irish question. Never have I spoken on it from first to last. Many of the measures rendered necessary by the situation are condemned by my whole past attitude; but they have really been made inevitable by blunders for which I had no responsibility, and which I should not have been allowed to condemn."[12]

Dilke's judgment that he had permanently sacrificed

_____

¶ Sir Mountstuart Grant Duff, 1828–1906, had just been appointed Governor of Madras, after serving for two years as under-secretary at the Colonial Office. For several years after his Madras appointment Dilke kept up an intensive correspondence with him.

Gladstone's confidence proved pessimistic. Either the Prime Minister was more forgiving or Dilke was more powerful than had been anticipated. Throughout the summer and autumn of 1882 there were strong rumours of Gladstone's impending retirement. At the beginning of July Chamberlain was persuaded that he was going immediately and in November Dilke was even more certain. "Mr. G. has finally decided not to meet Parliament again in February," he wrote, "Hartington is to be P.M."[13] In the event, however, the reconstruction, which came in December, merely involved Gladstone shedding the Exchequer to Childers, who had until then been Secretary of State for War, and a series of consequential changes. These created two new Cabinet vacancies, for Hartington succeeded Childers at the War Office, and was himself succeeded at the India Office by Kimberley, who had been Colonial Secretary since the formation of the Government, and Chancellor of the Duchy of Lancaster since the resignation of Bright in July, 1882. The Colonial Office went to Derby. He had been Foreign Secretary under Beaconsfield until 1878, and, despite a rapid subsequent move towards the Liberal party,** his earlier assumption of office might have seemed inappropriate.

The other vacancy, it had been decided, was to go to Dilke. Gladstone probably neither understood nor liked him very well, at this or any other time. He greatly preferred Bright, and even after the latter's resignation, in protest against his own Egyptian

---

** Already by the summer of 1879 Derby was sufficiently Liberal to act as Dilke's host when the latter went to Liverpool to make a political speech. But Dilke was unimpressed by the amenities offered. "Nothing," he wrote, "not even £100,000 a year 'clear' would induce (me) to live in such a stink of chemicals as Knowsley." (D.P. 43903, 246.)

policy, he could still remark: "Just compare his (Blight's) high principles with those of Chamberlain and Dilke and the new style of radicals, who are all opportunism."[14] Gladstone was nevertheless capable of treating Dilke with great courtesy and consideration—when the latter was ill for a few weeks in 1880, for instance, the Prime Minister had been quick to pay a call of enquiry to 76, Sloane Street—and he had slowly acquired a great respect for Dilke's parliamentary and administrative ability, if not an equivalent one for his "high principles." Indeed, at about this time, if we are to believe the testimony of Lord Acton, Gladstone began to look on Dilke as a possible successor, at least as leader of the House of Commons. Looking to a time when he himself would have retired and Hartington would have become Devonshire, Gladstone is reported as saying: "The future leader of H. of C. was a great puzzle and difficulty. Sir Charles Dilke would probably be the man best fitted for it; he had shown much capacity for learning and unlearning, but he would require Cabinet training first."[15]

If this was Gladstone's view it was obviously sensible that he should make the "Cabinet training" available as soon as possible. Early in November Dilke was confident that promotion was very near, and he wrote to Mrs. Pattison discussing the prospects of his re-election for Chelsea.[††] On the 16th of that month he had an interview with the Chief Whip, Lord Richard

---

[††] Until 1918 Cabinet (but not junior) office disqualified a member from sitting in the House of Commons until he had successfully sought re-election by his constituents. Amongst other disadvantages this produced an inconvenient few weeks at the beginning of most Governments when the senior minister with a seat in the House of Commons was the Financial Secretary to the Treasury.

Grosvenor, who asked Dilke whether he thought that the Queen would now be prepared to have him in the Cabinet. Dilke replied saying that he believed she would (perhaps his "jingo" attitude to the Alexandria riots in June had helped), and he had the authority, for what it was worth, of the Prince of Wales and the Duke of Albany for saying this. What in fact proved to be the case was that the Queen was prepared to have Dilke in the Cabinet, but only in an office which minimised his contact with her. The Chancellorship of the Duchy of Lancaster she did not regard as being within this category; it was a "peculiarly personal" post, she held, and one which should be filled by "a moderate politician." The original plan by which Dilke was to take over this sinecure office from Kimberley (and use it to become a general parliamentary spokesman of the Government) had therefore to be abandoned.

There was then a great searching around for alternative arrangements. On December 12th the Prime Minister (whose talent for rubbing Chamberlain the wrong way was always considerable) suggested to Dilke that he should approach his Birmingham friend with a view to a switch of offices. "Would you take the Duchy and let me go to the Board of Trade, you keeping your Bills?"[16] Dilke wrote. This course was also strongly pressed by the Prince of Wales, who, Sir Sidney Lee has told us, "engaged with infinite zest in (these) confidential negotiations."[17] It was not a course which commended itself to Chamberlain. He received Dilke's letter at Highbury on the morning of December 13th and replied immediately:

"Your letter has spoilt my breakfast. The change will be loathsome to me for more than one reason and will give rise to all sorts of disagreeable commentaries. But if it is the only way out of the difficulty, I will do—what I am sure you would have done in my place—accept the transfer. . . . Consider however if there is any alternative. I regard your *immediate* admission to the Cabinet as imperative, and therefore if this can only be secured by my taking the Duchy, *cadit quaestio*, and I shall never say another word on the subject."[18]

Chamberlain went on to suggest two possible alternative courses of action. The first was that they should try to force the Queen to accept Dilke for the Duchy by both threatening resignation unless she did so. "Personally I would rather go out than take the Duchy," Chamberlain added. The second was that Dodson, the President of the Local Government Board, might be persuaded to switch to the Duchy. "He *might* like an office with less work, and he *might* be influenced by the nominally superior rank," Chamberlain wrote hopefully. Dilke, somewhat surprisingly, appeared satisfied with this highly grudging reply. "I have your letter which is exactly what I expected and exactly what (I hope) I should have written if the places had been changed,"[19] he wrote in turn. Fortunately Chamberlain was not called upon to pass what he described to Morley as the hardest test to which friendship was ever put. The Queen saved him by announcing firmly that as an attempt at a moderate politician she regarded him as no improvement on Dilke. The Prince of Wales then came on the scene with a much more attractive suggestion. "What he would like to see," Francis Knollys wrote to Dilke on December 15th, "would be Lord Northbrook at the India Office and you at the Admiralty."[20] But the India Office was already filled, and in any event, Northbrook showed no desire to abandon the amenities of Admiralty House. So the Prince tried again, and arrived at the solution which Chamberlain had suggested as one of his alternatives four days earlier. "H.R.H. thinks matters might be arranged as follows," Knollys wrote again on the 17th. "Mr. Dodson to go to the Duchy of Lancaster, you to the Local Government Board, and Chamberlain to remain where he is. What do you say to this arrangement?"[21]

Dilke did not say anything very enthusiastic, for the prospect of the Local Government Board did not excite him. But the situation was becoming too difficult for any solution to be excluded, and in the outcome it was the Prince's (or perhaps Chamberlain's) plan which was adopted. By December 23rd it had been accepted by the Prime Minister, the Queen and Dodson.

> "Dodson 'put himself in Mr. G.'s hands,'" Dilke wrote to Mrs. Pattison from the Foreign Office that evening, "so I shall be in the Local Government Board by Wednesday I think, as I shall not after Chamberlain's kindness put him into an office which he likes less than the Board of Trade. Shan't I hate it after this place—but it will 'knock the nonsense out of me.'"[22]

Dilke's appointment was announced on December 23rd, and he took up his new duties on December 27th. He was fortified with a letter from Gladstone dealing with the delicate subject of the new minister's relations with the Queen.

> "Notwithstanding the rubs of the past, I am sanguine as to your future relation with the Queen," the Prime Minister wrote. "There are undoubtedly many difficulties in that quarter; but they are in the main confined to three or four

Departments. Your office will not touch them; while you will have in common with all your colleagues the benefit of two great modifying circumstances which never fail, the first her high good manners, and the second her love of truth. I am the more desirous to do her justice, because, while she conducts all intercourse with me in absolute and perfect courtesy, I am convinced, from a hundred tokens, that she looks forward to the day of my retirement as a day, if not of jubilee (*sic*), yet of relief."[23]

There were some immediate difficulties, but these were mostly removed by a combination of Lord Granville sending again to Sir Henry Ponsonby, the Queen's private secretary, a copy of a slightly unctuous little letter‡ which Dilke had written, nominally to Granville but in fact for royal eyes, at the time of the

---

‡ The letter was as follows: "Dear Lord Granville: When I was asked my views upon republicanism during the recent elections I gave a public answer which formed, I hope, a complete refutation of the suggestion of disloyalty to the Queen. I said that I thought that the republican might be the best form of government in many new countries, and I viewed with pleasure the consolidation of a new republic in France, thinking that government adapted to the conditions of a country which was making as it were a fresh start in national life after a great convulsion, and where there would have been rival claimants to a throne supposing one to have been again set up. It would be folly, I thought, to apply such reasoning to England, where we possessed a well-established constitutional monarchy, and where the true constitutional theory had been so much strengthened by the illustrious occupant of the throne. The traditions and the feelings of the country were on the side of constitutional monarchy, and the existing order of things contained every guarantee for freedom and the possibility of reform. Believe me, dear Lord Granville, sincerely yours, Charles W. Dilke." (D.P. 43878, 38.)

Government's formation; and by Dilke himself, in his campaign for re-election in Chelsea, making speeches which were mild and narrowly restricted in the subjects which they covered. He secured his re-election, unopposed, on January 8th, having kissed hands on his appointment and been sworn of the Privy Council, at Windsor, a few days previously.§§ He was thirty-nine years of age and the youngest member of the Cabinet. His nearest rivals in this respect were Chamberlain, who was forty-two, and Hartington, who was forty-nine. His post was not exciting, but members of the

Cabinet were in those days concerned relatively less with their own departments and more with the business of the Government as a whole; and the prospect before him was extremely promising. Amongst his letters of congratulation was a rather quavering note from old Lord Barrington, who had been Disraeli's Whip. "I like watching your political career," it ran, "as besides personal

---

§§ Dilke's thoughts on this occasion were more occupied with reservations about the oath he was taking than with reflections on the majesty of the Queen's presence. "I could not but think that the portion of the Privy Councillor's oath which concerns keeping secret matters treated of secretly in Council is more honoured in the breach than in the observance; but when Mr. Gladstone chose, which was not always, he used to maintain the view that the clause is governed by the first part of the oath, so as to make it secret only in respect of the interests of the country and the position of other members of the Council. There is nothing in the oath about any limit of time, but it has always been held in practice that a time comes when all political importance has departed from the proceedings of the Council, and when the obligation of secrecy may be held to lapse. . . . It is difficult, therefore, to say that the oath in practice imposes any obligation other than that which any man of honour would feel laid upon him by the ordinary observances of a gentleman." (D.P. 43936, 286.)

feeling, it makes me think of what my dear old Chief used to say about you, viz: that you were the rising man on the other side."[24] So, indeed, appeared again to be the case after a period, not perhaps of setback, but of hesitation, in Dilke's career.

Chapter Eight

A Radical amongst the Whigs

Dilke's entry into the Cabinet coincided with the median point of Gladstone's second administration. Its first half had been singularly barren of liberal achievement. Ireland, Bradlaugh, and the perpetually festering split between Whigs and radicals had combined to put an almost complete stop to controversial domestic legislation. Had the Government resigned at the beginning of 1883 it would have been remembered for the occupation of Egypt and for little else—an ironic achievement for a Prime Minister who had swept to office on an anti-Beaconsfield platform. The prospect for the future was a little more encouraging. In the autumn of 1882 important amendments to the rules of the House of Commons had been made. After much controversy a procedure of closure by simple majority, strongly supported by Harcourt and Chamberlain within the Cabinet and by Dilke outside it, had been carried; and a system of delegating work at the committee stage of legislation to "Grand" or

"Standing" committees of the House was instituted. At the beginning of 1883 there seemed a good chance that the work of Parliament would be less clogged by Irish disputes and Irish tactics than in the preceding years. Furthermore, the Prime Minister's mind was turning towards a great measure of franchise reform which would extend the vote as widely in the counties as the Act of 1867 had done in the towns.

The mind which was turning was temporarily a tired one. Gladstone had not been sleeping well, and in the middle of January, having refused the Queen's hopeful offer of a peerage, he left for six weeks' rest at Cannes. Dilke was at Toulon for his post-Christmas holiday, and he several times travelled along the coast both to dine and to attend church with the Prime Minister. Before the end of January he returned to England to join with Chamberlain in an attempt, by correspondence, to persuade the Cabinet to give priority for the session to the franchise bill. They were unsuccessful. The Whigs, worried by the strengthening of Parnell which would inevitably follow from the extension of household suffrage to the Irish counties, all said that a franchise bill might needlessly endanger the life of the Government and that a measure of local government reform should be the first objective. Weakened by the absence of the Prime Minister, the radicals were forced to yield. But Dilke's self-confidence was not abated. "My first Cabinet," he recorded on February 6th, "I wrote most of the Queen's Speech."[1]

This claim was neither quite so extravagant nor quite so arrogant as it appears, for much of the legislative programme which it announced touched upon Dilke's departmental responsibilities. There was to be a general local government bill, which, according to the draft subsequently supplied by Dilke, provided for the setting up of both district and county councils; there was to be a separate Government of London Bill; and there was also to be a Corrupt Practices Bill, rather surprisingly entrusted to Dilke and not to the Home Secretary. This was the only measure of the three to pass into law, and proved almost as important as the Ballot Act of 1872.

The Government of London Bill foundered on the violence of Harcourt's opposition to placing the Metropolitan Police under local control. The existing position (which still prevails to-day) was that the City Corporation, like a provincial town council in an incorporated borough, managed its own separate force through a Watch Committee, but that outside the square mile of the City itself there was direct Home Office control. The difficulty arose out of the Government's intention to change the nature of the City Corporation and to extend its jurisdiction to cover most of what is now the County of London. To continue with two separate police forces within the same local authority area would be manifestly absurd. To deprive the City of a control which it had exercised for fifty years would neither be popular nor in accordance with any obvious liberal principle. But the third solution, that of giving the extended Corporation authority over the whole Metropolitan force, was totally unacceptable to the Home Secretary, who, in Dilke's words, "thought himself a Fouché." Harcourt's own justification was that London as a capital was too liable to political crime for popular control to be contemplated. "Suppose, for example," he wrote, "that news arrived either from America or Ireland which required instant and secret action by the police throughout London against a Fenian outbreak. Is it to be contended that a meeting of the Watch Committee is to be summoned . . . a debate to be raised and a vote taken?"[2] Dilke's reply was to point out that Liverpool was "by far the most Fenian town in England," but that control by Watch Committee worked quite satisfactorily there. "To this reasoning (of Harcourt's)," Dilke noted, "neither Mr. Gladstone nor Chamberlain nor I yielded."[3] But Harcourt proved equally unyielding, and after three months of his irascible but determined opposition the whole bill was abandoned in the early summer.

At this time Dilke found Harcourt equally difficult on other issues. "*What* a beast Harcourt makes of himself," he wrote to Chamberlain at his first Cabinet meeting. "He's quite as objectionable as I thought Fawcett would be."[4]

"Informal Cabinet in Mr. G.'s room (in the House of Commons) which I am using till his return," he wrote in his diary two weeks later. "Harcourt fought against Lord Granville, Childers, Carlingford, Northbrook and Kimberley for his violent views about Ireland. Carlingford said to him at last: 'Your language is that of the lowest Tory.' Harcourt then cried out: 'In the course of this very debate I shall say that all this proves that there must be no more Irish legislation and no more conciliation and that Ireland can only be governed by the sword.'* 'If you say that,' replied Carlingford, 'it will not be representing the Government, for none of your colleagues agree with you.'"[5]

And in May, when a few cases of cholera had been reported in the Thames Estuary, Dilke noted: "My cholera committee met to please Harcourt. He is as frightened now about cholera as

---

* Beside this part of the account Dilke noted: "He *didn't*. He made a very good speech."

he used to be about dynamite."[6]

Harcourt's bursts of violent enthusiasms and antipathies and the concentration of his interest upon police questions to which they led during this period had certain advantages for Dilke. He was always eager for more work and the power which went with it. In consequence he greatly welcomed Harcourt's decision in March that the time of the Home Secretary should be fully occupied with police and security matters and that such normal Home Office subjects as the inspection of mines and factories, the operation of the Artisans' Dwelling Acts, and the control of fire brigades, should be handed over to Dilke and the Local Government Board. This change was strenuously opposed by the permanent officials of the Home Office, who frustrated the original plan for a legislative transfer and substituted a personal and temporary arrangement between Harcourt and Dilke. Rosebery, who was at that time under-secretary in the Home Department, was also markedly unenthusiastic about the new arrangement. Rosebery was discontented about most things at this stage; in June he resigned from the Government and departed from British politics for half a year's voyage around the world.

It was not only Harcourt's sudden passion for repression which produced bitterness in the Cabinet. Dissension continued on almost every possible subject. Hartington, usually with the solid support of the Whig phalanx, could be relied upon to defend the rights of landowners, whether in Britain or in Ireland. But sometimes he over-reached and isolated himself, as in his opposition to a mild Agricultural Holdings Bill in the spring of 1883. "Much heat between Derby and Hartington," Dilke wrote after a Cabinet on April 21st. "All my lords very radical indeed to-day except our Marquis, who was ferocious to the highest point, being thoroughly at bay. He gave us to

189

understand that Derby was a mere owner of Liverpool ground rents, who knew nothing about land."[7] Occasionally, also, Chamberlain put himself in a position, and not necessarily a radical one, to which neither Dilke nor anyone else would follow him. After a Cabinet in this same April at which the Explosives Bill, one of Harcourt's anti-terrorist weapons, was discussed, Dilke noted: "Chamberlain was the only man in favour of making it retrospective!!!"

The most striking feature of Cabinet proceedings at this time was the frequent inability of the Prime Minister, "dictator" though he was considered to be by the Queen and by many others, to get his own way. Sometimes it was on important matters, as in the dispute with Harcourt over the London police, or Egypt or Ireland; and sometimes it was about matters small in themselves, but which were not in consequence less successful in filling the Prime Minister's mind. "The removal of the Duke of Wellington's statue from Hyde Park Corner," Dilke wrote after a meeting on August 9th, 1883, "was the cause of the most severe fight that Mr. G. had ever known in Cabinet—as he said. The Cabinet voted, and the numbers were taken down by him three times over. He was in favour of the old statue and against removal. I supported him. A majority against us, and Mr. G. (was) trying to get his own way against the majority."[8] On another occasion, when the opposition wished to put down a vote of censure, Gladstone was against giving time to debate the motion, but found himself in a minority of one in the Cabinet. But he out-manoeuvred his colleagues by the simple if dangerous expedient of getting the Liberal back-benchers to vote against the Government. The proposal to give time to the vote of censure was defeated in the House of Commons. "How splendid is the discipline of our party," the Prime Minister said

190

complacently to Dilke on the Front Bench. "Not a man but voted against us. . . ."[9]

Such devices were not always open to Gladstone and he frequently sustained Cabinet defeats which he could not circumvent. He even achieved a certain equanimity in accepting them. "At dinner at Lord and Lady Cork's in the evening," Dilke noted on one occasion. 'I was astonished to see in what excellent spirits Mr. Gladstone was, although he had been entirely overruled in his own Cabinet in the afternoon." Sometimes the Prime Minister sought to overcome his difficulties by postponing issues on which he could not get his way. "Matter adjourned as usual when Prime Minister in the minority," Dilke wrote after a discussion on New Guinea in July, 1884. But these tactics were more destructive of good government than of Gladstone's opponents. The best summing-up came from Lord Granville. "I think you too often counted noses in your last Cabinet," he said to Gladstone in 1886. Dilke would have agreed, for he, like Granville himself, was more often than not on the Prime Minister's side. In foreign and imperial affairs, and notably in the case of Egypt, Dilke was too much of a jingo and Gladstone too much of a pacifist for each other's taste, but on the other principal issues which pressed for decision—Ireland, franchise reform, redistribution of seats, local government and the control of the police—Dilke was more closely in accord with the head of the Government than with any other member of the Cabinet except Chamberlain.

In a sense both the radicals counted themselves as Gladstone men. They regarded him as an essential counter to the Whig influence, and thought it their duty to safeguard his position, even, in certain circumstances, against their own immediate interests. Thus, at the beginning of 1885, when Harcourt, the inveterate retailer of rumours, told Dilke that Gladstone's resignation was imminent and that Hartington, who would succeed, intended to offer the Exchequer to Chamberlain and the Foreign Office to Dilke, the latter wrote: "But, great as were the offices proposed, Chamberlain and I could not have consented to remain in if Mr. Gladstone had gone out notoriously dissatisfied. If he had gone out on grounds of health alone, it would, of course, have been a different matter."[10]

Dilke nevertheless recognised that there was a vast range of subjects on which he was about as closely in agreement with Gladstone as with the Queen. "Constructive radicalism"— State intervention to remedy the most pressing evils in the condition of the people—of which Gladstone always spoke with severe and slightly incredulous distaste, was the centre of Dilke's political creed. But the issues which arose out of this did not, for the most part, fall for settlement in the Parliament of 1880. It was, after all, a period in which John Morley, than whom no radical was less of a social reformer, worked in the closest alliance with Chamberlain. Politically, therefore, Dilke could believe firmly in the tactic (and even the principle) of support for the Prime Minister.

Personally his views were more equivocal. He would never have gone as far as Chamberlain, who, after a trying interview in the autumn of 1884, came rushing into Dilke's room in the House of Commons saying of the Prime Minister: "I *don't* like him, really. I hate him.[†][11] But, given the fact that Dilke was

---

† In less exasperated moments, Chamberlain could take a lighter view of Gladstone. At a Cabinet in May of the same year he scribbled and tossed to Dilke the following snatch of verse:

naturally disposed to admire great men, his attitude towards Gladstone was remarkable more for its cynical coolness than for anything else. "As we went home Chamberlain told me that before the last Cabinet Lord Granville begged his colleagues to remember who Mr. Gladstone was and not to push him too hard in discussion," he wrote in 1882. "In other words told them to remember that they were dealing with a magnificent lunatic." "The old gentleman's storm has blown over,"[12] he added tolerantly a few days later. Another fairly typical comment on the Prime Minister can be found in one of Dilke's letters to Chamberlain at the time of the negotiations over the entry of the former to the Cabinet. "He's another Bishop to make, so he'll be happy,"[13] Dilke wrote. Nor was Dilke ever loath to record any gossip about the Prime Minister which came his way, particularly in relation to that strange figure, Mme. Olga de Novikof. "She is going to Birmingham to-morrow and Mr. G. wants Chamberlain to cut the Cabinet to go with her though he doesn't know her. Chamberlain won't," he wrote in November, 1882; and a few weeks later: "I breakfasted with Mr. G. to meet the Duc de Broglie. That horrid beast Mme. de Novikof was there and of course the Duc took me into the corner to ask if all the scandal about her and Mr. G. was true. . . ."[14]

There was a difference in age of thirty-four years between

"Here lies Mr. G., who has left us repining,
  While he is, no doubt, still engaged in refining;
  And explaining distinctions to Peter and Paul,
  Who faintly protest that distinctions so small
  Were never submitted to saints to perplex them,
  Until the Prime Minister came up to Vex them."

(D.P. 43886,154.)

Dilke and the Prime Minister, and with it went an almost unbridgeable psychological gap. Gladstone probably never ceased to regard Chamberlain as an overrated social upstart with ideas above his station. He did not put Dilke in this category. For one thing Dilke had very much the same social origin as himself. For another Gladstone had the highest respect for his parliamentary and administrative ability. But he was not a man with whom it is possible to imagine the Prime Minister engaging in intimate discussion. Neither would have begun to understand the mainspring of the other's mind; and Dilke would, in addition, have suffered in the Prime Minister's estimation from being neither a Whig patrician like Granville nor a fine old "moral force", pacifist, provincial radical like Bright.

In the spring of 1883 Ashton Dilke died in Algiers. He had been ill with tuberculosis for some years, and there was no element of surprise about his death; but it was a blow to Charles Dilke, for it left him without any close family connection. A few months before his death Ashton Dilke resigned his parliamentary seat at Newcastle-on-Tyne, and was succeeded there, largely as a result of Chamberlain's intercessions with Charles Dilke, by John Morley. The other dispositions which Ashton Dilke had to make related to the guardianship of his three children and the administration of his estate, then substantially bigger than that of his brother because of the development of his journalistic properties. "You know Maye (Mrs. Ashton Dilke) well," he wrote on these points to Charles Dilke in the January before his death. "Would it be safe to leave her in charge, or should I ask Eustace Smith (her father)?" "I think I had sooner you did not put in any of the Smiths—unless Maye wishes it," Charles Dilke replied. "How would it be to leave Maye and myself executors with full powers to manage the literary property?"[15] In the event however,

194

Mrs. Dilke herself retained almost complete control over the "literary property," although Charles Dilke was given certain responsibilities in regard to the children.

Dilke suffered another loss with the death of Gambetta, which preceded that of his brother by less than two months. But the interval was sufficient for Ashton Dilke to supply his own summing up of the Frenchman. "Gambetta's death will I believe be an advantage to France in the long run," he wrote. "He meant mischief if he could have got power, and his doctrines always seemed to me thoroughly unsound. But he was a great man." "I agree with what you say about Gambetta," Charles Dilke surprisingly replied. "I agree *exactly* on all points."[16] Political disillusionment had not affected Dilke's personal friendship for Gambetta, however. He had remained Dilke's principal friend in Paris, and after his death his place in this respect was filled, for many years, by his former secretary, the deputy and historian, Joseph Reinach. Reinach was both a son-in-law and a nephew of the Baron Jacques de Reinach whose death in 1892 set off one of the most unsavoury scandals of the Third Republic, but was himself to be one of the most courageous and distinguished of the Dreyfusards. Dilke's French visits, both to La Sainte Campagne‡ and to Paris were becoming less frequent. He had less time for foreign travel, and he was proceeding rapidly with plans for building two small villas in the country. The first was at Dockett Eddy, a small island in the Thames near Shepperton, which was designed as a centre for his sculling activities and a replacement for the "village pothouses" of which he had complained to Mrs. Pattison. It was completed in 1885,

---

‡ He sold this house in 1882.

and was thereafter used as a summer week-end house. Pyrford Rough, only six miles away, was to be a winter house. It was four hundred feet up on a sandy Surrey heath and, Dilke averred, had a climate quite different from Dockett. Both houses were architecturally hideous but he remained devoted to them until the end of his life.

In the autumn of 1883 he suddenly contemplated a retirement from the political battle. The Speakership was falling vacant with the resignation of Sir Henry Brand, who had been a rather weak occupant of the chair since 1872 and for whose knighthood Dilke had been inadvertently responsible in 1881.§ There was no obvious successor. Courtney was suggested by Harcourt, but Dilke objected on the ground that he dropped his h's, which more than neutralised his radicalism. Childers, the Chancellor of the Exchequer, was then mentioned and so were Dodson and Goschen, but none of these proposals came to anything. "Dear Lady," Dilke wrote to Mrs. Pattison at this stage, "I suppose you would not like me to go out of active politics for some years . . . by taking the Speakership?"[17] What Mrs. Pattison liked is not on record, but this plan (based apparently on Dilke's very odd view that he might re-engage in party politics as an ex-Speaker) also fell through. The intention then was that Campbell-Bannerman should have the job, but an offer was first made to Arthur Peel, a former Government Chief

---

§ At that time Dilke thought it desirable that the services of another Brand, who was President of the Orange Free State, should be recognised by the Government. "'I think Brand should be knighted.—Chas. W.D.," he wrote with characteristic brevity on a paper which was circulated to the members of the Cabinet. They almost all added initials of approval; and the Speaker received the G.C.B., (D.P. 43933, 183.)

Whip and the fifth son of Sir Robert, in the confident but false belief that he would refuse. Peel was elected and presided over the House until 1895.

So far from disengaging Dilke was in fact taking on more work than ever at this stage. He retained, at Granville's wish apparently, a curious informal position as a second Cabinet adviser on foreign affairs, and saw far more of the telegrams than were normally circulated. In addition, the work of his own department and that of the Home Office was proving unusually onerous. In November Harcourt at last gave way on the question of the London police, and it was possible to draft a Government of London Bill and bring it before the House early in the session of 1884. It secured a second reading, but then died from lack of positive support. "One unfortunate thing about the London Bill," Dilke wrote to his constituency agent "is that no one in the House cares about it except Dilke, Firth, and the Prime Minister, and no one outside the House except the Liberal electors of Chelsea,"[18]

More general local government reform was being considered by a strong Cabinet committee, composed of Chamberlain, Kimberley, Childers, Carlingford, and Dodson, with Dilke as chairman. The scheme which the committee produced, and which was mentioned in the Queen's Speech as one of the principal measures for the session of 1884, foreshadowed most of the reforms of 1888 and 1894. The main difference was that Dilke's. bill provided for no aldermanic seats on the county councils. But it did not greatly matter, for this bill made still less progress than the London one. It was abandoned as being too controversial to be introduced in the same session as franchise reform.

The third and somewhat more productive of Dilke's

197

departmental activities was the setting up of a Royal Commission on the Housing of the Working Classes. Conditions in London and the other large cities were appalling, and were widely acknowledged to be so. Cross's Acts of 1875 and 1879 had produced only the slightest amelioration, and a further step forward was canvassed on all sides. Lord Salisbury was anxious for an enquiry and even the Queen, under the influence of a highly-charged pamphlet entitled *The Bitter Cry of Outcast London*, became almost a social reformer.

> "The Queen has been much distressed by all that she has heard and read lately of the deplorable condition of the houses of the poor in our great towns," she wrote to the Prime Minister on October 30th, 1883. "The Queen will be glad to hear Mr. Gladstone's opinion . . . and to learn whether the Government contemplate the introduction of any measures, or propose to take any steps to obtain more precise information as to the *true* state of affairs in these overcrowded, unhealthy and squalid bodies."[19]

Gladstone passed the letter on to Dilke, who was both delighted and surprised to receive a spur to action from Balmoral. He devoted much of the autumn to a personal investigation of the worst areas in London—some of them owned by Lord Salisbury—and gave as much publicity as he could to his findings. In this way opinion was prepared for the announcement of the Royal Commission.

The decision was made by the Cabinet on February 8th, and Gladstone immediately asked Dilke to accept the chairmanship himself. The membership was distinguished, but this did nothing to lessen the difficulties of appointment. The Prince of Wales was anxious to serve—there was even a most unsuitable suggestion that he should be chairman, but this was quickly withdrawn—and Gladstone and Dilke were both delighted to have him as an ordinary member. He was not perhaps the most assiduous of the participants,¶ but his membership underlined both the importance of the Commission and its non-party inspiration. Cardinal Manning was Dilke's first nomination for membership. He accepted with alacrity, but considerable difficulty arose over his precedence. Was he to come before or after Lord Salisbury, who was also to be a member? The Queen ruled that he was entitled to precedence not as Archbishop but as a Cardinal, i.e. a foreign prince. Harcourt, who as Home Secretary was nominally responsible for the Commission, reacted with radical horror to this suggestion. "This will never do," he wrote. "The situation is very awkward. . . . Whether as Archbishop or Cardinal he would rank first after the Prince of Wales and before Lord Salisbury."[20] Dilke therefore consulted Salisbury himself, who replied at the time that he did not in the least mind, although six years later, when it was suggested that his complacency had betrayed the rights of every marquess in the kingdom he wrote to a newspaper indignantly but falsely denying that he had ever been consulted.

For the moment, however, the difficulties were out of the way. Manning became the Commission's second princely member, and proved a good deal more assiduous than the first. But Dilke

---

¶ "Although the Prince's attendance subsequently was somewhat fitful," Sir Sidney Lee informs us, "he was present at 16 of the 38 meetings when witnesses were examined. In May he cut short a visit to Royat in order to attend." (*Life of King Edward VII*, i., p. 550.)

was not impressed with the wisdom of his suggestions. "Manning is our only revolutionary," he wrote on one occasion. But he was soon adding to this judgment, which was not in itself intended to be unfavourable:

"On Friday the 16th May at the Commission the Cardinal handed me his list of suggestions, which were not only revolutionary but ill-considered, and I have to note how curiously impracticable a schemer, given to the wildest plans, this great ecclesiastic showed himself. He suggested the removal out of London, not only of prisons and infirmaries (which no doubt are under the control of public authorities), but also of breweries, ironworks, and all factories not needed for daily or home work, as a means of giving us areas for housing the working class; suggestions the value or practicability of which I need hardly discuss."[21]

The next difficulty arose from Dilke's desire to break precedent and have a woman member of the Commission. He nominated Miss Octavia Hill, but Harcourt refused to sign the warrant if there were a woman's name upon it. The matter accordingly went to the Cabinet. "Mr. G. sided with me, but Hartington siding with Harcourt, and Lord G. saying that he was with me on the principle, but against me on the person. Mr. G. went round, and said the decision of the Cabinet was against me. . ."[22] The best that Dilke could do was to appoint Lyulph Stanley (who turned out to be a great time-waster) as a fraternal representative for Miss Maude Stanley, who would have been his second choice as a woman member. Dilke always had the strongest views in favour of the political rights of women. A few months after the appointment of the Commission he almost forced himself out of the Government by abstaining on a suffrag-ist amendment to the Franchise Bill, supported for tactical reasons by many Tories. Hartington wanted Dilke turned out for this offence, but Chamberlain, although not with his ally on the merits, made common cause, and the offence was passed over. A year later, in June, 1885, Dilke returned to the issue with Chamberlain and wrote with singular lack of prescience: "I had a curious talk about women's suffrage with Chamberlain to-day, as that is the only question of importance on which we differ and the only question which seems likely ever to divide us."** Sometimes Dilke was able to strike more practical blows for the cause. With doubtful but unchallenged legality he appointed several women members to the Metropolitan Asylums Board; and, although Harcourt frustrated him in the case of factory inspectors, he obtained the appointment of several female Local Government Board inspectors.

The other members of the Housing Royal Commission included Goschen, Cross, Lord Carrington, Lord Brownlow, the Bishop of Bedford, McCullegh Torrens, Chamberlain's hench-man Jesse Collings, and the former stonemason Henry Broadhurst. Bodley was secretary. It was generally thought a most distinguished Commission, so much so that even the Queen wrote to congratulate Dilke on the excellence of his choice. Dilke himself thought that he had not done badly, but he expressed his

---

** "The only political question" was no doubt Dilke's meaning, for within a few weeks of this talk they had exchanged notes, at a Cabinet, about their respective religious beliefs. Chamberlain had written: "I do not know that we differ much except that I am more impatient than you of the *forms*, Religious people, and cannot stand Church or any other service." Dilke noted: "But we did differ very much." (D.P. 43887,77.)

own satisfaction in less rounded terms. "Completed, my Royal Commission with fewer fools on it than is usual on Royal Commissions,"[23] he wrote on February 16th.

The Commission began work in March, and met twice a week for some months. It occupied much of Dilke's time, because apart from the sittings he found all the witnesses, corresponded with them about the evidence they would give, and prepared for the examinations-in-chief, which he himself conducted. The Commission's labours continued into the session of 1885, and culminated with visits to Edinburgh in April and to Dublin in May. The latter visit gave Dilke his only direct experience of the country for which he had so nearly been made responsible in the House of Commons.[††] On the whole Dilke found the work unexciting. "But the Commission kept up its character for dullness," he wrote after a session at which Chamberlain had given evidence and when a memorable clash had been expected between the witness and Lord Salisbury, "and nothing noteworthy occurred." Its reports led on directly to some minor legislation, and indirectly to a new wave of concern with slum conditions which expressed itself in housing trusts, university missions, a series of private investigations and a generally bad conscience on the part of the more sensitive sections of the upper and middle classes. For Dilke himself the results were a fortification of his reputation for hard, highly competent, painstaking work and the beginning of a cross-party friendship with Lord Salisbury.

[††] His inexperience in this respect was, however, no greater than that of his Chief. Gladstone devoted the best part of twenty-five years to Irish problems but only three weeks to an Irish visit, which unique event took place in the autumn of 1877.

This friendship was within a year to become important in connection with the Distribution of Seats Bill, but at the beginning, early in 1884, its chief result was the election of Dilke, on Salisbury's proposal, to Grillion's. Grillion's was (and is) a dining club composed mostly of senior politicians of both parties, which had been founded in 1812 and had since enjoyed an illustrious life.‡ Indeed Dilke wrote sharply that "the Club considers itself such an illustrious body that it elects candidates without telling them they are proposed." Rather typically—he did the same at the Athenaeum a month or two later—he refused membership. "I was elected on Saturday to Grillion's, which is a mere dining club which dines every Monday," he scribbled on a note tossed to Chamberlain at a Cabinet meeting. "I had not solicited the honour—most Cabinet ministers and ex-ditto belong to it. I have declined to take up my membership, as I think these things a bore." Chamberlain replied to this not very tactful note—the President of the Board of Trade had never been asked to join—by more particularised acerbity: "Yes, it is no great inducement to dine with Hicks Beach or to see Cross drinking himself to death."[24] But Carlingford remonstrated with Dilke, told him that nobody before had ever rejected membership, and persuaded him to send a letter (albeit a rather ungracious one) withdrawing his previous refusal. Within a year or so he had become a regular attender, and towards the end of his life Grillion's was one of his centres of interest.

At the beginning of 1884 the Egyptian question again became

---

‡ Not the least remarkable of the .occasions associated with the club was that when Gladstone arrived to dine, found himself by an unusual accident the only member present that night, and entered himself in the club books as having consumed one bottle of sherry and one bottle of champagne.

important in British politics. Since 1881 a movement of religious revolt under Mahommed Ahmed, called the Mahdi, had been in progress in the southern Soudan. The Egyptian hold over the area had always been loose and the government was of an appallingly low standard; but these facts did not make the Khedive's ministers in Cairo any more anxious to evacuate. In the autumn of 1883 they sent an Egyptian army under the command of a British officer, Hicks Pasha, to attack the Mahdi in his own territory. The result was a dismal failure. The army was almost annihilated. A new set of problems were thereby created for the British Cabinet. Egypt was in effect a British protectorate, and Sir Evelyn Baring, who two months before the defeat had been appointed agent and consul-general, the real ruler of the country. Responsibility for Egyptian policies had eventually to be taken in London. This applied as much to the Soudan as to Egypt itself, even though there was nominally no British control there.

After Hicks's defeat there were two possible courses for the Cabinet. They could mount a full-scale British offensive to crush the Mahdi and establish effective control as far south as the Equatorial Province—the policy pursued under Kitchener fourteen years later; or they could arrange for the evacuation of Khartoum and the other scattered garrisons and abandon the whole area south of Wadi Halfa. The choice was overwhelmingly for the latter alternative. Hartington and Selborne might have preferred the more forward policy, but no one else in the Cabinet was with them. Gladstone saw in the Soudanese, as he had failed to see in the Egyptians, "a people rightly struggling to be free," and was violently against incurring either the expense or the moral opprobrium of a campaign of conquest. He was strongly supported by Granville and Harcourt; and the majority of the Liberal back-benchers took the same view. The radical imperialists—Dilke and Chamberlain—did not dissent. They were to have their differences with Gladstone on the issue, but about the execution rather than the conception of the policy. Evacuation seemed to them both inevitable and desirable. This was partly because they regarded the Soudan as a useless and burdensome piece of territory, which, at least through the agency of Egypt, we were incapable of administering efficiently; and partly because Dilke, at any rate, was by no means a universal imperialist. "I am as great a jingo in Central Asia," he was to write in 1885, "as I am a scuttler in South Africa."[25] What he liked was a decisive, perhaps rather ruthless policy, whether it was backwards or forwards. And a firm resolve to evacuate seemed to fulfil this qualification.

Dilke's views on the issue were more important than Chamberlain's, for he was more directly involved. On December 12th he noted: "Soudan dealt with outside Cabinet by Committee at War Office: Ld. G., Hartington, Northbrook, Carlingford, and self, in order that Mr. G. might avoid writing to the Queen about the matter and get Hartington to tell her verbally."[26] This was the origin of the Committee which, a month later and without the assistance of Carlingford, was to appoint and brief Gordon. How a Government resolved on retreat came to commission for the purpose such an unlikely agent as Charles Gordon is still shrouded in mystery. He was not asked for by Baring, who, on the contrary, at first resisted his appointment. He was not desired by Gladstone, who gave only a rather sceptical acquiescence from Hawarden. And Gordon himself had made it clear, in an interview given on January 7th to Stead of the *Pall Mall Gazette*, that his views diverged sharply from those of the Government. The probability is that Granville, having rather imperfectly informed himself about Gordon, decided that the appointment would be a good sop to public opinion, and found it easy to get the support of Hartington, who cared little for public opinion, but who on military matters was much under the influence of Lord Wolseley; and Wolseley favoured Gordon. Dilke, who two days earlier had protested to Granville against the idea of sending any British officer to conduct the retreat from Khartoum, appears to have offered no resistance to Gordon's appointment. Whether this was because he had changed his mind in the course of forty-eight hours, or because he did not understand that Gordon was going to Khartoum, is not clear. In his confidential diary for January 18th he wrote: "Cabal at the War Office as to Khartoum . . . decided to send Colonel Gordon to Suakim to report on the Soudan."[27] But in his memoir entry for the same day—the memoir, it should be noted, was written up several years later— Dilke wrote: "Meeting at War Office summoned suddenly . . . Gordon stated danger at Khartoum exaggerated, that two Englishmen there had too much whisky. He would be able to bring away garrisons without difficulty. . . ."[28]

After another three days, however, Dilke had become more apprehensive that it was Khartoum that Gordon had in view. "I am alarmed at Gordon's hints to the newspapers," he wrote to Lord Granville on January 21st, "for I fear they must come from him. While I was at the War Office I heard nothing of his going to Khartoum, or anywhere except to Suakim. But if he goes up towards Khartoum, and is carried off and held to ransom—we shall have to send a terrible force after him even though he should go without instructions."[29] By this time Gordon was already on his way across the Mediterranean. He had left Victoria Station at 8 p.m. on the day of the War Office meeting, and had travelled overland to Brindisi, interspersing his journey with "a series of decrees which he telegraphed to us and we telegraphed to Baring." The result of them was, first, to make it quite clear that Gordon was intending to go to Khartoum and not merely to Suakim, and secondly, to secure his appointment as Governor-General of the Soudan—a curiously executive post for an officer whose mission was only to report. What they did not make clear, in Dilke's view, was that Gordon had already abandoned evacuation as a policy, although a subsequent re-reading of the decrees convinced him, with the hindsight which he then possessed, that this was already Gordon's intention.

The discovery of Gordon's deceit, had different effects upon Dilke and Gladstone. "Mr. G., from the first moment when Gordon broke his orders," Dilke wrote, "was for disavowing him, stating that he was acting in defiance of instructions, and leaving him to his fate. Hartington was equally strong for an expedition."[30] Dilke was on Hartington's side. He was firmly for evacuation, and he had no great respect for Gordon, of whose insubordination he was convinced, but he did not believe that the latter could be abandoned. On the contrary he was prepared to work hard for an expedition to cover Gordon. "Met at night with Hartington and Chamberlain," he wrote on February 7th, "and decided on more vigorous action."[31] This secret and ill-assorted meeting was intended to prepare the ground for the Cabinet on the following morning. But it failed to secure a decision: "Cabinet called at our wish," Dilke reported. "I, Hartington, 2, Self, 3, Harcourt, 4, Chamberlain, 5, Northbrook, 6, Carlingford were for asking Gordon if a demonstration at Suakim would help him. Mr. G. and Lord G. very strong the other way, broke up the meeting sooner than agree."[32] Four days later, at another Cabinet, Granville weakened and Gladstone, standing alone, was overruled. A decision in principle to send British troops to Suakim was taken.

A decision in principle, however, proved quite different from a directive to action. It was August before the expedition sailed. It was October before it was ready to leave Wadi Halfa and advance into the Soudan. The intervening months had been passed in almost endless Cabinet discussion of what exactly was to be done. There was the dispute about Zebehr, the former slave-trader whom Gordon wished to commission as his principal lieutenant, a course which Gladstone—most strangely—was at first alone in favouring. There was a proposal that a minister should be sent out to Egypt to make decisions on the spot: "Chamberlain . . . suggested that I should go," Dilke wrote. ". . . Hartington evidently thought that somebody should go, and thought he had better go himself. Lord Granville would not have either, as might have been expected, for it was doubtful which of the two propositions would make him the more jealous."[33] There was the question of timing, with five members of the Cabinet (Gladstone, Granville, Harcourt, Kimberley and Dodson) arguing until April that an autumn expedition would be premature. There was the associated question of its scope, in their approach to which ministers were greatly influenced by their varying views of the objects it was to achieve. Dilke and Chamberlain, who wanted a neat evacuation, were divided from Hartington, who wanted a prolonged occupation and consequently favoured a larger-scale enterprise. Indeed, in Dilke's view, Hartington's desire to mount a major offensive was an important cause of the long delay. "Hartington was determined to give Wolseley his big job," he wrote after a discussion on May 31st. "If the early suggestion for an expedition by 1,000 picked men, or Roberts's suggestion of a wholly Indian expedition, had not been vetoed by Hartington and Northbrook, Gordon would probably have been saved."[34]

There were the questions of the interest on the Egyptian foreign debt, of whether the Cairo government should be made bankrupt, of whether the powers should agree to "cut the coupon," of whether an international conference should be summoned. All these matters formed part of the Government's Egyptian agenda and most took precedence over Gordon and the Soudan. At the beginning of August, Dilke wrote to Chamberlain: "We always have two subjects—(a) Conference, (b) Gordon"; and the latter replied: "The first always taking up two or three hours, and the second five minutes at the tag end of business."[35] Cabinets were frequently acrimonious and almost invariably long drawn out. Northbrook, the First Lord of the Admiralty, to whose views Dilke was usually opposed, was a particularly difficult man with whom to argue. On one occasion, "instead of sleeping (his usual practice at a Cabinet)," he fainted and had to be carried out.

As a background to these deliberations and delays, innumerable and confusing telegrams from Gordon poured into London. "Twelve telegrams from Gordon of the most extraordinary nature,"[36] Dilke recorded on March nth. "We were evidently dealing with a wild man under the influence of that climate of Central Africa which acts even upon the sanest men like strong drink,"[37] he summed up the situation at this time. Six months later the story was still the same. "A telegram from Gordon which shows he's quite mad," Dilke wrote in September, adding with faint surprise: "Some of the other telegrams from him sent at the same time are sane enough."[38] But by then the story was nearly over. Communications with Khartoum became increasingly sporadic and eventually ceased altogether. Meanwhile the expeditionary force was slowly making its way up the 850 miles of river between Wadi Haifa and Khartoum. It took three months to cover the distance, arriving on January 28th, 1885. The citadel had been stormed and Gordon killed on January 26th.§§

Early on the morning of February 5th the news became known in London, and, in the words of Sir Philip Magnus, "Gladstone's reputation touched the lowest point in his whole career." The Queen sent him her famous unciphered telegram, which would be memorable for its syntax if for nothing else:

---

§§ In view of the controversies which have since developed around the character and personal habits of Gordon, the following vivid account, written many years later by Joseph Reinach (formerly Gambetta's secretary) and contained in an unpublished letter amongst the Dilke papers, is perhaps worth appending. "J'ai beaucoup connu Gordon," Reinach wrote. "J'ai fait sa connaissance en Janvier 1880 sur un bateau qui faisait la service entre Alexandria et Naples. Nous passâmes plusieurs journées à Naples. Il me mena chez Ismail. Je le menai un soir au théâtre à San-Carlo. Il n'etait pas allé au théâtre depuis vingt ans. On donnait un ballet Sardanapale, avec beaucoup de petites femmes à demi-nues. Il se scandalisa. 'And you call that civilisation!' me dit-ii et il rentra à l'hotel. Je l'y trouvais vers une heure du matin en déshabille, lisant le Bible et ayant vidé une demi bouteille de whisky. Il buvait terriblement de brandy. Plus tard, à Paris, il venait souvent me voir le matin. Et, au bout de cinq minutes, il demandait du cognac.

"C'etait un héros, à très courte vue comme beaucoup d'héros, un mystique qui se payait de phrases, et aussi, comment dirai je? Un peu 'un fumiste.' Vous savez ce que nous appelons ainsi. Il s'amusalt à étonner les gens. Il ne croyait pas tout ce qu'il disait. Dans les lettres de lui que j'ai conservées, il traitait volontiers Dizzie et ses amis de *Mountebanks*. Il était, lui-même, *Mountebank. . .*" (D.P. 33921, 186.)

"These news from Khartoum are frightful, and to think that all this might have been prevented and many precious lives saved by earlier action is too fearful."[39] This was handed to Gladstone at Carnforth Junction when he was on his way to London from Holker, where he had been taken by Hartington to stay with the Duke of Devonshire. His reaction, Dilke tells us, was a mixture of annoyed dismay and a shrewd inquisitiveness about the Carnforth station-master's politics and hence the probability of the contents of the telegram becoming known. But it was not the displeasure of the Queen alone that the Prime Minister and the Government had to face. Public opinion, particularly in London, became hysterically jingo. There were crowds in Downing Street and outside the House of Commons, ready to hoot at Gladstone on every possible occasion; and he was execrated in innumerable music halls as the murderer of Gordon. In the House there was a general collapse of Liberal morale and some defection. A vote of censure against the Government's Egyptian policy had been defeated by the fairly comfortable margin of forty-four in the previous May; but when a similar motion was put at four o'clock on the morning of February 28th, the Government majority fell to fourteen. Dilke wished to go out on the issue. "Mr. G. now *wishes* to be upset," he had written to Grant Duff on February 20th. "He thinks the party will permanently suffer by the Soudan war if in power at the elections (Nov.-Dec, I fancy), and had sooner be out soon and come in again after them."[40] Dilke tended to agree with this view, particularly as Chamberlain, violently opposed to Hartington's desire for full pacification and a long-term occupation of the Soudan, had been in a resigning humour for some time. Believing this, Dilke was inclined to interpret the cryptic "that will do" with which Gladstone greeted the result of the

211

division as meaning that it was enough of a blow to justify resignation.

In Cabinet at noon the next day, the Prime Minister presented quite a different face. He appealed to the "manhood" of his colleagues and carried the day for continuance in office against the opposition of Granville, Derby, Hartington, Chamberlain, Northbrook and Childers. The Government had received a most damaging blow, for which the only compensation—the accession of Rosebery¶—was hardly adequate. Internal dissensions were worse than ever. But there was still a majority in the House of Commons; the Parliament was more than two years short of its term; and the Prime Minister, aged seventy-five and at the nadir of his popular fortunes, preferred power to repose. Gladstone's second Government had a few months still to live.

¶ One of the more attractive strands of Rosebery's strange contradictory character led him to place himself unreservedly in Gladstone's hands as soon as the news of the fall of Khartoum came through. Three months earlier he had contumaciously refused the Office of Works with the Cabinet. Now he was quite willing to accept this or even a lesser post. In fact he got the Privy Seal as well.

Chapter Nine

A Dying Government

During the summer of 1884 the Government—and particularly Gladstone—had been much more occupied with the problems of the franchise than with those of General Gordon. The third of the great reform bills of the nineteenth century, conducted mainly by the Prime Minister himself, completed its passage through the House of Commons on June 27th. It increased the electorate from three to five millions; household suffrage was extended from the towns to the counties; and for the first time since 1829 Ireland was treated upon a basis of full equality.

Neither Lord Hartington nor the Conservative party liked the bill. But just as the Whig leader thought it undesirable to carry his public opposition beyond a few growling speeches in the country, so the Tories judged it unwise to provoke a head-on collision upon the issue. Resistance in the Commons was half-hearted, and attention became concentrated upon what the Lords would do. On July 8th they gave their answer. They would

213

decline to pass the franchise bill until the Government also presented them with a measure for the redistribution of constituencies. On the face of it this was not an extreme challenge. The Government was already committed to redistribution, and if the Lords had not existed, the Liberal party—and particularly the radical element—would have been almost as anxious for this as for the franchise bill itself. It was nevertheless a clever manoïuvre, and one which Disraeli had recommended for exactly these circumstances. A redistribution bill would take some time to draft, and even longer to pass. It would arouse great local jealousies, in the midst of which both bills might founder. Furthermore, any period of delay carried with it the possibility that the Government itself might collapse. "The Tory game," Dilke had written as early as May 24th when the first bill was still in the Commons, "is to delay the franchise bill until they have upset* us upon Egypt...."[1] The possibility of Gordon destroying Gladstone had not diminished by the time that the Conservative peers came to take their decision.

The apparent moderation of the Lords did not therefore make their attitude acceptable to the Government. There quickly developed a stronger tension between the two Houses than had existed since the great days of 1831–2. Gladstone earned an early rebuke from the Queen for the strength of his language against the peers, and was little comforted by her assuring him that the Lords reflected the "true feeling of the country" better than did the Commons. But the violence of the

---

* Dilke's normal use of the verb "to upset" was always in the sense of "to overturn." If he used it in the more common modern sense of "to disturb" he added inverted commas, and frequently a deprecating parenthesis—"as the servants say" or "to use housemaid's language."

Prime Minister's attack was as nothing compared with that which Chamberlain was to mount during the late summer and early autumn. He began, somewhat surprisingly, at a house dinner of the Devonshire Club, and he continued with a series of speeches at Bingley Hall in Birmingham, at Hanley, Newtown and Denbigh. He denounced the "insolent pretensions of an hereditary caste he threatened to lead a march of a hundred thousand Midland men upon London, and, if necessary, to give Lord Salisbury a broken head on the way; and he was implicated in the organised radical attack on Lord Randolph Churchill's meeting in Aston Park, which led to one of the worst political riots in recent British history, to several serious casualties, and to the narrow escape from the mob of Churchill and Sir Stafford Northcote. John Morley was giving full expression to the Chamberlain point of view when he coined "mend them or end them," the most memorable slogan of this period. The Queen's anger at Chamberlain's pronouncements made her even less grammatical than was her habit. "The Queen will yield to no one in TRUE LIBERAL FEELING," she wrote to the Prime Minister, "but not to destructive, and she calls upon Mr. Gladstone to *restrain, as he can,* some of his wild colleagues and followers."[2]

Dilke gave full encouragement to Chamberlain. "Speak as strongly as possible to-night and to-morrow," he telegraphed to Highbury before the Hanley and Newtown speeches. He acted frequently as a buffer for complaints which Gladstone relayed from the Sovereign. Furthermore, he greatly strengthened his ally's position whenever, as at the end of October, the Queen wanted Chamberlain's dismissal, by insisting that, if this happened, he would go too. Beyond this, however, he played no part in the agitation. The reason seems clear. He was an eager advocate of the franchise bill, and wished to see it passed quickly into law, both because this would be a blow to the prestige of the Whigs, and because it would improve the electoral prospects of the radicals. In addition, he had no respect for the pretensions of the peers, and would have been delighted to see them sustain a clear defeat. At the same time the terms which Lord Salisbury offered to the Government had great attractions from Dilke's point of view. The franchise bill had been the work of the Prime Minister, assisted by Harcourt and by James, the Attorney-General. Dilke had not been closely concerned. But a redistribution bill would be a different matter. He was to be the minister with the primary responsibility. The work of drafting a scheme, of negotiating with the Opposition leaders, and of piloting the bill through the House of Commons would give him a far greater opportunity than he had previously enjoyed. He would be the central figure of the next session. And the task would be most neatly fitted to his talents. It would call for hard work, a grasp of detail, and an ability to negotiate smoothly with those with whom he did not agree.

Even without the Lords, of course, there was a probability that the Cabinet would decide to proceed with redistribution. But there would not be the same urgency. The Government was manifestly rickety—no one was more aware of this than was Dilke—and it was by no means impossible that the second measure, which Lord Hartington liked little better than the first, would be left to await a new Parliament. Dilke was therefore influenced by two conflicting motives. Acting on the one, and on his constantly held belief that thorough preparation never did any harm, he began, early in July and without instructions from the Cabinet, to draft a rough scheme of redistribution.

Within a few days he received retrospective sanction from

Gladstone, and then felt able to set to work Sir John Lambert, the authoritative permanent secretary to the Local Government Board. Between them they produced a scheme for the Cabinet at its meeting on August 9th, a few days before the prorogation of Parliament. The Cabinet set up a committee—with Dilke in the chair, and Hartington, Childers, Chamberlain, Kimberley and Lefevre as members—to consider the matter further. "I soon got rid of the committee and went on by myself with Lambert," was Dilke's comment on this. His second and more detailed draft was ready for the Cabinet by September 18th, after only one meeting of the committee. Boroughs with less than 10,000 inhabitants were to lose their separate representation and be merged in the counties. Two-member boroughs with between 10,000 and 40,000 inhabitants were to lose their second member. The seats gained by this final demise of the semi-rotten boroughs were to be distributed partly to London, partly to the under-represented industrial boroughs, and partly to the counties, which were to be split up for the first time and were to enjoy a net increase of 53 members. Lancashire and Yorkshire, on the somewhat surprising assumption that they were urban throughout, were to be divided into single-member divisions. The remaining English counties were to be split (if their size warranted it) into two-member districts. Ireland, Scotland and Wales were to be somewhat over-represented on roughly the same basis.

This scheme was much less radical than Dilke would have liked. But he was restricted by Gladstone's instinctive conservatism on the one side, and by Hartington's concern for Whig electoral interests on the other. Gladstone's conservatism made him a passionate defender of university representation (which Dilke would like to have abolished) and a rearguard fighter for

217

the rights of ancient boroughs. The Prime Minister believed in the theory of popular democracy, but thought that it should be accomplished within the framework of an electoral map as similar as possible to that which he had known in his youth. Hartington's approach was more hard-headed. The basis of Whig strength was the two-member constituency. It sustained the practice of the double-harness Liberal team—one advanced candidate to enthuse the faithful and one moderate to broaden the appeal. But in a single-member division a choice would have to be made, and Hartington and his advisers were in no doubt that in these circumstances the faithful, who mostly chose the candidates, would prefer radicals to Whigs.

Dilke's most useful ally proved to be Lord Salisbury. There was an element of extremism in Salisbury's character. It was to enable him first, in 1885, to outflank the Liberals by the extent of the concessions he was prepared to offer the Irish and then, from 1886 onwards, to preside over the most ruthlessly repressive government in the history of the union. In 1884, on redistribution, it enabled him to follow the example set by Disraeli in the franchise struggles of 1866–7. Once he had accepted the need for a change he was prepared for a drastic one. He had less natural respect for the traditional and the familiar than had Gladstone, and he had no interest in pulling Whig electoral chestnuts out of the fire. Pushed on by Randolph Churchill, he was prepared for the moment to put his faith in Tory democracy.

Salisbury's views became known in September. "Now that Salisbury is going in for electoral districts," Kimberley wrote to Dilke, "it will become a sort of open competition which party can go farthest. I should not be surprised if he were to trump us by proposing to abolish the House of Lords."[3] This was a fairly typical Government reaction, and it made Dilke's task in strengthening his measure a great deal easier.

Informal discussions with the Opposition began towards the end of the month. They were conducted principally by Hicks Beach for the Conservatives and by Hartington and Dilke for the Liberals. They led to little result, although Beach proposed at one stage the abolition of separate representation for towns with a population of less than 25,000 and the loss of the second seat up to 80,000. Much of the difficulty arose because Beach was not fully authorised as a negotiator by his party. Sometimes he was flying a kite for Lord Salisbury, sometimes he was flying one for himself, and sometimes he was speaking for the whole Conservative party; but it was not easy to tell which occasion was which. The titular leader of the Opposition in the Commons—Northcote—was a constant source of weakness. Gladstone (whose private secretary Northcote had once been) believed that the latter had let him down so badly at the time of the "closure" negotiations in 1881, that it was useless, on grounds of feebleness not of duplicity, to deal with him. Salisbury was the key figure, but it was not possible at this stage to entice him into direct negotiation.

Later in the autumn this deficiency was repaired. Salisbury agreed on November 4th, in response to an initiative of the Queen, that there should be direct meetings between the party leaders. The first of these took place on the 22nd of the month, although there had already been informal discussions between Salisbury and Dilke on the Housing Commission. The formal meeting took place in Downing Street and was attended by Gladstone, Hartington and Dilke from the Government side and by Salisbury and Northcote for the Opposition. "There never was so pleasant and friendly a meeting," Dilke wrote enthusiastically; and added in a letter to Chamberlain: "It looks as though Lord Salisbury is really anxious that we should pass our Bill."

Chamberlain received this information rather sceptically, and within the course of a day or so it looked as though he might be right, for Salisbury suddenly demanded the grouping of small towns, so that the county divisions should be made more completely rural. Dilke was horrified by this proposal, for, independently of its psephological merits or demerits, it would have involved going back on a laboriously reached agreement about the number of county seats. Salisbury, however, withdrew from this position as rapidly as he had occupied it. He also abandoned a demand for minority representation in the towns, to which Chamberlain, not unreasonably, had taken particular objection. This behaviour did not impress Dilke. "All this shows great indecision," he noted, adding later: "Lord Salisbury did not seem to me thoroughly to understand his subject."[4] But it certainly assisted the progress of the negotiations.

There was a further meeting of the five negotiators on November 26th, after which the heads of agreement could be put before the Cabinet.

"I announced . . . that the Tories proposed and we accepted single-member districts universally in counties," Dilke wrote, "boundaries to be drawn by a commission who were to separate urban from rural as far as possible, without grouping and without creating constituencies of utterly eccentric shape. The names of the commissioners had been settled, and both sides were pledged to accept their proposals, unless the two sides agreed to differ from them. The Tories proposed single-member districts almost everywhere

220

in boroughs, and only positively named one exception—the City of London—but were evidently prepared to make some exceptions. They made our agreement on this point the condition of passing the Franchise Bill, of giving up the decrease of the Irish members from 103 to 80 which they urged, of giving up all forms of minority vote, and of giving up grouping. My own opinion and that of the Prime Minister were in favour of agreement."[5]

The Cabinet was not so favourably disposed. Apart from Hartington, who was inevitably hostile to single-member districts, Childers threatened resignation on this point; and the Chief Whip, Grosvenor, who had been called in, was equally critical. "We had the enormous advantage, however," Dilke wrote, "that Chamberlain and I and Mr. Gladstone were the only three people who understood the subject, so that the others were unable to fight except in the form known as swearing at large."[6] This opposition did not prove very effective, and the Cabinet eventually sent Dilke to tell Salisbury that agreement should be possible, and authorised the three plenipotentiaries to continue their negotiations with the Conservative leaders that afternoon. Following this afternoon meeting documents were exchanged between the parties. On the next day, November 28th, Salisbury and Dilke, in a series of four final meetings, put the finishing touches to the work. These meetings took place at Salisbury's house and the agreement which emerged became known in consequence as "the Arlington Street compact." The principal last-minute change was that the Conservatives, as a compromise, agreed to keep the two-member constituency for those boroughs outside London which had previously possessed and were still to retain two members. This arrangement persisted in some form until 1950, although its *raison d'être*, the easing of the Whig position within the Liberal party, was to disappear within eighteen months.

The "compact" gave considerable satisfaction to the leaders of the Government. Mary Gladstone, Sir Philip Magnus informs us, observed the Prime Minister, Hartington and Dilke behaving like boys out of school at luncheon on November 27th, and at tea on that day she found her father "splitting and chuckling." In the evening he wrote a letter to the Queen to thank her for "that wise, gracious and steady exercise of influence on Your Majesty's part which has so powerfully contributed to bring about this accommodation and to avert a serious crisis of affairs";[7] and his gratitude to Dilke was at least as lively, if less rotundly expressed. As for Dilke himself, he was fully but not unreasonably satisfied with his own work. He had decisively re-drawn the electoral map of Britain. Despite the subsequent changes of 1918, 1950 and 1955, to-day's pattern is recognisably based on that of 1884, and on no earlier arrangement. The modern county constituency and the modern divided borough are both Dilke's creations.

In addition to making a long-term settlement Dilke had also looked after immediate radical interests. He had obtained more seats for London (an increase from 22 to 55) and the other big towns than he had originally believed possible, and he had in consequence produced a much nearer approach to the equal weighting of votes than had ever before been attempted.[†]

[†] He had not, of course, abolished plural voting, although he would like to have done so. At the first general election following the act based on his scheme, Dilke himself had nine votes, scattered over the different constituencies in which he held property. He made several special journeys in order to exercise these votes, and when this was not possible he attempted

Furthermore, on most prognostications, he had strengthened the electoral prospects of the Liberal party generally and of the radical wing in particular, and he had done it all without a fatal breach with Hartington and in agreement with Salisbury. This last point gave him peculiar pleasure. "Lord Salisbury had always been so extremely soft and sweet to me," he wrote with satisfaction three weeks after the conclusion of the negotiations, "that it is a revelation to find him writing to Spencer in the style of Harcourt or of Chamberlain in a passion."[8]

Dilke's triumph had been secured without much help from Chamberlain. At times, indeed, he had found it almost as difficult to persuade the President of the Board of Trade as to prevent a breach with Hartington. In part this arose out of differences between Dilke and Chamberlain about the merits of particular proposals. Chamberlain, for example, was much more attached to the double-member constituency than was Dilke. But in part, also, it arose from doubts on Chamberlain's side as to the wisdom of engaging in negotiations at all. The difficulty was that any discussions with the Opposition about redistribution inevitably merged into the possibility of a compromise on House of Lords resistance to the Franchise Bill; and Chamberlain, having nailed his flag with a great public flourish to the mast of victory over the Lords, was against any such arrangement. Suggestions that Gladstone was preparing for compromise roused him to bitter private denunciation and the threat of resignation. Morley and he engaged in a spate of condemnatory correspondence. "For weeks," Garvin informs us, "Chamberlain did not realise that even Dilke was undergoing a modification of mind."[9]

---

to make "pairing" arrangements with Tory politicians whom he knew to own property in the same area.

When he did realise it and the practical advantages which might follow, Chamberlain withdrew much of his opposition. But he remained somewhat sceptical throughout, and as late as November 27th Dilke recorded that, in the midst of his negotiations with the Conservative leaders, he had to conduct parallel ones with his ally, who was in another room at 10, Downing Street and "somewhat hostile." Dilke had kept up his sleeve the card of a seventh seat for Birmingham, and this ace, played at the decisive moment, did much to bring Chamberlain along. When the compact was complete Chamberlain wrote to Morley outlining and defending the arrangement. But his final comment—"Not bad for a Tory Bill!"—was resigned rather than enthusiastic.

The conclusion of the compact by no means completed Dilke's work on the subject. First he had the task of appointing the Boundary Commissioners. The English ones gave rise to no difficulty, but the Irish ones led him into sharp conflict with Spencer and a charge of having appointed them over the head of the Lord Lieutenant and without any consultation with Dublin Castle. The Scottish appointments gave rise to still more trouble, but here it was with the Conservatives and not with a Cabinet colleague. "Perhaps I may take the opportunity of mentioning that I have been asked by some of our friends in Scotland about Mr. Crawford's appointment," Northcote wrote to Dilke on December 18th. "They say he is the Lord Advocate's Political Secretary, and that, if we are to be bound by the decisions of the Commission, his weight will tell heavily. We were not, I think, consulted as to his appointment."[10] Crawford was a distant family connection of Dilke's. His wife, whom he had married in 1881, was a younger sister of Mrs. Ashton Dilke.

Apart from these appointments there was the task of preparing the bill and piloting it through the House of Commons. At first the plan was that Hartington, whose succession to the leadership of the party was generally regarded as imminent, should share with Dilke the responsibility for this work. With this end in view Dilke went for a few days in January to visit Hartington at Hardwick Hall. He was impressed by the splendours of the Elizabethan mansion, which justified its local description of being "all window and no wall" to the extent that, "in spite of heavy hanging curtains, the candles are blown out if you go near the windows," but little useful business was transacted.‡ The house was full of other guests, and Hartington showed no eagerness to concentrate upon the details of redistribution. The result was that when the bill came before the House the responsibility remained with Dilke. Sir Henry James was deputed to help, but he did not in practice do much, and, in any event, as he was not in the Cabinet, his rôle was a junior one.

The parliamentary task was neither easy nor brief. The agreement of the Conservative leaders had been secured, but this was far from guaranteeing that there was to be no opposition from private members, a great number of whom were to find their seats abolished under them. On several occasions, acting under pressure from his back-benchers, Northcote tried to re-negotiate points in the compact. "Our men are getting

---

‡ Dilke also recorded, in characteristic terms, his impressions of one of the pictures. "The portrait of the first Cavendish—who was usher of Cardinal Wolsey, and who married Bess of Hardwick, the richest lady of the day—is exactly like Hartington, but a vulgar Hartington—fat and greasy—a Hartington who might have kept a public-house." (D.P. 43939, 34.)

hard to hold, and having twice walked through the lobby almost alone, I have no taste for repeating the operation,"[11] he wrote on March 15th. Dilke, however, showed no disposition to help Northcote out of his difficulties, even though the point at issue at this stage—the Tory desire to get rid of the remaining double-member boroughs—was one on which he personally preferred the rebel view. Where points remained to be settled he was conciliatory and flexible. But he would discuss no departure from the principles of the Arlington Street arrangements. He believed that a rigid adherence to these was the only way to get the bill through in the session, and he was no doubt right. Even with this rigidity, and driving so hard that for some time he had the bill in committee four nights a week, all the stages were not complete when the Government resigned on June 9th. The main bulk of the work was done, however, and the Salisbury administration completed the job in time for the royal assent to be given at the end of July.

In the autumn of 1884, in the midst of the Salisbury nego-tiations, Dilke had become engaged to be married. A few months earlier, in July, Mark Pattison had died after a prolonged period of ill-health. His widow, as has been seen, had long been on very close terms with Dilke, and their engagement followed almost automatically. Arrangements were made for Mrs. Pattison to spend the summer of 1885 in Madras with the Governor and Mrs. Grant Duff, and for the wedding to take place in Christ Church Cathedral, at Oxford, on her return in October. Perhaps because of the recentness of Pattison's death, perhaps because of a certain taste for mystery which was endemic in Dilke's character, the engagement was not made public. Only six or seven people were told, of whom Chamberlain alone was politically prominent. On receiving the news the President of the Board of Trade wrote to Mrs. Pattison. He began with the curiously constructed sentence: "Dilke has told me his great secret, and I sympathise with him so warmly in the new prospects of happiness which are opening for him that I have asked leave to write to you and to offer my hearty congratulations"; and he went on to refer to Dilke's friendship as "the best gift of my public life." "I rejoice unfeignedly," he continued, "that he will have a companion so well able to share his noblest ambitions and to brighten his life."[12] A self-conscious and heavy-handed benignity was the keynote of the entire letter, but it so impressed Dilke that he referred to it later as "the best letter of his (Chamberlain's) life."

The "secret," not unnaturally, soon began to leak out. Lord Granville offered Dilke his congratulations, which were coolly refused. Bodley, Dilke's secretary, found that by the spring he was constantly asked to confirm the rumour of Dilke's engagement, and developed the practice of asking in reply: "Do you think he would have time to get married? "At the end of April Dilke was writing to Mrs. Pattison, who had already left for India, and saying: "I hear that the subject of congratulation has been in a cheap and nasty society paper called *Society*." But he still persisted in his attempt at secrecy. One reason now driving him in this direction was his belief that someone was plotting against him, and his fear that news of his impending marriage might drive them to redoubled efforts. At the turn of the year, when he was at his house in Provence, he wrote to Mrs. Pattison in terms of unspecified foreboding. "I slept very badly last night as I had horrible nightmares of (you) unhappy," he wrote on January 1st.[13] And six months later he was further disturbed by the continued arrival of anonymous letters. "I had another of those dreadful letters a day or two ago," he wrote to her on June 10th. "They always suggest conspiracy, but why should those who conspire let me know. I fancy it must be some lunatic."[14]

There were familiy worries also.

"I am so distressed at having from time to time to bother you with unpleasant subjects . . ." Dilke wrote, again to Mrs. Pattison, on March 6th. "Maye (Mrs. Ashton Dilke) has discovered that her sister Mrs. Crawford is carrying on a correspondence with an officer now at Dublin and is in half trouble already with Crawford and likely to get into worse trouble. Maye consults me as to whether she shall write to the man and in the form of calling on him to discontinue writing to her sister to try to frighten him. . . . I have told her that, as I feel sure that if she writes she will write wisely and with good feeling, perhaps it would be right as well as wise that she should do so."[15]

At this stage, however, Dilke could not spare much time for these private concerns. The first half of 1885 was a period of unusual political fluidity. When the year began Gladstone was weary and depressed and the air was heavy with rumours of his early retirement. It was assumed that Hartington would succeed, but there was little reason to believe that the Government could long survive the disappearance of its chief. Into this atmosphere of decay Chamberlain threw the challenge of the Unauthorised Programme. This was based to a large extent upon a series of articles which had been appearing in the *Fortnightly Review* over the previous eighteen months. But the ideas contained in the articles were given a far sharper cutting edge when expressed by

Chamberlain, both because of his position as a member of the Cabinet and because of his command of trenchant, insolent language. He launched his programme in a series of three January meetings, the first and the third in Birmingham, and the second at Ipswich. Amongst its principal features were manhood suffrage, the payment of members, small-holdings for agricultural labourers, a restriction of game-preserving, a drive for better working-class housing and the full recognition of the rights of local authorities to acquire land on fair terms. The impact of Chamberlain's speeches, however, owed as much to their form as to their substance. At Birmingham on January 5th he asked "what ransom will property pay?" At Ipswich, nine days later, he proclaimed: "We are told that this country is the paradise of the rich: it should be our task to see that it does not become the purgatory of the poor." And at Birmingham on January 29th he announced:" I hold that the sanctity of public property is greater even than that of private property, and that if it has been lost or wasted or stolen, some equivalent must be found for it and some compensation must be fairly exacted from the wrongdoer." The period in which the speeches were made was one in which politicians habitually used strong language against each other, but it was not one in which Cabinet ministers were expected to challenge the sanctity of private property. Chamberlain's words were accordingly received with a sharp thrill of horror. From Windsor to Hatfield and from Chatsworth to Hawarden the ruling figures of England recoiled from their purport. They saw in Chamberlain's appeal the threat of a direct class conflict at the centre of politics, and they did not like the prospect.

Gladstone wrote a letter which was courteous in form but which hinted strongly to Chamberlain that a continuance of his agitation would lead to trouble in Parliament, Whig replies and the possibility of a break-up of the Government. Chamberlain answered that he was quite ready to resign, and set off for London to see Dilke. Dilke approved of the Unauthorised Programme, but he did not want it used, at least at that stage, as a reason for radical resignations. He was anxious to complete his seats bill; furthermore, at a time when Gladstone's retirement from politics seemed imminent, he saw little sense in provoking an open quarrel with the G.O.M. and, in effect, handing over to the Whigs the political bones of the saint. He therefore advocated restraint, and was probably the more successful in so doing because of the arrival on February 5th of the news of the fall of Khartoum and the death of Gordon. On the one hand this diverted attention from Chamberlain's excursions and on the other made it more difficult for any minister to leave the Government. Resignation was abandoned, but the shadow of the Unauthorised Programme continued for the rest of the year to lie heavily upon the minds of both Whigs and Tories.

Despite this tactical difference Dilke and Chamberlain were still basically agreed, and in the spring they moved together towards a new approach to the Irish problem. For several months past Chamberlain had been negotiating through O'Shea for Parnell's acceptance, as a final settlement, of a scheme of advanced local government, under which a single national board would be responsible for most purely domestic Irish affairs. There would be no question of a separate parliament. It is now clear that Chamberlain and Parnell were never near to reaching a full agreement. The Irish leader was prepared to accept a national board as a step towards a parliament, and perhaps pay the price of a limited renewal of coercion, but he would not consider it as a final settlement. "But no man has the right to fix the boundary of the march of a nation," he had announced at Cork on January 21st. On there terms, Garvin has told us,[16] Chamberlain would not have been prepared to make an offer. He wanted the Irish vote for the Liberal party and he wanted it on a long-term basis, which a final settlement alone could secure. O'Shea, the inveterate go-between, succeeded not in smoothing out this difference, but in pretending that it did not exist. For several months he deceived Chamberlain into believing that agreement was near. And Chamberlain, in turn, passed on the false optimism to Dilke.[§]

In April the prospect seemed still brighter. Manning, who was anxious to overcome British Government opposition at the Vatican to Dr. Walsh, his candidate for the vacant archbishopric of Dublin, took a hand in affairs. He urgently requested an interview with Dilke. When it took place the Cardinal announced that he spoke on behalf of Archbishop Croke of Cashel, of Archbishop McEvilly of Tuam, and of five other Irish bishops who had all been staying with him on their way to Rome. They were unanimous in being prepared to accept Chamberlain's scheme and then "to denounce, not only separation, but also an Irish Parliament"; and they believed that they would be supported

---

§ This Garvin version is disputed by Henry Harrison in his polemical but often convincing *Parnell, Joseph Chamberlain and Mr. Garvin* (pp. 96–101). Harrison accepted O'Shea's untrustworthiness, but believed the objective evidence pointed strongly to Chamberlain being far more aware of Parnell's real state of mind than he subsequently admitted. Mr. Conor Cruise O'Brien (*Parnell and His Party*, p. 91) reserves judgment on the point. What is in any event clear is that Chamberlain and Dilke both believed at this stage in the possibility of a great step forward on Ireland.

by the whole Irish hierarchy. Further meetings between the Cardinal and Dilke took place. Then Chamberlain called at Archbishop's House, and so, later, did Parnell and Sexton. Everything seemed to be going well, and on May 8th Dilke wrote excitedly to Grant Duff: "Chamberlain and I have a big Irish Local Government scheme on hand, which is backed by the R.C. Bishops, and which may cither pacify Ireland or break up the Government."[17]

The next day the scheme was discussed in Cabinet. It was supported by the Prime Minister but opposed by Spencer and Carlingford and seemed more likely to wreck the Government than to settle Ireland. Harcourt, at first hostile, swung over to support, and the final alignment was that all the commoners except Hartington were in favour, and all the peers except Granville against. This was too indecisive a result for action, and the scheme was effectively shelved. The Prime Minister was not pleased with his Whig colleagues. "Within six years, if it pleases God to spare their lives," he said to Dilke on leaving the room, "they will be repenting in ashes."[18]

Despite this setback Dilke remained in the closest touch with Manning. The Cardinal dined at Sloane Street on May 13th, and on the 17th he was urgently requesting another meeting:

My dear Sir Charles,

The General Election is not far off, and I am very anxious to talk with you upon the point which will determine the Catholic vote. I seem to see a safe and open way. But no time (must) be lost. The Liberalism of England is not yet the aggressive Liberalism of the Continent, but it may become so, and then the breach with us and with Ireland will be irreparable. I am most anxious for all motives that you should avert this. Hitherto you have been safe: and you can keep so. I would come to you at the L.G.B. any day at 2 1/4 after to-morrow.

Believe me always yours very truly,

H. E. C. Archbp.[19]

The negotiation was already yielding dividends from the Cardinal's point of view, for Dr. Walsh's appointment as Archbishop of Dublin had been announced, Spencer's opposition being to some extent neutralised by Dilke's support.

Dilke then proceeded to behave with a similar but greater lack of judgment than that which he had resisted in Chamberlain at the end of January. The alternative which the Whigs put forward to Chamberlain's Irish scheme was another land purchase bill. The radicals were sceptical about the merits of this bill, and were in any event opposed to its introduction because this could be a symbol that the Government had chosen agrarian rather than constitutional reform. In conversation with Chamberlain on May 18th, however, the Prime Minister understood that the former would agree to a short-term land measure. On the afternoon of May 20th, Gladstone, without further consultation, announced to the House of Commons that this was his intention. Dilke heard the announcement and immediately resigned. Chamberlain was furious at Dilke's precipitate action, not entirely reasonably, for he had not informed Dilke of his conversation with Gladstone and he had previously both written and spoken to Dilke in favour of resignation. Despite his anger, Chamberlain decided to follow Dilke. He sent in his own resignation the same evening, and Shaw Lefevre, equally reluctantly, did the same.

Dilke may have been influenced by having received from Randolph Churchill, at dinner on May 17th, the first news that the Tory party would bid for the Irish vote by coming out against coercion. He no doubt realised then that the Irish stakes were to be substantially raised. Nevertheless, his choice of an issue on which to go was extraordinarily inept, and Chamberlain was right in seeing this. It was so inept, indeed, that the suspicion that Dilke's judgment had been temporarily clouded by personal worry cannot be avoided. Perhaps he had received another anonymous letter. Perhaps it was merely the general and slightly malicious stir to which the spreading news of his engagement was giving rise. "Pray do not vex yourself about the gossip here,"[20] Chamberlain had written to Mrs. Pattison on the day on which Randolph Churchill told Dilke of Lord Salisbury's Irish intentions.

Manning, who preferred his political friends to be ministers, was also opposed to Dilke's action.

> "No third party (is) possible at this moment," he wrote to him on May 26th. "Two parties and two parachutes will only make us (as) weak and useless as the French Chamber. The just demands of Ireland are a destiny to which Whig and Tory must give way. But if you and the like of you leave the Whigs they will fall back and unite in resisting you. So long as you are in contact with them they will yield to reason. These are the thoughts of an Old Testament Radical."¶[21]

¶ Dilke noted on this letter: "But the Old Testament Radical went on to make proposals to me with regard to the Roman Catholic vote in Chelsea which would have astonished the Old Testament prophets."

When Dilke received this letter he was in Dublin. His position there was ambiguous in two respects. In the first place he was half in and half out of the Government. The radical resignations were not generally known, and to all appearances Chamberlain (who had gone to Paris for a Whitsun holiday) and Dilke were still members of the Cabinet. Gladstone, who was also beset by a conditional resignation from his Chancellor of the Exchequer, felt unable for the moment to do more than put their letters into suspense. Secondly, Dilke was nominally in Ireland on Housing Commission business, but he was in fact more concerned in canvassing the Lord Lieutenant, his host at Vice-Regal Lodge, in favour of Chamberlain's scheme. His urgency became greater as the visit—the only one he ever paid to Ireland—proceeded. What he saw turned his mind increasingly towards a drastic constitutional solution. It was not the glowing prospect of a union of hearts which impressed him, but the utter hopelessness of the existing system.

"Early in the morning of Saturday, the 23rd," he wrote, "before the meeting of my Commission at the City Hall, I had had a long talk with Spencer, and I felt, more strongly than I ever had before, that his position in Dublin was untenable, and that he ought to be allowed to go. On Whit Sunday I attended church with Spencer, and in the afternoon took him for the only walk which he had enjoyed for a long time. We passed the spot where Lord Frederick Cavendish was killed, and accompanied by a single aide-de-camp, but watched at a distance by two policemen in plain clothes, and met at every street corner by two others, walked to the strawberry gardens, and on our return, it being a lovely Sunday when the Wicklow Mountains were at their best and the hawthorn in bloom, met thousands of Dublin people driving out to the strawberry gardens on cars. In the course of the whole long walk but one man lifted his hat to Spencer, who was universally recognised, but assailed by the majority of those we met with shouts of 'who killed Myles Joyce?'** while some varied the proceedings by calling 'murderer' after him. A few days later, when I was driving with Lady Spencer in an open carriage, a well-dressed bicyclist came riding through the cavalry escort, and in a quiet, conversational tone observed to us, 'who killed Myles Joyce?' At his dinner party on the Sunday evening Spencer told us that a Roman Catholic priest who was present . . . was the only priest in Ireland who would enter his walls, while the castle was boycotted by every Archbishop and Bishop. On Monday morning . . . I paid a visit to the Mansion House at the request of the Lord Mayor of Dublin, taking by Spencer's leave the Viceregal carriages there, where they had in his second Viceroyalty not been before, and was received by the Lord Mayor in state. . . ."[22]

Altogether it was not surprising that Dilke summed up his impressions by writing to Mrs. Pattison: "What a life is Spencer's—cut off from nearly the whole people—good and bad! What sense of duty, what high-mindedness, and what stupidity!"[23]

On May 27th Hartington arrived in Dublin, and Dilke had two Whigs instead of one with whom to argue. But Hartington

---

** Myles Joyce, aged eighteen, was amongst those hanged for the Maamtrasna murders. All the others died protesting his innocence.

was not a man for argument; after a few hours of it he pronounced himself suddenly ill and stayed in bed. Dilke left the following evening, slept on the boat in Kingstown Harbour, crossed on the Friday, spent a few days at Dockett Eddy, and returned to London on Tuesday, June 2nd, ready for the last week of the Government's life.

Rarely, if ever, can an Administration have been quite so ripe for its end. The death of Gordon and the proclamation of the Unauthorised Programme, while at first they tended to neutralise each other, were both in the longer run weakening factors. Then in the spring there was a crisis over Afghanistan. The Russians had recently annexed Turkestan and were engaged in a boundary dispute with the Amir, who was under British protection. On March 31st, the Russians broke in upon the Afghans at Penjdeh and heavily defeated them. Gladstone became suddenly bellicose, and for a time war seemed near. The Prime Minister was strongly supported in his firmness by Dilke, who knew a great deal more about the subject than any other minister, but not by Harcourt, and the issue became yet another cause of dissension within the Cabinet. At the beginning of May the Russians unexpectedly withdrew and the crisis was over. But by that time the Government was quarrelling hard about Ireland on the one hand and the Budget on the other. In the four weeks from the middle of April the Prime Minister received resignations in one form or another from no less than nine of his colleagues.

In the event, however, it was not the greater issue of Ireland but the lesser one of the Budget which precipitated the Government's end. When the Chancellor of the Exchequer had brought forward in March a proposal to increase the beer duty this had met with radical hostility, and Dilke had predicted that it would kill the Government. What the radicals wanted was an increase in direct taxation, as was suggested in the Unauthorised Programme, and when Childers offered the compromise of limiting the beer increase to one year and compensating by raising the wine duty, Dilke took the lead in resisting this also. He argued that it would cause needless trouble with the French, and carried with him all the Cabinet except for the Chancellor himself. The defeated Childers then offered his resignation and walked out of the room.

When the Finance Bill was presented to the House for second reading on June 8th it was without the wine proposal and the Government was almost without a Chancellor. His resignation had not been withdrawn, and his position was as indeterminate as that of Dilke and Chamberlain. The Cabinet was in no position to sustain a challenge. This came in the form of a reasoned amendment moved by Hicks Beach and regretting amongst other things the increased duty on beer without any corresponding increase on wine.

The Government case was argued by Childers, Dilke and Gladstone, but in vain. The division was taken at 2 a.m., and the Government was defeated, unexpectedly, by 12. The result was the first fruit of the Irish-Tory alliance. Thirty-nine Parnellites voted in the Opposition lobby, and proclaimed the result with shouts, not of "cheaper beer," but of "no coercion." But these votes alone would not have sufficed to defeat the Government. There were also six Liberals who voted for the amendment, and more than seventy, mostly radicals, who abstained or were absent unpaired.

The issues were confused and the cross-currents were numerous, but it was not possible to doubt that the Government had had its day. None of its members questioned this. At the Cabinet on the following day they reached a decision to resign with a speed and unanimity that they had shown on few other issues. There were a few more Cabinets to dispose of routine business, but by June 24th Lord Salisbury had kissed hands as head of a minority Government. On the same day Dilke left his office at the Local Government Board, having handed over to Arthur Balfour, the new President.

Chapter Ten

Mr. Gladstone's Successor?

Dilke Left office without regret. Partly this was because he was tired and had been complaining for the past month that he was without energy, although quite well. Mainly, however, it was because his political confidence was high. His ambition was unlimited and his prospects were far brighter than those of most ex-Cabinet ministers. First there was his status as a foreign affairs expert. His position in this respect was one which has rarely been paralleled in British politics. There was hardly an area of the world about which Dilke did not have detailed knowledge. When a dispute arose, perhaps about some small piece of territory, Dilke would know exactly where the frontier ran and what the terrain was like. He would know where the old frontier had been prior to the convention of 1837 and all the other diplomatic antecedents. In addition the leading statesmen on both sides of the dispute were likely to be familiar figures to him, as he would be to them. In France, in Germany, in Greece, in Russia, in Afghanistan, in Australia and in many other places his repute was far greater than could be accounted for by the ministerial offices which he had held.

The danger of such an excess of expertise is that it makes its possessor a glorified civil servant rather than a major politician. This was not a very pressing danger in Dilke's case. As the former leader of English republicanism and as the unshakable ally of Chamberlain, the most controversial figure in politics, he could hardly be accused of a bureaucratic preoccupation with facts as opposed to policies. He not only knew a lot, but he stood for definite objectives as well. He was a leader and not merely a political encyclopedia. As such he was something more than the best qualified candidate for the Foreign Office in another Gladstone ministry. Should the G.O.M. retire he was also a strong possibility for the leadership of the Liberal party. Disraeli's prophecy that Dilke would be Prime Minister, made more than five years before, had not become less likely with the passage of time.

But what made it likely? Why should an ex-President of the Local Government Board in a defeated Government, and a man moreover whom most people regarded as less forceful than his ally Chamberlain, view the future with especial optimism? The question needs to be answered on a number of different levels. First, what were the prospects of the early return of a Liberal Government? Here Dilke was completely confident. He regarded the Tory hold on power as slight, even with the temporary Irish alliance. There could be no elections until the late autumn when the new constituencies and electoral registers would be ready. These should ensure a Liberal victory at least as decisive as that of 1880. "We shall be in office again in January," Dilke wrote to Grant Duff on June 16th; and his prophecy was

241

to be true about his friends although not about himself.

Under whose leadership was such a Government likely to come in? Gladstone was seventy-five, and his retirement, which had been strongly rumoured for some time, was clearly made more probable by the end of his premiership. But Dilke, who in the previous winter would have been indifferent, had become suddenly convinced that a continuation of Gladstone's leadership was highly desirable. On the evening of the resignation of the Government he had proclaimed this in a much-publicised speech at a dinner of the City of London Liberal Club. The battle of the future must be won, he said," not only with his (Gladstone's) great name, but under his actual leadership." This faith did not prevent him, two weeks later, from engaging in one further brush with the G.O.M., about a baronetcy conferred upon Errington, the unofficial representative of the Foreign Office at the Vatican. Dilke regarded this honour as a highly undesirable public expression of the late Government's gratitude for Errington's activities against Dr. Walsh, and threatened in consequence to withdraw from his seat on the Front Opposition Bench and sit below the gangway. But the terms in which he withdrew his threat were significant.

> ". . . (Harcourt) tells me that you have accepted a proposal to stand again for Midlothian," he wrote to Gladstone on June 29th. "This is so great a thing that smaller ones must not be allowed to make even small discords, so please put my letter of Saturday in the fire, and forgive me for having put you to the trouble of reading and replying to it."[1]

Dilke's new-found enthusiasm for Gladstone's leadership was probably due more to Ireland than to anything else, to his conviction that a quick solution had become essential, and to a final impatience, as a result of the negotiations of the spring, with the perpetual delaying tactics of Hartington and the Whigs. "There is no liking for Ireland or the Irish," he had also told Grant Duff in his letter of June 16th, "but an almost universal feeling now that some form of Home Rule must be tried. My own belief is that it will be tried too late, as all our remedies have been."[2] Dilke thought that Gladstone's new mood on Ireland offered the best chance of driving hard enough to avoid this fatal delay. And if the "almost universal feeling" did not extend quite far enough for all the Whigs to accept this hard driving, there would be some advantages in that. He was a shrewd enough tactician to see that Gladstone was an invaluable ally in the battle against Hartington. The Unauthorised Programme could obviously not be implemented until the Whigs were driven out of the Liberal party. But this could be accomplished more safely under Gladstone than by Dilke and Chamberlain; and once it was done the way would be open, when Gladstone came to retire, which it was thought could not in any event be long delayed, both for the radical programme and for radical leadership.

Even if this tactic failed, however, and Gladstone handed over to Hartington, there would still be great strength in the radical position. Hartington would probably have to compensate for his own whiggery by giving the highest posts, next to the premiership, to his radical colleagues. Indeed, at the time of Gladstone's rumoured retirement in the previous January, Dilke had been informed by Harcourt that it was Hartington's intention to offer him the Foreign Office and Chamberlain the Exchequer.[3] Admittedly this was before the launching of the Unauthorised Programme, but as Hartington's appointments

243

would have been dictated by the need for a balance of power rather than by love of the radicals, there is no reason to suppose that he would have made less generous offers at a later stage. Dilke and Chamberlain were likely to possess the same paradoxical power in his Cabinet which the Whig magnates had enjoyed under Gladstone. Nor would even the Foreign Office and the Exchequer be the limit of their possible advance. Hartington was an indolent man; and it might well be that after a short period of leading liberalism from the extreme right he would find the strain too great and throw in the Whig hand. In this event the way would be equally wide open to a radical leadership.

Both in these circumstances, and in those of Gladstone forcing Hartington out of the Liberal party before his own retirement, a choice between Chamberlain and Dilke would have had to be made. In retrospect Chamberlain looks the more obvious candidate. His speeches were more memorable; he was the favourite of the constituencies; and he had broken more new political ground with the Unauthorised Programme than Dilke had ever done. In fact, however, Dilke was the more likely choice. He had far fewer enemies; he would have been more acceptable to Gladstone; and he was on much better terms with Whigs, Tories and neutral "establishment" opinion. Whether consciously or not he had outflanked Chamberlain to the right during the previous winter, but he had done it without impairing his own radical credentials. The negotiation of the seats bill was a far better preparation for an early premiership than the proclamation of the Unauthorised Programme.

This position was recognised by one significant development which occurred immediately after the fall of the Government. The radicals of Cabinet rank—Dilke, Chamberlain, Trevelyan,

Shaw Lefevre and Morley—decided to meet in regular conclave. This "cabal," as they referred to it, assembled as often as twice a week and concerned itself both with the issues of day-to-day politics and with longer-term radical strategy. The meetings had been suggested by Chamberlain, but they were all presided over by Dilke. Furthermore, at least according to Dilke's own testimony,[4] Chamberlain at this stage recognised the fact that Dilke would be a more acceptable leader than he would be himself, and suggested an agreement with Dilke to this end. In addition, Dilke tells us, Gladstone expressed a clear wish that Dilke should be the future leader. Altogether, at midsummer, 1885, Dilke's prospects of becoming Prime Minister were almost as good as those of anyone who is neither the leader of his party nor a universally acclaimed crown prince can ever be.

With this future to contemplate, his life in the six weeks or so after the resignation of the Government was agreeable and relaxed. He had no lack of things to do. He became more socially active and went out a great deal. He dined often at Grillion's. He spent long and frequent days on the Thames, either at Dockett or at the houses of friends. He presided at the concluding meetings of the Housing Commission. And he tried to complete his plans for a visit with Chamberlain to the Roman Catholic bishops and archbishops in Ireland, in order to discover, in direct discussion, what were their real wishes.* These plans went awry, but this was a matter of much greater moment to Chamberlain than to Dilke.

---

* The Anglican Dilke and the erstwhile Unitarian Chamberlain consistently over-estimated the power of the Roman Catholic hierarchy in Irish politics.

Manning had promised introductions, but with the change of Government and the unfolding of the new Conservative policy, he grew cool. "What am I to do?" the prince of the church wrote to Dilke on June 25th. "I am afraid of your Midlothian in Ireland. How can I be godfather to Hengist and Horsa?"[5] Dilke was disappointed, but allowed himself neither to quarrel with the Cardinal nor to be deflected from his plan. He tried to secure the introductions from the new Archbishop of Dublin, and Dr. Walsh responded to the extent of writing two encouraging letters. But the reaction of the nationalist press to the proposed visit was hostile in the extreme. "We plainly tell Messrs. Chamberlain and Dilke that if they are wise, they will keep out of our country . . ." was the advice of *United Ireland*.[6] In the authoritative opinion of Mr. Conor Cruise O'Brien, the current of anti-radicalism, always important in Irish politics, was at this time running strongly and close to the surface. Archbishop Walsh was infected by the prevailing mood, and soon withdrew from his attitude of welcome. At the end of July he wrote to say that he, too, could give no introductions, as such an action would be interpreted as hostile to "the excellent tenor and promise of Lord Carnarvon's Conservative regime."[7] By this time Dilke was too concerned with other matters to care, but Chamberlain, always more prickly, was bitterly affronted. He had finished with Irish nationalism. He believed himself to have been deceived by Parnell in the negotiations of the early spring, and to have been spurned by the Church and the popular press in his overtures of the summer. These experiences led on directly to a new note of hard hostility to Ireland, which he struck in his Warrington speech of September 8th, and to his subsequent actions.

Dilke, even before his attention was distracted, reacted less sharply to these rebuffs than did Chamberlain. He never expected to be acclaimed as a hero by the Irish people, and he was consequently less disappointed when difficulties arose. In any event he had much else to occupy his mind. On June 30th he wrote to Mrs. Pattison a strange disquisition upon the subject of power in politics. After some rather conventional remarks about the unattractiveness for him of the minutiae of the game, he continued:

> "It is in old age that power comes. It is possible for an old man in English politics to exert enormous power without effort, and with but little call upon his time, and no drain at all upon his health and vital force. The work of thirty or more years of political life goes in England to the building up of a political reputation and position. During that period no power is exercised except by irregular means, such as the use of threats of resignation. It is in old age only that power comes that can be used legitimately and peacefully by the once strong man."[8]

When he wrote these words Dilke was more than half-way through the long journey to full power, but he was never to reap the rewards which he saw ahead of him. In the third week of July his career was shattered. He was struck by a blow from which he never recovered.

The week had begun well enough. The Sunday he spent on the river at Dockett. On the Monday he presided at his Royal Commission and dined at Grillion's. Later in the week he went to parties at Lady Salisbury's, at the Austrian Embassy and at the Duchess of Westminster's. He had a meeting about electoral organisation with Harcourt and Chamberlain. On the Friday evening he gave the last of his major political dinner parties at 76, Sloane Street. On the Saturday morning he presided at a meeting of the "cabal." On the Saturday evening the Reform Club paid him the unusual compliment of organising a banquet in his honour, to congratulate him upon the passing into law of the redistribution bill. The former Lord Advocate proposed the principal toast.

He returned home late, with the intention of going next morning to Taplow Court for another quiet day upon the river. But this Sunday, July 19th, was not to be a quiet one. At Sloane Street on the Saturday evening there awaited him a note from Mrs. Rogerson, a close friend, asking him to call on the following morning as she had some grave information to give him. He went early and learned that Mrs. Donald Crawford, the sister of his brother's widow, had announced to her husband that, soon after her marriage, Dilke had become her lover; and that Crawford, in consequence, was proposing to sue for divorce, and to name Dilke as the co-respondent.

Chapter Eleven

Mrs. Crawford Intervenes

I t would be difficult to exaggerate the seriousness for Dilke of the charge. Divorce, other than by private Act of Parliament, had been possible in England only since 1857, and during this twenty-eight year period there had been no case involving a prominent politician. The nearest parallel had been the Mordaunt case of 1870, in which the Prince of Wales had been cited as a co-respondent. This case, indeed, bore some striking resemblances to the Crawford case, as will emerge later. Lady Mordaunt, aged twenty-one, had made a confession to her husband shortly after the birth of her first child. "Charlie, you are not the father of that child," she had said according to her husband's court evidence; "Lord Cole is the father of it, and I am the cause of its blindness." Sir Charles Mordaunt's account continued: "She sat silent for a quarter of an hour, then burst into tears and said, 'Charlie, I have been very wicked; I have done very wrong.' I said, 'Who with?' She said, 'With Lord Cole, the Prince of Wales and others, often, and in open day.'"[1] Lady Mordaunt, however, was declared mad by her father and a number of doctors. This, combined with the Prince appearing in the witness-box and denying on oath that there had ever been anything improper in his association with her—a denial which was greeted with a burst of applause in the court—resulted in the husband losing his case.[*] But the incident did the Prince's reputation a great deal of harm, and was one of the factors, ironically enough, which made it possible for Dilke to mount his republican offensive of the following year.

Earlier there had been cases, not involving divorce, but touching a politician as prominent as Lord Melbourne. Melbourne had twice appeared in the courts, once while Prime Minister, and had denied, with legal success if not with complete public acceptance, allegations concerning his relationship with Lady Branden (an Irish peeress) and Mrs. George Norton. But the 'eighties were a different decade from the 'thirties. The Court had become much more puritanical, and, more important for Dilke, middle-class nonconformity had become an essential ally of the Liberal party. When the Parnell case broke five years later, Gladstone, Harcourt and Morley forced the Irish party to renounce its leader, not because they were shocked by his adulterous relationship with Mrs. O'Shea, of which they had known for at least seven years, but because of the feelings of the National Liberal Federation, which was in session at Sheffield, and the thunderings of the Rev. Hugh Price Hughes.

Quite apart from any changes in the moral climate, however, Dilke's position was much more vulnerable than Melbourne's

---

[*] Nevertheless, Mordaunt was successful in another petition five years later, when Lord Cole was cited as the sole co-respondent.

had been. To many people he was still a dangerous radical, and an ally of that even more objectionable politician, Chamberlain. If he could be ruined what a blow it would be to the left-wing forces in the Liberal party and how much less potent would appear the dreadful doctrines which Chamberlain had enunciated in the Unauthorised Programme. This was the reasoning of many people who, in other circumstances, would have been Dilke's natural defenders against the moralists. Furthermore, the Queen and her entourage were most willing to take the blackest view of his actions. Even before the charges were made she had received him into the Cabinet only with the greatest reluctance. How right she had been! How gratifying to discover that radical views and a republican past were associated with the blackest moral turpitude. No doubt the Queen would have looked askance at anyone who had become involved in divorce court proceedings, but she would have been a good deal more inclined to make excuses for, say, Hartington than for Dilke.

There was another factor which made the charge against Dilke unusually damaging—still more so, for example, than that which was to be made against Parnell. This was the nature of Mrs. Crawford's accusations. These would have done a great deal of harm to the most unassailable of politicians in the most tolerant of decades. They were made to her husband on the night of Friday, July 17th, 1885.[†] He arrived home at their London lodgings, then in George Street, Bryan-ston Square, at

---

[†] The account which follows is a summary of the evidence which Donald Crawford gave in the divorce court on February 12th, 1886. Whatever view is taken of the other parties to the case there is not the slightest reason to believe that Crawford did not tell the truth according to the best of his recollection.

about 11.30 that night, and found a letter waiting for him. It was anonymous—one of a series which he had received[‡]—and in the following terms: "Fool, looking for the cuckoo when he has flown, having defiled your nest. You have been vilely deceived, but you dare not touch the real traitor."

Crawford then went to his bedroom where his wife was waiting for him. She asked if he had received the letter and what were its contents. He told her, and then said: "Virginia, is it true that you have defiled my bed? I have been a faithful husband to you." She replied: "Yes, it is true, it is time that you should know the truth. You have always been on the wrong track, suspecting people who are innocent, and you have never suspected the person who is guilty." Crawford answered: "I never suspected anybody except Captain Forster," and Mrs. Crawford replied: "It was not Captain Forster. The man who ruined me was Charles Dilke."

She then related how, a few months after their marriage in 1881, when she was aged eighteen, Dilke had called upon her at Bailey's Hotel in the Gloucester Road, where they were staying

---

‡ The first of these, received as long ago as the spring of 1882, began by warning Crawford that his wife who, with her sister, was visiting the latter's husband in St. George's Hospital, had "been carrying on flirtations" with the students there. It concluded, on a quite different tack, with the words: "Beware of the member for Chelsea." The second anonymous letter reached Crawford in March, 1885. It told him that his wife was Dilke's mistress, that she was a frequent visitor to 76, Sloane Street and was known to the servants there; it gave, in fact, most of the details of her subsequent confession. The third was received in June of the same year and referred to Mrs. Crawford having lunched with a Captain Forster at the Hotel Métropole.

after their wedding trip.[§] On this occasion "he made love to me and kissed me but nothing more." There was no further meeting until the following February, because the Crawfords were away in Scotland. On their return, however, Dilke again called upon Mrs. Crawford, this time at a house in Sydney Place, Chelsea, which they had taken for the session. In the course of this call (on February 23rd, 1882) he persuaded her to meet him that afternoon at a house "off Tottenham Court Road." There they spent about an hour together, and she became Dilke's mistress. Their liaison continued, Mrs. Crawford said, for two and a half years, until the summer of 1884, although in a somewhat spasmodic way. She went only once again to the house near Tottenham Court Road, but in February, 1883, when she came to London from Scotland before her husband, she spent two nights in Dilke's Sloane Street house, returning home on one morning at 4 o'clock and on the other at 7–30. In addition there were frequent but brief adulterous meetings, both at Sloane Street and at the Crawfords' rented house in Young Street, Kensington, during the sessions of 1883 and 1884. These meetings took place between eleven and twelve in the mornings and lasted sometimes half an hour and sometimes an hour. In Sloane Street she mounted to Dilke's bedroom, but in Young Street they remained in the drawing-room. In the late summer of 1884, Mrs. Crawford said, Dilke tired of her and their clandestine meetings ceased, although they saw each other occasionally at family tea parties during the following autumn. She admitted that she had been "too familiar" with other men, including Captain Forster, but

---

[§] Some of the details of this "confession" were supplied to Crawford, not on the night of July 17th, but two days later when he interviewed his wife at the house of her sister, where she was then staying.

solemnly denied that she had committed adultery with anyone other than Dilke. About Captain Forster she was quite specific. "He had always treated her like a lady," and, less ambiguously, he was not and never had been her lover.

This was the skeleton of Mrs. Crawford's confession; but she embellished it with a number of details which contributed greatly to the sensationalism of the case. She said that Dilke's hold over her was such that, had he come into the room while she was making the confession, "I believe I should have to do whatever he pleased." She announced that he had told her that he was first attracted by her likeness to her mother, whose lover he had been many years before. She described how, at Sloane Street, she used to be dressed by a maid named Sarah whose silence was thought to be guaranteed by her status as an old mistress of Dilke's. She told how Mrs. Rogerson—also, she implied, a former mistress of Dilke's—had at his instigation gradually become a confidante of hers. And, most sensationally of all, she described the role of "Fanny." Fanny, she said, was a servant-girl of about her own age who, Dilke told her, used to spend almost every night with him at Sloane Street. Dilke, Mrs. Crawford said, was most anxious to see both herself and Fanny together. After one or two unsuccessful attempts to introduce Fanny into the room while she was there, her resistance was overcome and they all three shared the same bed. "He taught me every French vice," Mrs. Crawford added. "He used to say that I knew more than most women of thirty."

Dilke became aware of the greater part of Mrs. Crawford's story on the morning of Sunday, July 19th, at Mrs. Rogerson's. His informant had seen Mrs. Crawford on the previous day, after she had finally left her husband's house, and had obtained her version of what had happened. "19th. Early. Heard of charge against me," was Dilke's laconic diary entry. But he had no doubt of the seriousness of the threat to his whole future. He behaved, however, with surprising composure. First, he established contact with J. B. Balfour, the former Lord Advocate, Crawford's chief and the proposer of his own health at the Reform Club banquet on the previous evening. He arranged to meet him on the following afternoon. Then he took a train from Paddington and fulfilled his plans for spending the day at Taplow Court. While there he wrote two letters to Mrs. Pattison. They afford our best glimpses into his state of mind on that day. It should be remembered that the mail to India then took six weeks, and that they were not intended to break the news; a telegram sent by Chamberlain in the following week was to perform this task.

"The blow long threatened in the wicked letters has fallen at last," Dilke wrote in one of his letters. "The instrument chosen by the conspirators is Donald Crawford. . . . I shall at once leave public life for ever after doing everything that can be done through the late Lord Advocate whose secretary he was and who is very fond of him to stop it . . . In my belief the conspiracy comes from a woman who wanted me to marry her—but this is guesswork. I only know that there is conspiracy, from one of two women, perhaps from both."[2]

The other letter was still more despairing, at least about his political prospect.

"The only thing I can do in future," he wrote, "is to devote myself entirely to you and to helping in your work. To that the remainder of my life must be dedicated. I fancy you will

255

have the courage to believe me, whatever is by madness and malevolence brought against me, and to live a lifelong exile with me, which *if you can do at all* will be a dream of happiness. You may be ill when you get my telegrams— and they may kill you! I don't think ever man was so unhappy as (I) and the only ray of hope is that you may be willing to believe (me) whatever happens."[3]

On the Monday Dilke was back in London. He saw first Chamberlain and told him the whole story. He next called on J. B. Balfour, whom he asked to arrange for an independent, private investigation of the charges to be carried out by a commission of two, one being a friend of Crawford and the other a friend of Dilke. Balfour said that he would consult Crawford about the proposal and let Dilke have an answer in the course of a few days. Meanwhile Chamberlain had been to see James, the former Attorney-General, and had arranged for him to advise Dilke and, should this become necessary, to conduct the case. On the Tuesday morning, however, whether with or without James's consent, Dilke took a further and most unwise step. At nine o'clock—his habits had become earlier since the blow had fallen—he went, "boiling with rage" to use his own phrase, to his sister-in-law's house and demanded to see Mrs. Crawford. What took place then is in dispute. Mrs. Ashton Dilke said that he tried to bribe her sister into arranging a quiet separation from her husband without a divorce. Dilke denied this and said that he merely pointed out that Mrs. Crawford was telling lies and demanded that she withdraw the charges against him. What is common ground, however, is that at this interview he tried and failed to obtain a written retraction from his accuser. On the Wednesday he was informed that Crawford had refused the private enquiry suggested through Balfour.

These two setbacks reduced Dilke to a state of near despair.

"You always said that that family would lead us to shame," he wrote to Mrs. Pattison in a letter which he finished on Friday, July 24th, but which he had begun earlier in the week. "You could not have guessed to what shame. I believe I shall have to let the Crawford suit at the last moment go without defence, on condition that nothing is said, because otherwise they not only *press* the adultery with the mother . . . (but also) a mass of other charges supported by conspiracy and perjured evidence. Mrs. Cd. has got up my bedroom (!!!) having gone over it with Mrs. Chatfield I find! It is madness, but I will do my very best for us. I believe your love can forgive even shame and exile. 76 (Sloane Street) must be got rid of after you have cleared out the things from it. I can't see it again after this thing gets out, which may be to-day. . . . Chamberlain is very dear. He is writing to you."[4]

In the same mood of renunciation and resignation Dilke, on the Thursday, walked out of the House of Commons.

"Left for the last time the H. of C.," he recorded in his diary, "in which I have obtained some distinction. It is curious that only a week ago Chamberlain and I had agreed at his wish that I should be the future leader, that only three days ago Mr. G. had expressed the same wish. A sudden fall, indeed! Such a charge—even if disproved—which is not easy against perjured evidence picked up with care, is fatal to supreme usefulness in politics. In the case of a public man a charge is always believed by many, even tho'

257

disproved, and I should be weighted by it throughout life. I prefer therefore to at once contemplate leaving public life for ever."[5]

By the beginning of the following week Dilke's morale had improved a little. Partly, perhaps, this was due to the mere passage of time, and partly, also, to the fact that the hurdle of publication had been surmounted. Lord Granville, for example, on the news becoming known, had written an agreeable little letter, which while it did not express quite the burning faith in his innocence which Dilke was later to demand, was at least comfortingly tolerant. "Do not be too much discouraged," Granville had written. "After all you are not the Archbishop of Canterbury and continuous action on public affairs will soon cause a nine-day wonder to be forgotten."[6] And Dilke replied, on Monday, July 27th: "Things look better and I am quite well again."[7] Two days later—on what evidence it is not clear—he wrote again to Granville, in still more optimistic terms: "Your kind letter prompts me to tell you that the lady has changed her mind and declares that her 'confession' was hysterics, and as there never was or could be anything else in the charge but this so-called 'confession,' I hardly see how the gentleman can go on—though he still believes it, I am told."[8] But while it is true that Mrs. Crawford was hesitating a good deal at this stage as to what she should say and what she should sign, she never committed herself to such a withdrawal.

On Thursday, July 30th, Dilke went to Birmingham to stay

[¶] At the side of this last comment Dilke noted, many years later: "Chamberlain overpersuaded Hoya (Mrs. Pattison) and through her me, but he was wrong."

at Highbury. Chamberlain was not only "very dear," but had also abandoned some meetings at Hull in order to take him there. The first part of the visit was brief, for on August 3rd Chamberlain took Dilke back to London and made him attend the House of Commons for a week and speak in the debates on the Housing of the Working Classes Bill. While in London Dilke received some bad news—Crawford's divorce petition was filed on August 5th[**]—and some encouraging letters. John Morley wrote to say that ". . . whatever the result may be you will find that a good many of us shall stand firm by you. You have been a staunch friend, and it would be a shame if you were not to find others as staunch to you. If anything happens amiss to you, it will be as unfortunate a thing for English Liberalism as any contingency that I can imagine—let that other be what it may."[9] There was also a warm letter from Cardinal Manning asking if he could call at Sloane Street; Dilke readily acceded to this request, and claimed that when the visit took place he told the Cardinal "everything," a claim which was to some extent borne out by a letter which Manning wrote several years later.[††]

[**] T. M. Healy recounts in his memoirs that, before this stage was reached, Gladstone tried, through Labouchere, to buy Crawford off. Crawford proved unyielding, but Labouchere, always generous with invention, reported to Gladstone that he wanted a judgeship. "A Scottish judgeship, I presume," Gladstone replied; but on being told that it was an English judgeship which was required was undismayed. "Can any good reason be brought forward against his being made an English judge?" was the G.O.M.'s next answer, as he contemplated the possibility of a bargain. (Healy, *Letters and Leaders of My Day*, I, p. 215.) The story is uncorroborated from any other source.

[††] See *infra* p. 368.

Meanwhile Mrs. Pattison had received the news at Ootaca-mund in the Madras Hills, where she was convalescent from a severe attack of typhoid fever. She related that Mrs. Grant Duff brought the opened telegram in to her saying: "Of course this must be Mrs. Smith's doing."[10] Despite the nature of the news and the state of her health Mrs. Pattison reacted defiantly. Immediately and on her own responsibility she telegraphed to *The Times* the news of her engagement to Dilke. The announcement duly appeared on August 18th: "We are requested to announce that a marriage is arranged between the Right Hon. Sir Charles Dilke, M.P., and Mrs. Mark Pattison, widow of the late Rector of Lincoln College, Oxford."

This development produced a fresh crop of letters to Dilke. There was one from the Prince of Wales, whom Dilke had informed privately before the announcement (and who was later to join Manning amongst those to whom "everything" was told), which referred to the Prince's "trust that the painful ordeal you have lately had to undergo may soon be a thing of the past."[11] There was also a letter from Rosebery, which Dilke gave to Bodley, having noted upon it: "Perhaps we had better keep this of Rosebery's, because *she* is odd as you know."[12] Gladstone also wrote, several weeks later, offering his congratulations but making no reference to the divorce case. To this letter Dilke added the slightly aggrieved comment: "He's gone on writing about business until now without saying anything."[13]

These letters Dilke received at Highbury, where he had returned with Chamberlain on August 13th. He stayed there with a short break until the middle of September. Life in Birmingham involved a routine of almost breathless sporting activity, although Chamberlain himself, whose attitude to exercise was always hostile, participated only occasionally. Dilke described the pattern in letters to Mrs. Pattison.

"I rise at 8 with my letters," he wrote on August 28th. "Breakfast with Austen at 8–30. Write letters. 10–15, Boxing lesson with Austen. 10–45, Fence with rapiers, 11, Fence with foils. Dress in breeches. 11–30, Ride with Austen. . . . After lunch we have some pistol shooting and some lawn tennis, and then I get to work on the Local Government Bill."[14]

Another letter contained a similar account with mild deprecatory references to Chamberlain's lack of participation and general grandeur. "Breakfast with Austen at 8–30 (J. King does not get up till much later)," it ran. . . after lunch I play tennis with the King in person—I sett (*sic*) is all he will do."[15] This regime did much to restore Dilke's physical health and something to restore his equanimity. His weight, which had fallen from 13 stone 13 to 12 stone 4 in the fortnight after he had received the news of Mrs. Crawford's action, quickly went back to normal. But he remained subject to neurotic fears. He was afraid that his letters to Mrs. Pattison, who by now was on her way home from India, would be intercepted and used in some obscure way against him. He wrote to Aden, but with apprehension. Perhaps the Crawfords would obtain possession of the letter and use it for the basis of a libel action. He wrote to Naples, but only after great doubt that, if he addressed it care of the ship it might not be sent on board, and if he sent it *Poste Restante* she might not have time to go and fetch it. He wrote to Marseilles, where she was to disembark, but only after making most elaborate arrangements for his Toulon gardener to collect the letter from friends who kept the *Buffet de la Gare* and take it to the ship.

During the same period, however, he was able to write calmly and almost confidently to Cardinal Manning, and even with Mrs. Pattison herself to engage in quite a sensible discussion of his longer-term plans. Austen Chamberlain, writing many years afterwards, commented on Dilke's self-control while at Highbury during that summer. ". . . he showed me *nothing* of what he was suffering," Austen wrote, ". . . and at meal times he delighted me with talk of foreign politics, of France, French history and customs, so that he left on my mind the memory of a most inter-esting companion." Austen Chamberlain went on to testify to his recollection of his father's "anguish of mind" on Dilke's behalf at this time, and to his conviction, based both on memory and on a subsequent reading of contemporary letters to Morley,‡‡ that Joseph Chamberlain was absolutely convinced of the falseness of Mrs. Crawford's charges.[16]

In the middle of September Dilke crossed to Paris to await the arrival of Mrs. Pattison. There had been some dispute as to whether, in the circumstances, the wedding had not better be celebrated in France than in England. Eventually Chamberlain came down decisively in favour of a marriage in London. The original plan of a ceremony in the cathedral at Oxford had been abandoned, and Chelsea parish church was substituted. They were married there on October 3rd, Dilke having returned from

---

‡‡ Perhaps the most significant of these was in the following terms: "F. Harrison's sources of information are tainted. Please tell him from me for what it is worth that I am *certain* Dilke is innocent of the charge brought against him. I do not answer for his whole life—nor for my own—nor for any man's—but the particular charge and its accompaniments are false." (Letter written on October 22nd, 1885, and quoted in Garvin, *op. cit.*, Vol. II, p. 45.)

Paris two days before, and Mrs. Pattison having followed him twenty-four hours later. Chamberlain was best man, but in other respects the ceremony was as austere as Dilke's first marriage, nearly fourteen years before.

After the wedding the Dilkes did not use 76, Sloane Street for some time. They went first to the Oatlands Park Hotel, near Weybridge, and remained there, except for occasional visits to London (during one of which they stayed, a little strangely, at Bailey's Hotel) until the beginning of November. They then returned to Sloane Street and Dilke began his election campaign. His constituents had remained friendly, and he found it possible to abandon the earlier plan, by which, if the case should not have been heard when the campaign began, the chairman of his local Liberal Association should fight in his stead. His meetings were well attended and enthusiastic, and the result satisfactory. Under Dilke's own redistribution act Chelsea had become a one-member seat with its boundaries roughly the same as those of the present constituency. In those days there were proportionately many more working-class electors within these boundaries than there are to-day. The new borough, therefore, offered Dilke a fair radical prospect, although it was a seat which he would have done well to win even without the complication of the divorce suit.[§§] He had shed the Tory wastes of South Kensington, but he had also lost the electorally more encouraging areas of Hammersmith and Kensal Green.

Furthermore, the big towns—particularly London, Liverpool

[§§] At this stage the details of Mrs. Crawford's confession were not generally known. What had been published was that Crawford was suing his wife and citing Dilke as co-respondent.

263

and Manchester—swung heavily against Gladstone at this election. A few days before the beginning of the campaign, Parnell, after several weeks of hesitation, decided that he preferred the prospect held out by Lord Salisbury's Newport speech to that which emerged from Mr. Gladstone's tortuous Hawarden letter-writing, and instructed the Irish in England to vote against the Liberals. This decision is generally thought to have swung up to forty urban seats to the Tories. In the counties the movement was the other way. The newly enfranchised electors were not much interested in Ireland, and they went mostly for the party which had given them the vote. On balance, however, the Liberals emerged from the election in a weaker position than they had achieved in 1880. Then they had 347 seats and an absolute majority of 42 over any possible alliance of Conservatives and Irishmen. In 1885 they had 335 seats, which was enough to equal, but not to surpass, the combined Tory and Parnellite vote. In Chelsea, Dilke polled 4,291 against 4,116 for his Conservative opponent.

This result was declared on November 25th. Some of the others dragged on until the third week in December. But the general pattern was clear by the beginning of the month and a most complicated manoeuvring for position then set in.

During the week-end of December 5th-7th the radicals—Chamberlain, Dilke, Shaw Lefevre and Morley—met in conclave at Highbury. Chamberlain was in a difficult mood. He had brooded over his grievances against the Irish for six months, he was disappointed and embittered by the result of the election (which added to his anti-Irish feeling), and he felt no glimmer of loyalty towards Gladstone. Indeed his opportunist pro-Gladstone feeling, which he had shared with Dilke during the previous summer, had largely evaporated by the early autumn.

Correspondence in September convinced him that Gladstone would never accept the greater part of the radical programme. Furthermore, the G.O.M. was becoming much too preoccupied with Ireland for Chamberlain's post-Warrington taste. These suspicions were not lessened when Gladstone unexpectedly summoned Chamberlain to spend a few days with him at Hawarden in early October.¶ The visit was not a great success, for both the habits of life and methods of thought of the two men were too dissimilar for easy contact. It ended without Gladstone having confided his new thoughts about Ireland to his guest.

When the radical cabal assembled, therefore, Chamberlain's mood was one of unwillingness to promote a third Gladstone premiership. He thought it better for the Liberals to sort out their differences in opposition than to take office dependent upon Irish votes. Indeed he had written to Dilke a week before saying, "I should like the Tories to be in for a couple of years before we try again, and then I should 'go for the Church.'"¹⁷ This offered no basis for agreement at Highbury. No one except Chamberlain himself wanted to hitch the radical wagon to the star of disestablishment, and Morley at least was preparing to give enthusiastic support to Gladstone's Irish policy.

Dilke, however, was moved by the Highbury discussions to give public expression in an extreme form to the Chamberlain view. On December 12th he addressed the Eleusis Club in

----

¶ G. W. E. Russell, who had been a junior minister under Dilke at the Local Government Board, first suggested that the invitation should be sent. He recorded that Gladstone "could not have looked more amazed if I had suggested inviting the Pope or the Sultan." (*Cornhill Magazine*, Sept., 1914.)

Chelsea and argued strongly, on radical grounds, in the favour of keeping the Tories in. This meant shelving Gladstone, and it directly provoked a counter move from the leader's camp. Gladstone himself remained isolated at Hawarden, but on December 14th Herbert Gladstone went to London and, on his own initiative, announced to the press his father's conversion to Home Rule. This flying of the "Hawarden Kite," as it was known, was directly attributed to Dilke's speech, and further exacerbated Gladstone-Chamberlain relations. By the turn of the year Chamberlain had come down still more decidedly in opposition to his nominal leader. "For myself I would sooner the Tories were in for the next ten years," he wrote to Dilke on December 27th, "than agree to what I think the ruin of the country."[18]

What accounts for the sudden switch of the radicals between the summer when they wanted to keep Gladstone because he could deal with Ireland, and the autumn when they wanted to get rid of him for the same reason? In Dilke's case it was not due to a sharp revulsion from Home Rule. Indeed he subsequently attributed his Eleusis Club speech to his failure to realise "how far Mr. Gladstone was willing to go in the Home Rule direction" and to a consequent underestimate of the chances of "securing the real support of the Irish party."[19] This was an *ex post facto* explanation, although supported by the facts that at the Eleusis Club Dilke went rather too far for Chamberlain, but that six days later, when he had seen the "Hawarden Kite" and knew of an even more decisive letter which Gladstone had written to Hartington, he did not go far enough. In this second speech Dilke announced "that we ought not to allow ourselves to be driven either forward or backward from the principles we have put forward with regard to Ireland, and that our course should be to continue to propose the measures which we had previously proposed without reference to the Parnellite support of conservative candidates."[20] This earned from Chamberlain the cool comment: "Your own speech was most judicious."

Chamberlain was able to carry Dilke with him in his fear that Gladstone's obsession with the Irish problem might lead to the formation of a purely "Home Rule" government which would have no time for constructive radicalism at home, but not in his growing opposition to Home Rule as such.

What emerges most clearly from their interchanges of this period, however, is not the extent to which Dilke was in agreement or disagreement with Chamberlain but the collapse of his influence. This was partly because he was not consulted by the leadership. Gladstone, who in the previous few years had conducted most of his negotiations with the radical wing through Dilke, began to deal with Chamberlain instead. In the early autumn correspondence between Hawarden and Highbury had become much more frequent, even if not noticcably more inti mate; but this led more to misunderstanding than to a meeting of minds.

Much of the decline in Dilke's influence, however, came less from the actions of others than from the growth of his own abstraction. He had always been a less profuse letter-writer than Chamberlain, but this had never previously made him a passive participant in the correspondence. It had been his habit to return hard, sharp answers, forcibly expressing his own point of view. But from the letters of this autumn there emerges the impression of a flood of tentative views from Chamberlain breaking over the head of an almost indifferent Dilke. The importance of this can hardly be exaggerated. With Dilke either indifferent or making occasional rather thoughdess interventions—as at the Eleusis Club—Chamberlain's old dislike of Gladstone and new dislike of the Irish were given a free rein. The consequences of this determined the course of English politics for the next twenty years.

On New Year's Day, 1886, Chamberlain arranged a quadri-partite meeting at Devonshire House. The other participants were Hartington, Harcourt and Dilke. Dilke described the meeting in the following terms:

"I did not see my way clearly, and did not say much; the other three arguing strongly against Mr. Gladstone's conduct in having sent Herbert Gladstone to a news agency to let out his views for the benefit of the provincial press in such a way as to put pressure on his colleagues. It seemed to me that the pressure, though no doubt unfair and indefensible, had nevertheless been pretty successful, as neither Harcourt nor Chamberlain saw their way to opposing Mr. Gladstone, although both of them disliked his scheme. Hartington only said that he 'thought he could not join a Government to promote any such scheme.'"[21]

At this stage, therefore, the alignment was that Hartington was firmest in his opposition, that Chamberlain and Harcourt were disaffected but more uncertain, and that Dilke was most inclined, although perhaps without enthusiasm, to go along with Gladstone. Chamberlain was forging no alliance with Hartington, but the mere fact that the meeting had taken place showed that he had moved a little since December 17th, when he could still write: "The Whigs are our greatest enemies."

On January 11th Gladstone at last came to London. A few days later there was a meeting of Liberal leaders at 21, Carlton

House Terrace, where the G.O.M., always ready to borrow a house, had temporarily established himself. Chamberlain was out of London, but Dilke attended, although, in his own view, he was not welcomed by Gladstone.

"I know you think me over-sensitive, but you've not tried what it is," he wrote to Chamberlain on January 18th. "After Hartington's second very kind note I thought I ought to go, but I was not wanted; I got there with Grosvenor and Harcourt, and I heard Mr. G. whisper to Harcourt, 'This is very awkward. 'That's a pleasant position to be put in. . . . Please let Harcourt know that I did not thrust myself in at 21, Carlton House Terrace, but went on two very kind letters of Hartington, which grew out of the Devonshire House meeting."[22]

Despite this discouraging reception Dilke attended another similar meeting of ex-Cabinet ministers at Lord Granville's on January 21st. By this time Parliament had met, the Queen's Speech had been presented, and Salisbury seemed prepared to carry on. Chamberlain and Dilke would still like to have kept the Conservatives in for some time—a course which was obviously in Dilke's personal interest and which would have postponed Chamberlain's final decision about Ireland—but they decided that this was no longer possible. The best that could be done was to avoid turning the Government out on an Irish amendment. With this end in view the two radicals drew up the "three acres and a cow" amendment, which was quickly accepted by the meeting on January 21st. Five days later it was moved by Jesse Collings. Gladstone was then convinced that it was his duty to return to office. Earlier that day Hicks Beach had announced a new coercion bill. This led Gladstone to tell Harcourt that he was prepared to go ahead without Hartington, without Chamberlain, if necessary without anybody. Late that night the Collings amendment was put to the vote, and although Hartington, Goschen, James and fifteen other Liberals voted with the Tories, the Government was defeated by seventy-four. Salisbury resigned on the following day, and Gladstone kissed hands for the third time on January 30th.

Neither the weakness of his parliamentary position nor the magnitude of his Irish task made the new Prime Minister zealous in his cultivation of the radicals. Perhaps he thought it was enough to have John Morley as Chief Secretary. Chamberlain was first offered the Admiralty, but was reluctant to accept, partly because he was unattracted by the post itself and partly because he was asked to commit himself to an enquiry into the possibility of Home Rule, although to nothing more. On the following day, after consultation with Dilke, who was clear that he ought to join in some capacity, Chamberlain saw Gladstone and asked for the Colonial Office. The Prime Minister's reply was a classical example of his ineptitude in dealing with Chamberlain. "Oh!" he said with surprise, "a Secretary of State." "Chamberlain is furious and will never forgive the slight,"[23] Dilke recorded. Nevertheless, without forgiveness and with personal resentment added to political misgiving, Chamberlain did join the Government. On February 1st he accepted Dilke's old post as President of the Local Government Board.

No offer was made to Dilke himself. His case was due to be heard as soon as February 12th, but Gladstone made no effort to hold a post vacant against the possibility that his name might be cleared. Instead he wrote a courteous but unyielding letter.

My dear Dilke,

I write you, on this first day of my going regularly to my arduous work, to express my profound regret that any circumstances of the moment should deprive me of the opportunity and the hope of enlisting on behalf of a new Government the great capacity which you have proved in a variety of spheres and forms for rendering good and great service to Grown and country.

You will well understand how absolutely recognition on my part of an external barrier is separate from any want of inward confidence, the last idea I should wish to convey.

Nor can I close without fervently expressing to you my desire that there may be reserved for you a long and honourable career of public distinction.

Believe me always,

Yours sincerely,

W. E. Gladstone[24]

Dilke received this letter with reasonably good grace—better than that with which Chamberlain had accepted the Local Government Board—and returned a friendly answer to Gladstone. But his exclusion was damaging not only to his political prospects but also to his private reputation. It created in the public mind a greater presumption of his guilt than had hitherto existed; and he can hardly have failed to reflect on the mischance that the formation of the Government could not have been delayed for two weeks. Had this been so, and had he in the interval secured even a formal verdict in his favour, it would have been much more difficult to exclude him. But the mischance occurred, and the exclusion took place. What it meant to Dilke emerges most clearly from a letter which he wrote to Chamberlain immediately after the latter's acceptance of office:

> "I feel that our friendship is going to be subjected to the heaviest strain it has ever borne, and I wish to minimise any risks to it, in which, however, I don't believe. I am determined that it shall not dwindle into a form or pretence of friendship of which the substance has departed. It will be a great change if I do not feel that I can go to your house or to your room as freely as ever. At the same time confidence from one in the inner circle of the Cabinet to one wholly outside the Government is not easy, and reserve makes all conversation untrue. . . . I intend to sit behind (in Forster's seat), not below the gangway, as long as you are in the Government. There is one great favour which I think you will be able to do me without any trouble to yourself, and that is to let my wife come to your room to see me *between* her lunch and the meeting of the House.*** The greatest nuisance about being out is that I shall have to go down in the mornings to get my place, and sit in the library all day. . . ."[25]

At this stage, however, Dilke's thoughts were too concerned with what was about to happen at the Law Courts to be much occupied with events either at Westminster or in Whitehall.

*** Self-pity was not normally one of Dilke's vices, but the tone of this part of the letter would have been more appropriate had he been going to gaol rather than on to the back benches.

Chapter Twelve

An Inconclusive Verdict

The case of Crawford v. Crawford and Dilke was heard
before Mr. Justice Butt on Friday, February 12th. Dilke
appeared with a formidable array of legal and personal advisers.
Sir Henry James, out of office like Dilke himself, although for
different reasons, remained his principal but unpaid counsellor.
James's skill and experience, however, were fortified by those of
Sir Charles Russell, who had been appointed Attorney General
ten days before* and who was then the foremost advocate at the
Bar. Russell had more divorce court experience than James. But
he did not stand in the same position of friendship to Dilke, and
his services were not available for nothing. On the contrary, his
brief was marked with the figure, phenomenal for those days, of
300 guineas; and the junior, Searle, had in consequence to be

---

* It was then both permissible and usual for the law officers to accept private
briefs. Russell's appearance for Dilke implied no official backing.

rewarded with a proportionate fee. Chamberlain was also in court, to give support and to be available for consultation on any nontechnical point.

During the morning Crawford went into the box, and was led by his counsel through the confession which had been made to him. Mrs. Crawford was not in Court. Two witnesses only were called to offer corroborative evidence. The first was Anne Jamieson, who had been parlourmaid in the Crawfords' house from the beginning of 1882. She stated that, in February, 1883, when Crawford came to London later than his wife, Mrs. Crawford spent the two intervening nights away from home, returning on the first occasion at about 7–30 in the morning, and on the second at some unspecified hour. Anne Jamieson also said that, during the session of 1883, she remembered Sir Charles Dilke paying a series of morning calls upon Mrs. Crawford. He came about once a fortnight at noon or 12–30. The visits lasted approximately half an hour, and while he was there his carriage waited in the street. Mrs. Crawford received him in the ground-floor drawing-room and gave orders that, during the visit, no one was to be admitted. Under cross-examination by Russell, Anne Jamieson said that Mrs. Crawford, in July, 1885, had told her "to tell Mr. Crawford all that I knew about Sir Charles Dilke." She also admitted a series of visits to the house from Captain Forster, first stating that these began in 1883, but later correcting this to 1884.

The second witness was George Ball, who had been butler to Mrs. Harrison, one of Mrs. Crawford's elder sisters, at her house in Cromwell Road. Mrs. Crawford had told Anne Jamieson that she had spent the nights away from home at this house. Ball was called in order to refute this. He was not cross-examined.

This was the case for the plaintiff, and it was one which put

Dilke and his advisers in a position, as it appeared to them, of extreme difficulty. No evidence of any legal force had been offered against Dilke. This was fully recognised by Mr. Justice Butt. In the course of his summing-up he was to say: "I cannot see any case whatever against Sir Charles Dilke. By the law of England, a statement made by one party in the suit—a statement made not in the presence of the other—cannot be evidence against that other. I cannot see the shadow of a case."[1] In these circumstances, should Dilke be put into the witness-box to deny upon oath the uncorroborated story which Mrs. Crawford had told to her husband and which he had repeated to the court? There was no legal advantage to be gained. The purpose of such a course would be to convince the public not the judge. But there were two objections. The first was the belief, held by all Dilke's legal advisers and expressed by Russell, that if their client went into the box he would be open to cross-examination about the whole of his past life and about his relations with Mrs. Crawford's mother in particular; and the fact that Crawford was known to have spent a good deal of money—employing two men and two women in the task——trying to hunt up pre-1882 evidence against Dilke's general character may have added to their fear. But it was a curious fear, for there seems no doubt that under the rules of evidence as they existed in 1886 (and as they exist to-day) such questions would have been inadmissible. They would have dealt with matters not at issue and, as such, were excluded by the Evidence Further Amendment Act of 1869.[†] If Dilke had been

† In the relevant section of the Act there occurs the following passage: "The parties to any proceedings instituted in consequence of adultery, and the husbands and wives of such parties, shall be competent to give evidence in such proceedings provided that no witness to any proceeding, whether a

asked about his adultery with Mrs. Eustace Smith an objection from Sir Charles Russell would almost certainly have been enough to rule out the question.‡

The second difficulty is one which (quite naturally) Russell did not mention in court and which is not discussed, as is the first, in the Dilke papers relating to the case, but of which J. L. Garvin makes much in his biography of Chamberlain.[2] The aspect of Mrs. Crawford's story which was likely to make most public impact was that relating to the girl, Fanny. In the unanimous view of Russell, James and Chamberlain, according to Garvin, it was impossible for Dilke to make an effective answer to the charges unless Fanny herself could be put into the box, able to deny the allegations about her own role and to stand up to cross-examination. For reasons which will be discussed later, Fanny was not available. Consequently, Garvin states, Russell and James decided to let the case rest where it was, and Chamberlain, most reluctantly, saw the force of their reasoning and concurred.

The argument is not altogether convincing. It is obvious that a firm rebuttal by Fanny as well as by Dilke would have

---

party to the suit or not, shall be liable to be asked or bound to answer any question tending to show that he or she has been guilty of adultery, unless such witness shall have already given evidence in the same proceeding in disproof of his or her alleged adultery."

‡ Bigham P. was to take a contrary view in *Hall v. Hall* (*The King's Proctor showing cause*), 1909 (25 TLR 524), but the decision was disapproved and not followed by McCardie J. in *Hensley v. Hensley and Nevin*, 1920 (30 TLR 288), and Hill J. in *Mourilyan v. Mourilyan*, 1922 (38 TLR 482). For a full discussion of the point and the conclusion that the judgment of Bigham P. "cannot be supported," see Rayden on *Divorce*, Seventh Edition, pp. 437–7.

been an advantage, but, it is not clear why the latter without the former should have led, as Garvin assumes, to the certainty of a verdict against Dilke. Whatever their chain of reasoning, however, the facts are that during the luncheon adjournment Russell, James and Chamberlain met and decided that the case should be left where it was, and that Dilke should give no evidence. When this decision was taken Dilke was not present. He was waiting in another room. Chamberlain was deputed to go and tell him what had been decided. Dilke accepted what he was told.

When the court reassembled after luncheon Sir Charles Russell announced the course which had been resolved upon. He did so in somewhat hesitant terms:

"Ought we to take upon ourselves the responsibility of putting Sir Charles Dilke in the witness-box where he might be put through the events of his whole life, and in the life of any man there may be found to have been some indiscretions—ought we to take upon ourselves that responsibility? After an anxious consideration of the matter we have come to the determination to leave the case where it stands. . .

Mr. Justice Butt, however, showed no hesitation in his subsequent remarks:

"Nothing can be clearer than the law on this subject—that is that the unsworn statement of a person in the position of Mrs. Crawford is not entitled to be received or even considered in a Court of Justice as against the person with whom she is alleged to have committed adultery. . . . Under these circumstances I have no hesitation whatever in saying that

277

counsel have been well advised in suggesting the course which they have induced Sir Charles Dilke to take."[3]

His Lordship then proceeded to dismiss the case against Dilke and to order the plaintiff to pay his costs. But he also gave Crawford his divorce. In law both decisions were no doubt correct but to the public they seemed ridiculously paradoxical. The verdict appeared to be that Mrs. Crawford had committed adultery with Dilke, but that he had not done so with her.

Nevertheless, Dilke was at first reasonably satisfied with the result. In his diary for February 12th he wrote:

"My case tried. I left myself absolutely in the hands of counsel and they took the right course in saying with the judge 'no case.' But Russell did it clumsily and (without my permission) talked of 'indiscretions.' He *said* possible indiscretions, but of course most of the newspapers left out possible.[§] But for this blunder the case stood well. Nothing could be stronger than the judge's words, and 'costs' mean that Crawford had no ground for 'reasonable suspicion,' as in similar cases where there had been such ground costs had been left to be paid by each side."[4]

---

§ Dilke's objection to Russell's statement was slightly amplified in the memoir which he later wrote up from his diary: "The way in which Sir Charles Russell spoke of 'indiscretions,'" he wrote, "looked to the public as though he was alluding to something more recent than this old story of capture in 1868 and recapture for two months in 1874–5—the winter in which I was mad." (D.P. 43940, 117.) This is the only available written comment of Dilke's upon his relations with Mrs. Eustace Smith.

He noted also that for several days letters of congratulations arrived in great quantities from all sorts of people. "Even the wary politician Harcourt congratulated warmly," he added. Furthermore, James reported on February 13th: "I have seen a great many people at Brooks's, the Reform and Turf Clubs. Everyone seems satisfied." Dilke's reply to this was somewhat severe: "The Turf Club," he said, "was hardly the place to gauge opinion."[5]

Dilke's view of the whole position, indeed, was rapidly becoming less favourable. The verdict of the court was showing itself to have been a false release. It did not prevent the mounting against him of a considerable newspaper campaign. This was begun by the *Pall Mall Gazette*.

The *Pall Mall Gazette*—a London evening newspaper—was at that time under the editorship of W. T. Stead. Stead had been born in Northumberland in 1849, the son of a Congregational minister. He died in 1912, just over a year after Dilke's own death, but in more dramatic circumstances. He was a victim of the *Titanic* disaster. He became editor of the Darlington *Northern Echo* at the age of twenty-two, and then moved to London in 1880 to serve under Morley on the *Pall Mall*. He succeeded to this editorial chair in 1883 when Morley became a member of Parliament. But Stead was a very different type of journalist from Morley. His interests were narrower, his mind was less cultivated, and, although he was a Liberal (and often an extreme one), his political affiliations were not of primary importance to him. He had force and courage, but he was an extreme egotist who became obsessed with a sense of his own power.[¶]

¶ Any picture of Stead should perhaps be supplemented by a postcard which Bernard Shaw wrote in reply to a request for his views on the subject from

279

Furthermore, he possessed to an unusual degree the essential ingredients of moral intolerance—he was a puritan fascinated by sex. Professionally he was a sensationalist, and a pioneer of the highly personalised approach of modern journalism. He was the originator of the technique of the interview, and at the beginning of 1884 he had applied it with brilliant success by himself going to Southampton and obtaining an important statement of view from General Gordon who had just returned to England. This interview marked the beginning of the public agitation for the despatch of Gordon to Khartoum.

In the following year Stead applied his talents for personal investigation to a different field and in a more extreme form. He was anxious to promote a bill which would raise the age of consent from twelve to sixteen and generally make more difficult the abduction of young girls for purposes of prostitution. His method of drawing attention to the evil which he wished to combat was a direct one. For the sum of £5 he himself succeeded in purchasing and carrying off from her parents a child of thirteen. He published a full account of his activities in the *Pall Mall Gazette* and later re-published them as a pamphlet entitled *The Maiden Tribute of Modern Babylon*. The effect was considerable, and a change in the law was quickly carried through. Stead,

---

Robertson Scott, who was writing a history of the *Pall Mall Gazette*. "I never spoke to Stead in my life," Shaw wrote, "nor even saw him except once at a public meeting, where he behaved so outrageously that I walked out in disgust. I was a contributor to the *Pall Mall* under his editorship; but as my department was literature and art, and he was an utter Philistine, no contacts between us were possible. Outside political journalism such as can be picked up in a newspaper office he was a complete ignoramus. I wrote him a few letters about politics which he acknowledged very sensibly as 'intended for his instruction'; but he was unteachable except by himself.

however, had committed a technical offence and, with some of his associates, he was brought to trial at the Old Bailey in November, 1885. Most of the others were acquitted, but Stead himself, perhaps because he insisted on conducting his own defence, was convicted and sentenced to three months' imprisonment. He bore the punishment with a good deal of self-righteous pride** and emerged from it just in time for the hearing of the Dilke case.

To this case he devoted (and was to continue to devote for years to come) the closest possible attention. At first, before the trial, he appeared as a friend. Dilke had said in a letter to his constituents in August, 1885, that he would disprove the charge against him before attempting to continue his public career. This attitude, Stead announced, was an honourable one. He indicated his belief that Dilke was most probably innocent and offered him all possible assistance in demonstrating the fact. It was perhaps consistent with this attitude that Stead should express horrified disappointment at the course which was followed at the February trial; and even after the extremely harsh comments which he then printed about Dilke there were moments in the ensuing months when he still presented himself as a well-wisher, eager that Dilke might yet be vindicated by some fresh turn of events. Lady Dilke, willing no doubt to clutch

---

** His attitude was illustrated by the fact that for many years afterwards, on the anniversary of his conviction, he wore his convict suit, an attire which attracted a good deal of attention as he travelled up in the suburban train from Wimbledon and walked across Waterloo Bridge to his office. The gesture would have been more justified had he not been treated as a first-class misdemeanant for all but the first two days of his sentence, and allowed to wear ordinary clothes.

at any straw, corresponded with Stead and even went to see him during this period. But her intercessions did more harm than good. They merely served further to whet Stead's appetite for the case, and offered ground for misrepresentation. After their meeting Stead recorded that "at one point she said plainly that a heavy burden lay on her heart because she had brought all this trouble on her husband by trying to wean him from his worldly life; that if she had only let him go on with his intrigues and life of pleasure, none of the trouble would have come upon him; and it made her doubt whether it was not better to let men go on in their vice rather than try to raise them to a higher life." "It was pitiable, ghastly," Stead added, "to see her sobbing."[6]

Apart from the inherent improbability of Lady Dilke making these confessions to a sensational journalist who had already shown himself a determined traducer of her husband, Stead's reliability as a recorder of impressions and sifter of evidence is well indicated by the fact that he proceeded immediately afterwards to cite the private view of Sir George Lewis—"who was his own solicitor as well as Dilke's"—as decisive testimony against Dilke's innocence. There might have been some force in the point, were it not that Lewis in fact was Mrs. Crawford's solicitor, and not Dilke's.[††] After this it is not necessary to attach

---

[††] Stead's remarkable inaccuracy in writing about a case in which he was so closely interested is more than matched by that of his admirer, Robertson Scott. Scott, in summarising the proceedings, showed not merely inaccuracy but a formidable imagination. "Mrs. Crawford," he wrote, "was the respondent in the divorce suit brought by a Scottish M.P. in which Sir Charles Dilke, the Duke of Marlborough and Shaw, Captain of the London Fire Brigade, were co-respondents." (*The Life and Death of a Newspaper*, p. 82n.)

too much weight to Stead's similar assertions that Dilke had been excluded from Lord Randolph Churchill's house because of "his forwardness, to use no stronger word," to Lady Randolph, and that Sir Charles Mills (later Lord Hillingdon) believed that he habitually "had six intrigues going on at once."

These and other stories which Stead was subsequently to relate (and print) about Dilke may or may not have been true, but the fact that they came from Stead is certainly no testimony to their veracity. It is impossible to read the files of his paper for the weeks after the February trial without believing that his main interest was to print anything which would keep the case alive, and enable him to go on exploiting its sensationalism for some time to come. The *Pall Mall's* circulation had been dropping, its poor financial position was a current cause of dissension between its proprietor and himself, and it badly needed to attract new readers.

Later, however, Stead's general interest in the case was replaced by a more particularised emotion. He became seized with an abiding but self-righteous vindictiveness towards Dilke. He saw himself as the chosen instrument of public morality, protecting the innocent citizens of Britain against the impudent attempts of a shameless adulterer to climb back into their favour. He felt the same pride in his work as he expressed with unusual self-revelation about his similar (but possibly better-founded) attacks upon a man called Langworthy. "The fact that Langworthy was hissed off a platform in the interior of the Argentine because of what we had published," he wrote in this connection, "abides with me as one of those permanent consolations with which a man can comfort himself in the days when he is depressed and disheartened."[7] This spirit caused Stead, later in the year 1886, to take Mrs. Crawford on to the staff of his paper (presumably in order that she might be available for closer consultation‡‡) and to continue for many years, with unabated ferocity, his attacks upon Dilke. Even in the early 'nineties he was still distributing pamphlets, addressing meetings and engaging in long controversy in obscure magazines upon the subject. It is against the background of this knowledge that the opening of the newspaper attack against Dilke, with the *Pall Mall Gazette* at its centre, should be considered.

On the morning of February 13th, the day after the trial, the position was not too discouraging. *The Times* was censorious. The decision of the court was unintelligible, Dilke ought clearly to have gone into the box, and it was possible that his failure to do so would injure his future public career. But it was all put in rather tentative terms, and was more than counterbalanced by the *Daily News*, which declared unequivocally: "His character has now been vindicated after full and open trial, and he will be welcomed back to public life with a fervour increased by the sympathy excited by the imminent peril in which he has stood for the past six months." The *Daily Telegraph* was also reasonably friendly. All this was too much for the *Pall Mall Gazette*. It swung into action that evening. After a characteristic expression of regret at having to comment at all, it announced that the *Daily News* verdict was the reverse of the truth. Dilke had made no attempt to clear his name. He had broken his pledge to his constituents. By not going into the witness-box he had indicated that he had something even worse to hide than that with which he was charged. "His friends expected more, his foes in their most sanguine moments never looked for worse."

---

‡‡ Although it should be noted in fairness that she was far from laching in literary talent. (See p. 332 *infra*.)

After this the general comment became less favourable. On February 15th the *Manchester Guardian* condemned Dilke's behaviour at the trial and announced that "to ask us on the strength of this evasion to welcome him back as a leader of the Liberal Party is too strong a draft on our credulity or our good nature." The *Statesman* commented in similar terms. It was reported that in Glasgow one of the Liberal Associations had passed a resolution declaring against Dilke's inclusion in any Liberal Cabinet; to admit him would be to weaken party interests by condoning "unrighteousness and wrong." Fortified by this support the *Pall Mall* returned to the attack with renewed vigour on the evening of the 16th. Its front page headline demanded to know why Dilke had not offered his resignation as member for Chelsea. This must be done at once, if his honour was to be in any way retrieved. The charges against him might still be false, but if they were true he was "worse than the common murderer who swings at Newgate." He must still seek to disprove the allegations, which would otherwise continue to envelope him with "a black and hideous suspicion."

Perhaps feeling that he had reached the limit even of his own capacity for denunciation, Stead then changed his tack. He began to attack Chamberlain instead of Dilke, and for a time his enthusiasm for this new task became so great that Dilke, by contrast, appeared almost as a wronged innocent. The new line started on February 19th with a small paragraph announcing that "the man really responsible for the fatal blunder committed by Sir Charles Dilke in not going into the witness-box is Mr. Joseph Chamberlain." Three days later this was blown up into two front-page articles, one of them curiously entitled "The Case for Sir Charles Dilke, by One Who Knows It." Two days after this there was another article which reached the conclusion that "Mr. Chamberlain . . . seems to prefer that his intimate associate should remain for ever under this crushing burden of suspicion rather than that he, Mr. Chamberlain, should admit a simple error of judgment." Then, on February 27th, Stead published both sides of an acrimonious correspondence which had taken place between Chamberlain and himself during the previous week. Chamberlain had accused Stead of blackening Dilke's character in order to maintain the sensational nature of his paper, and Stead had replied that Chamberlain had ruined the career of one who "broken in nerve and health had placed himself in your hands. You overruled his personal desire to enter the witness-box and the responsibility was, therefore, not his but yours."

Chamberlain greatly disliked these attacks. He wrote to Dilke on February 22nd saying: "I am only too glad to be able in any way to share your burdens and if I can act as a lightning conductor so much the better"[8]; but he was worried, as Garvin makes clear, that so much of the public responsibility for what was now obviously a wrong decision (although Dilke generously denied this) should be placed upon his shoulders. In order, no doubt, to shift some of this weight he made in the course of this same letter of February 22nd a suggestion for fresh action to Dilke. "Of course," he wrote, "if *you* were quite clear that you ought to go into the box, it is still possible to do so—either by an action for libel or probably by intervention of the Queen's Proctor."[§§9] It is difficult to gauge how decisive

---

§§ The Queen's Proctor is a legal official who acts in the capacity of solicitor on the Crown's behalf in the Probate and Divorce division of the High Court. He can intervene between the granting of a decree *nisi* and its being

286

was this suggestion. Garvin discounts it. He points out, quite correctly, that Stead had put forward a similar idea in his issue of the same day. Indeed the latter had gone further and reported, probably on no authority, both that the Queen's Proctor had begun to move and that Dilke had instructed his solicitors to place all available information before that official. And it hardly seems likely that Dilke, preoccupied with his troubles, would not have read any relevant item in the *Pall Mall* at the earliest opportunity. This opportunity, it seems, must have occurred before the receipt of Chamberlain's letter, because this was a reply to a letter of Dilke's (the correspondence was delivered by messenger) which itself commented upon another passage in that same evening's issue of the paper. On the other hand Dilke himself afterwards wrote on Chamberlain's letter: "This was the first suggestion made to me of any rehearing of the case, and, although Brett, who was taking a great interest in it, was violently opposed to this course, and though Hartington and James and Russell were all under the impression that I should find no further difficulties, it was the course which I ultimately took."[10] On this point, therefore, we have Dilke's own testimony against the thesis (of Chamberlain's lack of responsibility for the next step) which Garvin was so anxious to prove, with the objective evidence, on this occasion, rather on Garvin's side. But whether or not the first hint came from Chamberlain, there is no doubt which was likely to have the greater effect upon Dilke's mind—a rumour printed by Stead or a suggestion, even if hedged about with counterbalancing considerations, from his closest friend.

---

made absolute, and if he can show that the court was deceived or that relevant facts were kept from its notice, the interim decree can be upset.

At first, however, Dilke did not respond favourably to the prospect of a Queen's Proctor's intervention. This was partly because he was not clear what that official's role was likely to be. The obvious purpose of an intervention would be to show that there had been no adultery between Dilke and Mrs. Crawford and that the divorce had therefore been given contrary to the facts of the case. But on March 2nd Dilke recorded:

"I became aware that the Queen's Proctor had put on detectives to try to prove the truth of a portion of the statements which had been made by Mrs. Crawford to her husband and I wrote to James to ask him how the Queen's Proctor could intervene except in the other sense. James replied: 'Stephenson (the Queen's Proctor) is a brute and cannot be acting in accordance with any principle. It cannot be right for the Queen's Proctor to intervene in order to prove that a woman *is* entitled to a divorce.'"[11]

Dilke was also influenced by the fact that Manning, as well as his own legal advisers and Hartington, was against any action. The Cardinal was in close contact with Dilke at this time. On February 17th he had written rather archly:

My dear Sir Charles Dilke,

Mr. Bodley has just been with me and you know with what we have been occupied. I have not forgotten any part of our conversation last summer and it has been constantly in my mind these last days. My first impulse would be to come to you, but I did not know what would be in accordance with your wish. You know how truly,

I am always faithfully yours,

Henry E. C. Archbp.[12]

A week or so later Lady Dilke had asked Manning to inter-vene with Stead, who claimed to be an intimate friend of the Cardinal's and who had certainly received his support at the time of the Maiden Tribute case. Manning responded at least to the extent of asking Stead to go and see him. It is possible that this interview may have had something to do with the shift of the *Pall Mall's* attack to Chamberlain, although Stead was much later to claim that throughout he had Manning's support for his strictures on Dilke. After the interview Manning wrote to Lady Dilke advising that Dilke should for the time being keep as quiet as possible and that he should neither leave the country nor, unless his constituents should demand it, attend the House of Commons. In the same letter (dated March 2nd) he also discoun-tenanced any action by Dilke to reopen the case. "All active attempts, such as Mr. Stead seems to propose," he wrote, "would only more widely spread and keep alive the excitement . . . which will lose its intensity if met by silence. . . . In trials so great all human efforts fall short."[13]

Dilke took neither of these pieces of advice. The first he rejected with remarkable alacrity, and on March 3rd he made his first appearance in the new Parliament, being welcomed with particular cordiality by Joseph Cowen, the member for Newcastle, but less warmly by many others.¶ He kept silent in

---

¶ Three months later, for instance, Dilke wrote to Chamberlain: "Mr. G.'s friendliness comes to me a little late. After sitting in front of me in the House for several weeks he suddenly discovered my presence (now some

the House, however. Against the second piece of advice Dilke acted three weeks later. Towards the end of March he offered to place all the information in his possession at the disposal of the Queen's Proctor. In mid-April, having received no response, he wrote formally and publicly to that official stating that the charges made against him were not only unsupported but untrue, and that he was prepared to deny them on oath. In consequence of this letter he was able to inform a meeting of 2,000 of his constituents held at Preece's Riding School in Knightsbridge at the beginning of May that he had succeeded in inducing the Queen's Proctor to intervene in what he described as "the natural and proper way," that is to attempt to show that the divorce had been given upon the basis of an adultery which had never taken place. Dilke noted: "My part in procuring this intervention had been the chief one, but it had been contrary to the advice of my friends."[14]

During this spring Dilke's spirits revived again. He received a number of unexpected expressions of goodwill. One was the offer of the freedom of the borough of New Romney, which he accepted with alacrity. Another was a letter from Lord Randolph Churchill, which is perhaps worth quoting in view of the statement of Stead which was cited earlier. Churchill wrote from Connaught Place on April 8th:

My dear Dilke,

Please be certain that if you think that at anytime any

---

time ago) and turned round and shook hands suddenly and warmly—which was very awkward and might have got into the papers, but luckily didn't. The people whose kindness and friendship—and in your case something more—I shall remember will be those who did not wait" (D.P. 49610.)

opinion of mine could be of any value to you I should be only too glad to be of service. I have felt great sympathy for you in the recent troubles and worries that you have had to encounter, but I did not like to speak about them to you for fear of being thought intrusive. I hope you will not take the smallest notice of the newspaper persecution which is going on. "The majesty of the law" is a very tawdry and poor sort of affair if the deliberate investigation of accusations by a Court of Justice and a clear judgment on such accusations cannot afford complete and adequate protection to the person against whom such accusations have been made.

Believe me to be,

Yours sincerely,

Randolph S. Churchill[15]

The investigations of the special solicitor—Ernest Humbert—whom Dilke was employing for the case also appeared to be going well. He had found Fanny Stock, the witness to whom Chamberlain attached so much importance at the time of the February trial, and obtained a fairly satisfactory statement from her; and he was in a position to prove, as had not been the case in February, the adultery of Mrs. Crawford with Captain Forster. This was likely to be of great importance because at the second trial it would not be possible for Mrs. Crawford, any more than Dilke himself, to escape the witness-box. The prospect of her being subjected to rigorous cross-examination by Sir Charles Russell would in any event have been an encouraging one for Dilke and his supporters. With this new evidence at his disposal, which directly contradicted what she had told her husband, there was every hope that Russell would be able to completely destroy her as a witness of the truth. An elaborate and powerful list of suggestions for Russell's cross-examination, incorporating this and many other points, was drawn up. Inspired by this outlook, Dilke took part in a debate in the House of Commons and went so far as to write to Chamberlain: "Things are changing so fast that I do not believe that at this moment Crawford himself believes me guilty. It will still be a *hard* and a *long* fight, but I am not now hopeless of coming out right. . . ."[16]

It was another false dawn. Dilke had assumed—a natural enough layman's assumption—that if the case were re-opened he would still be a party and his counsel would still enjoy the full rights of cross-examination. More surprisingly James and Russell appeared to share this view. It was quite false. Dilke had been finally dismissed from the case by Mr. Justice Butt in February. In a future hearing he could appear only as a witness, as indeed could Mrs. Crawford, and the only counsel who would have the right of cross-examination would be those representing Crawford as the successful plaintiff in the first case on the one hand, and those representing the Queen's Proctor, who was attempting to upset the verdict, on the other. The realisation that this was the position came as an immense blow to Dilke. "If I had known that I should not be allowed to be represented (at) the intervention," he wrote later, "I could not have faced it—the hardships of the course taken proved too great. But no one, of all these great lawyers, foresaw this."[17]

In an attempt to retrieve the position Dilke lodged an application to be reinstated as a party to the suit. It was heard, together with a similar but more surprising application from Mrs. Crawford and a motion relating to the jury, before Sir James Hannen, the President of the Probate, Divorce and Admiralty Division of the High Court, sitting in chambers, on June 11th. The applications of both Dilke and Mrs. Crawford were dismissed. The motion relating to the jury came from Crawford. He wished to have none on the ground that the public speeches about the case which Dilke had made might create bias in his favour. This was countered by counsel for the Queen's Proctor asking for a special jury,[***] in view of the complicated issues involved. To this latter request the judge readily agreed.[18] Dilke then took his application to be reinstated in the case to the Court of Appeal. It was again rejected, on June 30th.

The prospects for the trial were then about as unfavourable for Dilke as can easily be imagined. His future was to turn on whether or not the Queen's Proctor could prove a negative. The task of this official was to demonstrate to the court that there had been no adultery between Mrs. Crawford and Dilke—a type of proposition which, by its very nature and whoever the principals and whatever the circumstances, could never be a very easy one to prove. He was not to be assisted in this task by Dilke's own well-briefed legal advisers; and the issue was to be decided by a City of London special jury—a body of men who would no doubt wish to be fair but who were likely to have strong political prejudices against Dilke.

The decision that Dilke's own counsel could not appear in the case was made particularly damaging by two special factors. First, Crawford had engaged Henry Matthews, Q.C.,[†††] who had not appeared at the February trial, one of the most powerful and aggressive cross-examiners at the Bar. He was a Roman

---

[***] Special juries, abolished by the Criminal Justice Act of 1948, were chosen from persons with a relatively high property qualification.

[†††] Born 1826; Conservative M.P. for Dungarven, 1868–74, and for Birmingham, East, 1886–95; Home Secretary, 1886–92; created Viscount Llandaff, 1895; died, unmarried, in 1913.

Catholic and a Tory, and neither his religion nor his politics inclined him to treat Dilke with much consideration. In a case which would inevitably turn, more than on anything else, upon the relative performance under cross-examination of the two principal witnesses, it was essential that he should be matched by an advocate of equal toughness and skill. This Sir Charles Russell would undoubtedly have been. Equally undoubtedly it was what the leading counsel briefed by the Queen's Proctor was not. Sir Walter Phillimore was a lawyer of considerable repute who enjoyed a large practice, particularly in the ecclesiastical courts and in matters touching international law. He was later to be a judge of distinction. But as an advocate and cross-examiner he was not in the same class as Matthews or Russell. Furthermore, he was quite unused to the rough and tumble of a major divorce court case. Even had he possessed exactly the right qualities for his task, however, he could hardly have discharged it well in the circumstances in which he was constrained to act.

This was the second special factor. The Queen's Proctor, Sir Augustus Stephenson, showed throughout the most marked antipathy towards Dilke. This may partly have been due to his desire to guard himself against any charge of favouritism. The public suggestion that he might be asked to intervene, followed by the announcement that he was doing so, created in some people's minds the impression that he had re-opened the case, not because a miscarriage of justice might have occurred, but because of Dilke's political prominence. But Stephenson's behaviour surely went much farther than could have been justified by any fear of this sort. As early as March he provoked such a bland and genial Whig as Henry James to quarrel with him at a public dinner. In April he replied to Dilke's letters in a tone of strident discourtesy, and then, having brusquely refused to carry on any further direct correspondence, adopted the same tone, combined with extreme dilatoriness, in his replies to Dilke's solicitor. Throughout the weeks when the case was being prepared, information obtained from the Dilke side was quickly passed on by Stephenson to the Crawford side. Much of that coming from the Crawford side, however, was not communicated to Humbert, and none was communicated with alacrity. It was July 10th, for instance (with the case due to open on July 16th), before Humbert received a copy of Mrs. Crawford's proof; and it was July 14th before any meeting took place between Stephenson and Dilke. Even then Phillimore was not present. He would no doubt have regarded his presence as a professional impropriety. Neither he nor the Queen's Proctor conceived of their roles as being to represent Dilke, and it would indeed have been impossible for them to have done so, in view of the paucity of the contact which they allowed themselves with him.

In these circumstances it was not surprising that Dilke's buoyancy of the spring had evaporated by the beginning of July. The outlook for the case had become exceedingly gloomy. But before it began he was to receive yet another heavy blow. The period between the two trials had been politically one of the most decisive in recent British history. It had seen the preparation of the first Home Rule Bill, the resignation of Chamberlain from the Government, the introduction of the Bill to the House of Commons, a period of fevered negotiations in an attempt to patch up a last-minute agreement, the Prime Minister's sudden rejection of any compromise, and, in consequence, the defeat of the Bill on second reading. There followed the dissolution of the six-months-old Parliament, a

295

general election in which Chamberlain made common cause with Hartington, and the reduction of the Gladstonian Liberal party to a rump of 191 members. Dilke viewed these events almost as an outsider. When the time came he took his decision in favour of the bill and against Chamberlain, but throughout he saw the unfolding of the picture much more in terms of its impact upon his relationship with Chamberlain than upon the general political scene. His part can be described almost completely from their correspondence and from Dilke's notes on their meetings.

On March 4th Dilke wrote:

"I went to Chamberlain's house, he being too cross to come to the House of Commons, and held with him an important conversation as to his future. I tried to point out to him that if he went out, as he was thinking of doing, he would wreck the party, who would put up with the Whigs going out against Mr. Gladstone on Home Rule, but who would be rent in twain by a Radical secession. He would do this, I told him, without much popular sympathy, and it was a terrible position to face. He told me that he had said so much in the autumn that he felt he *must* do it. I said, 'Certainly. But do not go out and fight. Go out and lie low. If honesty forces you out, well and good, but it does not force you to fight." He seemed to agree, at all events at the moment."[19]

At the end of March Dilke had to attend a meeting of the Chelsea Liberal Association on the Irish question. He tried to steer a middle course by drafting a resolution "that while this meeting is firmly resolved on the maintenance of the union between Great

Britain and Ireland, it is of the opinion that the wishes of the Irish people, as expressed at the last election, should receive satisfaction." Chamberlain, to whom the resolution was sent for approval, wrote back surlily that the two things were inconsistent. On the day after the Chelsea meeting his own and Trevelyan's resignation from the Government were announced, and one bridge was down.

Dilke then set himself two objects. The first was to prevent Chamberlain, whatever he thought about Home Rule, from moving too close to the Whigs.

"I think you must let it be known that you are not satisfied with the Whig line," Dilke wrote on April 7th. "I hate the prospect of your being driven into coercion as a follower of a Goschen-Hartington-James-Brand-Albert Grey clique. . . . I believe from what I see of my caucus, and from the two large *public* meetings we have had for discussion, that the great mass of the party will go for Repeal, though fiercely against the land.[‡‡‡] Enough will go the other way to risk all the seats, but the party will go for Repeal, and sooner or later now Repeal will come, whether or not we have a dreary period of coercion first. I should decidedly let it be known that you won't stand airs from Goschen."[20]

Dilke's second object, against his own preference on the merits, was to get Gladstone to abandon the plan for the

---

[‡‡‡] The land purchase scheme which Gladstone at this time, largely on the advice of Spencer, was endeavouring to run in double harness with Home Rule. Dilke was as strongly opposed to this as was Chamberlain.

exclusion of Irish members from Westminster, His hope, which appeared not ill-founded, was that this might persuade Chamberlain to vote for the second reading of the bill. There was not much in the circumstances that Dilke could himself do with Gladstone, but he encouraged Chamberlain to ask for the concession, and gave him some extremely good (but unheeded) advice about the desirability of negotiating direct with a well-disposed member of the Cabinet, such as Herschell, the Lord Chancellor, instead of carrying on tortuous and pointless correspondence with Labouchere and O'Shea.

Chamberlain was trying to exert his own pressure upon Dilke at this stage. He wanted him to join in voting against the second reading, and he sought to achieve this by impressing upon Dilke how strong the opposition was likely to be. "The Bill is doomed," he wrote on April 30th. "I have a list of III Liberals pledged against the second reading. Of these I know that 59 have publicly announced their intentions to their constituents. I believe that almost all the rest are certain; but making every allowance for desertions, the Home Rule Bill cannot pass without the changes I have asked for."[21] He concluded by asking Dilke to go down to Birmingham and discuss the matter. This invitation Dilke declined. He was much occupied with preparations for the case, and, perhaps, was unwilling in his insecure circumstances to expose himself to the force of Chamberlain's determination. Instead, there took place in the first week of May their last major exchange of political letters.

Dilke wrote from Pyrford on May 1st. He explained why, although he still believed that Gladstone would agree to keep the Irish members at Westminster and although he (Dilke) would certainly accept the concession if it were made, he could not possibly demand it as a condition of voting for the second reading, because his real position was that he would much sooner be rid of the Irish. But he would remain uncommitted for as long as possible, if that was of any help. He concluded:

"The reason, as you know, why I am so anxious for you (which matters more than I matter at present or shall for a long time) to find yourself able if possible to take the offers made you, and vote for the second reading, is that the dissolution will wreck the party, but yet leave *a* party—democratic, because all the moderates will go over to the Tories; poor, because all the subscribers will go over to the Tories; more Radical than the party has ever been; and yet, as things now stand, with you outside of it."[22]

Chamberlain replied two days later in a harder and cooler tone:

"My pleasure in politics has gone, and I hold very loosely to public life just now. The friends with whom I have worked so long are many of them separated from me. The party is going blindly to its ruin, and everywhere there seems a want of courage and decision and principle which almost causes one to despair. I have hesitated to write to you again, but perhaps it is better that I should say what is in my mind. During all our years of intimacy I have never had a suspicion, until the last few weeks, that we differed on the Irish Question. . . . You must do what your conscience tells you to be right, and having decided, I should declare the situation publicly at once.

"It will do you harm on the whole, but that cannot be

helped, if you have made up your mind that it is right. But you must be prepared for unkind things said by those who know how closely we have been united hitherto. The present crisis is, of course, life and death to me. I shall win if I can, and if I cannot I will cultivate my garden. I do not care for the leadership of a party which should prove itself so fickle and so careless of National interests as to sacrifice the unity of the Empire to the precipitate impatience of an old man§§§—careless of the future in which he can have no part—and to an uninstructed instinct which will not take the trouble to exercise judgment and criticism."[23]

The letter ended: "Yours very truly, J. Chamberlain," a form which he had not used in his correspondence with Dilke for many years past.

Dilke replied at length and with pained agitation on May

"I need not say to you who know what I am what it has been to receive from you a letter which ends with a form of words intended to be cold by the side of that which for so great a number of years you have used to me. Your letter must have been written just at the moment when I was trying to express something of what I owe to your affection, which it seems that at this very time I had lost. . . . I care so much (not about what you name, and it is a pity that you

---

§§§ This letter, it should perhaps be noted, was written six weeks before the publication of Lord Randolph Churchill's election address which contained, amongst other pieces of invective, the memorable phrase: "An old man in a hurry."

should do so, for one word of yourself is worth more with me than the opinion of the whole world)—not about what people will say, but about what you think, that I am driven distracted by your tone. I beg you to think that I do not consider myself in this at all, except that I should wish to so act as to act rightly. . . . My seat here will go, either way, for certain, as it is a Tory seat now, and will become a more and more Tory seat with each fresh registration. If I should make any attempt to remain at all in political life, I do not think that my finding another seat would depend on the course I take in this present Irish matter. This thing will be forgotten in the common resistance of the Radicals to Tory coercion. . . . As to inclination, I feel as strongly as any man can as to the *way* in which Mr. Gladstone has done this thing, and all my inclination is therefore to follow you, where affection also leads. But if this is to be—what it will be—a fight, not as to the way and the man and the past, but as to the future, the second reading will be a choice between acceptance of a vast change which has in one form or the other become inevitable, and on the other side Hartington-Goschen opposition, with coercion behind it. I am only a camp follower now, but my place is not in the camp of the Goschens, Hartingtons, Brands, Heneages, Greys. I owe something, too, to my constituents. . . . If I voted against the second reading, unable as I should be honestly to defend my vote as you could and would honestly defend yours, by saying that all turned on the promise as to the retention of the Irish members, I should be voting without a ground or a defence, except that of personal affection for you, which is one which it is wholly impossible to put forward."[24]

Chamberlain wrote again the next day. It was a letter which began with a half apology—"I must have said more than I supposed, and perhaps in the worry of my own mind I did not allow enough for the tension of yours"—and finished "Yours ever sincerely," which, while it was not his usual ending, could at least be considered an improvement on "Yours very truly." But he was still full of complaint against those who would not agree with him, combining this, however, with a self-confident appreciation of his own political future: "On the whole—and in spite of all unfavourable symptoms—I think I shall win this fight, and shall have in the long run an increase of public influence!"[25]

Thereafter the correspondence dragged on for several weeks, but there was no longer any hope of its promoting real agreement. Sometimes it was acrimonious (on Chamberlain's side at least), and sometimes it was apologetic. Thus, on May 20th, Chamberlain complained bitterly about some of the speeches at a meeting of the London Liberal and Radical Council, over which Dilke had presided; but on the next day he wrote: "Your note makes everything right between us. Let us agree to consider everything which is said and done for the next few weeks as a dream."[26] During this period, however, Chamberlain was moved steadily away from the course which Dilke hoped he might follow. On May 16th, although racked with toothache, he attended a meeting of Hartington's support-ers at Devonshire House and advised Whigs and radicals to sink their differences in a policy of common resistance to Gladstone. On May 27th he refused to attend a meeting of the Liberal Parliamentary party which the Prime Minister had summoned at the Foreign Office. On May 31st he held his own decisive meeting of dissentient radicals in a committee room of the House of Commons. Of an attendance of a little more than fifty, forty-eight pronounced in favour of a straight vote against the second reading. In view of this, concessions by the Prime Minister on the retention of Irish members at Westminster would have been of little moment. They were not in any event forthcoming. Gladstone was unwilling to risk alienating Parnell for the doubtful prospect of conciliating Chamberlain. The vote in the House took place at one o'clock on the morning of June 8th. Chamberlain went into the "No" lobby with 92 other Liberals—46 of them his own radical followers—and 250 Tories. Dilke went into the "Aye" lobby with 229 other Gladstonians and 83 Irish Nationalists. The bill was defeated by a majority of thirty, and the third Gladstone Government, having failed in the sole task which it had set itself, was effectively at an end. So was the Dilke-Chamberlain political partnership.

Dissolution followed almost at once, and Dilke set about the task, which he would have regarded as hopeless even had his energies not been otherwise engaged, of defending Chelsea. His result there was declared on July 5th. He was out by 4,304 votes to 4,128. If anything this was better than he had expected. "The turnover in Chelsea was very small, smaller than anywhere else in the neighbourhood, and showed that personal consider- ations had told in my favour, in as much as we gained but a small number of Irish, it not being an Irish district, and had it not been for personal considerations should have lost more Liberal Unionists than we did."[27] This was a reasonable appraisal, and one which was fortified by comments in many of the letters of commiseration which reached Dilke. "No one but your husband could have polled so many Gladstonian votes," Sir Henry James wrote to Lady Dilke. "London is dead against the Prime Minister."[28]

Even if we discount a little both this and Dilke's own comment it is clear that the seat was not lost because of the divorce case. Nevertheless, the case meant that it was lost at a time when it would be exceedingly difficult to find another. The situation was quite different from that which prevailed in 1878 when Dilke was receiving pressing offers to stand for Manchester, or in 1884 when he could have chosen any part of the old Chelsea division. Furthermore, for a man in middle age to lose a seat which he has held since the age of twenty-five is at the best of times a considerable blow. When it happens eleven days before the commencement of legal proceedings upon which his whole future depends and the omens for which look increasingly dark, it is apt to seem an almost insupportable further trial. It is not surprising that he awaited the outcome with deep foreboding.

"I had at this moment," he wrote of the period between the election and the opening of the case, "through worry fallen into a condition of mental despondency. . . . I had made up my mind that untruth would triumph, that Stead, who had been professing to be strongly friendly to me since the Queen's Proctor's intervention had been asked for by myself, as he professed on his bidding, would turn round and insist on my prosecution for perjury; and, lastly, that in the then state of London opinion I should be convicted by a London special jury, and sent to penal servitude away from my brave and devoted wife for as many years as my strength might last—till death in fact."[29]

This was the mood in which Dilke presented himself at the Law Courts on the morning of Friday, July 16th.

Chapter Thirteen

The Case for Dilke

The case was heard before Sir James Hannen (who was referred to in the transcript as "the Right Honourable the President"*) and a special jury. The Queen's Proctor was represented by Sir Walter Phillimore, Q.C., H. Bargrave Deane and Marshall Hall, the last-named then so junior that he was allowed to take no part in the proceedings. For Crawford there appeared Henry Matthews, Q.C., Inderwick, Q.C. (who had led in the first trial) and R. S. Wright. Mrs. Crawford had Lockwood, Q.C., and H. F. Thompson. Murphy, Q.C., held a watching brief for what was rather mysteriously referred to as "a person interested

---

* He was the President of the Probate, Divorce and Admiralty division of the High Court. Later, as Lord Hannen, he became a Lord of Appeal in Ordinary. He was the father of Nicholas Hannen, the actor, and was known as the most handsome judge on the bench. Born in 1821, he died in 1894.

in the proceedings" and who was in fact Captain Forster. Dilke was described by *The Times* as having been refused leave to appear, but as "sitting in court with the Attorney General, Q.C., the Rt. Hon. Sir Henry James, Q.C., and Mr. Searle." The array of legal talent was formidable. The court, it need hardly be said, was crowded to the doors.

Almost at the beginning the odds were further weighted against Dilke. At the conclusion of his opening speech Sir Walter Phillimore proposed that Mrs. Crawford should immediately be put into the witness-box. The following interchange then took place:

> The Right Hon. the President: "No, you must leave that entirely to me."
>
> Sir W. Phillimore: "Then I shall have to ask your Lordship at what time Mrs. Crawford shall be called, and certainly I shall have to ask that Sir Charles Dilke shall not be called until after Mrs. Crawford."
>
> The President: "I may say at once I cannot assent to that. The issue lies on the Queen's Proctor to lay such evidence before the Jury as he thinks will establish the case."
>
> Sir W. Phillimore: "If your Lordship pleases. Then that is a settled matter which was a matter of some difficulty in my mind with regard to the conduct of this case."

No decision could have underlined more thoroughly the curious form which this second trial was to take, or done more to undermine Dilke's interests. Had the form of the case coincided with its substance—was Dilke guilty of the accusations made against him or was he not—the natural course would have been for Mrs. Crawford to specify her charges, for Dilke to answer them as best he could, and for the court to decide between them. The reversal of this procedure meant that Dilke in his evidence had to seek to controvert allegations before they were fully made and to demonstrate, not merely that specific charges were false, but that he could never have had an adulterous relationship with Mrs, Crawford. Furthermore, Mrs. Crawford was given the inestimable advantage, if she wished to fabricate a story, of sitting in court and hearing Dilke's defence before she formulated her attack. She could, if she desired, shape her evidence to circumnavigate his rebuttals.

Before Dilke was put into the box the evidence given at the first trial was read to the court, and so were the last two anonymous letters which Crawford had received, together with a correspondence between Mrs. Crawford and Crawford's solicitor, Stewart, all of which had been "put in" in February. The correspondence had taken place in July, 1885, after Mrs. Crawford's confession to her husband, when Stewart was endeavouring to persuade her to go to his office and make a written statement. This she hesitated to do, and Stewart attempted pressure, first by informing her that Dilke denied the charges and alleged a conspiracy, which allegation she would have to meet. She replied to this by writing: "I am horribly frightened at the prospect of Sir Charles Dilke fighting the case, as it complicates it so dreadfully." Stewart then adopted a more threatening tone.

> "I wish to say," he wrote, "that your husband is resolved, at all costs, to obtain a divorce, and that it will depend on you whether it is obtained quietly, without unnecessary exposure and without implicating others, or after offensive investigations, and with the painful, but unavoidable

necessity of making charges against many others whom you may wish to protect—I mean female relations of your own—and another co-respondent, Captain Forster. It will depend on you, therefore, which course is adopted. If you will assist in supplying the necessary information, a great deal which is painful to yourself and incriminating (to) others will be avoided, which will not be the case otherwise."

Dilke then took the stand. For the remainder of the morning and a short time after the luncheon adjournment he was examined-in-chief by Phillimore. Early in the afternoon his cross-examination by Matthews began and was continued for the remainder of the day and for a short time on the Saturday morning. Matthews asked him 453 questions. Phillimore then re-examined him for half an hour.

Dilke was an almost impossibly bad witness.[†] He was vague in his recollection of simple facts, he was full of verbose explanations, and he showed an extreme reluctance to answer a question with a straightforward affirmative or negative. His favourite method of denying a fact was to omit to say "no" but to explain why it was inherently improbable. The interventions of the President during the examination-in-chief indicate the way things were going. "Sir Walter, I think you must put the question," Hannen said after a quarter of an hour. "It is natural that Sir Charles should go into the question with greater detail than is necessary." Half an hour later he interjected again: "It

---

[†] Perhaps the expectation of this was an additional, unspoken reason which weighed with James and Russell in February.

will be much better if Sir Charles allows himself to be conducted by you in the material parts of the case. All the details of the business of the House of Commons are immaterial. It is the time he was there." And then again: "We do not want the reasons."

The examination-in-chief was directed to meeting the points put forward by Mrs. Crawford in her proof. It dealt with six principal issues. The first was Dilke's degree of acquaintanceship with Mrs. Crawford. He had known her slightly as a child, when she was probably brought to 76, Sloane Street by her parents to call upon Mrs. Chatfield, Dilke's grandmother. He believed that he had not attended her wedding, but he might have paid a family call on her at Bailey's Hotel some time afterwards, although he had no distinct recollection of this. He might also have called once at the Crawfords' house in Sydney Place during the session of 1882, but he had no recollection of the interior of the house, and believed they were not at home. Mrs. Crawford, he thought, had called at Sloane Street on perhaps two or three occasions in the years 1882–5, while he was at breakfast between 11 o'clock and 11–30, which was the normal time for family and other callers. That was all. There had certainly been no impropriety between them.

The second issue was that of the house off the Tottenham Court Road where Mrs. Crawford alleged that Dilke had taken her, and the address of which—65, Warren Street—she had specified in her proof. Dilke said that he knew the house well, although he had certainly not taken Mrs. Crawford there. It was the house where Anna Dessouslavy, a Swiss woman who was a pensioner of the Dilke family, lodged. The pension had been originally granted to Rosalie Dessouslavy, Anna's elder sister, who had been twenty-three years in the service of the family, and had been Dilke's own nurse. She had lived to enjoy it only for two years, and it had then been transferred, by Dilke himself, to Anna. Anna had at times assisted in the nursery and had returned to the Dilke household, in which two of her younger sisters had also at times been employed, when she was out of a job elsewhere. Her health had become bad, and Dilke used to call upon her at Warren Street perhaps once or twice a year.

The third issue was that of Dilke's general pattern of life and the domestic arrangements at 76, Sloane Street. The point here was whether Mrs. Crawford's statements were to prove compatible with these. Dilke described his day as beginning with the newspapers and tea being brought up to his room, followed by the arrival of the fencing party at 10 o'clock. This consisted (besides himself) of the fencing master and an average of two or three other people, who came without notice, as they chose, for the invitation was a general one. The fencing took place on a terrace at the back of the house if the weather were fine, or in the dining-room which led on to it if it were wet. It lasted until 11 o'clock. Dilke did not fence all the time, but used to spend part of the hour sitting in the dining-room reading Foreign Office telegrams which were brought to him by messenger. The messengers, several of whom would come on a normal morning, used to sit in the hall waiting to take the telegrams on to the next person on the list. In addition, one of his two footmen used invariably to be on duty in the hall, for the period from 10 to 11–30 was a busy one, with the arrival of the fencers, the messengers and other callers causing the door-bell to be constantly rung. When he joined the Cabinet at the end of 1882 he continued to see the telegrams; and the Foreign Office messengers were supplemented by others from 10, Downing

Street and the Local Government Board.

By 11 o'clock Dilke would have dressed himself, and from then until 11–30 he breakfasted in the room adjoining the dining-room at the front of the house. During the meal he continued to read telegrams and deal with work prepared by his private secretary, Bodley, as well as to see callers, who frequently came at this hour. At 11–30, according to a standing order, his coachman brought his brougham to the front of the house, and at this time or a few minutes later he left home. As a rule he drove straight to the Foreign Office (or later the Local Government Board), but he occasionally paid brief calls before doing so.

He usually remained at his office until it was time to go across to the House of Commons, which met at 4–30; sometimes, if the pressure of work were light, he would go out to luncheon. In the evenings, if he were dining away from the House of Commons, he would dress in his room there, or if the House were not in session in his room at the Foreign Office or the Local Government Board. He rarely returned to his own house until late at night.

This house he described as being "a very old house" with only one staircase. On the first half-landing was the "blue room," which had curtains and no door, and into which callers were normally shown. On the first floor proper were two drawing-rooms, leading into each other and again without doors. Above the blue room was Bodley's room, which looked straight out to the staircase. This room had a door, but it was invariably left open. Off the passage-way leading to it was another, smaller and doorless room which was used by Ireland, Bodley's clerk. Ireland used to arrive at about eight in the morning, Bodley somewhat later, but before Dilke was up.

Above the drawing-rooms were a suite of three rooms which were used by Dilke's son when he was at home (which was not often) or by Dilke's great-uncle when he came from Chichester to pay his one month's annual visit. On the third half-landing, above Bodley's room, was Dilke's own sitting-room, which he chiefly used for keeping his letters and other papers. Then, above his son's suite, came his own bedroom, together with another, unused room, which communicated with it, but which was kept locked. On the floor above, the top floor, were the servants' quarters.

The fourth issue was that of Dilke's movements on February 23rd, 1882, the day on which Mrs. Crawford alleged that she had gone to Warren Street and he had first seduced her. With the help of his engagement book he was able to recount these in some detail. The fencing and the departure from home at 11–30 he deduced from his unvarying practice, although he was able to recall that his great-uncle, who was staying with him at the time, had been present at breakfast. At the Foreign Office he had evidence of unusual activity. There were eight parliamentary questions for him to answer that afternoon, of which five were new that morning. The answers had to be prepared and cleared both with Granville and with the permanent under-secretary. There were also a great number of notes and minutes which passed during the day between Dilke and Granville, and which Dilke had brought with him and was prepared to show to the court. In addition, the day was particularly busy because a bill relating to the French commercial treaty negotiations, which Dilke had been conducting during the previous autumn, had been introduced that morning into the Chamber of Deputies. Lord Lyons, the Ambassador in Paris, had been telegraphing about it at frequent intervals.

On top of everything it was a "levée day," which meant that Dilke had to attend at Buckingham Palace in uniform. He described the procedure which this involved. On levée days he always ordered his brougham to be at the Foreign Office with a footman and his levée clothes at 1–25. That enabled him to be changed and at the Palace before two o'clock. As he was not then in the Cabinet he had not the privilege of the entrée, and had "to pass in with other gentle-men." It must therefore have been at least 2–40 before he could have passed through the three rooms and escaped. He could not have been back at the Foreign Office and changed before three o'clock or a little later. On levée days he had "lost his luncheon," but had tea and dry toast at the Foreign Office. He then checked the final version of his answers to questions which had to be completely ready and copied out for distribution to the newspapers by four o'clock. At 4–25 he left for the House of Commons to be ready to give the first answer of the day. He sat on the bench until the end of questions and then, at about 5–45, was asked for information without notice about what was happening in Paris. He was unable to answer fully at the time, but after returning to his room in the House, where there were boxes waiting for him both from the Foreign Office and from Granville in the House of Lords, he was able to interpose a statement at about eight o'clock. He dined at the House of Commons.

The fifth issue was that of Dilke's movements on February 13th and 14th, 1883, the dates on which Mrs. Crawford alleged that she had spent nights at 76, Sloane Street, and the only others specifically mentioned in her proof. In view of the times involved it was inevitable that Dilke's alibis for these dates should be less complete than for February 23rd of the previous year; but he was able to state that, on the 13th he had attended a Cabinet meeting in the afternoon, which had lasted from one o'clock until four or five o'clock, and in the evening at eight he had addressed his constituents at the Kensington Town Hall, the meeting lasting, with questions, until about 10–45, and the speech being reported, verbatim, in the newspapers the following morning. On the 14th he had attended, in uniform, the ministerial dinner for the reading of the Queen's speech (it being the eve of the opening of the new session of Parliament) and had gone on afterwards to a party at Lady Granville's. He denied resolutely that Mrs. Crawford had slept at his house on these nights, or on any other occasion.

The sixth and last main issue was that of Dilke's relations with his former servant, Sarah Gray, who had been mentioned in Mrs. Crawford's confessions, and with Fanny, who was Sarah Gray's sister, although Mrs. Crawford apparently did not know this. Sarah had been his principal woman servant for thirteen years, from 1872 to 1885. She had been engaged by his first wife and had left after his second marriage when he took over Mrs. Pattison's servants in place of his own. He had never given Sarah instructions to let Mrs. Crawford in, to dress her, or to show her out. There was certainly never any relationship between himself and Sarah "except that of master and servant." About Fanny he knew much less. She had been in his service, as under nursery-maid, for a short time, about seven years previously. He was not directly aware that she had subsequently been in the habit of coming to his house, to see her sister, almost every Sunday, because he was usually away from Saturday to Monday; but he had recently been told that this was so. Fanny had never been his mistress, and he had certainly never shared a bed with her and Mrs. Crawford. He had never given his solicitor any special instructions about Fanny. Humbert had been left to make what arrangements he thought fit, although Dilke knew that at one stage he was in touch with her.

Phillimore then proceeded, in a most circumlocutory way, to put his final question. He referred to his doubt about how the matter stood under the Evidence Further Amendment Act of 1869 and asked for the President's ruling. The President ruled that he could without doubt put the question he had in mind to "a willing witness," and Phillimore then said: "Then, Sir Charles, I put the question to you—have you ever committed adultery with Mrs. Crawford?" Dilke answered, "Certainly not"; and the examination-in-chief was at an end. Phillimore asked whether, if any further specific dates were alleged, he would be at liberty to recall the witness, the President agreed, and Dilke was handed over to Henry Matthews.

Matthews' cross-examination was hostile, skilful and effective. Bodley referred to him later as having vilified Dilke "with a coarseness unknown in the courts since the disappearance of Kenealy," but this was an exaggerated view. Matthews did his job as a highly-paid advocate, who was no respecter of persons and was determined to get a verdict for his client by discrediting the evidence of the principal adverse witness, and he did it with great success. Charles Russell would no doubt have attempted to do the same to Mrs. Crawford; but he was not allowed to try.

Matthews began by asking Dilke what he believed about Mrs. Crawford's state of mind and her reasons for making the allegations. It was an excellent choice of opening. Even a much more succinct witness would have found difficulty in dealing with this subject by means of question and answer. Dilke was

315

soon floundering hopelessly:

> Question: Did you believe at the time of the last trial that Mrs. Crawford was in her sound mind?
>
> Answer: Yes, I did, and do now.
>
> Q.: Did you believe that she had any motive for making this confession about you if it was untrue?
>
> A.: Yes.
>
> Q.: What motive?
>
> A.: I believe that she desired—finding that she was near discovery in a course of adultery with other persons—that she desired to fix upon a person already agreed between her and others for that purpose.
>
> Q.: Wait a minute; who were the others?
>
> A.: The persons with whom she had at various times confessed to having committed adultery.
>
> Q.: Who are they, Sir Charles?
>
> A.: They are Dr.—I am very sorry to have to mention the names of persons who are probably innocent—Dr. F. Warner, spoken of as "Freddy Warner," and her own brother-in-law, Dr. Robert Priestley. This I utterly disbelieve.
>
> Q.: Kindly mention the names.
>
> A.: I hardly like to mention the names.
>
> Q.: I am asking the names of persons whom you allege or believe she was conspiring with.
>
> A.: No; you misunderstand me entirely.
>
> The President: I so understood it.
>
> Mr. Matthews: He said so.
>
> The President: Who were the persons whom you allege?

Mr. Matthews: I understood you to answer me, Sir Charles, that you believed she was a perfectly sane woman, who, conspiring with others, had, in order to get rid of her marriage tie, invented this story about you?

A.: Yes.

Q.: I ask you who those others are with whom you allege she was conspiring?

A.: She herself has mentioned, or believed, that the anonymous letters proceeded from her own mother. I do not know—it is impossible for me to know from whom the anonymous letters proceeded—but the author of the anonymous letters would be one whom I mean, whoever that may be.

Q.: You say the author of the anonymous letters, whoever that was?

A.: Yes.

Q.: Do you say you believe it was her mother?

A.: I do not know. I have no means of knowing.

Q.: With whom else was she conspiring?

A.: The last of this series of lovers.

Q.: Let us have the names, if you please—let us have no false sense of delicacy about it?

A.: Captain Forster.

Q.: I understand you to allege that Captain Forster, Mrs. Smith and Mrs. Crawford conspired together to invent the story about her and you?

A.: No, I do not say that at all. I say the author of the anonymous letters. I have no means of knowing who the author of the anonymous letters was.

Q.: That the author of the anonymous letters, Captain Forster and Mrs. Crawford conspired together to get up this story against you without a shadow of truth?

A.: The case appears to me to point to that.

Q.: And you thought that at the time of the late trial?

A.: I thought so.

Q.: So that at the time of the late trial you thought it was a deliberate conspiracy by a wicked person to deceive the Court, and to get a divorce from Mr. Crawford without the slightest foundation for the allegations made?

A.: Without foundation for the allegations made as regards myself but with a great deal of foundation for the allegations as regards other people, also made in a similar way.

Q.: Other people—you now put several.

A.: I said so just now—you stopped me. I understood you wished for a list of names. I was giving that list of names when you stopped me.

Q.: You were giving a list of the names of people with whom Mrs. Crawford had committed adultery.

A.: With whom Mrs. Crawford had confessed she had committed adultery.

Q.: To what people?

A.: I believe several.

Q.: Give me one.

A.: Mrs. Rogerson.

Q.: Mrs. Rogerson has repeated it to you?

A.: Yes, and to many other people. I believe the whole of this is in the possession of the Queen's Proctor. I have every reason to believe so.

Q.: I did not ask you that; if you will kindly answer my questions I shall be obliged to you.

A.: You are asking me matters of opinion.

The President: Be good enough to follow the questions the learned Counsel puts to you; if any improper questions are put to you your Counsel will protect you.[‡]

Matthews then suggested that with these thoughts in his mind it was most improper for Dilke not to have gone into the box at the first trial. On Dilke's reasons for not doing so, he asked: "Is it true or untrue that there are acts of indiscretion in your life which you desired not to disclose on cross-examination?" Dilke answered: "Acts which came to an end eleven and a half years ago"; and Matthews said: "Then it is true?" And Dilke said "Yes." Later in the cross-examination (on the following day) Matthews reverted to this point:

Q.: Was it true that you had been her mother's lover?

A.: I was yesterday asked a question of a somewhat similar kind, and I replied to it. I must decline to answer that question.

It does not appear that Matthews, or the President, or Phillimore was keeping Section 3 of the Evidence Further Amendment Act very closely in mind at this stage.

Following his earlier reference to this point Matthews went on to question Dilke about his visit to Mrs. Crawford at Mrs. Ashton Dilke's house on the Tuesday after the confession. Here he wished to suggest that Dilke had offered Mrs. Crawford money if she would agree to a quiet separation from her husband. The witness's unfortunate method of answering questions, which was

<hr />

[‡] It was a remarkable slip on the part of the President to assume that Dilke had counsel to protect him, and one which caused great resentment.

particularly in evidence in this passage, greatly helped Matthews in his suggestion.

Mr. Matthews: Did you go on to say to Mrs. Dilke that if Mrs. Crawford had not income enough to live apart from her husband you would make up her income for her?

A.: Certainly not.

Q.: Or anything of that sort?

A.: No, certainly not.

Q.: Did you also tell Mrs. Ashton Dilke that you wished her sister to sign a retractation of the confession she had made?

A.: I do not think so. I do not know what I might have said of that kind, because I was very angry indeed at the foul charges which had been made against me by her. I do not think so, but it is possible I may. With regard to the money it is absurd, because Mrs. Dilke is far richer than I am.

Q.: I am not speaking about Mrs. Dilke. I am speaking about Mrs. Crawford.

A.: Mrs. Crawford was living with Mrs. Dilke. If she wanted to be provided for she would be provided for by her; the suggestion is absurd on the face of it.

The President: That is not within the limits of an answer; it is irregular.

Mr. Matthews: I am not asking you the question without reason. I put it to you distinctly. You said that in substance you urged a separation, so that the matter should be secret instead of being public—a voluntary separation—and if there was any difficulty about Mrs. Crawford's income you would make it up,

A.: I believe a separation was offered.

Q.: I am asking you, did a conversation about separation take place between you and Mrs. Dilke?

A.: You have been asking me a great deal about what I believe.

Q.: Now I am asking you about the conversation.

Sir W. Phillimore: I think, Sir Charles, you had better answer the question as to the conversation.

Mr. Matthews: Did Mrs. Ashton Dilke express indignation, and advise you to say nothing of the kind to Mrs. Crawford?

A.: I just told you I said nothing of the kind.

Q.: Then did Mrs. Crawford come down, and did you see her, and have an interview with her in the drawing-room, Mrs. Dilke standing some little way off?

A.: Yes, which is in itself inconsistent with what you have been asking.

Q.: Never mind, Sir, we shall see whether it is inconsistent or not by and by.

Matthews ridiculed Dilke's suggestion that his behaviour on this occasion was to be accounted for by the fact that he was "boiling with rage." "This was Tuesday," Matthews asked, "you had been boiling with rage since Sunday? "He then passed to an involved exchange about the conversation which had occurred when Mrs. Rogerson told Dilke, as Matthews alleged, of the anonymous letters received by Crawford. Dilke denied that such a conversation ever took place, but Matthews pressed him hard to admit it and to agree that Mrs. Rogerson added: "You see your sin has found you out." Dilke not only denied this on his own behalf, but added that, to his certain knowledge, Mrs. Rogerson denied it also. This got him into further trouble with the President, who interjected sharply: "You are

321

not here to tell us what Mrs. Rogerson said or will say. You are here to answer for yourself."

The next point of substance related to Mrs. Dessouslavy. Here again Dilke was on weak ground, because he was unable to specify periods of any length when she had been in his own or his father's service and which could provide an apparent justification for a continuing payment of forty pounds a year. It would have been much better if he had said firmly that the pension was not directly related to her own services, rather than attempting an unconvincing search for dates. Then, after Dilke had rejected repeated suggestions that he had paid very frequent visits to the Warren Street house and had met a lady or ladies there, Matthews turned to asking him about Fanny. Did he not know that Fanny had been living at Warren Street with Mrs. Dessouslavy from June, 1884, to July, 1885? Did he not see her when he called there? The answer to both these questions being no, the following interchange took place:

Q.: Had you any mistress called Fanny in the years 1882, 1883 or 1884?
A.: No.
Q.: Or any mistress whom you called "Fanny"?
A.: No.[§]

Matthews concluded this section of the cross-examination by suggesting that, in the autumn of 1885, when Fanny had been sent to a farm-house in Essex where Humbert used to stay for shooting, Dilke had been paying for her keep, and that Mrs. Ruffle, the farmer's wife, had been employed to try to get

---

[§] Again, the Act of 1869 seems to have been forgotten.

Fanny to swear to an exculpating statement. The substance of Dilke's reply was that these were matters which he had left to his solicitor.

The next issue was that of Dilke's morning habits. Matthews was most anxious, for the sake of Mrs. Crawford's story, to create an impression of greater elasticity.

> Q.: With regard to your going out after breakfast, there again it may have been twenty minutes earlier, and sometimes twenty minutes later?
>
> A.: I should doubt its varying twenty minutes later. I never went out before half past eleven; my brougham came round as a matter of course without being ordered.
>
> Q.: I dare say your brougham came round.
>
> A.: You said earlier.
>
> Q.: Never before half past eleven?
>
> A.: Yes.
>
> Q.: Might have run on until twelve?
>
> A.: Very seldom, if ever.
>
> Q.: But occasionally?
>
> A.: Very seldom, except on Saturday, when I was staying in town.
>
> Q.: Occasionally it might?
>
> A.: On Saturday, when I was staying in town, it might.

Matthews then attempted to break down Dilke's alibi for February 23rd, 1882. He asked to see Dilke's diary for that day and noted that the entries were confined to "levée" and "dined at the House." He refused firmly to look at the morning's letters to and from Lord Granville, which Dilke kept proffering him, and instead embarked on a line of questioning which could hardly have been expected to produce positive answers:

Q.: Have you any document, or any entry, that will show at what hour you reached the Foreign Office that day?

A.: No. With regard to that, or any specified day, I have a great many letters passing between Lord Granville and myself.

Q.: You have nothing whatever in writing to show what hour you reached the Foreign Office that day?

A.: I have a great many letters passing between Lord Granville and myself which will show that the answers to the questions were settled in the morning.

Q.: Show me anything to fix the hour at which you arrived at the Foreign Office.

A.: No, nothing will fix the hour; they only show that I was there before the levée and did a great deal of work.

Q.: Whom did you first see when you arrived at the Foreign Office?

A.: Always my private secretary; he was the first person I should see.

Q.: Is there any person you can mention as having seen earlier?

A.: It is impossible for me to fix the first person I saw any day.

Q.: Then you cannot fix it.

Matthews did not cross-examine on the evidence about February 13th and 14th, 1883, the only other dates mentioned in Mrs. Crawford's proof, but he introduced several new dates, the 5th and 6th of May, and December 7th, 1882. "Where were you on the 5th or 6th May, 1882?" he asked suddenly. Dilke immediately applied for the President's protection. This was a date which had not been mentioned in the examination-in-chief. Surely he ought not to fix the hours before Mrs. Crawford had given her evidence? Phillimore supported him. "I do think, my Lord," he said, "that considering the nature of the cross-examination, and of certain questions I shall have to address to Mrs. Crawford, your Lordship ought to hesitate before hearing the defence on that part of the case before the attack." But the President gave no help. Indeed by this stage his hostility to Dilke had become marked: "I must conduct the case on known principles," he replied. "I know of no principle on which I can exclude this cross-examination."

> The witness: Of course I shall take your Lordship's direction absolutely. Shall I state the matter definitely as to hours?
>
> The President: Be kind enough to answer the questions put to you; that is the only advice I can give you; if any improper questions are put to you the learned counsel who represents the Queen's Proctor will take the objection, but until that objection is taken you must answer.
>
> The witness: Of course I shall do what I am directed, the reason I was going to give——
>
> The President: You must excuse me. I do not desire to hear any reason from you except it be in explanation of a question which is put to you."

The cross-examination continued. Matthews concentrated on May 6th and having asked to see Dilke's diary for that day found the following entries: "Earle," "Duchess," "Greenwich dinner," and "Evening party." He was most interested in the morning; and, having discovered that "Earle" meant a luncheon engagement at Mrs. Charles Earle's in Bryanston Square at 1–30 or 1–45 and that Dilke had left home by 11–45, he thought he had discovered a lacuna. But Dilke explained it by saying that he had gone to Mrs. Earle's at twelve o'clock in order to meet his present wife who was staying there and who had returned from France that morning.[1] Dilke was also able to volunteer the fact that May 6th was the day of the Phoenix Park murders and, for this reason, was particularly clearly fixed in his mind.

Matthews then asked, rather casually, about May 4th and May 5th, and in looking at the entry for one of these days was struck by the condition of the diary. It was remarkable, like that of all Dilke's engagement books, for many years both previously and subsequently. His habit was to buy these books in half-yearly units, with a large page to each day and a perforation running down the centre. Entries were made in duplicate, and at the beginning of each day one side of the page was torn off to be carried about by Dilke and destroyed when the day was past, while the other remained on a table in Bodley's room and was kept as a permanent record. In addition, however, the permanent pages were frequently lacerated, sometimes by the excision of large segments, sometimes by the cutting out of neat little circular holes. It was an unfortunate habit for someone who was to appear in the Divorce Court, and it excited a good deal of incredulous questioning from both Matthews and the President:

Mr. Matthews: I suppose these pieces have been cut out since?
A.: I always reduce it in bulk as much as possible. It is done in the morning, and I cut it so as to make it as small as possible.

---

[1] When the cross-examination was resumed on the following day, Matthews repaid Dilke by a delicate piece of innuendo for this explanation. The following interchange then took place: Q.: Sir Charles, you said yesterday that on the 6th of May, 1882, you had lunch with the Earles, and you met your present wife? A.: Yes. Q.: Was she then married, and was her late husband then living? A.: Yes. Q.: When did he die? A.: I think in July, two years ago. Q.: July, 1884? A.: I think so."

Q.: Do you mean you cut holes like that?

A.: Yes; it would be an engagement that has gone off.

Q.: You mean that when an engagement goes off you cut a hole like that.

A.: Yes; you will find it done everywhere.

Q.: What do you mean by an engagement going off?

A.: I mean to say if I have made an engagement to see a person, and that person did not come, I should cut it out.

The President: Do I understand you to say that you carried that very book which we see out with you?

A.: No.

The President: Then I do not very well see why it is necessary to cut it so as to reduce it in bulk as you say.

A.: Because it goes into my letter-box; if you like to send to my house now you can get any of my boxes.

Mr. Matthews: When was it you cut the holes?

A.: If any of my engagements go off, I take the scissors and cut it out.

Q.: You sit down with scissors or a penknife and cut it out and cut holes in your diary?

A.: I should naturally cut it out, not cutting the diary through— cutting the part off—I should cut it out.

Q.: If I really understood you rightly that because an engagement goes off, instead of just striking a pen or pencil through it, you would sit down with a penknife and cut a hole in it like that?

A.: I sometimes strike a pencil through it, but the blot of a pen is a trouble. I always sit with scissors by my side.

It all sounded most unconvincing and helped to deepen the bad impression which Dilke had already created. In fact,

327

however, it was undoubtedly a habit of long standing, in which Dilke indulged freely and publicly, certainly in front of Bodley and Ireland. In later years he habitually sat in the House of Commons library with a pair of scissors at his side, and his passion for laceration (or "reducing the bulk," as he would have called it) was such that he frequently cut off the tops and bottoms of letters, without disturbing the text, before putting them away for keeping.

December 7th, 1882, was the other new date which Matthews suggested. Dilke in answering first looked at his diary for the previous year and denied that he was in England. Matthews put him right with unconcealed pleasure—"Just think, Sir Charles"— and then elucidated that he had met Harcourt to discuss the Government of London Bill in the morning and had dined at 143, Piccadilly, in the evening. Dilke obviously had no idea what was being alleged for this day, but Matthews eventually put the point to him direct—asking whether he had met Mrs. Crawford in Hans Place that evening and taken her home with him—and received a clear denial.

The next point upon which Matthews decided to cast doubt— and managed again to get the witness floundering—was the plausibility of the degree of acquaintanceship with Mrs. Crawford to which Dilke admitted.

Q.: This was a young married woman with whom, as you say, your relations had been extremely slight since her marriage. What did she come to see you for in the morning?

A.: We got to know each other better, as I had seen her, as I said, some two or three times a year, and her sister, Mrs. Dilke, used occasionally to call on me in the morning.

Q.: I am not asking you about her sister, Mrs. Dilke, but Mrs. Crawford; what on earth did Mrs. Crawford, a young married woman, come to the house of a bachelor about eleven o'clock for?

A.: She looked upon me as I looked upon her, I should think, as a member of the family.

Q.: Looked upon you as a member of her family. Did you ever speak of these visits to Mr. Crawford?

A.: Whenever I met him after I always asked after her by her Christian name.

Q.: Sir Charles Dilke, is that an answer to my question? Did you ever speak to her husband of these visits of a young wife to your house in the morning?

A.: It never occurred to me for one moment that he was not aware of them, if there were more than one.

Q.: You know from his evidence that has been read that he was not aware of it. . . . You cannot suggest any legitimate business she came to you about?

A.: If you want topics of conversation I can give some of them. I do not remember that particular occasion when she called upon me.

Q.: That is what I am talking about. I want you to tell us what business this young woman came to your house upon, by herself, without her husband?

A.: The topics of conversation she occasionally started on two or three occasions I saw her had relation to what she was trying to do in Whitechapel and sometimes to her husband's position.

Q.: What do you mean by "sometimes to her husband's position"?

A.: She was very anxious indeed that Mr. Crawford should obtain a permanent place in any Scotch Home Rule arrangement.

Q.: Do I understand you to say that she came to you about her husband having a permanent place?

A.: Yes, I do. I won't say she ever came for that, to press his claims for such an appointment; but she was certainly anxious that those claims, which were great, should be considered.

Q.: Had Mr. Crawford ever asked you for a place?

A.: No, he never asked for any services from me except on the last occasion but one when I saw him.

Q.: Do you suggest that was the purport of these visits?

A.: I do not know. I had my suspicions.

Q.: You had your suspicions.

Another section of Matthews's cross-examination was apparently based on some straws of information obtained from Dilke's servants. He asked whether Dilke had ever told his footman that Mrs. Crawford was coming to the house. Dilke denied it, and Matthews went on:

Q.: If they say that, then that is untrue.

A.: Yes.

Q.: Have you ever told your footmen that a lady was coming to look over the house, and you wished the windows cleaned?

A.: There have been people who went over the house to see the pictures, but I have no recollection of any particular lady, or having the windows cleaned.

Q.: I am afraid you will oblige me to repeat my question. Have you told your footmen, any day when Mrs. Crawford was coming, that a lady was coming to the house?

A.: No, no, no.

Q.: You are not in doubt about that, you are positive?

A.: Yes. I do not think Mrs. Crawford is a lady who would be interested in pictures or things of that sort.[**]

Dilke was then asked whether a housemaid of his, Mary Ann Gray (Sarah Gray's niece) had not "come upon a lady with her outer garments off" in his bedroom at 11–30 in the morning and whether this servant had not in consequence been forbidden by Sarah to go to that part of the house? Dilke returned negative answers to both these questions, and Matthews proceeded, without much success, to insert some insinuations about the witness's relations with Sarah.

The last main point in the cross-examination was concerned with a quarrel which had taken place between Dilke and Captain Forster at Mrs. Rogerson's flat in Albert Mansions in June, 1885. Mrs. Rogerson had asked Dilke to go and see her and had told him that Forster was extremely angry, having heard that Dilke had written a letter to the War Office which mentioned the captain's intrigue with Mrs. Crawford and was designed "to blast his military prospects." When Dilke was leaving Forster came out of another room and accosted him on the stairs, using very violent language and challenging him to fight. According to Dilke, Forster said: "I know that you are a good fencer, and boxer, and a good shot or so forth, but I am one of Angelo's pupils." Dilke implied that he laughed the whole thing off as being utterly ridiculous, denied that he had written to the War

---

[**] This was an astonishing answer, for as Dilke in fact knew Mrs. Crawford was a trained painter and had a highly intelligent artistic and literary appreciation.

Office about Forster, and said that the only person to whom he had mentioned Forster's relations with Mrs. Crawford, of which he had been told by Mrs. Ashton Dilke, was his present wife.

At this stage the court adjourned. The first day's sitting was at an end. On the following morning, Matthews took only another quarter of an hour, mostly reverting to points of the previous day to which he had no doubt given further thought during the evening. He ended with a characteristic innuendo, based obviously on one phrase in Mrs. Crawford's confession, which Dilke tried hard to repulse:

Q.: Have you spent a good deal of your time in France?

A.: Not of late years.

G.: But in youth and early manhood?

A.: No, not in youth. I first bought a small property in France in 1876.

Q.: Since that you have been frequently to France?

A.: From 1876 to 1880 I was in France each winter for two and a half months.

Q.: And you are familiar with French habits and ways?

A.: I can hardly say that, because my property is away in the extreme south, and manners there are very different to the ordinary French ways. I am familiar with the habits in Provence on the coast, where they do not even speak French, but speak a different language.

Phillimore then re-examined briefly. He made a few rather half-hearted attempts to throw out life-lines to Dilke, but the latter grasped at them incompetently, continuing his habit of diffuse and inconclusive answers. Then, at last, he was able to step down. His five hours in the witness-box had not only been a formidable personal ordeal. They had also, without doubt, been immensely damaging to himself and his cause. The case for the Queen's Proctor was already looking weak.

Over the next two and a half days, Phillimore called twenty-three other witnesses. The first of these was Sarah Gray, who was then aged 41 (much older than her sister, Fanny, who was at that time 21) and whose difficulties in the box were greatly increased by her deafness. She had seen Mrs. Crawford once at 76, Sloane Street, but that was in old Mrs. Chatfield's time and before her marriage to Crawford. She had never seen her since. She had certainly never let her in, let her out or dressed her. She herself had never been Dilke's mistress, nor had Fanny. She had never seen Fanny and Dilke together.

Most of her cross-examination and all the evidence of the next two witnesses, Humbert, Dilke's solicitor, and Mrs. Ruffle, the farmer's wife from Stebbing in Essex, was concerned with the Fanny mystery. From the answers of the three it was possible to piece together the following story. At the end of July, 1885, Fanny came with her father to see Humbert. She had been badly frightened by the visit of two detectives working for Crawford. They had threatened her with a prosecution for perjury if she did not agree to appear in court and give the evidence which was required. She had wished to leave her father's house, where she had been staying, in case they came again. Humbert accordingly arranged for Mrs. Ruffle, as a special favour to him, to take her on as a housemaid for a short time. She stayed at the Ruffles' for four months, and at the end of November was married from their house to a local journey-man coach-builder called Stock. Sarah attended the wedding. Fanny then left with her husband, and her whereabouts were unknown until a week after the first trial, when she appeared at the house of a married sister at Forest Gate. She was seen there by Sarah and by Humbert, and she also went, at this time, to stay for a few days at Stebbing. Contact was again lost (as a new trial was not contemplated at this stage Humbert had no particular interest in preserving it), but in April she arrived with her husband at an address near King's Cross, and wrote to Humbert to say she was there. Humbert in consequence took a statement in writing from her and sent it to the Queen's Proctor. At Humbert's request Mrs. Ruffle twice came up to London to see Fanny and to endeavour to persuade her to appear in court and swear to her statement. This Fanny refused to do. She was also seen by Sarah during this "King's Cross" visit to London. After ten days she left without notice, and had not been heard of since.

There were several loose ends to this story. It was difficult to see who had paid the Stocks' expenses on their April visit to London—Stock being at the time an out-of-work journeyman, and Humbert denying resolutely that he had done so. There was another mystery about where Fanny had lived in the year or so before she went to Warren Street. Sarah, whom she had visited constantly during this period, believed that she had been in service in Brixton, but was unable to state at what address or with whom. Mrs. Ruffle and Humbert, on the other hand, both stated that Fanny declined to account for her movements during this period. The general impression that there was a good deal to hide was accentuated by the fact that Sarah gave her information with obvious reluctance, only admitting the Forest Gate meeting, for instance, after sustained probing by Matthews.

There followed the examination of Dilke's other servants. First came the three footmen: Samuel Goode, who had been at 76, Sloane Street for two years until August, 1882; William

Goode, his brother, who replaced him and stayed until December, 1884, and Henry Shanks, who was there from March, 1882 to April, 1885. All three received a rough handling from Matthews, with the worst treatment being reserved for Shanks, who was most unwell and had just come out of an infirmary. Nevertheless, they gave practically no corroboration for Mrs. Crawford's allegations. Samuel Goode had let her in one morning in 1882. Dilke came out into the hall to meet her (he might have seen her coming through the breakfast-room windows) and took her to the blue room. Goode let her out after a quarter of an hour. Shanks had let her in twice, again in the mornings, in the summer of 1884. On the first occasion Dilke saw her in the breakfast-room, and she left after a quarter of an hour. On the second occasion he saw her in the blue room and she left after ten minutes. It was possible that he had let her out on one other occasion when he had not let her in. Once during his service he was told by the other footman that a lady was coming to look over the house and asked to clean the windows. He cleaned those of the dining-room, the blue room and the drawing-room. He had no idea whether the lady came or who she was. He was pressed very strongly by Matthews to confirm some slightly more incriminating statements which the latter believed he had made to Stewart, Crawford's solicitor, in the autumn of 1885. He resolutely refused to do so, and made it clear, on re-examination, that Stewart had taken no statement from him in a regular form.

William Goode had let Mrs. Crawford in on two occasions, both, he thought, in the spring of 1883. On these occasions Dilke saw her in the breakfast-room, and she went into no other room. On the first she left after eight or ten minutes, and on the second after fifteen to twenty minutes. He denied having passed on to

Shanks any message about cleaning the windows. All three of the footmen fully confirmed Dilke's own description of his morning habits.

Next came Ellen Drake, who had been under-housemaid from April, 1880, to March, 1883. She had never seen a lady in the house (other than Mrs. Ashton Dilke) except for one occasion, in the evening, when she came up from the basement and found Sarah in the hall talking to someone who was dressed in black and wore a large black hat. But Ellen Drake was not certain that this person "was a lady. She might have been a friend of Sarah's." Ellen Drake further testified that she normally cleaned Dilke's bedroom with Sarah, sometimes while he was at breakfast, sometimes after he had gone out. There was no fixed time, and there was no prohibition on her being in any part of the house at any particular time, except that when she was first engaged, Mrs. Chatfield, still alive for her first year's service, had impressed on her that Sir Charles disliked seeing housemaids about the house. Matthews made no impression upon her in cross-examination.

The last of this group of witnesses was Charles Grant, who had been Dilke's coachman for fourteen years. His evidence was slightly against Dilke so far as Sloane Street was concerned (because it suggested that the latter's 11–30 departure was not always very punctual) but very much in his favour on the point of his visits to Mrs. Crawford. He could not remember ever having driven to Sydney Place, but he remembered five or six visits to Young Street in the course of two years. Sometimes Dilke did not stay at all. He was ready to leave by the time that Grant had turned his horses. On the other occasions he remained only ten or fifteen minutes. Grant then stood the brougham at the door, and from his place on the box he could see through Mrs. Crawford's drawing-room (which had windows at either end). He saw Dilke and a lady inside, and there was certainly no impropriety.

Next came Dilke's three private secretaries. Bodley was first, and was subject to a rigorous cross-examination from Matthews—a fact which may partly have accounted for his later strictures upon this advocate's methods. The main point was to challenge the witness's statement that he invariably sat in his room at 76, Sloane Street with the door open, and that he would therefore have seen anyone who used the staircase in the morning. "Was that to facilitate a view of the house-maids going up and down with the slops?" Matthews asked. But Bodley, whose answers were at once adroit and arrogant, emerged comparatively unscathed from this and other questioning. H. G. Kennedy, whom Bodley had replaced, then told the court that he was aware of the pension to Mrs. Dessouslavy, and had indeed been responsible for a number of years for seeing that it was paid.

H. A. Lee, Dilke's official private secretary at the Foreign Office, was last in this group. He testified to Dilke's punctuality and regularity—"the most regular man I think I have ever met"—and to his almost invariable habit of arriving at the Foreign Office within a few minutes of twelve. He also said that he had referred to the Foreign Office library and had discovered that, on February 23rd, 1882, Dilke had dealt with and initialled about thirty despatches and drafts, in addition to the parliamentary questions; but there was nothing to show whether they had been done before or after the levée.

Mrs. Dessouslavy was next put into the box. She was an even worse witness than Dilke himself, for she was ill, deaf, had an imperfect understanding of English, and was probably rather stupid as well. Matthews showed no patience with her infirmities; on the contrary he assumed for her benefit his most brusque and intimidating cross-examination manners. "Now, Mrs. Dessouslavy, do answer something. I do not much care what it is if you will only answer," he said on one occasion; and earned his one half-rebuke of the case from the President, who intervened: "If that is the case I think you might as well leave it." The facts of her life, as Mrs. Dessouslavy presented them (although in an extraordinarily muddled way) appeared to be that she had been born near Neuchâtel in 1837; that after a period of service in England she had gone back to Switzerland and married in 1867 and lived with her husband until he died in 1876; that she had inherited property from her father and her elder sister which, together with the Dilke pension, enabled her to live without earning, although until her health deteriorated in 1881 she attempted various forms of work, such as keeping a cigar shop off the Brompton Road, taking in lodgers, and looking after a priest's house at Petersham; that by 1884 her health had become still worse and that she therefore arranged for another sister to come from Russia (where she, too, was in service) in order to be with her; but that there being delay in the development of this plan she met Fanny by chance in the Tottenham Court Road and asked the girl to come and live with her, as a sort of companion-maid, until her sister arrived.

Matthews devoted himself to casting doubt on this story in order to suggest that her life had been passed in the indulgence or organisation of immorality. He tried to minimise her property and to make nonsense of her periods of employment in order to suggest that she had throughout been kept by Dilke. He insinuated that her lodging-house had been a disorderly

338

one and that she had taken in Fanny so that the attractions of the house in Warren Street, already available for assignation, might be increased. Her memory for dates and figures and her slowness of reaction was such that he had some success in all these endeavours, and certainly reduced her to a state of utter confusion about her past life. But he failed completely to shake her denials that Warren Street had ever been used by Dilke, or anyone else, as a place at which to meet women; and throughout there was the impression that Matthews was overplaying his hand, and for once was losing the sympathy of the President.

A handwriting expert—G. S. Inglis—was then called to give his view that the last anonymous letter to Crawford, received on July 17th, 1885, had been written by Mrs. Crawford herself in a disguised hand. He was also asked to look at an earlier anonymous letter, that written on June 10th and referring to Mrs. Crawford's luncheon with Forster at the Hotel Métropole. He could not say that this one had also been written by Mrs. Crawford, though he was by no means certain that it had not. The reasons he gave for his belief were highly confusing, and he did not give the impression of convincing the court.

Sir Julian Pauncefote, permanent under-secretary at the Foreign Office and later ambassador to Washington, then made a brief appearance to testify to the fencing habit in the mornings at 76, Sloane Street, to the fact that there were normally five or six people present, and that they could attend on any morning they wished without previous notice. He was the first witness not to be cross-examined.

Mrs. Rogerson, whose curious status in the case emerged increasingly as that of a professional confidante, was next examined. In the summer of 1884, Mrs. Crawford, who was then ill, had written to her and asked her to call. She had done so, had found Mrs. Crawford in a very depressed condition, and had seen a great deal of her in the course of the next few weeks. During this time Mrs. Crawford made a "confession" to Mrs. Rogerson about her relations with Sir Charles Dilke. She told her some but not all the details which she later specified to her husband. She also told her, a little later, about her relations with Captain Forster. She said that she was in love with Forster; but that between herself and Dilke there had never been any real affection. She also told Mrs. Rogerson of adulterous relations with several other men, whose names Mrs. Rogerson was asked not to give.

Mrs. Rogerson said that she was a close and long-standing family friend of Dilke's. She half believed Mrs. Crawford's story about her relationship with him, because she could not otherwise imagine why it had been told her; and half disbelieved it because of its inherent improbability. But to be on the safe side she advised Mrs. Crawford immediately to break off the intimacy. This advice Mrs. Crawford apparently took; she did not afterwards see Dilke except at family tea-parties. Towards Forster Mrs. Rogerson was more accommodating. In the following spring he and Mrs. Crawford frequently met at her house, and after Mrs. Crawford's confession to her husband, Forster sent from Dublin a letter for Mrs. Crawford to Mrs. Rogerson, which the latter forwarded. She did not tell Dilke about Mrs. Crawford's original story, but when, in the spring of 1885, Crawford received an anonymous letter dealing with his wife's relations with Dilke, Mrs. Crawford told Mrs. Rogerson about it, and Mrs. Rogerson told Dilke. This was the occasion on which she was alleged to have said to him: "Your sin has found you out," but she was adamant that she had not. She might have said that the sins of the anonymous letter-writers

340

would find them out.

Immediately after Mrs. Crawford left her husband she came to see Mrs. Rogerson and told her the full details. Mrs. Rogerson then took it upon herself to see Crawford and tried to persuade him to agree to a quiet separation or to anything which would prevent such a case coming before the public. Shortly after this she began to suffer from an illness which affected her reason and from which she did not recover for nine months. She could remember very little of what occurred during this period, and during the latter part of it she was under restraint. Soon after she recovered she received a copy of a statement which her brother—who was Stewart, Crawford's solicitor—claimed to have taken from her at the beginning of her illness, together with a threatening letter from him stating that if she deviated from this statement in the witness-box she would have a very hard time.

Matthews put to her that she was the writer of the anonymous letter mentioning Mrs. Crawford's Métropole lunch with Forster, basing himself on the somewhat flimsy support of its being written in magenta-coloured ink, as was a letter which she had sent to Stewart from Gmünden in the summer of 1885. She rejected this allegation, and he was not able to make very much of his other lines of attack. Her defence of having been out of her mind during the period about which he was asking was a more effective one than he had previously encountered in the case.

Three of Mrs. Rogerson's servants were then examined— two Dalgleish sisters, her lady's maid and housemaid, and Albert Talbot, her footman. They all testified to Mrs. Crawford having met Forster frequently at Mrs. Rogerson's during the spring of 1885, and to their having been alone together in the house on some occasions. There was evidence of their having been seen sitting together on one chair. In addition, there was an occasion when Mrs. Crawford was staying in the house, when she left after dinner and did not return until nine o'clock the following morning. Matthews confined his cross-examination to asking the Dalgleishes whether they had not been dismissed for drunkenness by Stewart (after Mrs. Rogerson had been placed under restraint) and to suggesting that they had all three been suborned by Dilke through the agency of Mrs. Rogerson. Two private soldiers from the Duke of Cornwall's Light Infantry were then called. They gave evidence of a visit by Mrs. Crawford to Forster in Dublin at Easter, 1885. They were not cross-examined.

The next witnesses were Lady Dilke and her niece, Gertrude Tuckwell, later to be Sir Charles's joint official biographer. Their brief evidence was designed to substantiate Dilke's alibi for May 6th, 1882. Lady Dilke said that on that day her future husband had been with her at Mrs. Earle's from before noon until half-past two or a little later. Miss Tuckwell gave evidence of Mrs. Crawford's arrival in Oxford, for, ironically enough, the Crawfords were staying that week-end as the guests of Mark Pattison in the Rector's Lodgings at Lincoln College. They reached the tennis courts near the museum at about five o'clock, which meant that she must have come by the train due in at 4–5 p.m.

The last witness for the Queen's Proctor was Samuel Barnett, Vicar of St. Jude's, Whitechapel. He testified that in the early part of 1884, when Mrs. Crawford was doing charitable work in his parish, she had received a letter there "from some officer in barracks." The witness had reported this fact to Crawford. After Dilke himself had been recalled briefly on one or two points not of major importance, Sir Walter Phillimore said: "That will be the case, my Lord, for the Queen's Proctor."

It was by no means a wholly satisfactory case, but it was one which made look implausible several aspects of the story Mrs. Crawford was expected to tell. Furthermore, it offered convincing evidence of her adultery with Forster, which she had hitherto denied. How she would deal with these difficulties remained to be seen.

Chapter Fourteen

The Case for Mrs. Crawford—and the Verdict

The normal procedure at this stage would have been for Matthews to make his opening speech and then to call such witnesses as he wished, perhaps beginning with Mrs. Crawford. Instead he appealed to the President for permission to call Mrs. Crawford immediately, on the ground that he could not tell what she was going to say in reply to some of the evidence which had just been offered. This, he said, would make it very difficult for him to open first. After a moment's hesitation the President agreed.

Mrs. Crawford then went into the box. She was twenty-three years old at the time and an attractive, although hardly beautiful young woman. She had been brought up as a member of a large family. She was the sixth of ten children and the fourth of seven daughters. As a child her home had been partly in London and partly in Northumberland, where her father, Eustace Smith, was a rich Tyneside ship-repairer, the son of the founder of Smiths' Docks. Her education, however, had been mainly in France, where, although not a Roman Catholic, she had been sent to a convent school. She returned to England at the age of seventeen ready for the season of 1880. She had married fifteen months later, having apparently refused one earlier proposal. Despite this one refusal her marriage had been dictated, not by any love for her husband, but by a determination to get away from her parents' house, where her mother, a woman of strong but difficult character, followed a habit of making life impossible for all the daughters in turn.

Mrs. Crawford was a woman of lively mind and considerable intelligence. At the trial she created an immediate impression of clarity and incision. She was not strictly Matthews's witness—it was her husband, not she, who was his client—and this necessitated the following procedure. The President himself conducted her through a four-question examination-in-chief. Was she willing to give evidence? Had she read her husband's evidence at the last trial? Was it true? Was it in particular true that she had committed adultery with Sir Charles Dilke? When she answered "yes" to each of these questions he handed her over to Matthews, who then began what was in part a supplementary examination-in-chief and in part an extremely courteous cross-examination. Matthews asked her 332 questions, and another thirty-five on re-examination. Phillimore in cross-examination asked her 551 questions. Her ordeal was a little longer than Dilke's, but considerably less gruelling. She was rarely at a loss for a satisfactory answer, she showed no signs of distress, and she apparently impressed the court as a truthful and straightforward witness. Whether the story she told was in fact the truth remains to be seen.

Matthews first asked her about her visit to Warren Street on February 23rd, 1882. She said that she returned to London that winter on February 13th and went to stay with her parents for a short time. On Monday, February 20th, she moved into 3, Sydney Place, the house which she and her husband had taken for the session. On the following morning Dilke came to see her there. Her evidence continued:

> He asked me to meet him at another house. I refused for a long time. I did not know what he meant. Then he explained, and at last I promised to go. He gave me the address, but he would not allow me to write it down. He made me repeat it, and he described the house to me.
>
> Q.: What description did he give you of the house?
>
> A.: He told me the number of the house, but in case I made a mistake he told me it was a house on the north side of Warren Street—that there were two tall narrow houses together just alike, and the one I was to go to was the one which had three bells to it. I was to ring one of those bells.
>
> Q.: Did he fix the date on which you were to go?
>
> A.: Yes, he asked me to go on the following Thursday, at half past eleven.
>
> Q.: Did he tell you how to go?
>
> A.: He told me I was to drive there, and that I was to drive in a hansom, and that I was to change hansoms on the way, and that I was to get out at the corner of Warren Street and walk up to the house, and that when I arrived at the house I would be let in by a woman, and that I was to go straight upstairs to the back room on the first floor and not to speak to anyone, and that he would be there waiting for me.

346

Q.: Did you go on the Thursday?

A.: Yes, I went.

Q.: And found the house he had described?

A.: I found the house, yes.

Q.: Do you remember who opened the door to you?

A.: A woman opened the door, but I did not look at her; I did not speak to her; I went straight upstairs.

Q.: Which room did you go into then?

A.: It was a bedroom. There was a large bed standing against the wall on the same side as the door. The fireplace was opposite the bed, and I think there were two windows at the end of the room. It was furnished like a bedroom.

Q.: Was Sir Charles Dilke there when you arrived?

A.: Yes, he was waiting for me.

Q.: In that room?

A.: In the room. The curtains were drawn, and there were lights in the room.

Q.: Did you ask him or did he tell you anything about the house?

A.: I asked him what house it was, and he said it belonged to an old servant of his, and that he made use of the room when he wanted it.

Q.: I am sorry to be obliged to put the question to you directly. Did he commit adultery with you on that occasion?

A.: Yes, he did.

Q.: You said that it was a Thursday. What was the day of the month?

A.: The 23rd, I think. I know it was two days after I had seen him at Sydney Place.

Q.: Will you refer to your diary for Thursday, 23rd February?

A.: Yes, Thursday, 23rd.

347

Q.: Who wrote "C.W.D."?

A.: I did.

Q.: Does that stand for Charles Wentworth Dilke?

A.: Yes, it does.

Q.: Did you write that at the time—on the day?

A.: I think I must have done so.

Q.: About how long did you stay in the house that Thursday?

A.: I think it was an hour.

Q.: Who left first?

A.: I left first.

Q.: Why did you leave first. How did that happen?

A.: He told me to.

Q.: You left him in the room, did you, when you went away?

A.: Yes.

Q.: Do you remember whether you saw anybody as you went out or did you let yourself out?

A.: I cannot remember that. I did not speak to anyone.

This account varied in two respects—one of them certainly important—from her confession as re-told by her husband at the February trial. It was then stated that she had gone to Warren Street on the afternoon of the day on which Dilke called upon her at Sydney Place. It was also stated that he had taken out a piece of paper and written the Warren Street address on it for her.

Mrs. Crawford continued her evidence by saying that she did not meet Dilke again, except at one or two parties, until May 6th. He told her that he was not well and "gave that as an explanation of my not seeing him." On that day she again went to Warren Street, at about 11.30 a.m., and the same pattern was followed. She then went back to Sydney Place to fetch her luggage and left by train for Oxford. Her account of her movements after arriving in Oxford was in accordance with Miss Tuckwell's evidence.

This was the last occasion on which she went to Warren Street, but throughout the summer there were one or two calls by Dilke at Sydney Place and five or six visits by Mrs. Crawford to Sloane Street. On these occasions she always arrived between quarter and half-past eleven. Why was this, Matthews asked:

> A.: It was the hour Sir Charles asked me to come. Mr. Crawford had to be at the Home Office at eleven, and Sir Charles had not to be at the Foreign Office until twelve, so it was the most convenient hour.
>
> Q.: Did your husband know you were going to Sir Charles Dilke?
>
> A.: No, he never knew. I never went until after he had started to go to the Home Office.
>
> Q.: When you got to Sir Charles Dilke's, who let you in—was it always the same person, or different persons?
>
> A.: Sometimes I rang the bell and was let in by the footman. It was not always the same footman.
>
> Q.: Sometimes the footman and sometimes who else:
>
> A.: Sometimes Sir Charles let me in himself. He used to tell me not to drive up to his house in a hansom, as the servants would be sure to hear. I always used to go in a hansom and get out at the corner of Pont Street, just close to his house and walk down to his house. Sir Charles has a conservatory over his door and he used to stand in the conservatory. The two lower panes of glass are shaded so that you cannot see through. One could just see his head, but he used to watch until I came round the corner there

349

and I could see if he was there and then he used to let me in without my ringing the bell; as soon as I came on the doorstep he opened the door from inside. Sometimes when I rang the bell Sir Charles would be in the dining-room and then he would come to the door and let me in himself, but he always came with his hat and gloves in his hand, to look as though he was going out in case it was not me.

Q.: Where was the dining-room? Do you mean the front room or the back room?

A.: The breakfast-room—the front room.

Q.: From the front room we understand a person coming to the door could be seen?

A.: He used to call out at the top of the stairs to the servants it was all right, and then the servants did not come up.

Q.: Are those the only persons who let you in when you called in the morning—either Sir Charles himself or the footman?

A.: Yes.

Q.: When you got into the house admitted in this way where did you go as a rule?

A.: I almost always went up to the blue room on the staircase, whether Sir Charles let me in or the footman, except once or twice when Sir Charles had not quite finished his break-fast I sat with him in the dining-room, but I almost always went into the blue room, whether Sir Charles or the footman let me in. The footman used to take my name, and show me into the blue room.

Q.: From the blue room where used you to go?

A.: Sir Charles always came to me in the blue room.

Q.: And did you go from there to any other part of the house?

A.: Yes, he used to take me up to his bedroom.

Q.: Was anything done to prevent your being seen? Just describe how you used to go up.

A.: We always used to talk a little in the blue room first, and then he used to go upstairs to see that there was no one on the staircase, and to shut Mr. Bodley's door. He always said "Bodley leaves his door open; I must go and shut it." Then he used to come down and fetch me up. I used to run upstairs as gently as I could, and there were very thick carpets to all the stairs, so I do not think anyone could hear.

Q.: I presume I need not ask what you went to the bedroom for. I suppose he used to commit adultery with you?

A.: Yes.

Matthews asked her to describe the bedroom, which she did in some detail. She also told how, after Dilke had left, Sarah would come and help her to dress and they would wait, sometimes as much as an hour, until Bodley and the clerk had gone and Sarah could safely take her down and let her out.

The next incident related by Mrs. Crawford occurred on December 7th, 1882, when, at the end of the autumn session, Crawford travelled north a day before her. Dilke called on her in the morning at Sydney Place, and discovering this was the position, asked her to spend the night at Sloane Street. Mrs. Crawford dined with her sister, Mrs. Harrison, in Cromwell Road and left to meet Dilke in Hans Place at 10 p.m. He conducted her into his house and up to his room. Between three and four o'clock in the morning Sarah was summoned down from the floor above, helped her to dress, and let her out. She then returned to her own house.

On February 13th, 1883, she returned to London, again

travelling twenty-four hours in advance of her husband. Dilke called to see her that morning at 27, Young Street—their house for the ensuing session—and arranged for her to come to Sloane Street that night. On this occasion she arrived at his house on her own, for Dilke was addressing his constituents at the Kensington Town Hall. She did not ring the bell, but Sarah met her at the door at nine o'clock exactly and took her to Dilke's bedroom. She went to bed and was asleep when he arrived at about eleven. This time she stayed until morning. At 7–30 Sarah brought her some breakfast and she left a little before eight o'clock, returning home in a hansom and being let in by her parlourmaid. These two nights were the only ones that she spent at Dilke's house. This again was an important variation from the story which her husband said she had told him. His evidence at the first trial referred to two consecutive nights in February, 1883. When Matthews put this discrepancy to her she explained it by saying "that was a mistake by Mr. Crawford."

During the spring and summer of 1883 the liaison continued on the basis of morning visits by Dilke to Young Street and by Mrs. Crawford to Sloane Street. There were perhaps six of the former and eight or ten of the latter. At Young Street Mrs. Crawford used to pull down the blinds, so that the room could not be seen through as Dilke's coachman had suggested. At Sloane Street the pattern followed was the same as that in 1882.

Mrs. Crawford was then asked about Fanny:

Q.: During that year, 1883, did Sir Charles ever mention a person named Fanny to you?
A.: Yes, I think it was in the summer of 1883 that he first mentioned Fanny to me.
Q.: What did he say to you about her?

A.: He told me about her first by degrees—he said that she was a girl that used to sleep with him and spend the night at his house.

Q.: What else had he said to you about her?

A.: He told me that she was very nice and quite young; he said that she was about my age, no more than me, I think, and he asked me if I would not like to see her at his house. I said I would not like to see her at all, and he talked to me about her several times. He said that she was supposed to be in service. I asked him how he had got hold of her, and he said he had got hold of her through Sarah, his house-maid; that she was supposed by her parents to be in service at Brixton, and (that) he used to make her write letters to her parents saying that she was getting on very nicely in her place at Brixton, and that she used to live in lodgings close to Sloane Street, and that she used to be let into his house every evening, I think about nine o'clock, when the other servants were at supper. She was let in by Sarah, and she spent the nights at his house, and Sarah used to let her out again in the morning.

. . . . .

Q.: Did you ever see the person whom he called Fanny?

A.: Yes.

Q.: When did you first see her?

A.: I cannot remember the exact date; I think it must have been in August, 1883; I have nothing to tell me the exact date.

. . . . .

Q.: I must ask you to tell us the circumstances under which you saw her; where were you, to begin with?

A.: I was at Sir Charles Dilke's house. He had asked me to see her several times, and I never would. He said that he wanted to see us together, and one day when I was at Sir Charles Dilke's house he took me into the sitting-room and said she was in the house then, and he asked me if I would see her, and I did not want to at all, I said I would not, and then we went upstairs, and after I had been in the room upstairs—in the bedroom—for a little, he brought Fanny in from the next room.

Q.: Was she dressed or undressed?

A.: My Lord, is it necessary I should give all the details?

Q.: Very well, I will not ask. What happened when he brought her into the room?

A.: He wanted me to talk to her, and I would not. She stayed only a few minutes, and I burst out crying, and asked Sir Charles to send her away, because I could not bear having her there, and he sent her away, and told me I should never see her again as I did not want to see her.

.   .   .   .   .

Q.: When did you see her again?

A.: I saw her again in the spring of 1884, when I came back to London . . . he brought her into the room one day when I was there, and she remained, I think, a minute or two, and I asked him to send her away, and he sent her away.

Q.: Did you ever see her again?

A.: Yes, I saw her, I think, about a week or a fortnight after.

Q.: Again at Sir Charles Dilke's house?

A.: Yes, in the same way; he told me I was very silly not to like her, and not to let her stop; he was rather vexed about it, and so to please him I let her stop longer, and she was in the room, I think, about ten minutes or so with Sir Charles Dilke and me, and then when Sir Charles Dilke left she helped me to dress.

Q.: One moment, please, were you all three in bed together?

A.: Yes.

Mrs. Crawford added that she had a little conversation with Fanny, but that she did not discover her surname or the fact that Sarah was her sister. She was next asked to look at a photograph and say whether she recognised it. She replied: "It is Fanny."

During the session of 1884, apart from Fanny, the pattern of visits continued, although they were perhaps less frequent. Mrs. Crawford said that as late as that summer she had affection for Dilke, but in the autumn, largely as a result of Mrs. Rogerson's advice, she implied, she broke off the intimacy. She had been very friendly with Mrs. Rogerson during that summer, but she now believed her to have written the "Métropole" anonymous letter. She based her belief partly on the handwriting and partly on the fact that Mrs. Rogerson, to whose house she and Forster had gone to tea on the same day, was the only person who knew of their Métropole luncheon. So far as the last anonymous letter—the one which precipitated her confession—was concerned, she would not like to give any opinion about its authorship. But when she saw it she thought it looked by the form of the envelope to be an anonymous letter, and she decided to end her dissimulation and tell her husband "the real truth." She had been very miserable with her husband, with whom she had never been in love and whom she had married because she had been unhappy at home. She had told Mrs. Rogerson a little time before the confession that she could not much longer go on living with him.

Towards the end of Matthews' examination one or two loose ends were gathered together. Mrs. Crawford said that she had never been unfaithful to her husband before her first visit to Warren Street. She told how Dilke had visited her at her sister's house on the Tuesday after her confession, and had tried to get her to withdraw her statements, threatening that he would otherwise make public her relations with other men, and ruin herself and her family; but she did not suggest that he had tried to bribe her. Finally she described how she was able to identify the Warren Street house so many years after she had forgotten the number. In November, 1885, she accompanied Mrs. Ashton Dilke on a shopping expedition to Maple's in Tottenham Court Road. While there she decided to try to find the house She succeeded, recognising it from the outside, and went back to her sister with the address written down.

Sir Walter Phillimore then began his cross-examination. It was much less aggressive and effective than Matthews' cross-examination of Dilke had been. Phillimore was frequently doubtful about his facts, which meant that he often realised neither the strength of his own case nor the weakness of Mrs. Crawford's. Sometimes he appeared to be cross-examining without point and merely leading Mrs. Crawford through a repetition of the statements she had already made in reply to Matthews. At other times he would pursue a poor point with greater enthusiasm than he would show for a good one.* As a result her cross-examination occupies a much less central position in the case than does that of Dilke. It was probably less important in its effect upon the court than her examination by Matthews.

Phillimore attempted to make three main points. The first was to bring out the adulterous nature of Mrs. Crawford's relations with Forster, and perhaps with others as well. About Forster he put the direct question to her, and, after an attempt to avoid it, she admitted the position for the first time:

Q.: Have you not had guilty relations with Captain Forster?
A.: My Lord, must I answer that question?
The President: If the question is pressed you must answer it.
Sir W. Phillimore: Yes, my Lord, I must press it.
A.: Yes, I have.
Q.: When did these relations begin?
A.: In 1884.

She also admitted that at Easter, 1885, she had gone to Dublin to see Forster, telling her husband that she was staying with Mrs. Rogerson.

So far as her relations with other men were concerned the principal evidence against her was that of her diary. The space for February 23rd, 1882, contained the initials "C.W.D." faintly

---

* Thus he devoted much time to suggesting that, on May 6th, 1882, Mrs. Crawford would have found it difficult to remain at Warren Street until nearly 12.30, to go to Sydney Place to collect her luggage, and to catch the 2.15 train from Paddington to Oxford. Nearly twenty questions elicited from Mrs. Crawford the admission that she might have sacrificed her luncheon.

pencilled in her own handwriting close against the line. Matthews had drawn attention to this in his examination. Phillimore drew attention to similar entries. For May 25th, 1882, "F.W." was written in this way, and for November 20th of the same year there was "R.C.P." For June 4th, 1884, there was "H.F." Mrs. Crawford was asked who were designated by these initials and replied that "F.W." was Mr. Frederick Warner, "R.C.P." Mr. Robert Priestley (who had subsequently become her brother-in-law), and "H.F." Captain Henry Forster. Phillimore continued:

Q.: Now I ask you whether those three initials, May 25th, 1882, "F.W.," November 20th, "R.C.P." and June 4th "H.F." are not meant as records of committing adultery with these three people?

A.: No, certainly not.

Q.: None of them?

A.: No, none of them.

Q.: Or of appointments made with them?

A.: I do not remember what they refer to, but they must refer to their coming to the house, probably to tea.

Q.: Is that the way that you recorded visits of people coming to tea?

A.: Yes, apparently so.

Q.: You may have an opportunity of showing that. Can you turn now, or at any time, to any entries in your diary of people coming to tea, put in this manner?

A.: I do not remember any. I have sometimes put people down by their initials.

Phillimore then allowed her to leave this immediate point, and turned to asking her about the first anonymous letter which her husband had received and which referred to her flirting with

358

medical students at St. George's Hospital, where she was visiting a sick relative. She fixed the date of this letter as March, 1882, but denied the allegations both in general and in reference to Warner and Priestley; the latter, she said, had never been a student at St. George's.

Phillimore's second main point was the implausibility of Mrs. Crawford's story on what may perhaps be called psychological rather than circumstantial grounds. He asked her whether she resented Dilke's having made love to her at Bailey's Hotel, and she replied that she did. She was asked whether she had told her husband and whether there had been any communication between her and Dilke in the five months which followed this incident. She replied "No" to both these questions, and Phillimore continued, referring to Dilke's visit to her, at Sydney Place, on her return to London:

Q.: You expected him to come. Did you try to stop him coming, or take any precautions to prevent his coming?

A.: No.

Q.: And when he did come, was it on that very first occasion that he came to you that he and you made this arrangement that you should go to Warren Street?

A.: Yes.

Q.: Did you understand you were to go to Warren Street to be seduced by him?

A.: Yes, I did, when he explained.

Q.: And you say that on this occasion you made the arrangement to meet him in Warren Street knowing the object?

A.: Yes.

Q.: Without further interview with him or further pressing on his behalf?

A.: I did not see him any other time.[†]

Phillimore also pressed Mrs. Crawford on the accusations she had scattered around about other people being Dilke's mistresses and about her relations with these others:

Q.: Have you said that he told you that Mrs. Rogerson was his mistress?

A.: Yes, that Sir Charles Dilke asked me to make a friend of Mrs. Rogerson. He told me Mrs. Rogerson was his mistress.

Q.: He told you that?

A.: Yes, he told me so himself.

Q.: Was his mistress, or had been his mistress, or what?

A.: He implied to me that she was still.

Q.: That she was still his mistress—you really mean to say that?

A.: Yes, positively. He asked me if I should like to meet Mrs. Rogerson at his house. I said no, I would rather not.

Q.: Let me see, he told you Fanny was his mistress; he told you about your mother, and he told you about Mrs. Rogerson, and did he tell you about Sarah—that Sarah had been his mistress?

A.: Yes.

Q.: All those four?

A.: Yes.

Q.: And Sarah, who had been his mistress, was dressing you on every occasion when you went to his house, and

---

[†] Mrs. Crawford's method of dealing with difficult questions could hardly have been more different from Dilke's. She was less addicted to explanation.

bringing you tea and letting you out on those occasions when you slept there?

A.: Yes.

Q.: And Mrs. Rogerson, who was his mistress, was meeting you, and you were making statements to her?

A.: Mrs. Rogerson always denied it to me. Of course I was bound to believe Mrs. Rogerson.

. . . .

Q.: Did you send for Mrs. Rogerson when you were ill and ask her to come and see you?

A.: Yes, I did, because Sir Charles had asked me to make friends with her several times.

Q.: At that time you had not had Mrs. Rogerson's denial that she was Sir Charles Dilke's mistress?

A.: No.

Q.: So being ill, were you in low spirits?

A.: No, not particularly, I was dull of course, I was ill and could not go out, and my sisters were out of town, so of course I was dull.

Q.: Being ill and dull you sent for somebody whom Sir Charles Dilke told you was another of his mistresses to come and see you?

A.: He told me that Mrs. Rogerson wanted to make friends with me and asked me to make friends with her."

Mrs. Crawford also informed the court of her understanding that, in the spring of 1885, Dilke had asked Mrs. Rogerson to marry him, but that Mrs. Rogerson had refused. She further said that, until recently, it had not occurred to her that Mrs. Rogerson had written any of the anonymous letters. She had believed them to be all "contrivances" of her mother—Mrs. Smith.

Phillimore's third main point—and certainly his most important one—was to try to suggest reasons why Mrs. Crawford might have invented the story against Dilke. He got her to admit that she was Forster's mistress; that she was very much in love with him during the summer of 1885; that her husband had become suspicious to the extent of himself watching her movements as closely as he could and employing a detective to do what he could not do; that Forster had in consequence left London and been able to communicate with her only by sending letters to the Kensington Post Office addressed to Mrs. Green; that Forster and Dilke had quarrelled, as had been stated in previous evidence; that she and Forster were as a result very angry with Dilke; and that, after making her confession, she specifically asked her husband not to put Forster's name in as a co-respondent.

Phillimore also suggested that if, as she said, she had broken off a two-and-a-half-year intimacy with Dilke in August, 1884, it was very odd that, two months later, she should on her own initiative have taken lodgings for the autumn session at 61, Sloane Street, only fifteen doors from his house. She replied that she had done this because her husband had wished to be near the Lord Advocate, who lived in Cadogan Place, but it was not clear why this consideration had not applied in former years; the implication which Phillimore attempted to bring out was that she wished to be in a position closely to observe Dilke's house while she was concocting her story.

To complete the picture Phillimore put it to her that the last anonymous letter was phrased in what she knew would be the form most likely to provoke her husband—because it suggested that he would not dare to take action against Dilke, being too concerned for his own political prospects—and that she herself had written it. She admitted the former, but resolutely denied the latter. Phillimore also put it to her that when she made her confession she hoped to marry Forster. This, too, she denied. "No, there never had been talk of marriage," she said, "as Captain Forster was engaged at that time to be married to Miss Smith Barry; he told me, and I knew all along that he was engaged to her. . . ."

There were two other small points which emerged in the cross-examination and which should, perhaps, be mentioned. The first concerned the discrepancy between Crawford's original statement about the two nights she had spent away from home and her own evidence. She was able to explain her husband's evidence by saying that he had been confused at the time she made her confession, but there was the further point that Anne Jamieson, her maid, had sworn at the first trial to her being away on two consecutive nights in February, 1883. When Phillimore put this to her she made the startling reply: "I suppose that is what she was told to say," but Phillimore, even more surprisingly, did not follow up the point and ask by whom Anne Jamieson was told, or why she was told. The second small point related to a visit which Mrs. Crawford had paid to Edinburgh in December, 1885, in an unsuccessful attempt to see her husband. "I only want to help you, and I can do nothing unless you see me," she had written to him. Matthews assumed throughout that she had given her husband no help in his divorce proceedings, and took this as a clear refutation of the "plot against Dilke" theory.

On re-examination Matthews elicited only one important fact from Mrs. Crawford. This was that she fixed the date of her first meeting with Forster as February 15th, 1884, when she had been introduced to him at a ball. Then, before she stood down, the foreman of the jury handed up a written question to the President, who asked Phillimore to put it. It was a request that she should draw a plan of the bedroom in Warren Street, showing also the means of access to it and the shape of the staircase. This she did with apparent ease, and the result was passed from counsel to judge and from judge to jury.

Matthews then announced that as he had only a few witnesses to call he proposed not to address the jury until they had been heard. The President readily agreed to this course, and Mrs. Ashton Dilke, the first of these witnesses, was put into the box. She was affirmed and not sworn. Her evidence was directed principally to an account of Dilke's behaviour when he came to see Mrs. Crawford three or four days after the confession. Mrs. Ashton Dilke said that he offered money if a quiet separation could be agreed to and also made repeated attempts to get Mrs. Crawford to sign a retraction. Mrs. Dilke also said that the evidence given by her sister was exactly in accordance with the account which she had given her during the summer and autumn of the previous year. The witness had believed her sister's confession when she first heard it, but details which had subsequently come to light had made her even more convinced of its truth. She confirmed her sister's story of the expedition from Maple's to find the Warren Street house, although of course she was not present when it was discovered. She herself had no other knowledge of the existence of this house, although she knew the name Rosalie Dessouslavy. She was not aware of any family pension being paid to Anna Dessouslavy.

Phillimore in cross-examination was unable to move her on any of these points, although he elicited the information that there had been a certain interchange of servants between the households of Sir Charles Dilke and Mrs. Ashton Dilke, the suggestion being that this might have been a possible source of knowledge to Mrs. Crawford of the internal arrangements at 76, Sloane Street, and of the existence of Fanny. He also got Mrs. Dilke to admit that, despite her claim to believe her sister's story and despite her expressions of indignation at Dilke's conduct, she wrote to congratulate him on his marriage, left cards on Lady Dilke, and twice called at 76, Sloane Street.

George Lewis, the solicitor to whom Mrs. Dilke had sent her sister and who was subsequently to act for Parnell and in many other trials of great note, was then called. In effect he merely testified to the fact that Mrs. Crawford's evidence was in accordance with the story she had told him before the first trial; but he had taken no written statement from her until shortly before the second trial.

There followed a group of three witnesses whose evidence proved to be most damaging to Dilke. These were the members of the Hillier family—husband, wife and daughter—who had lived on the ground floor of 65, Warren Street, from April, 1882, to July, 1884. George Hillier was a tailor and he used to sit working in the window of the room which looked on the street. His evidence, and that of his wife and daughter, was that a man whom he now recognised as Dilke used to visit the house quite frequently. Hillier was extremely reluctant to define the degree of frequency, but under great pressure from counsel he agreed that it might have been once a month. When Dilke came, his visit, Hillier noted, was usually preceded by that of a lady. He would stay for half an hour to an hour, and would then leave the house first, turning up the collar of his coat, as though to avoid recognition, as he went. The lady left afterwards. Hillier was quite unwilling to give any description of the lady or to answer any question about her appearance. But he was perfectly certain that the man he had seen was Dilke. He rejected firmly a curious attempt by Phillimore to confuse him by getting a Swiss jeweller named Giuliano, who lived near Warren Street, was a friend of Mrs. Dessouslavy's and bore some superficial resemblance to Dilke, to stand up in court. Hillier placed the times of Dilke's visits as between 3–30 and 5 in the afternoon. They occurred mostly during the London season.

This evidence was confirmed by that of Mrs. Hillier and Miss Hillier, and they added some additional information. Mrs. Hillier said that the lady who used to come was tall and fair, and aged about twenty-eight, she thought. Both she and her daughter agreed that it was always the same lady who came, and that she was not Mrs. Crawford. They believed that Dilke used to be with her in the large back bedroom, the door of which Mrs. Hillier once or twice heard being locked, and that Mrs. Dessouslavy used to wait in the smaller front room. They agreed that the visits were always in the afternoon, generally between 3–30 and 5.

Matthews' next witness was Mary Ann Gray, a niece of Sarah's, who had succeeded Ellen Drake as housemaid at 76, Sloane Street in March, 1883, and remained there for two years. She stated that on one occasion she went into Dilke's bedroom at about 11–30 in the morning and caught a glimpse of a lady there; but she was not quite sure whether it was a lady or a gentleman. The lady, if it was a lady, was wearing a dress, but no coat. Mary Gray left the room immediately, but she was later reprimanded by Sarah for having gone there, and for a month afterwards she was not allowed into Dilke's room. On another occasion, after the first incident, she saw

Dilke conducting a lady upstairs. She thought this was in the afternoon. Phillimore, in cross-examination, was able to show, on Mary Gray's own fixing of the dates, that the incidents were very unlikely to have occurred before September, 1884. He also elicited the information that she had quarrelled with her aunt before leaving Sloane Street.

Another handwriting expert was then produced. He was an assistant in the manuscript department of the British Museum, but his evidence was almost as confusing as that of Phillimore's expert. Its burden was that the last two anonymous letters—the "Métropole" letter and the "cuckoo" letter—were both written by Mrs. Rogerson. Mrs. Rogerson's brother, Charles Stewart, also testified "with regret" to his belief that the "Métropole" letter at least had been written by his sister. Stewart, it will be recalled, was also Crawford's solicitor, and the main purpose of his being put into the box was to show that the statements he had originally taken from the footmen, Shanks and William Goode, were somewhat more incriminating to Dilke than the evidence they had given. Stewart appeared to be actuated by deep personal malice towards Dilke, and suddenly, at the end of his examination in chief, said that he wished to correct an inaccuracy in his sister's evidence. The President tried to prevent him, but he insisted on blurting out: "She (Mrs. Rogerson) stated Sir Charles Dilke was an intimate friend of my mother's. He was so at one time, but not latterly, for she became aware of his character."

This, combined perhaps with Stewart's general behaviour, provoked Phillimore into one of his few effective pieces of cross-examination:

Q.: Are you a solicitor of standing?

A.: Not of very long standing.

Q.: Have your professional studies told you or not that what you have been saying just now is not evidence?"

Phillimore then proceeded to discover that it was Stewart's practice, when taking statements, to repeat each sentence aloud as he wrote it, but not to read the whole document through to the witness at the end or to obtain a signature. This discovery destroyed the value of most of Stewart's evidence.

Donald Crawford was then called. He was asked to give his account of his meeting with Dilke, at the Reform Club, on the day after his wife's confession. Dilke, in evidence, had described this as being a perfectly friendly meeting. Crawford said:

"I was speaking to the hall-keeper at the lodge . . . and I suddenly heard Sir Charles Dilke's voice behind me saying 'How do you do?' or 'How do you do, Crawford?' I turned round and I said 'How are you?' I did not shake hands with him. I had an umbrella in my right hand and I looked down at the umbrella and came to a decision on a certain point, and I merely said, 'Sir Charles Dilke, how are you?' He then said, 'How is North-east Lanarkshire?'—that is the constituency I was about to stand for. I said, 'It is doing very well,' and I walked upstairs. That is the whole of the conversation."

He was also asked whether he now believed that he had made a mistake about the two consecutive nights, and he said that he did. Those were the only points which Matthews put to him. Phillimore then asked him about his attitude to Dilke and Forster at the time of his wife's confession:

Q.: At the time of your getting the last anonymous letter were you suspecting Sir Charles Dilke?

A.: Not in the least.

Q.: Were you suspecting Captain Forster?

A.: I was.

Q.: And taking steps to have your wife watched with regard to Captain Forster?

A.: Yes, within a fortnight—within a very short time previous to her confession—before that I had not even asked questions.

Q.: Did you—after your wife had made a statement to you with regard to Sir Charles Dilke—did you accept it until she gave the details?

A.: Yes, I did not doubt it for a moment when she made it to me.

Q.: Then when she made the whole statement?

A.: I did not doubt it at all in my mind from the time she said, "The man who ruined me was Sir Charles Dilke." From the solemnity of her manner I had no doubt at all.

Q.: Did you press her after that as to Captain Forster?

A.: Yes.

Q.: And she denied?

A.: Yes.

Q.: And with as much solemnity as she made her statement with regard to Sir Charles Dilke?

A.: Yes, very earnestly: there were certain things which seemed a little suspicious. She asked me not to make him a co-respondent. She said, "I do not want to ruin more men than one." It seemed in one interpretation as if it were not quite true.

Mrs. Rogerson's son-in-law was then called, and gave it as his opinion too that his mother-in-law had written the "Métropole" letter. Then came Forster, Matthews's last witness. He was apparently called in order that he might give his account of his quarrel with Dilke at Albert Mansions, where Mrs. Rogerson had her flat. He said that he went there because Mrs. Rogerson had asked him to go to castigate Dilke on her behalf. Dilke, she said, had slandered her by telling Mrs. Crawford that she had been his mistress. As to the form of the quarrel, Forster said that Mrs. Rogerson came to him in her dining-room and told him that Dilke was on the stairs.

"I followed him down," Forster continued, "and overtook him only at the bottom. There is a glass door there. As he was going into the street I said to him, 'Sir Charles Dilke, I believe?' He said, 'Yes.' I said, 'I wish to tell you you are a scoundrel and a liar.' I remember the words of his answer accurately—'I am afraid you must add a coward too.' He then said to me, 'Captain Forster, I understand that you are a gentleman—you would not take an unfair advantage of me—my political reputation is everything to me.'"

Phillimore interposed an objection to this evidence and the account was broken off there. Later both Mrs. Rogerson and Sir Charles Dilke were recalled briefly in order to refute this account. Dilke did so with characteristic circumlocution. If he had used the word coward it was with regard to Forster's conduct "in making a scene of that kind at the house of a lady." Mrs. Rogerson was more direct. She had never asked Forster to her house and she had never asked him to defend her from Dilke.

Forster was then available to Phillimore for cross-examination.

He asked him about his engagement to Miss Smith Barry, and discovered that it was first made in September, 1884, was broken off in January, 1885, and renewed at the beginning of July of that year. The marriage took place two months after the renewal. Phillimore also asked him the following questions:

Q.: Did you take Mrs. Crawford to No. 9, Hill Street, Knightsbridge?

A.: I have taken her there.

Q.: You know that house?

A.: I do.

Q.: Is it a house of ill-fame?

A.: I presume it is.

Q.: You have met Mrs. Crawford there?

A.: I have.

That was the end of the evidence, and Matthews proceeded to deliver his speech to the jury. He chose a high note of moral indignation and sought his verdict with a mixture of sustained invective against Dilke and scornful dismissal of the arguments upon which Phillimore had sought to build his case. He began with a reference to his client, Crawford, who "stood alone amidst all the mud and filth as a gentleman of stainless life and unblemished honour." What a contrast with Dilke, whose behaviour at the first trial he castigated with particular vigour.

"The Judge who tried the case had rightly decided that there was no legal evidence against Sir Charles Dilke: but was there not moral evidence of the strongest kind against him? He was charged by (Mrs. Crawford's) confession not merely with adultery, but with having committed adultery with the child of one friend and the wife of another. He was

371

charged with having committed with Mrs. Crawford ruthless adultery unredeemed by love or affection—he was charged with coarse brutal adultery more befitting a beast than a man, he was charged with having done with an English lady what any man of proper feeling would shrink from doing with a prostitute in a French brothel, and yet he was silent."

He could not shelter behind his counsel for the course which he had taken. Did the jury believe that they had not acted on instructions? Here Russell tried to interrupt, but the President silenced him with "I cannot allow you to interfere at all, Mr. Attorney-General," and Matthews swept on. What made Dilke change his mind? It was not a respect for the truth as such but the fact that the Press campaign against him had become politically inconvenient.

Mrs. Crawford's story was contradicted only by the denials of Dilke. All the other evidence went to strengthen her allegations; and if her account were a fabrication, what possible motive could she have for inventing such a traduce-ment of her own character? As for the value of Dilke's oath, was this not shown up by the evidence of the Hilliers, upon which Matthews said that he relied strongly? Did not Mrs. Crawford's ability to sketch the apartment in Warren Street powerfully bear out her account of what had occurred there? Nor was Matthews prepared to attach weight to the evidence against the possibility of adulterous meetings at 76, Sloane Street.

"As to the evidence adduced for Sir Charles Dilke with regard to the fencing in the mornings, it was of no importance. Sir Julian Pauncefote had been brought forward as

372

to that point. Like other witnesses brought forward by the Queen's Proctor, Sir Julian was a merely ornamental one. Who had disputed that there had been fencing in the mornings? Nobody. . . . Mr. Bodley, the private secretary, had been produced, and from his evidence it would appear that the occupation of a private secretary to a Cabinet Minister was of a most extraordinary character. Mr. Bodley, who, though he always sat with the door of his room open would not have it taken off, was constantly shouting to Mr. Ireland in an adjoining room, and Mr. Ireland was constantly shouting to him; and as to the Minister himself, though messengers were constantly arriving at his house with telegrams and written despatches, and every minute of his time throughout the morning was occupied with official business, except that which he spent in fencing and at breakfast, he found time to remove cancelled appointments from his diaries by cutting little round holes in those diaries instead of erasing the entries by the stroke of a pencil."

Matthews turned to Fanny. She was "so precious a vessel that she was not allowed to come into contact with anyone from the Queen's Proctor until her statement had been distilled in the retort of Mr. Humbert." But then she was lost. Her absence fixed guilt on Sir Charles Dilke. Mrs. Crawford had confessed adultery with Captain Forster, "but the dates showed that she had not done so till she had committed herself with Sir Charles Dilke." The suggestion that she had invented the story against Dilke because she wished to marry Forster was most implausible. She would hardly have helped her desire by falsely accusing herself of adultery with another man. And if she was party to a conspiracy against Dilke why had she not given her husband more help in his suit against him? Matthews moved to his conclusion.

"The burden of proof was on the Queen's Proctor, who, in order to be successful must show conclusively that Mrs. Crawford had not committed adultery with Sir Charles Dilke. The jury could only give a verdict against his client if they believed that Mrs. Crawford was a perjured witness and that a conspiracy existed to blast the life of a pure and innocent man. . . . He asked earnestly for a verdict which would deliver his client from the terrible burden which he had had to bear and free him from a marriage on which Mrs. Crawford had, unhappily, brought discredit and disgrace."

Sir Walter Phillimore's closing address was a much tamer affair. It had none of Henry Matthews's gusto. "There was no need," he began by saying, "for the advocate for the Queen's Proctor to use impassioned speech." Nevertheless he deployed some effective arguments in a quiet way. Could the jury believe that a guilty wife accusing herself of innumerable acts of adultery in three or four different places would be unable to produce more corroboration than had been heard during the case? Such evidence as had been produced against Dilke—that of the Hilliers and Mary Ann Gray—did not appear to refer to Mrs. Crawford. So far as her two specific dates for Warren Street were concerned, were not Dilke's alibis for the two days almost completely convincing, and might not that for the first occasion have been still more so had Mrs. Crawford not had the opportunity, after hearing Dilke's evidence, to change the time of the alleged meeting from the afternoon to the morning? As for the second occasion—May 6th—Phillimore had Mr. Earle (who was willing to testify to the time of Dilke's arrival at Bryanston Square) as well as Lady Dilke in court, but as she was not cross-examined there appeared to be no need to call him.

There was the difficulty about Mrs. Crawford's knowledge of the interior arrangements of both 76, Sloane Street, and 65, Warren Street. But might she not have picked up the former through her family connection and the interchange of servants between Sir Charles Dilke's household and that of her sister? As to Warren Street, who knew whether her plan was correct? Forster had admitted taking her to a house of ill-fame. Perhaps she had drawn the room there. For motive there was her desire to shield Forster. She had not admitted her adultery with him until it had been overwhelmingly proved against her, and at the time of her confession she was almost certainly unaware of the renewal of his engagement. What the jury had to consider was not whether Mrs. Crawford had been guilty of adultery—that was not in question, and whatever their verdict Crawford could without doubt obtain his divorce—but "whether she had been guilty of a double adultery, or whether, having fallen a victim to a man with whom she was enamoured, she had falsely accused Sir Charles Dilke." Phillimore concluded, a little unenthusiastically, by saying that "he was glad that his task had come to an end and (that) he now left the case in the hands of the jury and of his Lordship."

The President then summed up. He began by defining the issue, first in its legal and then in its practical form.

"The Queen's Proctor," he said, "is entitled to be successful in his intervention on one condition only, and that is if the decree has been obtained by reason of 'material facts not

375

having been brought to the knowledge of the court.'" He continued: "Mrs. Crawford has come into court and asserted upon oath that her confession to her husband was a true confession. Sir Charles Dilke has sworn to the contrary, and substantially you have to determine which of these two persons, who have been brought face to face before you, is telling the truth, and which is telling what is false."

Next he turned to the question of Dilke's behaviour at the first trial and led himself to a conclusion highly unfavourable to Sir Charles.

"Well, you must put yourselves in his place, if I may venture to suggest such an idea to you," he said to the jury. "If you were to hear such a statement made involving your honour, as it would do morally, whatever might be the legal view of the facts—would you accept the advice of your counsel to say nothing? Would you allow the court to be deceived and a tissue of falsehoods to be put forward as the truth and to be accepted as such by a court of justice?"

Sir James Hannen then considered Dilke's alibis for February 23rd and May 6th, 1882. He agreed that it would have been impossible for the latter to have gone to Warren Street during the afternoon of February 23rd. If Mrs. Crawford's allegation had been that originally stated by her husband, Dilke would have had an adequate answer. But there was nothing implausible in the suggestion that Crawford, in the stress of the moment, might have misunderstood her statement. As to the morning, if the time at which Dilke had arrived at the Foreign Office could have been fixed "at so early an hour as to render the drive to Warren Street and back impossible, such evidence would have been invaluable." In its absence his advice to the jury could merely be that they should decide between the relative truthfulness of Dilke and Mrs. Crawford. As to the alibi for May 6th, that depended upon "whether or not you can rely upon the accuracy of Lady Dilke." The President appeared to be unwilling to do so.

"It has been stated that Mr. Earle was here, but that it was not necessary to call him because Lady Dilke was not cross-examined. Now the meaning of that is this. In the view of lawyers when a fact ceases to be made the subject of cross-examination in the sense that you see it is no longer in dispute, it is not necessary to go on calling witnesses to prove that which you see from the action on the other side is not disputed. I must say I do not think that anyone would suppose that Mr. Matthews intended it to be taken that Lady Dilke was giving the hour of Sir C. Dilke's arrival correctly. I can easily imagine that he would be anxious not to keep that lady in the box longer than was necessary;‡ and therefore I can only say that it appears to have been a very great mistake not to have called Mr. and Mrs. Earle to prove what time Sir C. Dilke came to the house in corroboration of the evidence of his wife."

---

‡ The President was perhaps inclined to give greater weight to Matthews's sense of delicacy, as opposed to his diligence as an advocate, than would most other followers of the trial.

The President then considered the state of the evidence about the Warren Street house. He was prepared to accept Dilke's account of the pension paid to Anna Dessouslavy as being reasonable. But he clearly found the evidence of the Hilliers highly damaging to the veracity both of Dilke and of Mrs. Dessouslavy. He was also most unfavourably impressed by Phillimore's "theatrical" action in producing Giuliano and then not putting him into the box. The implication was that even if Dilke had not used Mrs. Dessouslavy's rooms as a place of assignation, Giuliano had. Furthermore, if Mrs. Crawford had not gone to the house under the circumstances described, how could she have known of its existence? Nor did the President think there was anything inherently implausible about Mrs. Crawford's account of her visits to 76, Sloane Street. It was not necessary to assume anything more than the perjury of Sarah. Mrs. Crawford did not claim to have been there sufficiently often that it was inevitable that she must have been seen by anyone else, other than the footmen on the occasions they had mentioned; and what, in any event, was the reason for her admitted visits at Sir Charles Dilke's breakfast time?

The President did not make a great deal of the nonappearance of Fanny, but he clearly thought that the detail relating to her added to the credibility of Mrs. Crawford's story: "That is a most revolting subject, gentlemen, and one which one would be glad to believe untrue; but the question for you in regard to that is do you think Mrs. Crawford invented the story?" "Which is the more probable," he asked later, "that a man should do such things or that a woman should invent them of him?" And it was clear what his own answer would be. He turned to Mrs. Rogerson: "I think it is vain to endeavour to put any intelligible construction on the conduct of an hysterical woman who seems to have acted with such grave indiscretion." But he thought the evidence pointed strongly to her having written the "Métropole" letter; and he was very sceptical of the theory that Mrs. Crawford had written the last anonymous letter herself or that it was part of a conspiracy to which she was privy.

He passed to the final words of his charge to the jury.

"You must bear in mind, as I have already pointed out to you, that on the former occasion it was for Mr. Crawford to prove that his wife had committed adultery with Sir Charles Dilke. On this occasion it is for the Queen's Proctor to prove that Mrs. Crawford did not commit adultery with Sir Charles Dilke. The onus is on the Queen's Proctor."

He added a further point. It had been suggested that the verdict would not greatly matter to Mr. Crawford as he would still be in a position to sustain an action against Captain Forster.

"That certainly ought not to influence your judgment in the least. But if it were entitled to a feather's weight in your judgment you will not forget this, that the difference would be that Mr. Crawford would be put to the enormous expense of these proceedings before he could begin again to take further proceedings against his wife and Captain Forster." "I believe I have now said all I need to say," Hannen concluded . . ." and I now commit the case to your charge."

After this summing-up there could be little doubt about the verdict, and little reason for the jury to take long in reaching it. They retired at 2.55 on the afternoon of Friday, July 23rd. They were back at 3.10. The clerk of the court asked them: "How do you find on the issue whether the decree *nisi* of the 12th of February last was pronounced contrary to the justice of the case by reason of material facts not brought to the knowledge of the court?" The foreman replied: "We find that it was not pronounced contrary to the justice of the case."

It only remained for the President to dismiss the intervention with costs against the Queen's Proctor, to make arrangements for the decree to be made absolute during the vacation, and to approve a suggestion that the jury should be renumerated at the high rate of a guinea a day. The case had gone as badly for Dilke as his worst fears could have foretold. His political future was clearly wrecked, and he faced other, more positive dangers as well.

Chapter Fifteen

The New Evidence

When the court rose Dilke returned with his wife to Sloane Street. Two of their most faithful friends—Mrs. Jeune, whose husband,* ironically, was later to fill Hannen's place as President of the Divorce Court, and Justin McCarthy, the novelist and Irish Nationalist M.P.—were waiting for them there. Dilke immediately set himself to writing (and issuing the same evening) an address to the electors of Chelsea. After outlining the way in which the form of the trial had told against him he concluded: "As far as public life goes, I have no option but to accept the verdict, while protesting once more against its justice. I can only, gentlemen, assure you, as I have already often solemnly assured you, and with equal solemnity sworn in court, that I am innocent of the charges brought against me, and respectfully and gratefully bid you farewell."

---

* Francis Jeune, later Lord St. Helier.

This message was published in the newspapers the following morning, together with a great volume of comment on
the case. Although less coldly pharisaical than *The Times*, the
Daily News was perhaps the most damning, in view of its
almost fulsome attitude after the February trial and of its
position as the principal Liberal organ. Its leading article
began with the wish that it might still be possible to believe in
Dilke's innocence.

> "But the case has been so thoroughly investigated," it
> continued, "that there is unfortunately no room for scepti-
> cism any longer to assert itself. No better tribunal for the
> trial of such an issue could well be found than Sir James
> Hannen and a special Jury from the City of London.[†] Sir
> James Hannen's ability is equal to that of any Judge on the
> Bench, and his experience in the divorce court has extended
> over fourteen years. No one can read his summing-up
> without being convinced that every consideration in Sir
> Charles Dilke's favour is fairly weighed, or that the result is
> irresistibly fatal to his innocence."

For the moment, however, Dilke's most pressing problem was
not whether people would believe in his innocence, but whether
criminal proceedings would be taken against him. Even before
the trial, as was seen, he envisaged the possibility of a

[†] Dilke himself, despite his dismay when it was originally decided upon, felt
no resentment against the special jury. ". . . the Jury decided as they could
not have helped deciding, and as I should have decided had I been one of
them," he wrote in his diary. (D.P. 46910.)

prosecution for perjury. After the trial, when it was clear that his evidence had not been believed, these fears greatly increased. Nor were they a product only of his own mind. They were shared by Chamberlain and, to some extent, by James. Chamberlain wrote to Dilke on July 27th: "James is absolutely convinced that in the present state of the evidence a conviction and a heavy sentence would be certain. . . . The whole question turns, as I have said, on the possibility of getting fresh evidence. Will you await this possibility in prison or in a quiet home abroad?"[1] Three days later he wrote advocating Dilke's departure from England in still more urgent terms: "I cannot see what duty is fulfilled or what interest served by facing a prosecution, which I fear must come, and which may end in a sentence of seven or even fourteen years' penal servitude."[2]

Dilke himself, however, had moved into a defiant mood. At first he had believed that his conviction for perjury might involve not only a prison sentence but also the confiscation of his goods. This, indeed, had been the state of the law until a few years previously, and it was a penalty which he was not prepared to face. Once he discovered that his property was not at stake he became less nervous. There was even an idea at one stage that he might himself invite a trial for perjury. James received this suggestion with dismay and replied saying: "You must do anything sooner than stand a trial *now*. The atmosphere must be cleared before justice would be done you, and as I have said before time may unravel much." This wise advice turned Dilke's mind away from the active course, but it did not persuade him to seek refuge abroad. He had to make a short visit to France, but this was to be in no sense a "flight." To underline the fact he wrote to the Attorney-General in the new Conservative Government, Sir Richard Webster, giving him his address and announcing that he would return at once if proceedings were started.

> "I intend to remain abroad as short a time as Emilia's arm, which is crippled with rheumatism, will allow," he wrote to Chamberlain on July 28th, "and if a prosecution is begun we shall return at once, arm or no arm. I have put off going till the 13th to 'face' prosecution, which I think Stead‡ and *The Times* will force on. I do not expect a favourable verdict, but Emilia and I decided three months ago that seven years' penal servitude is better for me, better for her, better for Wentie's future, and better above all for our love and happiness than life in Paris. Emilia is quite able to conduct the case while I am in penal servitude, and will conduct it better than I should."[3]

In the event any thought of a prosecution was abandoned before Dilke set off to take his wife to Royat. On August 5th Chamberlain was able to write decisively: "I have the best reasons for knowing that the present Government are most unlikely to initiate a prosecution for perjury." James also reported in the same sense. Dilke believed that the Government took this decision because of advice that there was no possibility of Mrs.

---

‡ The comments of the *Pall Mall Gazette* on the trial, curiously enough, were a good deal more favourable to Dilke than were those of most other newspapers. It pointed out that there were many inconsistencies in Mrs. Crawford's story. The issue was still in doubt. It could be resolved only by Dilke suing Mrs. Crawford for slander or by the Crown prosecuting him for perjury. Stead was still unwilling to drop the bone which he had got so firmly between his teeth.

Crawford being believed in a criminal trial.[§]—Matthews, who had become Home Secretary, would have been in a good position to assess this—but it seems equally probable that they were influenced by the obvious advantages of magnanimity over vindictiveness. No further blows were needed to destroy Dilke's political usefulness.

Social ostracism was also inevitable. Dilke's inclination was to recognise this by resigning from all his clubs, but he was dissuaded by Sir Henry James. There was also the question of his membership of the Privy Council. The Queen was extremely anxious that it should be terminated and assumed that Salisbury or Gladstone would see that this was done. Gladstone agreed with her to the extent of believing that continued membership was inappropriate, although he thought that the initiative should come from Dilke himself. But it did not come, for Dilke thought, and no doubt rightly, that such an act would be construed as an admission of guilt. Gladstone, in these circumstances, was prepared to take no further action; and Salisbury never wished to concern himself with the matter. Dilke therefore retained the designation "right honourable,"[¶] but he retained little else, so far as the general public was concerned, in the way of honour.

[§] In such a trial the onus would of course have been reversed. Furthermore, a higher standard would have been required—proof beyond reasonable doubt, and not just a balance of probabilities. Corroboration of Mrs. Crawford's story would have been required and—an added advantage—Dilke would under the law as it then stood have been ineligible to give evidence in his own defence. Despite James's view, it is perhaps a pity that the prosecution did not occur.

[¶] Not even the popular press suggested that Dilke should be deprived of his baronetcy. Perhaps they regarded it as an appropriate title for him to continue to bear.

The slow journey which he made across France to Royat was therefore a dismal one, still more so perhaps than if there had been the challenge of a prosecution still to face. He remained away for a month, returning to England in the middle of September and going straight to Dockett Eddy. After a few days he removed to Pyrford and stayed there until early November, when he and his wife again went abroad, this time to Paris for four weeks. In December they opened 76, Sloane Street for the first time since the beginning of August.

Dilke was trying to find ways of occupying his time. He wrote a series of anonymous articles on European politics for the *Fortnightly*, which, with the anonymity abandoned, were later published in book form, and he contemplated journalistic work of a more executive nature. "What I want is work on foreign affairs, or rather external affairs, or foreign and colonial," he wrote to his friend Thursfield of *The Times* in January, 1887. "I would prefer not to write, but to suggest and supervise foreign news, and to work up the subjects of leaders which others would write."[4] Dilke's idea was partly to gain experience with a view to starting a new London evening newspaper, but it came to nothing, which was hardly surprising if his proposal was that he should work for *The Times*.

He continued to see some friends, but not to any extent those who had been in his circle immediately before the crash. Lady Dilke's academic and professional connections were on the whole more faithful than his own acquaintances of the great world. James and Chamberlain were almost the only politicians of the front rank with whom he maintained any real contact. "You can't think how *dear* James has been to us and about us," Dilke wrote about the former. But the ex-Attorney-General, while always sympathetic and always available for consultation, was too *mondain* a figure to continue to fit easily into the rather dowdy atmosphere which had descended upon 76, Sloane Street. Even with Chamberlain intimacy became rather attenuated. Dilke saw him on October 1st, and received "an interesting picture of the political state." They met again at the end of the year, but on January 11th, 1887, Chamberlain was writing: "I have so much to do in London that I fear I cannot call at 76, this time. If you want to see me for anything will you call at 40, Princes Gardens on Saturday morning at 11–30? In this case send me a line saying you are coming."[5] He was not a man to smother in false delicacy the change in the balance of a friendship.

Dilke, it must be admitted, was probably not a very stimulating companion during this period. His mind was too exclusively occupied with the search for new evidence against Mrs. Crawford, and with the possibility that at some stage he might successfully confront her in yet another action and at last demonstrate his innocence. Even had his former political friends been available, he would probably have preferred to dine and correspond with those whose interest in the case was almost as great as his own. Fortunately he succeeded in collecting such a band of adherents. Their leader was F. W. Chesson, a former constituent of Dilke's who had long been active in a whole series of good causes. He developed the idea of forming a committee to investigate the case and to produce further facts to lay before the public. Dilke welcomed this plan enthusiastically and suggested that his former Trinity Hall friend, D. F. Steavenson, might be a useful legal member. Steavenson, in the earlier part of his life, had built up a £2,000-a-year practice at the Newcastle-upon-Tyne bar. Later he had moved to London, but had failed to achieve legal success there. In 1886 he was living quietly on his private money. He was able and willing to devote a great deal of time to work on the case. In 1891, Dilke, through the agency of Chamberlain, secured his appointment as a county court judge.

The other members of the committee were Howel Thomas, a Local Government Board official; W. A. McArthur, who had just become a member of Parliament and was later to be a Liberal Whip; Clarence Smith, former sheriff of the City of London and subsequently Liberal M.P. for Hull, East; and Canon MacColl, a clergyman whose political interests made him a frequent correspondent of both Gladstone and Salisbury. The last three were in no way close friends of Dilke. Chesson died in 1889, but the committee continued, and in 1891 a pamphlet incorporating some of the findings of its members was published. They did not publish everything because of an expressed wish not to involve "other persons besides those hitherto named in the case," and also, perhaps, because of a desire to avoid libel suits. In addition, Dilke himself, working through a solicitor and providing large sums of money for the employment of detectives, accumulated other new evidence. These two sources provide the information additional to that forthcoming at the two trials upon which any definitive view of the case must be based.

Before it is considered, however, it is perhaps relevant to give the facts about Mrs. Crawford's subsequent career. This, too, must be a factor in any final judgment. When she was divorced from her husband she was twenty-three years of age; she was in ill-health; she had enough money of her own to live on, but she was not rich; and she was the most notorious woman in England. Forster, whom she had probably wished to marry, was no longer available. It was not easy to see how she would shape her future life.

She did not remain long at her sister's house, but removed in the course of 1887 to a flat of her own in Oxford and Cambridge Mansions, in the Marylebone Road. In that neighbourhood she lived for more than forty years. At first, as has been said, she did some journalistic work under Stead for the *Pall Mall Gazette*. This arrangement did not last long. By the end of 1889 Stead had ceased to be editor and Mrs. Crawford's interests had moved in another direction. In the course of that year she became closely acquainted with Manning and was received into the Roman Catholic church by the Cardinal himself. Thereafter her religion was the centre of her life, although, as it appeared from outside, it was its social rather than its mystical aspects which primarily attracted her. She was associated with St. Joan's Social and Political Alliance, a Roman Catholic society concerned with securing, by means other than those which Mrs. Crawford had herself employed, a greater influence for women in politics. She became chairman of this body and also of the St. Joseph's Home for Girl Mothers. In 1909 she was one of the founders of the Catholic Social Guild and served for many years as its honorary secretary. But her social work, while clearly arising directly out of her religious beliefs, was not confined to Roman Catholic outlets. She was a member of her local Board of Guardians for thirty years, and in 1919 she was elected to the St. Marylebone borough council as its first Labour member. She remained on the council for twelve years, and played a major part in building up the borough's public libraries. In 1931 she moved to Kensington and lived on Camden Hill for the remainder of her life.

She had also a large literary output, partly on socio-religious subjects and partly works of criticism. In 1899 she wrote a series of essays on nineteenth-century European writers, including Daudet, Maeterlinck, Huysmans and D'Annunzio, which were published under the title *Studies in Foreign Literature.* In the following year she wrote a small book on Fra Angélico, and also published a work entitled *Philanthropy and Wage Paying. Ideals of Charity, Catholic Social Doctrine* and *The Church and the Worker* were the titles of her other works in this latter *genre. The Church and the Worker,* written as a textbook for the Catholic Social Guild, sold more than 50,000 copies before it went out of print. She also published a descriptive work on Switzerland and a life of Frederic Ozanam, a French Catholic thinker who had been one of the leaders of the Society of St. Vincent de Paul. This last book appeared as late as 1947. She died, at the age of 85, on October 19th, 1948. She had never re-married, and towards the end of her life had become extremely reluctant to discuss the events of the 'eighties. Perhaps she had forgotten that they ever occurred. To some of those who knew her in her later years she appeared a rather formidable old lady. But others were struck by her devoutness, by her untroubled mind, and by the force and sympathy of her character. "The day of her death was the feast of St. Peter of Alcantara," one who knew her well has written, "a saint whose human sympathy, charity and realisation of the spirit of penance were reflected in Mrs. Crawford's own life."

The first part of the new evidence which was accumulated between 1886 and 1891 concerned Mrs. Crawford's relations with Captain Forster and other men. At the second trial, it will be remembered, she admitted her adultery with Forster, but said that she had not known him prior to February 15th, 1884; and she resolutely denied that she had been guilty with others. In particular, she said that Frederick Warner—the "F.W." of her diary—was scarcely known to her. On this showing her statement that she had implicated Dilke because it was he who had "ruined" her had some plausibility; and Matthews, in his address to the jury, stressed the point that Dilke had been her first lover.

The first aim was to show that Mrs. Crawford's liaison with Forster had begun well before 1884. The evidence on this point came primarily, but not entirely, from those associated with 9, Hill Street, the house of assignation to which Forster had admitted in cross-examination that he had taken her. The witnesses were therefore, in Chamberlain's words, somewhat "tainted," but there were a sufficient number of them to render it highly unlikely that they were all lying. The house had been kept by a Mr. and Mrs. Harvey, who sometimes passed under the name of Murray. Harvey or Murray owned a number of other brothels as well, but at the end of 1884 he parted from his wife, which led to the closing down of 9, Hill Street. There was also some danger of police action against the house, and Mrs. Harvey, indeed, was subsequently prosecuted and fined £150. It was difficult to get her to produce a statement (which may have been because, as she eventually admitted, she had been given £100 by Sir George Lewis on Forster's behalf as the price of her silence), but she eventually signed a declaration that she remembered the visits of Forster and Mrs. Crawford as extending over a long period, although she was imprecise about the dates.

The other Hill Street witnesses were more specific. There were six of these. The first was Mrs. Sarah Anne Thomas, who had been a friend of Mrs. Harvey's and had stayed with her in February, May and December, 1882. She had a distinct recollection of seeing Forster and Mrs. Crawford (who passed under the name of Captain and Mrs. Green**) at Hill Street during the first and last of these visits. Mrs. Thomas's husband, John Thomas, signed a joint statutory declaration with a Mrs. Mary Ballard, who had been housekeeper at 9, Hill Street in 1880 and 1881, which went back even farther. They said that they had seen Mrs. Crawford (or Miss Smith as she then was) at the house in April or May, 1881. A Mrs. Emily Hallett, who had been temporary housekeeper, testified in a similar form to her having come with Forster on several occasions in the winter of 1882–3.

> "On one occasion," Mrs. Hallett stated, "the lady did not keep her appointment, and while waiting for her Captain Forster told me that the lady was married to an old man who she did not like and that she was always after him, Captain Forster, not he after her as he had another lady who he liked better."[6]

Mrs. Winifred Barzettelli, also an employee at the house, made a declaration in roughly similar terms, relating to the same winter. She added that she thought Mrs. Crawford had "a very nice voice," but "was a plain-looking woman with an ugly turned-up nose." The last of this group of witnesses was Mrs. Susan Etheridge, who had replaced Mrs. Ballard as permanent housekeeper at the beginning of 1882. Her evidence was regarded as of particular value, because she made her declaration in St. Bartholemew's Hospital where she was dying of

---

** Mrs. Green, it will be recalled, was the name under which Mrs. Crawford admitted having received letters from Forster at the Kensington Post Office.

tuberculosis. Her statement began with a dramatic reference to her awareness of her rapidly approaching end—which did indeed occur within a few days. She testified to frequent visits by Captain Forster, accompanied sometimes by Mrs. Crawford and sometimes by other women, between February, 1882, and June, 1884. At times they came together as often as twice a week.

From the sum of these statements several significant details about the Hill Street arrangements emerged. The meetings there between Mrs. Crawford and Captain Forster normally took place between eleven and twelve in the mornings. They were known in consequence as "the early people." They occupied two rooms while they were in the house, a sitting-room which led on to a bedroom. The curtains of the latter were always kept drawn, with the gaslight burning. Forster paid a sovereign for each occasion on which he used the rooms.

The statements also brought out one other fact of importance. They involved not merely Mrs. Crawford but her sister, Mrs. Harrison. This sister, Helen, was four years older than Mrs. Crawford; she was married to Robert Harrison, a partner in the stockbroking firm of Hickens, Harrison and Co., and a brother of Frederic Harrison, the positivist writer; and she becomes from this point a key figure in the investigation of the case. She was mentioned in the declaration of Mrs. Thomas as having been at Hill Street in 1880 and 1881, but not with Forster. Mrs. Harvey, however, said that she had been there with Forster and also with Mrs. Crawford, all at the same time. Dilke stated that it was Mrs. Harrison who, in the autumn of 1886, first gave him the Hill Street address, and it was probably on the assumption that she was the originator of the connection that he wrote later to Chesson: "I happen to know that (Mrs. Crawford) took Forster there—i.e., *she* was the *habitué* of the house."[7]

Mrs. Harvey, in her statement, cast the net still more widely over members of the Smith family. She said that Mrs. Ashton Dilke used also to visit Hill Street—accompanied by Forster. Dilke, however, appended a note at the side of this section of the statement saying that he did not believe it, although he had also received information *via* Chamberlain that Mrs. Dilke had at one period been living abroad with an unspecified man.

The next piece of evidence relating to Forster and Mrs. Crawford came from Captain Ernest Martin, who had been an intimate friend of Forster's. Martin stated: "Forster used to boast of his conquests over women and frequently confided to me . . . various particulars in reference to intrigues he was carrying on with ladies married and single.[††] He made no disguise of his illicit connection with Mrs. Harrison and spoke of her in contemptuous terms, and he mentioned Mrs. Donald Crawford as having frequently compromised herself with him. . . ."[8] Martin was apparently sceptical of Forster's success, and entered into a curious arrangement by which, in order that he might be convinced, a telegram should be sent to him informing him when Forster was at Hill Street with Mrs. Crawford. He would then go and watch them leave. Mrs. Hallett, the temporary housekeeper at 9, Hill Street, confirmed the incident, saying that she had sent the telegram. In response to it Martin went to Hill Street and, between noon and one o'clock on May 7th, 1883, observed the departure of Forster and Mrs. Crawford. It should be stated that the value of Martin's evidence is

[††] In 1885 Martin apparently wrote to Sir George Lewis saying that Forster had told him of affairs with four women—Mrs. Crawford, Mrs. Harrison, and two others.

diminished by the fact that, when he gave it, he had quarrelled with Forster, and, the latter claimed, had tried to blackmail him.

Another statement came from Catherine Ruddiman, who had been a parlour-maid in the service of the Crawfords at 3, Sydney Place in 1882. She had been subpoenaed as a witness for Crawford at the second trial, but Matthews had not called her. She stated that during 1882 there were frequent calls from both Forster and Robert Priestley (the "R.C.P." of the diary). Dilke called on only one occasion. When Forster or Priestley were in the house she was told to say that Mrs. Crawford was not at home to any other caller. On the occasion of Dilke's visit she was not so instructed.

The next group of evidence came from Mrs. Harrison's servants. The principal one was George Ball, who had been her butler at 73, Cromwell Road, from November, 1879, to March, 1885, and who had appeared briefly in the witness-box at the first trial. He joined with his wife and George Reeves, Mrs. Harrison's footman, in giving written testimony that in the summer of 1882, when Mrs. Crawford had told her husband that she was going to stay with her sister at Cowes (and when there was no suggestion that she had been with Dilke) she had not in fact appeared there. Ball also testified that Mrs. Crawford had been acquainted with Forster as early as January, 1882, and that, during the early months of that year he and she had frequently called on Mrs. Harrison at the same time. Mrs. Harrison, he believed, had first met Forster at a ball in Gloucestershire at the end of 1881.

George Ball, however, went much further in his testimony than this. He did not merely add to the already formidable pile of evidence that Mrs. Crawford had known Forster long before the date to which she had sworn in the witness-box. He also provided information about Mrs. Crawford's activities upon one of the specific dates which she had alleged against Dilke. This was February 13th, 1883, one of the only two occasions on which she said that she had spent the night at 76, Sloane Street. She had been free, she told the court, because she had returned from Scotland that morning, twenty-four hours in advance of her husband; and she had gone to Sloane Street, waited for Dilke until he had returned from addressing his constituents at the Kensington Town Hall, and stayed with him until 7–30 the following morning. Ball's testimony was as follows:

"I distinctly recollect that one night in February, 1883 (and on 13th February '83 to the best of my recollection and belief), Mrs. Crawford dined with Mrs. Harrison at 73 Cromwell Road about seven o'clock in the evening. I waited upon them at dinner and gathered from their conversation that Mrs. Crawford had just arrived from Scotland. Just before ten o'clock on that evening I was directed to call a hansom cab for Mrs. Crawford, which I did and handed her into it, at the same time asking her where I should tell the cabman to drive. She replied, 'Straight on—I will tell him where to stop.' My curiosity was rather excited and I made a move as if to return to the house but instead of doing so I remained on the pavement kerb and distinctly heard Mrs. Crawford tell the cabman through the trap in the roof of the cab as it was pulling off from the door to drive to Earls Court Gardens. When she said this I was standing behind the back of the cab, which drove off in the direction of Earls Court."[9]

Ball added that Earls Court Gardens was a significant address

396

to him because a messenger who had often brought notes from Forster to Mrs. Harrison had told him that he (the messenger) kept a lodging-house there.

This statement obviously offered a whole new line of enquiry which the Dilke partisans were quick to follow up. They discovered a Mrs. Julia Medland who, with her daughter, of the same name, kept a lodging-house at 32, Earls Court Gardens. She recognised photographs of Forster, Mrs. Crawford (who had "a peculiarly loud voice") and Mrs. Harrison, and linked them with a Mr. de Jersey,‡‡ who, she said, had lodged with her from December, 1882, to February, 1883, and had occupied a front sitting-room on the first floor and a back bedroom on the second floor. Forster, Mrs. Medland said, used frequently to be in de Jersey's rooms, and they were on many occasions visited by Mrs. Harrison and Mrs. Crawford. After de Jersey left the two sisters continued to visit a Mr. Stewart, who was another lodger in the house.

Mrs. Medland continued:

"I recollect on one particular occasion in the middle of February, 1883, Mr. de Jersey informed me that a friend of his who was a stranger in town was going to occupy his room for one night and would dine with him that evening. The ladies whom I have identified as Mrs. Harrison and Mrs. Crawford came to tea in the afternoon of the same day. About midnight the same night my door was opened

---

‡‡ De Jersey, it was discovered, came (a little confusingly) from Guernsey, was "something on the Stock Exchange" in addition to running a society for the recovery of lost property, and died in a brothel in 1891.

by a latchkey by Mr. de Jersey's friend and I distinctly heard the rustle of a lady's dress ascending the stairs talking very loud to the gentleman who was accompanying her. I heard them enter Mr. de Jersey's bedroom and heard the door closed and both my daughter and myself heard their voices in conversation for a very long time during the night. At about six o'clock in the morning I heard the bedroom door open and I heard both the lady and the gentleman descend the stairs. I heard the front door closed after the lady and the gentleman returned to his room and remained there until about two o'clock in the afternoon, and then he sent down to see if there was any breakfast for him. My daughter informed him that no breakfast was provided for him. I saw him leave the house about two o'clock in the afternoon and I recognise him as the same gentleman whose photograph is now produced and shown to me. . . ."[10]

This story was fully corroborated by Mrs. Medland's daughter. It was also to some extent supported by a Mrs. Castell, who kept another lodging-house at 28, Earls Court Gardens, and made a signed declaration that Forster engaged a room at her house for the night, but did not occupy it, returning in the middle of the following day in evening clothes and without an overcoat.

Unfortunately, however, from the point of view of neatness at least, Mrs. Medland's statement cannot be accepted in its exact form. C. J. C. Pridham, a solicitor who was in charge of this part of the enquiry, wrote to Dilke in 1891 to say that Forster was in fact much better known at the Medlands' house than the statement implies. He lodged there frequently when on leave, and he merely took a room at No. 28 in order to change because the house was full that evening. Later Miss Medland left to stay with

398

relatives at Acton so that a room might be freed for Forster and his guest. She and her mother were thus much more privy to what was going on than they admitted. "This is what the Medlands are ashamed of," Pridham wrote. But their evidence was nevertheless substantially true, he believed.

A further element of confusion was provided by Mrs. Harrison who, Dilke noted, "positively denies that Forster lodged in Earls Court Gardens at any time, and does so with so much vehemence, while admitting her own adultery with him both at Hill Street and at the British Hotel in Jermyn Street, that there seems to be some strong motive in the denial."[11] Whatever the motive there is no indication that it was ever discovered.

This completes the evidence touching on Mrs. Crawford's relations with Forster. It should perhaps be noted that the dates of his leaves from the Curragh, where he was in charge of the gymnasium in 1882–3, fit in well enough with the dates mentioned. In 1882 he was on leave from February 6th to 28th, and from July 7th to 30th (the time of the assumed Cowes visit); in 1883 he was on leave from February 1st to March 9th.

The next section of subsequently accumulated evidence concerned Mrs. Crawford's relations with men other than Forster, and was of a much more tenuous nature. The most important figure was Warner. He was traced with difficulty and found to be in practice as a doctor at 140, Fulham Road. He was described as very good-looking, lately married to a rich wife, and having previously "led a fast life." No information was apparently forthcoming from him. He had been a student at St. George's Hospital in 1882, and had come into contact with Mrs. Harrison there, and through her with Mrs. Crawford. Mrs. Harrison and to a lesser extent Mrs. Crawford had been frequenting the hospital because Robert Harrison, as a result of a riding accident in Hyde Park, had been a patient there for nearly two months. It will be remembered that the first of the anonymous letters received by Crawford, which ended with the phrase "beware of the member for Chelsea," had referred also to the flirtations which his wife and her sister were carrying on with students at the hospital. Crawford in his evidence at the first trial said that he received this letter while Harrison was a patient there, but that he thought the date was March or early April. Records showed, however, that Harrison had in fact left the hospital on February 23rd, the date of Mrs. Crawford's alleged first seduction by Dilke. This was thought to be of importance because it showed, first, that Mrs. Crawford's relations with Warner must have begun before February 23rd, and second, that the reference to "the member for Chelsea" could have been at most no more than a prophecy.

The investigations of an enquiry agent succeeded in producing the information that Mrs. Harrison, apart from her activities at 9, Hill Street (where, it was said, both she and Mrs. Crawford used to be taken by Mr. Hugh Hammersley and the Honble. A. Grosvenor of Moor Park, Rickmansworth), had rooms during her husband's period in hospital at 27, Chester Street. There both she and Mrs. Crawford were visited by several of the students from St. George's, "including Freddy Warner."

Rather harder evidence was forthcoming later when Dilke obtained possession of some letters from Warner to Mrs. Harrison. They were dated between March and May, 1882. There was a mystery about how the letters had been obtained, and there is a note in the papers saying: "Dilke cannot state the circumstances under which a large collection of Mrs. Harrison's letters came into his hands, but two persons are implicated in the larceny."[12] He made no attempt to conceal that he had them, however. He first showed them to Steavenson, who expressed the view that they were of great importance, so much so that had they been in the hands of the Queen's Proctor at the time of Mrs. Crawford's cross-examinations they would have been sufficient to win his case. Through solicitors Dilke then informed Mrs. Crawford that the letters were in his possession and asked her to meet him. She refused at first, but when he had sent her one of the letters she agreed to come. They met in Sir George Lewis's office, with Humbert also present. But the interview was ineffective. Mrs. Crawford said "she could do nothing and that I must do what I must."

Two of the letters pointed only to a liaison between Warner and Mrs. Harrison, but a third was in the following terms:

"My dear Nell: I found your letter . . . awaiting me . . . to-day and it kept me in roars of laughter. It was so characteristic of you in your supreme moment of bliss. Just as I was leaving I got your card asking me to tea to-morrow, which I shall be most happy to do, provided no one else besides yourself and Nia will be there. . . . With very much love to you pet and Nia."§§[13]

The letters were clearly much more damaging to Mrs. Harrison than to Mrs. Crawford, but they tended strongly to contradict the latter's assertion that her acquaintanceship with Warner was of the slightest nature; and their suggestion of a curious, tripartite relationship between Warner and the two sisters, together

---

§§ "Nia" was the diminutive of Virginia by which Mrs. Crawford was known to her intimates.

with other similar hints in the Hill Street evidence and the Chester Street report, was thought, perhaps rightly, to be of great significance, and to offer a possible explanation of Mrs. Crawford's "invention" of the sensational Fanny story.

There was also some further information relating to Robert Priestley, Mrs. Crawford's brother-in-law. This was contained in a letter from Mrs. Rogerson to Lady Dilke, dated September 22nd, 1886. The letter itself has a note of conviction, although Mrs. Rogerson cannot in general be regarded as a reliable witness of the truth, or indeed of anything else.

"I cannot for a moment go back from what I said that Mrs. Crawford had told me of repeated adulteries with Mr. Priestley," it ran. "She told me with the fullest particulars. She said that it had been so constantly *before* and in *August, 1884,* up till he went to Scotland or somewhere north. *A week later* he wrote he was engaged to her sister.¶ She also mentioned a Mr. Warner but quite casually. I feel I must now say this because she has denied having told me. of it. As I never knew there were such men till *she* told me, I can hardly be even confused. It was from herself and *no one else* I heard of these adulteries at first."[14]

Mrs. Harrison also referred to the liaison between Mrs. Crawford and Priestley as something which was beyond dispute. She said that Mrs. Ashton Dilke was aware of the relationship with Priestley, but not of that with Warner. There were also a

---

¶ This was a younger sister, Ida, who had been born in 1864 and who lived until 1943.

few snippets of information suggesting that at Edinburgh in the autumn of 1881 Mrs. Crawford had another lover—perhaps her first—called Captain Ernest Graham. The initials "E.G." had appeared in her diary for these months in the same way as the others already noted. In addition there was mention of another gentleman referred to simply as "Fleming," who appeared later in the period under review. But these suggestions were not supported by evidence. They complete the subsequently obtained information relating to Mrs. Crawford's conduct.

The next group of evidence related to 65, Warren Street, and Anna Dessouslavy. This began with a series of statements from a variety of apparently impeccable sources testifying to the relationship of the Dessouslavy family to the Dilke family being as Sir Charles had stated it in his evidence, to the pension paid to Anna being a perfectly open arrangement, and to the Dessouslavys being thought to be a family of excellent character. These statements were not of major importance, as the judge in his summing-up, even if not the public, had been prepared to concede at least the first two points to Dilke.

Next came a further series of statements from those intimately connected with Warren Street which were designed to show that the house could not have been used for immoral purposes. These were taken by McArthur and Howel Thomas from Mrs. Goudge, the landlady, from Mr. Collins, the beadle at Trinity Church, St. Marylebone, who had lodged there with his wife, and from Mr. and Mrs. Williams, who had also lodged in the house. Moreover, they all swore that the description of the interior of the house, supported by a plan, which Mrs. Crawford had given in the witness-box and which had so impressed the court, was wrong in every respect. She was wrong as to the position of the staircase (which was remarkable as it ran from the back of the house to the

403

front), she was wrong as to the position of the door leading into the bedroom, and she was wrong as to the shape of the bedroom and the position in it of the window. A surveyor's plan of the house was then made, which confirmed the accuracy of these witnesses and the inaccuracy of Mrs. Crawford.

Mrs. Goudge made one other statement which was thought to be of importance. She said that some time before the trial began (she did not specify which trial), two ladies whom she had seen wandering up and down the street on several previous occasions called and asked if Mrs. Dessouslavy lived there. The suggestion was that the two ladies were Mrs. Crawford and Mrs. Ashton Dilke, looking for the house with more difficulty and by a somewhat different method from that which Mrs. Crawford had described in her evidence. It was also pointed out in the papers, as was indeed confirmed by the author on a visit to Warren Street, that had Mrs. Crawford looked for the house, as she told the court, in the belief that it was one of two which were taller than their neighbours, she would indeed have found difficulty in identifying it; it is in fact one of a group of five which are all taller than the others in the street.

The Dilke investigators also reverted to the problem of Giuliano, whose production by Phillimore had failed so signally either to confuse the Hilliers or to impress the court. There was a statement by Chesson testifying that Giuliano, with his hat on, did in fact look remarkably like Dilke. There was not perhaps very much to this, and there may have been more value in the investigators' refutation of the judge's strongly made dialectical point that, when it was suggested by Sir Walter Phillimore that it was Giuliano and not Dilke who had been to the house under the circumstances described by the Hilliers, Sir Walter was apparently abandoning his attempt to defend Mrs. Dessouslavy's reputation to the court. Giuliano was shown by the new evidence to be a man of accepted respectability, well known to the other inhabitants of the house as a friend of Mrs. Dessouslavy's. His wife was also a close friend of Anna's and he used frequently to meet her in the latter's rooms. McArthur and Howel Thomas also took statements from Mrs. Hillier and Miss Hillier, who had been such important witnesses at the second trial. They both said that they regretted the certainty which they had then displayed about the man who frequently visited the house being Sir Charles Dilke. They were now extremely doubtful about his identity.

All this, so far as it went, was clearly in Dilke's favour, but one other subsequent development in regard to Mrs. Dessouslavy, had it been known, must have told the other way. On July 29th, 1890, she wrote to Dilke, in French, what appeared to be a letter of half-apology. She wrote that, as a result of delusions, she had been saying things about him to which "*il ne faut pas attacher trop d'importance.*" The only clue to the nature of these remarks comes from a note which Dilke attached to Mrs. Dessouslavy's letter.

"Anna went cracky (*sic*) (she has been so since her cross-examination but got much worse)," he wrote, "and at last wrote to me that I had seduced her sister, was the father of her son, and (had) induced her to give false evidence." He added, a little inconsequently: "The son was born in wedlock, the sister has been all along in place, and I have hardly ever set eyes on the one she means (Eliza, I think it is)."[15]

The only subsequent record of Mrs. Dessouslavy was in 1907

when she was writing to Dilke with complete friendliness and apparent sanity.

The next section of evidence related to Fanny Stock. First there was the signed statement which Humbert had taken from her in April, 1886.*** In this statement she denied the charge made against her. "I certainly never saw Mrs. Crawford at Sloane Street or any other lady, I did not even see Sir Charles Dilke. I never heard of Mrs. Crawford until the commencement of this case and I should not know her if I saw her." She insisted, however, that she was frightened to go into the witness-box and said that her husband was also most anxious that she should not do so. That was why they had disappeared for several months. She gave an account of the places where she had been in service which was complete except for the fifteen months before she went to Warren Street. About this period she was firmly reticent: "I decline to say where I was between March, 1883, and July, 1884—it has nothing whatever to do with this case.[16]

After this statement was taken the Stocks disappeared again, and sought on this occasion to cover their traces by assuming a false name. By the beginning of 1887 they had been tracked down by detectives employed by Dilke's solicitor. Chesson then

---

*** The original of this document found its way into the Dilke papers by a curious route. In 1931 Edward Marjoribanks sent it to Miss Tuckwell with the following letter: "I have been meaning to send you this document for a very long time; it is a proof taken by Humbert & Co. in the case of Crawford and Crawford from Fanny Stock before the trial. Marshall Hall stole this statement or failed to return it to the solicitors because I suppose of its unique interest; all the Marshall Hall papers were, I understood, to be destroyed, but I specially asked for this so as to send it to you if you wanted it." (D.P. 49612.)

went to see Fanny and wrote this account of his interview:

"On Tuesday, January 28th, 1887, Lady Dilke and I visited Fanny Stock (alias Archer) at Foot's Cray. We questioned her on the subject of her disappearance during the year 1883–4. Her story was as follows: when residing at 16, Curzon Street, as housemaid to Mrs. Charles Roundell she made the acquaintance of a man who visited at the house, and at his insistence she left her situation and went into lodgings somewhere, as it would seem, in the suburbs of London. She entered the service of a lady of his acquaintance, and passed a certain number of hours daily with her in doing needlework, and taking charge of her clothes. Both parties were married, but the lady's husband was away; and she and her paramour met, from time to time, at Fanny's lodgings. The lady lived about ten minutes' walk from Fanny's lodgings; and it would take about an hour to walk from Sloane Street to the place in question. She refused to give the name of either of the parties concerned in the intrigue. . . . She declared that she had never had relations of any kind with Sir C. Dilke, and could hardly say that she knew him; that she never saw Mrs. Crawford in her life; and that she met Anna Dessouslavy by pure accident when she went to Shoolbred's to buy a cloak. She was not in want, but was glad to take service with her, because having left Mrs. Roundell's for more than a year, she was without a character and would have found it difficult to get a place."[17]

A fairly implausible story it sounded, and so indeed it proved to be. Some time later Dilke's detectives discovered that the address at which Fanny had lodged was 14, Grafton Street, Fitzroy

Square. Her landlady there, Mrs. Anne Thorpe, made a declaration, supported by her husband, that from February, 1883, to July, 1884, Fanny Gray had occupied a bed-sitting room in her house. During that time, Mrs. Thorpe stated, Fanny "conducted herself with the greatest propriety." She received no visitors, but she often spent nights away, returning in the morning. She apparently did no work; she occasionally went out walking for a short time in the afternoons; but "the greater part of her time (was) spent in reading the works of Jane Austen, George Eliot and Sir Walter Scott."[18]

Enquiries were also conducted at Haslemere, where the Roundells had another house and where, rather than in Curzon Street, Fanny had passed most of her year in their service. These enquiries yielded the information that Fanny was believed to have become involved there with an artist, and to have left with him. His name, it was thought, was George Williams.

At this stage the investigators went back to Fanny. At the end of 1890 she made a sworn declaration—which she had not in 1887—admitting that what she had then told Chesson had been a fabrication. She stated that while at Haslemere she had become engaged to the artist and that he had taken the room for her in Grafton Street and had paid her £1 a week. She would not give his name and she would not state the circumstances in which the engagement had been broken off. Her husband stated that he fully believed her story and had the best of reasons for knowing that she was a woman of good character. At this stage the "Archers" seem to have assumed, correctly, that their part in the drama was over; they reverted to their real name and passed into obscurity.

The fact that Fanny had previously told a false story inevitably throws doubt upon her second version as well. Against this must be set the somewhat greater plausibility of the second story together with the fact that its skeleton came first from other sources and was merely confirmed by Fanny herself. Nevertheless a substantial element of mystery remains, one which existed in Dilke's mind as much as in anyone else's. "I have my doubts as to the story as to the meeting of Fanny and Anna," he wrote cryptically but inelegantly to Chesson; but we have no means of knowing what these particular doubts were or why they existed.

The next section of further information related to the Sloane Street servants and arrangements. The menservants appeared not to be of the most exemplary character. Henry Shanks, who had been footman from 1882 to 1885, was first given notice to leave because he was discovered to have stolen 30s.; was then reinstated for a time; but was finally discharged without a reference for admitting acquaintances into 76, Sloane Street, and gambling with them throughout the night. William Goode, who was footman from 1882 to 1884, took during the latter part of his service to spending most of his time at the local public house. He was eventually discharged for drunkenness and stole a cheque on leaving. William Ireland, Bodley's clerk, was also dismissed for drunkenness in 1884.

All these three servants, therefore, had possible grievances against Dilke, and there is certainly no reason to assume that their evidence at the trial was prejudiced in his favour. Admittedly there was some bribery, but it was self-cancelling. Both Shanks and Ireland, who were almost destitute, were paid 25s. a week by Humbert, but they were known also to have received money from the other side. Ireland, who had not been called at the trial, signed a statement saying that he was always in his room from 8 a.m. to 1 p.m. and again in the afternoons, and that he never saw or heard Mrs. Crawford going up or down stairs.

Shanks signed a statement (which was confirmed from other sources) saying that after Dilke entered the Cabinet three policemen used to watch the house each night.[†††] He was on duty in the front hall every second night (alternating with the other footman) from 8 to 10–30, and he used habitually to stand at the door talking with the policemen. He did not believe it possible that Mrs. Crawford could have come into the house at night without being seen. He also testified to the fact—supported by other servants—that the only bed in Dilke's room was a very small camp-bed with room for no more than a single pillow. The policemen who watched the house were apparently under orders to report anyone who entered or left at night, and the instruction was interpreted sufficiently strictly for the men who failed to report the entry of Shanks's gambling companions to be dismissed from the force.

A further statement was also obtained from Ellen Drake, who had been under-housemaid from 1880 to 1883 and who, at the trial, had been generally considered a truthful witness. She testified that it was her regular duty to take fruit and milk to Dilke's bedroom at ten o'clock at night. It was also her habit to be up and about the house by 6.30 a.m. She never saw Mrs. Crawford in the house, either at night or in the morning. There were also letters from Mr. Hanbury Tracey, M.P., and Baron d'Estournelles de Constant, who had become French Minister at The Hague. They had both participated in the fencing parties, and they wrote of their conviction that

---

[†††] This was at a time when there was some Irish terrorist activity; and when the Home Secretary, Harcourt, took his duties as a protector of public safety almost excessively seriously.

Mrs. Crawford's stories of her morning visits to Sloane Street were quite impossible. D'Estournelles said that he was frequently at the house until 11–30, and Tracey wrote that he often returned from Prince's, where he dressed, to pick up something he had left behind at Sloane Street. All the guests came and went quite freely both before and after Dilke's departure for his office.

The last group of post-trial information was concerned not with the contradiction of Mrs. Crawford's story, but with providing an explanation for her invention of it. First there was evidence to suggest that her illness in the summer of 1884 had in fact been the beginnings of syphilis, and that, by the time of her confession, the knowledge that she was suffering from this disease provided her with an additional and urgent reason for wishing to sever her connection with her husband. This information was first given to Dilke by Mrs. Rogerson, who was a good source in so far as she had been very close to Mrs. Crawford at the relevant period, and a bad source in so far as she was a highly unreliable witness. There was evidence that Mrs. Crawford had been treated at this period by Dr. Lee of Savile Row, Dr. Matthews Duncan, and Dr. Cumberbatch of Cadogan Place. To the last-named Mrs. Rogerson claimed that she herself had sent her.

Enquiries to these three doctors not unnaturally failed to elicit any information, but a further line was obtained when it was discovered in 1889 that Mrs. Crawford was still receiving treatment, at this time from Dr. Priestley, the father of her brother-in-law and one of the foremost specialists of the day on women's diseases. One of his prescriptions for her was traced as having been made up by an assistant (Caesar) employed by a chemist (Miles) in business at 165, Edgware Road, and was said

411

to confirm the nature of her disease. The theory was that she had contracted it from Forster, who, in Dilke's phrase, was "thereafter eaten away by the disease until he died of it a few years later," Forster having previously been infected by her sister, Mrs. Harrison. This would account for the revulsion from Mrs. Harrison which was known to have seized Forster, and also for a coolness which had sprung up between the two sisters; but it was all rather hypothetical.

There was also a view that, if Mrs. Crawford had invented the story, she must have been aided by allies other (and probably more powerful) than Forster. Bodley wrote to Dilke, on September 27th, 1887, commenting on a paragraph, friendly to Dilke, which had appeared in a journal entitled *Land and Water*, and which suggested conspiracy against him. Bodley's letter (a vital part of which is most unfortunately missing‡‡‡) starts several new hares.

> "There can be no doubt to whom the paragraph points," he wrote, "but I know nothing whatever to justify the suspicion. The combination of 'individual jealousy,' 'feminine hatred,' 'racial prejudice,' and 'great wealth' can only mean Rosebery and his wife.§§§ . . . I have never heard a word as to Rosebery's hostility to you except of course the very frequent and obvious observations that your being

---

‡‡‡ Many of the Dilke papers (not only his engagement diaries) are appallingly lacerated. It is not always clear whether this was done by Sir Charles himself, or whether it was the result of the censorship which Miss Tuckwell exercised before entrusting the papers to the British Museum in 1939.

§§§ Hannah Rosebery, who died in 1890, was a rich Jewess, the only daughter of Baron Meyer de Rothschild. She was a first cousin of the Miss (Alice) Rothschild referred to later in the letter. See also p. 113, *supra*.

out of the way was worth a good deal to him. . . . My impression would be that the writer has two different rumours mixed up in his head. As you took the line you did about the Princes Gardens incident[¶¶¶] I have never opened my mouth in this country regarding it. But there has always been the idea in the air that your hidden foe was of your own party—that is to say that you were betrayed by Chamberlain. Then the second rumour was that of Miss Rothschild's attachment to you. Of course I heard much about this in the autumn of '85 when half the women you knew in London wrote to me to ask if your marriage could not be stopped, and as they were all previously fettered themselves they invariably suggested that if marriage was necessary you should avail yourself of Miss R.'s disposition. But as you know I never had any intimacy with the Jew gang. I never heard they had shown any great hostility to you excepting of course the national line the tribe would take of kicking a man when he is down. As to the Princes Gardens incident I have always felt that. . . (here the break occurs) . . . said about you, and I find a most marked advance of feeling in your favour. Everybody of course connected with the F(oreign) O(ffice) wants you back, but amongst the rest there is a distinct change. If only something tangible could happen people would welcome it. . . . There is one individual who did not frequent that section of society in bygone days who does not share the sentiments I have described, indeed, I was told, he gets 'very mad' as the Americans say, when it is suggested that your return to public life is not an

---

[¶¶¶] See pp. 355–8 *infra*.

413

improbability. There is no need to give a name, but this fact assures me in my belief that if Mrs. Crawford's proceedings for the twenty-four hours preceding the confession could be ascertained, nothing more would be necessary than to publish them. However, the fact of the possibility of your speedy return exciting anger is a good sign, as if there were no chance of it you would still be the object of the devoted sympathy which did more than anything else to ruin you in '85.

> "Yours ever,
>
> J. E. C B."[19]

This fascinating letter although long is none the less cryptic. The references to Rosebery and to Chamberlain (it is to him again, of course, that the last section refers) are, however, clear enough. Rosebery, in whose guilt Bodley did not believe, can be dealt with first. The basis of the rumour was that some money had passed between the Roseberys and Mrs. Crawford. The position as Dilke understood it was most fully stated in a note which he wrote in April, 1894:

> "John J. Louden of Killudunyan House, Westport (one of Parnell's solicitors), wrote naming Mrs. Bridgmount, an Irish woman, as the author of the story of how Lord Rosebery found the bribe for Mrs. Crawford to lie about me. Mrs. Bridgmount lived with Rosebery both before and after his wife's time. I have never believed the story. Lady Rosebery found some money for Mrs. Crawford as we know, but that was a different matter."[20]

Dilke had felt a gust of suspicion against the Roseberys much earlier, however. On December 12th, 1885 he wrote to Rosebery in the following terms:

"*Secret*

My dear Rosebery,

Some time ago friends of mine who are also friends of Mr. Crawford and of yourself expressed surprise that he was staying with you. I replied that it was not unnatural, there being nothing I know of against him. To-day I have however a statement so incredible that I hesitate to repeat it to you even in a secret letter. It is that Mr. Crawford states that Lady Rosebery has promised him *help* in his case. Now, no doubt he believes the wicked and monstrous lies that have been told him, but no one else who has any acquaintance with the matter believed them, and I make no doubt but that the nature and authorship of the plot against me will be fully exposed. Still, it is not pleasant to have a colleague's name used in this way, and I think it best to write to you rather than to write to relations of Lady Rosebery's or to colleagues of ours or common friends.

Yours sincerely,

Charles W. Dilke."

Rosebery, replying on the following day, wrote: "I should have thought that even in this age of lies no human being could have invented so silly a lie as that you mention. But if you wish me to contradict it, I will only say that there is not a vestige of truth or even possibility about it." He added that when he "first heard" with the rest of the public "about this case" he was placed in an embarrassing position, and had decided to keep clear of it and treat Crawford and Dilke, who were both his friends, as though nothing had happened.

This letter (as Mr. Rhodes James makes clear in his recent

415

biography of Rosebery) contains a misstatement about the way in which Rosebery first heard of the case, but it appeared completely to satisfy Dilke. He answered at once:

"My dear Rosebery,

Your letter is all I could expect or wish. He (Crawford) thinks he has received the greatest of injuries at my hands. I have received none at his because I have never for an instant doubted his belief in what he was told.

Yours sincerely,

Chas. W. D."

Many years later Dilke wrote to Sir Wemyss Reid saying that his suspicions never revived. Rosebery behaved less generously. He severed all contact with Dilke after the second trial, and as late as 1909 he took the trouble to write the following note:

"I think it necessary to leave on record for the information of my children, in case Sir Charles Dilke should leave any records of his life speaking ill of me, that I was compelled to cut him dead, for having declared that my wife (then dead) had inspired Mrs. Crawford to make a false accusation against him in order to get him out of the way of my career.

AR."

Could one or both of the Roseberys have been party to a conspiracy?

Apart from the alleged payment of money by Lady Rosebery to Mrs. Crawford there are two factors which gave a certain superficial plausibility to the story. The first was that Dilke was undoubtedly a direct rival to the extremely ambitious Rosebery.

This was explicitly (and generously) recognised by Rosebery on February 3rd, 1886, the day on which he became Foreign Secretary. "You will know already," Rosebery wrote to Dilke, "that I have been appointed to the Foreign Office. . . . Had you not felt compelled to stand aside this office would have been yours by universal consent."[22] The second factor was Lady Rosebery's known capacity for trying to advance her husband's career by rather unfortunate methods. But there is a great difference between making scenes to Mr. Gladstone and bribing Mrs. Crawford to concoct a conspiracy. It is true that she was sometimes hysterically anxious for her husband's success and that Dilke stood directly in his way. But these truths do not even begin to prove that she attempted to remove the obstacle. The theory of a plot instigated by the Roseberys might be dramatically satisfying, but there is no hard evidence in its support.

A Chamberlain-instigated conspiracy would be still more dramatic, and this theory has at least a certain volume of circumstantial evidence in its support; but the question of motive would be more complicated in the case of Chamberlain than in that of Rosebery. Bodley, as his letter indicated, clearly believed in Chamberlain's guilt. But his mind had long been predisposed in this direction. Even before he had any evidence to go on he wrote to Dilke in terms which were bitingly critical of Chamberlain. The latter's behaviour in allowing Matthews to be elected for East Birmingham—"by his deliberate action he returned to Parliament in as strict a sense as the Duke of Bedford used to return the member for Tavistick the man who a week previously had vilified you . . . in the court"—aroused Bodley's special anger.

"More than this," he continued, "what you suffered on account of that association (with Chamberlain) in the autumn of '85 will be never known. Chamberlain had not then adopted the fashionable principles of the Primrose League on Irish affairs. His anecdotes about Foulon and similar sentiments had struck terror into the hearts of the 'classes' who now are for the moment his allies. Lady Salisbury's brutality on hearing of your disaster represented a very extended feeling; she said 'we liked Sir Charles Dilke, but we are delighted because it will smash Chamberlain.' At the time of the Birmingham election a man of the world whose opinion you respect said to me, 'It would certainly have been a strong order for Chamberlain to have chucked over the Ministry in the matter of Matthews, but not so strong as Dilke's insisting in 1880 upon the ex-Mayor of Birmingham going straight into the Cabinet.' There have it is true been single-minded patriots who have sacrificed friendship to the state ever since the days of Brutus and Cassius, but there have always been a few cynics inclined to criticise their lofty motives."[23]

Some time after this letter was written the Dilke investigators, to the knowledge of Bodley, obtained sight of the notebook of the detective—ex-Inspector Butcher—whom Crawford had employed to watch his wife during the last few weeks of her life with him. This revealed the astonishing fact that, on Wednesday, July 15th, two days before her confession, Mrs. Crawford had called at Chamberlain's house in London and had apparently remained there for some time, Ex-Inspector Butcher's notes—the narrative is not very smooth—read as follows:

"(Mrs. Crawford) returned home 4–20 p.m., changed her dress and came out again at 4–30 p.m. The servant called a cab (5017) and drove her to 40 Princes Gardens, S. Kensington, at 4–50 p.m. Just after arrival Mr. Chamberlain drove up to house in cab. Horse fell down and the watcher (Butcher) helped Mr. Chamberlain out and helped get up horse. 2 carriages with ladies and a cab with gent in the same house at 9–50 and 10 p.m. the carriages returned and the ladies got in and drove off. I believed the young person must have gone with the one closed carriage as I watched till lights turned out at 11 p.m. and did not see the young lady after."[24]

This was an astonishing story, first, because there was no overt acquaintance between Chamberlain and Mrs. Crawford; and, secondly, because Chamberlain never informed Dilke of the call. This can hardly have been through lack of opportunity, for within a few weeks of the incident they were to spend more than a month together at Highbury. Nor is it likely that the visit escaped Chamberlain's memory. During Dilke's period at Highbury the question of Mrs. Crawford's motive must surely have been frequently discussed. It is hardly conceivable that in the course of these discussions it should not have occurred to Chamberlain to tell Dilke of her visit to him. Why did he not do so? This was a question to which Chamberlain, in Dilke's view, never provided an adequate answer. Dilke recorded the explanation given by Chamberlain (after the detective's notebook had become available) and his view of it in three separate places. On the copy of the detective's notes he wrote: "Chamberlain confirms the call but says that she did not find anyone at home

419

or go in."[25] On Bodley's letter (the one which referred to both Rosebery and Chamberlain) he noted:

> "Keep in letter-box for memoirs: it is interesting as a specimen of the kind of advice one got from the ablest people. I do not reject all faith in human nature, and do not believe in the awful wickedness of bosom friends. The man who wrote this knew that Butcher, the detective of Crawford, when we bought his notes of what had passed before the confession, showed us that she had been at Chamberlain's house the afternoon before and had been lost there, but though the explanation was not satisfactory I do not believe one word of the innuendo."[26]

Then again apparently some years later, Dilke wrote a note saying:

> "I and Emilia (Lady Dilke) always rejected Bodley's view that Mrs. Crawford's visit to Chamberlain at that moment was more than a chance. What Bodley will not see and what Emilia and I can is that though a 'Red Indian' Chamberlain is loyal to friends and incapable of such treachery."[27]

Dilke's rejection of Bodley's suspicions was therefore based on faith in Chamberlain's character and not on any convincing, innocent explanation of the Princes Gardens incident.**** It

----

**** Dilke's act of faith was the greater in so far as he apparently believed that Mrs. Crawford herself posted the last anonymous letter to her husband—the one which provoked her "confession"—immediately after leaving

seems indeed as though Dilke was disinclined to believe Chamberlain's statement that Mrs. Crawford did not go into his house. This is not surprising, for it is almost impossible that had she merely rung the bell, spoken to the footman, and turned away from the door, a trained detective, operating in full daylight, could have lost her there. Equally difficult is it to believe that, had the call been of such a casual and ineffective nature, Chamberlain, while not remembering it in the following month, should have recalled it two years later when challenged by Dilke. The first part of Chamberlain's statement—that he was not at home when Mrs. Crawford called—is not in dispute. It is confirmed by Butcher's evidence that he arrived in a cab soon afterwards; and is in a sense doubly confirmed by Chamberlain having told Dilke that he could recall the incident of the cab-horse falling down to which Butcher referred. But this merely suggests that her call was pre-arranged with Chamberlain. Otherwise, being unknown to his servants, she would hardly have been admitted in his absence.

Of course, even a pre-arranged two-hour call, about which Chamberlain was first silent and then untruthful, would be

---

Chamberlain's house (D.P. 43933,85)). This story was still circulating as late as 1952, when Miss Gertrude Tuckwell related it, sceptically, to Mr. Harry Pitt, Fellow of Worcester College, Oxford. It is supported by the fact that, under the system of code numbers then used by the post office it would have been possible to tell from the envelope (which was available at the time of the trials) whether it had been posted, as was suggested, in the Princes Gardens pillar-box. But the story is made implausible by the dates not being right. Mrs. Crawford's visit to Princes Gardens was on the Wednesday afternoon, while the letter did not reach Bryanston Square until the Friday evening; and posts were somewhat quicker then than they are to-day.

far from proving that he was a party to a conspiracy. Even for those whose faith in Chamberlain's character is less firm than was that of Dilke's there would be difficulty in explaining why he should have wished to promote such a plot. Superficial reasons could easily be suggested. If there was to be a radical Prime Minister, Dilke and he were clearly alternative candidates, and Dilke's recent selection as chairman of their "cabal" strengthened his position.[††††] Dilke's own testimony, indeed, was that only a week before the case broke it had been agreed that he should be the future leader. On the other hand it was clear, first, that Dilke and Chamberlain united were far stronger than either without the other was likely to be; and secondly, that in any Dilke cabinet, Chamberlain, probably charged with a general supervision of home policy, would have occupied a commanding position.

[††††]It would also be well to have in mind at this point the thesis which was powerfully argued by Henry Harrison (1867–1954) in his previously cited *Parnell, Joseph Chamberlain and Mr. Garvin*. Harrison believed that in 1889, after the exposure as forgeries of *The Times* letters implicating Parnell in the Phoenix Park murders, Chamberlain found it essential to destroy the Irish leader, and played a decisive part in instigating O'Shea to start the divorce proceedings which achieved precisely this result. If Harrison's views are accepted (and he adduces much evidence in their support) there develops a temptation to treat Chamberlain with the suspicion which normally falls upon someone who has I cen present at the scene of an unsolved murder and is later found committing an almost exactly similar crime. Even if the lowest view is taken of Chamberlain's character, however, it is more probable that his knowledge of the Dilke case (and of Parnell's long-standing relations with Mrs. O'Shea) suggested to him a possible line of attack than that he was attempting to repeat his success in destroying a rival by acting against an enemy.

Some ambitious men would not have been satisfied with this. Disraeli might not have regarded it as the "top of the greasy pole." Even Gladstone might have felt that it showed a lack of divine confidence. But Chamberlain, as his whole career goes to show, was unusually interested in power as opposed to place. He could be brutal to enemies and ruthless with friends. But he had a clear-sighted judgment; and it is most unlikely that he would have wished to destroy a valuable ally on the hypothetical chance that this would secure to himself more of the trappings of office. If Dilke had been a serious hindrance to Chamberlain, the latter would have been a dangerous man for him to have as an intimate friend; but in the summer of 1885 this was hardly the case.[‡‡‡‡] Nevertheless, there remains a substantial element of mystery about this visit of Mrs. Crawford to Chamberlain. It is difficult to believe that it did not have some purpose which he was anxious to conceal from Dilke. Perhaps, even if he did not instigate her, he let slip a crucial opportunity of deflecting her from her purpose.

Others, who came to know even more about the case than Bodley, believed not in political but in private conspiracy. Steavenson, for instance, who had worked more on the papers and seen a greater number of the witnesses than anyone else, believed that Mrs. Rogerson was closely involved. As late as 1914 he wrote to Miss Tuckwell, Dilke's official biographer, to protest against her plan to ignore rather than refute the charges

---

[‡‡‡‡]Bodley, of course, contradicts himself when he suggests both that it was in Chamberlain's interest to smash Dilke, and that Dilke suffered because Lady Salisbury and many others welcomed his downfall as a weakening of Chamberlain.

in the projected work.

"A book would sell by the 100,000," he encouragingly began, "that could have for a hero (a man) in real life who was ruined, or even most probably ruined, by a conspiracy of two women. (1) Mrs. Rogerson who wanted to marry him and revenged herself when she found she could not. (2) Mrs. Crawford, a foolish woman, who was tired of her useless husband and was as putty in the hands of the other. The worst details were the invention of two shockingly immoral women."[28]

Lady Dilke, on the other hand, believed that Mrs. Crawford's mother, Mrs. Eustace Smith, was a more central figure. Lady Dilke knew that her husband had been receiving frequent anonymous letters for some years; that he remembered them as having begun in 1880 when he ceased to dine with the Eustace Smiths; that none of them mentioned any woman by name, but that one, probably received in 1882, mentioned "the house in Tottenham Court Road where you take your mistresses," and another, probably in the year 1884, referred to "the two women who live with you"; and that it was the firm belief of the Dilke investigators that they had traced the authorship of these letters, as well as of the earlier ones which Crawford received, to Mrs. Eustace Smith's maid, who acted as the agent of her mistress. On the basis of this knowledge Lady Dilke summed up her belief in the following words:

"The anonymous letters came from a source bitterly and revengefully hostile to Charles and they in the first instance suggested to Mrs. Crawford the opportunity of gaining her freedom while protecting her lovers. Later in the history of the case it is certain (if the opinion of experts is of any value) that she herself was the writer of anonymous letters involving my husband."[29]

What, at a distance of seventy-five years and from a less partisan standpoint, should the reader now believe?

Chapter Sixteen

What was the Truth?

In a sea of doubt one point stands out as being beyond dispute. Mrs. Crawford lied in the witness-box. She lied about Forster; she lied about Warner; and she lied about one of the nights she claimed to have spent in Dilke's house. This does not prove that all her other statements against Dilke were untrue; but it does mean that the impression she made upon the judge and jury must be discounted. They heard her contradict Dilke and they decided that she was a witness of truth. In this they were mistaken. It follows that no automatic reliance can be placed upon her uncorroborated evidence.

Furthermore, it seems overwhelmingly likely on the basis of the evidence of George Ball and others relating to February 13th, 1883, that she was on this occasion accusing Dilke not merely out of her imagination but by transference. What she claimed had occurred with him had in fact occurred with someone else. The possibility that this was so with regard to other dates as well cannot be excluded. There were three others which she specified. There was February 23rd, 1882, the date of the alleged first seduction at Warren Street. Dilke's alibi against her earlier version—that he had visited her at Sydney Place in the morning and arranged to meet her at Warren Street in the afternoon—was complete. Against her second version—a morning visit arranged a few days before—it was not formally complete, and was not accepted by the judge as such. But it was such as to make it highly unlikely that he could have found the time for such an expedition. Once it is accepted that Mrs. Crawford was capable of telling elaborate lies under oath the balance of plausibility in regard to this day is clearly heavily on Dilke's side.

The next date—again an alleged visit to Warren Street—was May 6th, 1882. Dilke's alibi for this occasion, as presented to the court, turned on his wife's evidence, which is not perhaps the most legally convincing that a man can have, and which was politely rejected by the judge. There is, however, a difference between legal and moral conviction. Lady Dilke might in the circumstances have been prepared to lie to the court. It seems much less likely that, had she not then been telling the truth, she would have written, four months later, in a private letter not intended for publication: "I can *never* be too glad that this woman fixed on the 6th May, for whatever may be the value of my evidence in regard to the public to *me* my certainty on this point is of the greatest satisfaction."[1] Lady Dilke, it should be remembered, was a woman of strong character and decided views.

It therefore seems highly likely that, of Mrs. Crawford's four allegations relating to specific dates, three were complete fabrications. The fourth—the suggestion that she also spent the night of December 7th, 1882, at 76, Sloane Street—cannot be rebutted with evidence of the same force. But it rests only upon the uncorroborated statement of Mrs. Crawford. If her three other allegations were false there seems little reason to believe this one either.

In addition there were her allegations, not related to specific dates, of constant adulteries at Sloane Street, at Sydney Place, and at Young Street. No corroboration for any of these charges was forthcoming. On the contrary, the evidence of Bodley, of the fencers and of Dilke's indoor servants was all strongly against the Sloane Street story; that of Anne Jamieson and of Catherine Ruddiman, Mrs. Crawford's own servants, was against the Sydney Place story; and that of Charles Grant, Dilke's coach-man, against the Young Street story. In these circumstances the conclusion of the Dilke investigators, in their pamphlet published in 1891, does not seem unreasonable. "Now, for a husband working in the dark to find evidence against a wife who denies adultery may often be difficult," they wrote; "but for a wife charging herself with adultery, extending over a lengthened period, at four different houses, on innumerable occasions, assisted by the ablest solicitor in England and a whole battalion of detectives, to be unable to find a vestige of corroboration seems impossible if the story were true."

There was of course some evidence against Dilke, which undoubtedly made an impact on the mind of the public. But it was all purely prejudicial. It may have been damaging to Dilke's character, but it was in no way corroborative of Mrs. Crawford's story. There was his admission of a liaison with Mrs. Eustace Smith. There was the statement of Mary Ann Gray that one morning she saw a lady in his bedroom; but she did not believe that it was Mrs. Crawford, and her recollection was such as to suggest that the incident occurred after the alleged relationship had ceased. There was the statement of Shanks, Dilke's footman, that he had been told to clean the dining-room and drawing-room windows because a lady was coming to the house; but there was nothing to suggest that the lady was Mrs. Crawford, and the preparations he was told to make were hardly the most obvious ones for a clandestine and illicit meeting. More important, there were the statements of the Hilliers that Dilke was in the habit of meeting a lady at 65, Warren Street; but they were certain that the lady was not Mrs. Crawford and that the visits took place in the afternoons and not in the mornings. Also, unknown to the public, there were Anna Dessouslavy's subsequent and sweeping accusations; but these, manifestly, in no way involved Mrs. Crawford.

One of the aspects of Mrs. Crawford's story which gave it a great air of verisimilitude was the wealth of detail which she was able to supply. Her account of changing cabs, of passing messages, of arranging meetings—the whole paraphernalia of deceiving her husband—carried a note of conviction. But once it is accepted that she had a considerable experience of intrigue with others and that she was ready to make what had in fact occurred with one man the basis of her accusations against another, this ceases to be even moral evidence against Dilke. This consideration may also be taken to apply to her sensational three-in-a-bed story. If it were not true how could she possibly have thought of it? This was the natural and general reaction. But it might have been less general had the details of her activities with her sister, Mrs. Harrison, and in particular their relationship with Warner, been known to the public.

Some of the details which Mrs. Crawford gave could not of course have been the result of "transference." Neither Forster nor Warner would have given her knowledge of the interior arrangements of 76, Sloane Street, or of the existence of a Dilke pensioner at 65, Warren Street. But there were several other sources from which she might have obtained these pieces of information. There was Mrs. Rogerson, who from her long-standing friendship with the Dilke family was probably well informed on both points. If, as Steavenson believed, she was party to a conspiracy, she could have briefed Mrs. Crawford most effectively; and even if she were not, she might have been a gradual source of much useful information. The same considerations apply to Mrs. Ashton Dilke. Alternatively Mrs. Eustace Smith might have planted the seed of the Warren Street idea in her daughter's mind. It is certain, as is shown by one of the anonymous letters which Dilke received in 1882, that there was some gossip about the nature of the Warren Street establishment; it is probable that Mrs. Smith helped to spread this; and it is unlikely that she would not have included her own family in the list of recipients. There is no difficulty in explaining how, if she had not gone there in the circumstances she described, Mrs. Crawford could have known of Warren Street.

There is more difficulty in explaining her "invention" of Fanny Gray. It can be seen how she might have conceived the idea of introducing such a character into her confession. Her mind might have been inclined by experience to move in such a direction, and she might have thought, intelligently and rightly, that the addition of this sensational detail would make her story appear more and not less plausible. It is also just possible to see how she might, perhaps from Mrs. Ashton Dilke's servants, have known of Fanny's existence. But it is difficult to see how she could have known from this, or any other obvious source, what a good choice she was making. The mysterious and nervous

Fanny, who would never appear in the witness-box because there was so much in her life which she wished to conceal, was the perfect victim of a false accusation.

What are we to believe? We should not of course exclude the possibility that on this point if not on others Mrs. Crawford was telling the truth. But there is no evidence to support her. On the contrary, there is a great deal of evidence against her story that Fanny was in the habit of spending almost every night with Dilke at Sloane Street. It also seems unlikely that, had either this suggestion or that concerning Mrs. Crawford been true, Dilke, while protesting his innocence, would have encouraged his wife and his friends to go chasing Fanny round the Home Counties, seeking statement after statement from her. But it seems equally unlikely that Mrs. Crawford, had she fixed purely by chance upon Fanny, should have been so singularly lucky in her choice. It is not entirely impossible that it was luck and nothing more; but it seems more likely, on the hypothesis that Mrs. Crawford was falsely implicating Dilke, that she had known or at least heard of Fanny through some other source, conceivably through Hill Street or through one of her lovers, and had realised that this girl, with her Dilke connection and her doubtful past, would be an almost perfect choice for the purpose.

Fanny Gray apart, it is therefore perfectly possible to sustain a view that Mrs. Crawford could have fabricated the whole of her charges against Dilke; and it is just possible, with a certain stretch of the imagination, to overcome the logical untidiness of Fanny. There still remains the question of whether it is psychologically plausible that Mrs. Crawford should have had the desire to perpetrate (and the nerve to sustain) this colossal fraud upon the British public. This question divides itself into three parts. First, could she have wished to do it? Second, could she have maintained her position throughout the period of public enquiry? And third, would she not subsequently, when her Roman Catholicism became the centre of her life, have felt it necessary to make public retribution to Dilke?

On the first point it was always easy to suggest a half motive for her action. She had become desperate to get rid of her husband, and she did not wish to implicate Forster. But this does not show why she wished to implicate Dilke, as opposed to some other victim. He was by no means the safest man to choose, for she must have known that by so doing she would provoke a national scandal, and subject her own conduct to the closest examination. Did she have some grievance against him? A French writer named Hector Malot wrote an imaginative reconstruction of the story which was published in England, under the title of *Josey*, in 1887. He assumed Dilke's innocence, and succeeded in building up a surprisingly convincing portrait of Mrs. Crawford's state of mind when framing the false charges. He did so, however, on the basis of an assumption that she had been in love with Dilke, had offered herself to him, and been contemptuously rejected. But Dilke never suggested that this was so.

Her other possible basis for a grievance against him was the part that he had played in getting Mrs. Ashton Dilke to warn her against Forster, and the rumour that he had intervened against Forster at the War Office. This might have made her bitter. It is difficult to believe that it would in itself have made her choose Dilke as the victim of her plot. It would have been so much easier to have chosen one of her earlier lovers. For Dilke to have qualified it seems likely that other considerations would have needed to be at work. First, a certain taste for notoriety in Mrs. Crawford, a positive desire that if her sins were to become known they should do so under the glare of the greatest possible publicity, and in association with one of the most eminent names amongst her acquaintances. Second, the existence of a climate of opinion or a body of rumour about Dilke which made him a not implausible victim of such a charge. It would not have done to have picked Gladstone, even allowing for his night prowling activities.* Third, some active outside encouragement, whether from a great personage like Rosebery or Chamberlain, or more probably from a small one like Mrs. Rogerson or Mrs. Eustace Smith. If it is accepted that some or all of these three considerations might have applied, there ceases to be any insuperable difficulty in explaining Mrs. Crawford's choice of Dilke as her victim.

Can we further believe that, having once made the charges, Mrs. Crawford would have had the nerve to sustain them? This is obviously a question to which no firm answer can be returned. Clearly she would have needed to be a woman possessed, to a most unusual degree, of cool, malevolent courage. But we know her to have been an accomplished liar, resourceful in the search for plausibility and unintimidated by the paraphernalia of the law. And if she had a curious, unbalanced taste for notoriety this might have made the ordeals which she inflicted upon herself, and which for most people would have been crushingly burdensome, into something of a stimulant.

The greatest difficulty arises from her subsequent

---

* Over a period of many years Gladstone tried to devote one evening a week to walks through the West End, interviewing prostitutes and trying to reclaim them. It was a work obviously open to misunderstanding. (See Magnus *op. cit.* 106–110.)

conversion to the Church of Rome. This occurred in 1889, and she was instructed by Manning himself. For reception into the Church and the hearing of her general confession he sent her to Father Robert Butler of St. Charles College, Bayswater. Nevertheless, her numerous conversations with Manning can hardly have failed to touch on her relationship with Dilke and the accusations, false or otherwise, to which she subjected him. Nor could the Cardinal Archbishop have failed to note what she said on these points. He had always given the closest attention to the Dilke case, and even had his interest shown any signs of flagging it would no doubt have been revived by Bodley, whom he would like to have chosen as his biographer and who was almost certainly his most intimate non-Catholic friend. Dilke, as has already been noted, claimed that in the summer of 1885 he "told everything" to Manning. At the beginning of 1889 he wrote to Manning again, sending him some notes which the Chesson committee had prepared upon the deficiencies of the trials. The Cardinal replied in distinctly friendly terms on February 26th:

> "I could hardly have believed that so many oversights and omissions, and all against you, could have happened as in these two trials.
>
> Nor how so many contradictions should have been possible. God grant that some light may spring up to clear you: and lift off from you the great suffering that is upon you."

This was shortly before Mrs. Crawford's confession. After it the Cardinal maintained his friendly relations with both Sir Charles and Lady Dilke. His only further known written comment, however, is contained in a letter which he wrote to Miss May Abraham (later Mrs. John Tennant) on March 9th,

1891. This was written within nine months of his death, and a great deterioration had taken place in his handwriting. Miss Abraham had written because Stead, still conducting his tireless anti-Dilke campaign, had again claimed that he had the Cardinal on his side. "Neither directly nor indirectly have I expressed either judgment or sympathy in what Mr. Stead has done," Manning wrote. "The relation of confidence in which I have stood to both persons involved has absolutely closed my lips."[3]

This was cryptic, and so far as written evidence is concerned Manning never cleared up the mystery. He left no paper which revealed his knowledge. In conversation he may have been less discreet. Sir Shane Leslie, whose work on a life of Manning had been interrupted by the war of 1914, wrote to Miss Tuckwell from Vermont in 1916 in the following terms: "There is no doubt the Cardinal thought your uncle innocent of the extreme charge. . . . Later I hope to be able to bring light from Manning's point of view which will be pleasant to you."[4] On another occasion he wrote in still more definite terms: "I have plenty of proof that Manning really believed in Sir Charles's innocence."[5] Sir Shane, however, when he eventually published his work on Manning, shone no new light upon the issue, but it appears that he based the conviction which he expressed to Miss Tuckwell upon conversations with Wilfred Meynell. Meynell was Manning's "familiar," who came as near as any man often does to knowing all of another's thoughts and beliefs. The Abbé Alphonse Chapeau, of the University of Angers, whose new life of Manning is eagerly awaited and whose knowledge of the Manning papers is now unrivalled, gives credence to any expression of the Cardinal's views which came *via* Meynell.

435

Perhaps more important than what Cardinal Manning believed, however, is what Mrs. Crawford did—or failed to do. It is impossible to believe that her reception into the Church of Rome was not of the deepest significance to her. It changed her whole life, to such an extent that the person who existed under her name after 1889 can hardly be reconciled with the one who existed previously. The teachings of that Church, it surely follows, must have had great influence upon her, particularly in the years immediately after her conversion. Yet the Catholic teaching on the Sacrament of Penance would clearly have imposed upon Mrs. Crawford, had she falsely accused Dilke, the absolute duty of doing everything possible to restore his good name. This, of course, she never attempted to do.

What force should be attached to this point? Should her failure to be truly penitent be taken as a final proof of her innocence and of Dilke's guilt? This would be a most extreme conclusion. Against the fact that Mrs. Crawford's behaviour may, from a religious point of view, have been incompatible with her having deceived the court must be set the equally salient fact that Dilke's behaviour, from a practical point of view, was equally incompatible with his having done so. Had he been guilty he might no doubt have strongly protested his innocence. But it seems most unlikely that he would have encouraged the closest possible investigation into the case, or continued, for almost the whole of the rest of his life, to keep the issue alive and to urge others to do so too.

No firm judgment can therefore be based on the subsequent behaviour of either Mrs. Crawford or Dilke, The one neutralises the other. We must go back to the evidence, that presented at the trials and that subsequently accumulated. On

436

this basis the balance of probability is against Mrs. Crawford. There seems little doubt that the greater part of the story she told about Dilke was false. It is just possible that there may at some stage have been a chance relationship, very different in form and of much shorter duration than that which she described. It might have taken place before her marriage, in the year between her return from a finishing school in Brussels and the beginning, in the summer of 1881, of her unhappy alliance with Crawford. If this were so, it would dispose of several difficulties. It would explain Dilke's strong and persistent sense of legal grievance (he committed neither a crime nor a civil wrong) accompanied by a certain moral unease. It would also explain Manning's failure to impose upon Mrs. Crawford the duty of restitution. The truth would have been almost as publicly damaging to Dilke as the falsehoods with which he was accused, and perhaps still more damaging to him privately. Silence, after so much noise, may therefore have appeared to the Cardinal to be the better course. Yet he still could have believed that Dilke had not perjured himself in the witness box[†] and was "innocent of the extreme charge." Yet all this is pure surmise. There is no evidence to support it. At best it can be considered as no more than a possibility. What is a probability, however, is that Dilke's general pattern of life was not nearly so innocent as his relationship with Mrs. Crawford. Even if not guilty of the charge made against him he may have laid himself open to it and prejudiced his defence by his other activities. He was, perhaps, by the public standards of his age, a guilty man, but he was nonetheless, in all probability,

---

[†] His denial of "adultery" with Mrs. Crawford, which was all that was directly put to him, was formally correct.

innocent of that of which he was accused and that which brought about his downfall. He was that rare thing, the victim of a conspiracy, the main lines of which we can see, but the exact details of which (and, indeed, the identity of the other participants in which) are shrouded in mystery and are likely always so to remain.

Chapter Seventeen

The Long Road Back

During 1887 and the immediately following years Dilke had to learn to live with his new situation in life. He still hoped that the fresh evidence which was being collected might form the basis for a decisive vindication of his name; but as time went by it became increasingly difficult to count upon this. Even if it did not happen he had to continue to live. He was only in his middle forties. He still had a restless energy and a great appetite for work. He had a new wife, with whom he was apparently very happy but who, perhaps because of her character, perhaps because of the circumstances in which he had married her, came to exercise an increasingly dominant influence upon him. His reputation had survived better abroad than in England, for although he had some staunch friends at home he also had a great number of enemies who were determined to prevent his return to public life. And he was still rich.

His plans for doing regular newspaper work came to little. He

439

worked for a few months for the National Press Agency, but he soon grew tired of this, and concentrated instead upon his own writing. He achieved a considerable output. Apart from his work, already mentioned, on the current state of European politics, he wrote a further series of articles for the *Fortnightly* which were published in the winter of 1887–8. These were on the British Army, and like those on European politics were subsequently collected and issued in book form. In addition, he wrote a major, two-volume treatise, entitled *Problems of Greater Britain*, which was published in 1890. This was intended as a sequel to his youthful and highly successful *Greater Britain*, but was in fact quite different both in tone and scope. The later work was not a travel book, but a detailed analytical survey of the political, economic and military problems of the British Empire. It was a heavy work, and a tribute more to Dilke's compendious knowledge than to anything else. The introduction, however, contained one penetrating shaft. In the second half of the twentieth century, Dilke thought, the powers of Central and Western Europe would no longer dominate the world scene; they would be replaced by the United States and Russia, although Britain might retain her place by virtue of her overseas connections. The book—"this record of the peaceful progress of Greater Britain which is made securer by his sword"—was dedicated to Field-Marshal Lord Roberts.

Dilke also did a good deal of journalism, mainly for American and Colonial papers, and was very highly paid—thirty guineas a column in the Colonies, he told Chamberlain—for anything he chose to write. He also travelled widely. In the autumn of 1887 he went to Turkey and Greece, and received almost a royal welcome in Athens. In the following year he went to India and stayed there for much of the winter, devoting many weeks to a study of the Indian Army under the guidance of Roberts, who was then commander-in-chief. He also pursued his military studies in Europe, being Gallifet's guest at the French manoeuvres in the autumn of 1891 and a frequent visitor to our own on Salisbury Plain.

In 1889 he paid a visit to Bismarck at his country house at Friedrichsruh and wrote a somewhat censorious account of the austerities practised by the Chancellor, in his last days of power, when he was away from Berlin.

"The coachman alone wears livery," Dilke wrote, "and that only a plain blue with ordinary black trousers and ordinary black hat—no cockades and no stripes. . . . The family all drink beer at lunch, and offer the thinnest of thin Mosel. Bismarck has never put on a swallow-tail coat but once, which he says was in 1835, and which is of peculiar shape. A tall hat he does not possess, and he proscribes tall hats and evening dress among his guests. His view is that a Court and an Army should be in uniform, but that when people are not on duty at Court or in war, or preparation for war, they should wear a comfortable dress. . . . The Prince eats nothing at all except young partridges and salt herring, and the result is that the cookery is feeble, although for game eaters there is no hardship. . . . A French cook would hang himself. There is no sweet at dinner except fruit, stewed German fashion with the game. Trout, which the family themselves replace by raw salt herring, and game form the whole dinner. Of wines and beer they drink at dinner a most extraordinary mixture, but as the wine is all the gift of Emperors and merchant princes it is good. The cellar card was handed to the Prince with the fish, and, after consultation with me, and with Hatzfeldt, we started on sweet champagne, not suggested by me, followed by Bordeaux, followed by still Mosel, followed by Johannesberg (which I did suggest), followed by black beer, followed by corn brandy. When I reached the Johannesberg I stopped and went on with that only, so that I got a second bottle drawn for dessert. When the Chancellor got to his row of great pipes, standing against the wall ready stuffed for him, we went back to black beer. The railway station is in the garden, and the expresses shake the house."[1]

The radical Dilke was clearly unimpressed with the style of living of his High Tory host; but they appear nevertheless to have got on well enough together. Bismarck thought that Dilke's knowledge of European politics was remarkable, and appeared to be attracted rather than repelled by the fact that his guest had become almost without influence. Dilke thought that the Chancellor was "dear in his polite ways," and was interested to discover how bad were his relations with the Emperor, and how he had turned against absolutism because he believed that it led to women having too great an influence on politics.

At home Dilke continued to suffer a great deal of ostracism and occasional insults. His name had become something of a music-hall joke, and a ribald ditty which ran as follows achieved a wide currency:

> Master Dilke upset the milk,
> Taking it home to Chelsea,
> The papers say that Charlie's gay,
> Rather a wilful wag.
> This noble representative,

Of everything good in Chelsea
Has let the cat, the naughty cat,
Right out of the Gladstone bag.*

On a similar level, obscene messages were frequently written across his doorstep in Sloane Street. Sometimes incidents of a more serious nature occurred. On one occasion he was refused communion at his parish church (at Pyrford, not in London), and on another Canon Barnett of Whitechapel (who had appeared as a witness in the case) rose to a fine height of self-righteousness by ostentatiously cancelling a lecture on the

---

* According to Mr. Guy Deghy's recent book on the history of Romano's restaurant (*Paradise in the Strand*), habitués of that establishment amused themselves by giving renderings of this verse in several languages. The French and the Latin versions he gives as follows:

> Mâitre Dilke a renversé le lait
> En l'apportant à Chelsea,
> Les journaux disent que Charlie est gai,
> Tant soit peu arceur
> Ce noble representant
> De tout ce qui est bon à Chelsea
> A fait sortir le chat,
> Le méchant chat,
> Du Gladstone sac.
> Effundit Carolus domum reportans
> Lac Dilkus media procax suburra
> Hunc salsum putat, urbs virum, et facetum,
> Eheu! nobilis hic patron us omnis
> quodcunque est mediae boni suburrae,
> Felem perdidit, improbam, ecce felem,
> Grandaevis foculis diu retentam.

châteaux of the Loire, accompanied by illustrated lantern slides, which Lady Dilke had been asked to give at Toynbee Hall. *The Times* offered competition to the Canon by trying to pretend that Dilke did not exist. It refused to print a word of any of his speeches, to review his books, or to mention him in any form. This agitated Dilke a good deal, as he regarded it "as a great check on usefulness of any form." He wrote to Chamberlain to ask him if he could do anything to get the ban removed. The latter replied in very friendly terms saying that he would prefer to wait until he had seen Buckle (the editor) in person. Two weeks later, however, on December 3rd, 1890, he wrote in less encouraging terms: "I have seen Buckle to-day and am not very hopeful—though I think I have shaken him. But Walter is behind and he is an obstinate old gentleman."[2] It was clear that Dilke could hope for no help from *The Times*.

The key question was when he might attempt a return to politics. In 1887 his part in public life was reduced to the chairmanship of the Chelsea Board of Guardians and member-ship of the vestry.[†] But the possibility of a re-entry to a much wider field did not seem too distant. In November, 1887, he received a warm letter from Mr. J. Cooksey, the editor of a local paper in the Forest of Dean, where there was a by-elec-tion pending, pressing him to pay a visit to the radicals there, and clearly holding out the possibility of the candidature. Three months later he received similar tentative offers from Merthyr Tydfil and the northern division of West Ham. All

---

[†] Prior to the establishment of the London County Council in 1889 the Chelsea vestry was the only local government authority for that part of the metropolis. Its powers were restricted in 1889 and it was swept away ten years later when the metropolitan boroughs were established.

three of the constituencies were safe radical seats.

Dilke might have been expected to leap at these chances. But he did not do so. This was partly because he knew that, as soon as he made a move, Stead and others would mount a great new campaign against him, the result of which would probably be the withdrawal of the tentative offers and great damage to his prospects of future success. Partly, also, it was because his sights were still fixed above the mere securing of another seat in Parliament. He wished to come back into the inner councils of his party, and this made it desirable that he should move only with the approval of Gladstone and the other leaders. This was not easy to obtain. Relations between Gladstone and Dilke were almost non-existent during this period, although there was an occasional indirect contact through James.‡ This contact was sufficient to make it clear that, for the time being, Gladstone regarded silence as Dilke's best policy.

In August, 1888, Chamberlain came to visit Dilke at Dockett and urged him to stand both for Parliament and for the newly established London County Council. The first elections to the County Council were to take place in November of that year. Dilke was strongly pressed to allow his name to go forward for Fulham, even though he would have left for India before the contest began. "Stead can't fight your shadow," a supporter encouragingly wrote. But Dilke declined; and perhaps he was right, for apart from what Stead might or might not have done, even the rumour of his candidature caused the publication of a petition of protest backed by influential signatures.

In the Forest of Dean a new Liberal member had been elected;

---

‡ James had become a Liberal Unionist by this time. The fact underlined the indirectness of Dilke's relations with his leader.

but Dilke continued to receive pressing invitations, at least to pay a visit and make some speeches. He replied saying that he would address no meetings outside Chelsea during 1888. Nevertheless in March, 1889, he was elected (with some opposition and in his absence) to the presidency of the body known in the Forest as the Liberal Four Hundred. Then, in May, he and Lady Dilke at last paid their long-awaited visit to the area, and were received with enthusiasm. This enthusiasm was not diminished by the fact that the sitting member, Samuelson, even though it was only two years since he had been first elected, was already unpopular.

The Forest of Dean, which politically had been carved out of the old West Gloucestershire division in 1885, was primarily a mining constituency. There was an electoral roll of just over 10,000, and there were more than 5,000 miners in the area—although some of these would have been excluded from the franchise. But it was not a typical mining seat. It was cut off from any other mining district, the collieries were small and scattered, and it possessed unusual scenic beauty. It was a wooded plateau, bounded by the Wye on the west and the Severn on the east. The principal towns were Cinderford, Coleford, Lydney and Newnham. It offered the prospect of being an ideal seat for Dilke. The miners were strong enough to insist on a member who would support their principal demands. Legislation to restrict the working day in the mines to eight hours was becoming the most important of these, and unwillingness to support this proposal was the main cause of Samuelson's unpopularity.

At the same time the Gloucestershire rural tradition which persisted in the area made a candidature from the Miners' Federation seem less attractive than in South Wales or

Northumberland. The Forest of Dean throughout its whole independent existence as a parliamentary division (which lasted until 1950) never had a member who had himself worked in the mines, and was in this respect unique amongst coal constituencies. What the Foresters wanted was a radical of some outside distinction; and if he could be rich as well this would be an added advantage, for their Liberal Association was con-stantly short of funds. They did not much care about the divorce scandal, not because they themselves were loose-living, but because the sense of independence and apartness which has always been a characteristic of mining communities gave them a certain indifference to the opinion of the outside world.

Dilke found the atmosphere there sufficiently encouraging for him to return to London with a more urgent desire to secure Gladstone's approval of his candidature. In June he wrote to James asking him to approach Gladstone and see if his views had changed. Gladstone responded by calling on Dilke at Sloane Street, but he did not find him at home. In consequence, and after a delay of several weeks, he wrote to Dilke and set out his views at length. His letter is given in full, not only because of its significance in Dilke's attempted rehabilitation, but because of the light it throws on the working of Gladstone's mind:

> *Hawarden Castle,*
> *Chester*
> *August 10th, '89*

My dear Dilke,

I was very sorry to find that my call in Sloane Street on July I was premature, I suppose by a few hours. Not indeed that I could have added much, or perhaps anything, to what you have stated

447

in your letter to Sir Henry James. But I should have been glad of an opportunity which would at least have sufficed to show friendly intention.

There is nothing, according to my belief, in which human beings either individually or collectively seem, and are, so small as in their judgments upon one another. The profound wisdom of the laconic precept "Judge not" comes home more and more every day: as does the prudence and necessity of arresting the mind on its course towards conclusions, and adopting the rational as well as Christian alternative of suspending judgment unless when we know facts and persons sufficiently well to go forward.

But you will perceive that the judgments of the world are in certain cases irresistible as well as inexorable, and must be treated as if they were infallible. It was in this view that I felt what, judging from your letter, you have felt still more strongly, namely that according to the dictates of prudence your abstention, whether a longer or a shorter one, should be absolute; and that (I should think) each year when the abstention is visibly absolute is worth several of any course of proceeding in which an acutely hostile criticism professes to detect any sign of resistance or impatience.

I deeply feel the loss we sustain in your absence from public life after you had given such varied and conclusive proofs of high capacity to serve your country. And I have almost taken for granted that with the end of this Parliament, after anything approaching the usual full term, the ostracism would die a kind of natural death. And I heartily wish and hope that you may have lying before you in the future a long and happy time of *public* usefulness.

And I now ask you to forgive my writing this letter (for it may

wear an appearance I should hate) and to believe that it springs
from the friendly feeling which is in every way your due from
me. . . . I know myself to be totally unfit to advise anything to
anybody by virtue of moral qualification. I found myself only on
that long experience of the world which often makes the social
sight get keener, even when the natural eye is growing dim.

And I will close by saying from my heart May God bless
and guide you.

Believe me sincerely yours,

W. E. Gladstone[3]

In so far as anything was clear from this remarkable letter it
was that Dilke might reasonably come forward as a candidate at
the next general election, but that he should postpone his adop-
tion until the latest possible moment. He was prepared for the
time being to take this advice. The Forest of Dean, where the
sitting member was still in the field, was not for the moment
available; and he found it comparatively easy to decline offers
from Dundee and Fulham which arrived during the autumn.

In the following summer—that of 1890—the situation in the
Forest took a decisive turn in Dilke's favour. The Miners'
Federation of Great Britain, in conference at Bristol, passed a
resolution instructing their members to support only those candidates who would commit themselves in favour of a Miners' Eight
Hour Day Bill. This sealed Samuelson's fate. He was in trouble
not only at the Miners' annual demonstration at Speech House,[§]
but also at meetings of the executive committee of the Liberal

---

§ An old inn in the centre of the Forest, which was a traditional meeting-
place, and which Dilke was later to make his headquarters on many
constituency visits.

Four Hundred. He stated his view fairly and courageously. He agreed with Bradlaugh, Morley, Labouchere, Broadhurst, Burt and Fenwick in believing that the eight-hour day should not be secured by legislation. He was prepared not to vote against the Bill, but he could not vote in its favour. This was not enough. In the following February he announced that he would not again contest the division.

Dilke was in no difficulty about the new policy of the Miners' Federation. He said that he had been converted to the legislative restriction of the hours of men workers by the proceedings of the Industrial Remuneration Conference in 1885, over which he had presided; and he had published his views, on this and a wide variety of other subjects, in a pamphlet "entitled *A Radical Programme,* which had appeared earlier in the year 1890. He did not believe that the hours of all workers could be limited, but he thought that there were many trades in which this was both feasible and desirable, and that the mining industry was in the forefront of them. The pamphlet also showed that on all home policy questions his radicalism had become still more pronounced. He was in favour of a wide extension of municipal socialism, into the trading and industrial as well as the social service fields. He saw great significance in the sharp decline in the rate of interest which had reached its nadir under Goschen's Chancellorship.

"While the interest on the capital of the rich, the rents of land, trade profits, and returns from manufacturing, on the whole, decrease, and while the rich save less, the poor will become more and more educated and more able to make use of every advantage they obtain. Great fortunes will be divided, new ones will become more hard to found, and only a few who personally minister to the wants of the democracy—inventors, engineers, newspaper proprietors, and journalists, highly-skilled surgeons, actors, singers and so forth—will grow very rich; a handful as compared with the numbers of human beings living in an organised society. British law, moreover, will not only cease to bolster up great fortunes by primogeniture, but may begin to imitate British colonial legislation, and, by progressive taxation, discourage their existence. There is reason to expect, then, that the worker will become king in Britain as he is king already in the British countries of Australasia."[4]

The prospect caused Dilke no dismay. The view that the rich were intelligent and the poor ignorant was a grossly exaggerated one:

"In a first-class carriage on many lines of railway men often find themselves among those of their fellows who are utterly incapable of following a close argument, or of reading with enjoyment any literature except that supplied by comic papers of an inferior kind. In a third-class compartment they will sometimes discover that, on the whole, the literature is of a nature better suited for general consumption."[5]

The poor still had a long way to go so far as education was concerned, but their rate of advance was remarkable. He could not see the distant form which it was desirable that society should take, or the extent to which he wanted it to be socialistic. But he was certain that early progress should be in that direction; and he believed all experience to show that there was far more danger of the advance being too slow than of its being too rapid.

451

"Order, and not chaos," he concluded, "lies before us, except, indeed, in the event of unsuccessful war, against which we should guard by all means in our power. As regards domestic change there is reason to expect a gradual evolution of society from an individualist to a collective state, and one accomplished without danger."[6]

With these views, Dilke found it easy to move into a position of close alliance with the Miners' Federation. In August, 1890, he addressed his first miners' meeting—at Cannock Chase; and in the course of the next twelve months he spoke to the miners of Yorkshire, Lancashire, Cheshire, Somerset, Fife, Ayrshire, Monmouthshire and Glamorgan. Many of these meetings were in strong Nonconformist districts, and it was remarkable that their inhabitants gave such a warm welcome to Dilke. In the Rhondda Valley the local "Lib.-Lab." member—William Abraham (or Mabon as he was better known)—organised a huge torchlight procession to greet Sir Charles and Lady Dilke; and Tom Ellis, the Liberal Whip who sat for Merioneth, the very heart of religious Wales, took them to his constituency to address a large meeting of quarrymen at Blaenau Festiniog. Everyone was not equally enthusiastic. Stead was at work in the Welsh valleys, and when Dilke addressed a Liberal rally at Cardiff in the following year it was noticeable that the meeting had been boycotted by most of the local Gladstonian members.

In the Forest of Dean, however, opposition to Dilke was very much a minority view. At the meeting of the Liberal Four Hundred to which Samuelson's resignation was announced, it was proposed by a Coleford business man and seconded by a Cinderford clergyman that the nomination should be offered to

Dilke. After what a local newspaper described as "considerable and sometimes heated discussion," this resolution was carried by a big majority. A deputation which included five Nonconformist ministers was appointed to wait upon Dilke in London. He received them at Sloane Street a week later and promised to make a statement about his position when he visited Cinderford in the following month. Even at this Cinderford meeting, however, he remained noncommittal. "The proceedings were characterised by strong pressure and deep pathos," the *Dean Forest Guardian* reported, "but the Right Honourable Baronet, although much moved, was still coy and the final answer was further postponed."

In fact, Dilke was in no way undecided. He wanted very much to become member for the Forest of Dean. But he feared that a good deal of latent opposition would be called forth by the proposal. He thought it better that this should develop before he was committed to the seat. His supporters, he believed, might counter it more vigorously if they were still trying to obtain his acceptance than if he had given this with obvious alacrity. Furthermore, his hold on the seat for the future was likely to be more secure if he were adopted by a Liberal Association which knew exactly what was involved in their choice. Dilke's tactics were therefore those of showing the greatest possible interest short of giving a definite answer. He and his wife remained in the Forest for most of the three months following the Cinderford meeting. They both spoke at a number of meetings, and they secured a wide distribution of the pamphlet based on the work of the Chesson-Stcavenson committee which was published at this time.

These tactics were brilliantly successful. The whole area was seized with a premature election fever. Would Dilke stand

453

or would he not? This became the burning question throughout the Forest. Stead, who had announced as soon as Dilke's
candidature was mooted that he would resist it to the utmost,
was decisively routed. He flooded the constituency with anti-
Dilke pamphlets, but the Foresters made bonfires at which
they were publicly burned. He allowed his chagrin to lead him
into denouncing the local inhabitants as "only ignorant
miners," and thus did a great deal to help Dilke's cause. Many
who had been hostile at an earlier stage, like the Rector of
Newent, became enthusiastic supporters. By the beginning of
June, 1891, Dilke judged that he had the Liberals of the Forest
overwhelmingly on his side, and on the ninth of the month he
gave his definite acceptance at a meeting in Lydney. "This
announcement," the *Dean Forest Guardian* wrote, ". . . was
received with wild and tumultuous cheering (and) the singing
of 'Auld Lang Syne.'" Mabon was present at the meeting, and
referred to Dilke as "not only a political leader, but a real
Labour leader."

The announcement was not received with equal enthusiasm
outside the Forest. *The Times* was displeased, and so, more
importantly, was Gladstone. His attitude had hardened since
his call at Sloane Street and his letter to Dilke two summers
previously. When he was asked publicly to state his view he
replied on several occasions that it was a matter exclusively for
the constituency, but he had written a private memorandum
on March 13th, 1891,[7] which he arranged to be brought to
Dilke's notice, and which made it clear that he was against the
latter's acceptance of the candidature. He argued that it would
weaken the position of the Irish Parliamentary party and make
it more difficult for him to bring the Home Rule struggle to a
successful conclusion.

The event which had made Gladstone adopt this more austere view was the Parnell divorce suit. This had been heard in November, 1890, and had substantially damaged the prospects of the Liberal party for the next election. After it, Gladstone wanted no more adulterers (or alleged adulterers) on his hands. And he assumed that his own view about the relative importance of Irish Home Rule and the resumption of the political career of Sir Charles Dilke would be shared by Dilke himself. It was a false assumption. Dilke had never cared much about Ireland, but he cared a great deal about his own political role. Gladstone's attempt at private pressure did nothing to deflect him. But it must have made it plain that, at least under a Gladstone premiership, his return to the House of Commons was unlikely to lead to his return to the Cabinet.

Chamberlain had also given Dilke a somewhat discouraging forecast.

> "The comments of *The Times* and other papers are only what we had to expect," he had written on June 22nd, 1891. "They represent the general feeling in the House and in Society which is undoubtedly hostile to your candidature. The question is can you live it down. I think you can but I do not conceal from you that it will be a *mauvais quart d'heure*."[8]

Six months later Chamberlain was writing in a similar vein and adding advice which, while apparently well-intentioned, was a little tainted because so obviously in accordance with his own prejudices:

> "It is not to your interest to arouse the prejudices of the

society in which you hope one day again to take your place. I do not mean fashionable society—but political society or the great majority of cultivated politicians. I think you go out of your way to offend them when you advocate evacuation of Egypt, and I ask you to consider if it is worth while. . . . Therefore my advice is: Be as Radical as you like. Be Home Ruler if you must—but be a little Jingo if you can."[9]

Unlike Gladstone, however, Chamberlain was prepared to be of some use and not merely to offer rather unwelcome advice. When Dilke wrote in the spring of 1891 to complain of the personal attacks which *The Scotsman*—a Liberal Unionist paper—was making upon him, Chamberlain took moderately effective action. A month or two later he obtained a county court judgeship for Steavenson. Then in June Dilke wrote with another complaint—he had heard a rumour that he was to be opposed by a Liberal Unionist in the Forest of Dean. He did not fear the electoral consequences of this, but, "for political reasons connected with the future of the Irish Question," he would not like it. Chamberlain replied the same day: "I do not believe a word of it—but I will make enquiries. If by any chance in the world such an act of folly *were* contemplated, I will stop it. But it is not true."[10]

It was not true. When the election came, in the summer of 1892, Dilke was opposed neither by a Liberal Unionist, nor by Stead, who had threatened to appear as an independent radical, but by a local Tory country gentleman named Colchester Wemyss. Wemyss himself eschewed the divorce issue and attempted to wage a purely political fight, but many of his supporters declined to follow his example. They were aided by the flood of Stead publications which poured into the constituency up to polling day. There is no evidence that these publications, or the platform innuendos, had any appreciable effect on the result.

Dilke had campaigned hard—he had been in the Forest for the greater part of the three or four months preceding the election—and his wife had proved a vote-winner at least as effective as he was himself. An election song was written for the campaign and was enthusiastically sung at all his meetings, and at some of the Tory ones as well. The words showed a somewhat misplaced trust in the welcome which Dilke would receive when he returned to Westminster, but they also indicated the faith which he had already aroused in his future constituents:

> We are the jovial Foresters,
> Sir Charles shall be our man;
> We'll send him back to Parliament
> To help the Grand Old Man.
> Of that there's not the slightest doubt
> The Tories ne'er shall turn him out
> For we will stick; his foes we'll lick
> And send him up a jolly brick.
>
> Sir Charles when up in Parliament,
> He soon again will spout;
> For he can catch the Speaker's eye,
> He knows his way about.
> And when we ask about deep gales[1]

---

[1] A local mining problem.

Sir Charles will open wide his sails,
And steer right through, with merry crew
A Bill, that will our hopes renew.

To him we will in future look,
And shall not look in vain;
For he will all our interests back,
And in our hearts shall reign.
When re-instated in the House,
What greetings there he will arouse!
What welcomes back to public life!
Thus end all strife—and won't his wife
Thank us, the jovial Foresters,
Whose trade is getting coal. . . .

Sir Charles and Lady Dilke's health
We'll not forget to drink
For we're the lads, when free from toil,
That can our glasses chink.
And this shall ever be our toast,
(And this shall ever be our boast),
Success to Sir and Lady Dilke
And he shall long our member be.

The result was as great a triumph as the campaign. Dilke polled 5,360 votes against Colchester Wemyss's 2,520; at the 1887 by-election the Liberal vote had been 4,286, and the Conservative 2,736. He had secured a safe and loyal seat for the rest of his life. He was to be overwhelmingly re-elected at five subsequent general elections, at one of which he was unopposed.

His hold on the constituency became such that, even at one of the opposed elections, he was able to confine his address to the admirably laconic:

Gentlemen,
　　I solicit with confidence the renewal of your trust.
　　　　Believe me, your devoted servant,
　　　　　　　　Charles W. Dilke

He had decisively re-established his position in a constituency. Whether he could repeat this in the national political life was a much more doubtful question.

Chapter Eighteen

An Independent Expert

The General Election of 1892 gave an almost equal number of seats to the Liberals and the Conservatives. Allied to the former, however, were 81 Irish Nationalists as against only 46 Liberal Unionists on the other side. There was therefore a small but clear Gladstonian majority in the new House of Commons. Nevertheless, Lord Salisbury waited to meet Parliament, and did not resign until he had been defeated on an amendment to the address. Gladstone kissed hands for the fourth and last time on August 15th.

The new Prime Minister made no offer of a post to Dilke. It is doubtful indeed if the question even presented itself to him as one for decision. In 1886 when he had left Dilke out he sent him a letter of apology and explanation. In 1892 Dilke did not even get a letter. He had clearly to prepare himself for a long period on the back benches. This exclusion was a heavy but not unexpected blow. He was, however, still only 48. He did not accept the exclusion as being necessarily permanent.

He had, nevertheless, to prepare himself for a considerable period of parliamentary life in which he would have no official position. Apart from any question of personal exclusion he was still sufficiently under Chamberlain's influence* to believe—and believe correctly—that for some time to come the Liberal party's share of power was likely to be small. This prospect led him to no lack of interest in the Parliament to which he had striven so hard to return. He found that he was tolerably well received, and he quickly attracted to himself that vague but persistent label of "a good House of Commons man." He was regular in his attendance at the House, so much so, that except on the occasion of the Forest of Dean miners' annual demonstration, he never left London during the session. He always sat in the same place—the next to the corner seat on the front bench below the gangway— and he was at the House at the beginning of each day's sitting in order to claim it.† He never appeared except in the most punctilious of parliamentary dress—tall silk hat and frock-coat—but

---

* Chamberlain had written to Dilke on March 31st, 1892: "My prediction is that unless the Gladstonians give up the idea of a separate Parliament (I do not say extended local government) they will not attain power—though they may attain office—for this generation. There is a bold prophecy for you—but it is my sincere opinion." (D.P. 43889, 87.)

† Labouchere had the corner seat, but unlike Dilke he never appeared at prayers in order to claim it in the accepted way. Sydney Gedge, Conservative member for Walsall, discovered how this was arranged. Dilke interrupted his devotions not only to slip a card into the back of his own seat, which was allowed, but also to slip another, on Labouchere's behalf, into the back of the next, which was not. Gedge drew the attention of the House to this, but secured no support for his objection. (Algar Thorold, *The Life of Henry Labouchere*, p. 477.)

he added a touch of eccentricity by using his hat as a receptacle for his discarded notes and documents, and habitually stuffed it to overflowing in the course of a speech.

He had a wide range of parliamentary interests, and he used his Privy Councillor's precedence in order to speak frequently about most of them. His oratory gained nothing in lightness as time went by, but the scope of his knowledge and the force of his reputation often gave him an attentive audience. He was an expert on the rules of the House, and he used this expertise both to instruct young members and to raise procedural points. Outside the chamber he became notable for the speed with which he moved through the lobbies and about the corridors— he was commonly to be seen with his coat-tails flying behind him; for his habit of sitting in the library snipping away at his papers with his scissors; and for the quantity of tea which he daily consumed in the tea-room. The smoking-room saw him less often, for although he had ceased to be a teetotaller in 1886 and was a great smoker of cigars, he believed that he had little time for such indulgences when the House was sitting. He quickly managed to fill in his time with a mass of detailed work, and to become a key figure in the life of the House of Commons, a man whose absence would be noted, who was pointed out to visitors, and whose features were a normal component of any picture or cartoon of the working of the House. Whether his diligence and his fame were matched by real influence is another matter. After nine months he recorded that "I had now regained the position which I had held in (the House) up to 1878, though not my position of 1878–80, nor that of 1884–5."[1] He never recorded any advance beyond this point.

The main business of the first session was the Home Rule Bill, in which Dilke took almost no part, intervening only once on a technical point concerning Irish electoral registration. Much of his interest was devoted to labour questions and in particular to the Miners 'Eight Hour Bill. On this latter point he tried to revive his old habit of co-operation with Chamberlain, acting partly on the assumption that a measure which was unwelcome to Gladstone and Morley, preoccupied with their political objectives, might *per contra* make a certain appeal to the Birmingham Unionist. But Chamberlain was as contemptuous of the labour leaders as he was of the Prime Minister—"I am . . . impatient of their extremely unpractical policy, and . . . I believe their real influence is immensely exaggerated and Dilke got little beyond a general expression of sympathy.

This was their last attempt to work together. While Dilke had been out of the House of Commons they had retained at least the shell of intimacy, and had pretended that the future was likely to bring them together again. Even during this period there had been difficulties. Dilke became somewhat disenchanted with Chamberlain after the Home Rule dispute and wrote in his diary on February 4th, 1887: "Chamberlain very sore and vindictive against Labouchere and others. I fear all this split has spoilt Chamberlain and that he will be very difficult for all men to work with in the future."[2] A couple of years later, however, Dilke could show a wistful regret for the old closeness with Chamberlain. "All day Sunday probably," he rather pathetically wrote to the latter in July, 1891, "I and Wentie will be at the Midland Hotel, Birmingham, if there is anything I can do for you."[3] Chamberlain, too, could show something of the same feeling, although in a slightly more patronising way. "In fact I have been thinking that owing to the changes in our lives and the pressure on both of us," he wrote from Highbury in November, 1890, "we have been slipping away from one another—and this I do not desire or intend."[4]

After the general election of 1892 a new situation presented itself. It could no longer be pretended that it was only circumstances which kept Dilke and Chamberlain apart. But Dilke's return to the House coincided with Chamberlain moving closer to the Conservative party. He sat on the front opposition bench and he excelled everyone in the mordancy of his attacks on Gladstone. The way was being rapidly paved for his acceptance of office under Lord Salisbury. Dilke found his former friend's debating power to be formidably improved, but thought that "he had sold his old true self to the devil."

Nor was there any return to personal intimacy—which, except on a firm political foundation, would probably have been impossible for Chamberlain. The nearest approach to this was in 1893 when Dilke consulted Chamberlain about the best wine-merchant from whom to buy champagne, and in 1894 when Chamberlain wrote to Dilke to protest against a rumour that the latter was to speak in Birmingham. "I can hardly believe the enclosed announcement to be true," he remonstrated. "I certainly should have declined to speak in your constituency, and as a general rule I think that personal friends might avoid what looks like direct attack."[5] Dilke replied that the announcement was false, and Chamberlain wrote again accepting the denial in terms which were still a little truculent: "I am glad that the report is untrue. When you have all the rest of the world to go to, I could not but regard it as an unfriendly act that you should address my political opponents in Birmingham."[6]

Almost the only subsequent letter of any interest in their correspondence (and this from the viewpoint of the rapid growth of Chamberlain's Toryism rather than of their intimacy) was one written in July, 1895, about university representation in the House of Commons. "Personally I doubt whether 'one man one vote' would do as much good to your Party as the wire-pullers suppose," Chamberlain complacently wrote, adding magnanimously, "but there is a great difference of opinion on the subject."[7] After this date most of the letters were in a secretary's handwriting. When Lady Dilke died, in 1904, there was a very distant expression of sympathy from Chamberlain, and one subsequent letter, written in February, 1906, six months before his stroke. Thereafter there was no correspondence and no other intercourse. When Dilke died, Chamberlain was an invalid. Austen Chamberlain attended the funeral.

Dilke never found another political friend to replace Chamberlain. He found loose allies like Labouchere and temporary disciples like Reginald McKenna, for whom, in 1893, he secured the Liberal nomination in North Monmouthshire. He found new men like Asquith—"a bold, disagreeable, strong man, of great intellectual power"—for whom he had some admiration but with whom he was never intimate. He maintained relations with old friends like Harcourt and Morley, to whom he had some nostalgic attachment but whom he most certainly did not admire. And he cultivated the new Labour leaders. But with none of these did his relationship approach the close and equal partnership which had once existed with Chamberlain.

The Labour leaders did not belong to any one group. "Mabon," who was authentically working class but rather right wing in that, like almost all the miners' leaders, he believed in working within the Liberal party, was a frequent dinner guest at 76, Sloane Street. So was Cunninghame Graham, the Scottish laird who had sat as a radical for Northwest Lanarkshire in the Parliament of 1886, but had been defeated at Glasgow, standing

465

as a Labour candidate, in 1892; he, however, was regarded as sufficiently athletic to be asked more often to Dockett Eddy. Hyndman, the Marxist old Etonian who had led and then split the rigidly sectarian Social Democratic Federation, was another occasional guest, as well as being a frequent correspondent.[‡] Through Hyndman, Dilke arranged to meet Jaurès, the French Socialist, who came to London in 1899. Keir Hardie, who was in the House of Commons from 1892–5 but was then out until 1900, also corresponded occasionally, sometimes during the latter period asking Dilke to put down a question on his behalf. In August, 1894, he had made a more surprising and important request to Dilke. He had asked him, if Dilke's testimony in his memoir is to be believed, to assume the leadership of the Independent Labour party, then in its second year of existence. Dilke tells us that he refused the offer, principally because he was at the time deeply concerned at the danger of war with Russia, and believed that if this occurred he would find an alliance with the Tories both more useful and more congenial than one with this new socialist organisation.

What is difficult to credit is not that the offer was refused but that it was ever made. In the first place, the I.L.P. was not a body which particularly required a leader. It had Hardie himself, its most dominant figure, as its first chairman. Hardie was not a good leader, as emerged in the next decade when he presided for some years over a parliamentary Labour party of twenty-nine

---

[‡] Hyndman's letters were not always full of obvious revolutionary content. In August, 1896, he wrote protesting against the appointment of Sir Edward Monson as British Ambassador in Paris on the grounds of his poverty, his failure to pay his bills, and the bad company which he had kept in Vienna.

members. But it was not for this reason that the chairmanship did not remain in his hands but rotated amongst other leading I.L.P. figures. It was because the I.L.P. was an aggressively democratic movement which resisted the idea of any one man's authority. Furthermore, the tone of the I.L.P. in its early days was bitterly anti-Liberal. "I would consider it a stain on the Labour party to have any dealings with the Liberals," Hardie had proclaimed at the inaugural Bradford conference. "I would as soon have dealings with the devil."[8] He went on contemptuously to reject the idea that the I.L.P. was ever intended to be "a halfway house between Liberalism and Socialism." But this was precisely what Dilke would have wished it to be. As a result he was much more in sympathy with the "Lib.-Labs." like Mabon, Broadhurst and Joseph Arch than with Hardie. Hyndman and some of the continental Marxists, with their heavy theory and their more "realistic" approach to questions of foreign policy, would also, in a way, have been more to his taste than the somewhat imprecise pacifist idealism of Hardie. Altogether, a marriage between Dilke and the I.L.P. would clearly have been a most unhappy affair.

More fruitful was Dilke's co-operation with the Trades Union Congress. When he had been in office, in the early 'eighties, he had begun the practice of starting each session with a luncheon for the Parliamentary Committee (the forerunner of the General Council) of the T.U.C. At this gathering they discussed the strategy for dealing with labour questions in the House of Commons during the coming year. Dilke revived the practice in 1898, and within a few years the luncheons began to be followed by a conference of the Parliamentary Committee and the radical and Labour members in the House. The conferences continued until 1906, when the great inflow of new Labour members made them inappropriate. The luncheons went on until Dilke's death, and in the last year were supplemented by a dinner at which the T.U.C. and not Dilke was the host, and at which a presentation was made.

One of the fruits of this consultation was the Trades Disputes Act of 1906. Immediately after the Taff Vale judgment of 1901, which made it possible for employers to compensate themselves for the effects of the strike by suing for damages the union concerned, Dilke was called in by the Amalgamated Society of Railway Servants. He secured the support of Asquith for the calling of a conference which led to a Liberal commitment to legislate in the union's interest. He also led a deputation which was received on behalf of the Cabinet by his old lawyer who had become Lord James of Hereford. They made some impression on him, but not enough. D. J. Shackleton, the Labour member for Clitheroe, introduced a private members' bill in 1903, and again in 1904 and 1905. It was defeated on second reading on the first occasion, and perished in committee on the latter two. A Liberal Parliament had to be awaited before further progress could be made. When this came, in 1906, it still remained to be decided how strong a bill was to be, pushed through. Most of the lawyers in the Government were in favour of one which would give only a qualified exemption to union funds. Dilke's influence was thrown strongly the other way. He urged the Labour M.P.s, who showed some sign of weakening, to stand out for the measure they wanted; he exerted great pressure on the Government, and he did something to neutralise Tory opposition. He was successful, and the bill which passed was one involving the complete reversal of Taff Vale. "In so far as (trades unionists) have now a charter invulnerable alike to the prejudice and the caprice of those who administer the law," Miss Mary MacArthur wrote in

1917, "it is largely due to the clear vision of Sir Charles Dilke, and to the skill and invincible courage with which he followed his aims."[9]

Dilke's main labour interest, however, was with those in the dangerous and sweated trades. In part this was due to the influence of his wife. Lady Dilke was long associated with the Women's Trade Union League and took her association sufficiently seriously to attend every Trades Union Congress from 1889 until her death. In trades like match-making and white lead the majority of the employees were women, and the statistics of industrial disease were appalling. The Dilkes between them succeeded in effecting a substantial improvement. In the china and earthenware trade, too (although this was not primarily a woman's trade), the industrial processes in the 'nineties involved a ten per cent casualty rate, with the victims suffering blindness, paralysis or death. Dilke kept up a constant pressure on the Home Office, raising the matter in the House year after year, securing the appointment of several committees, and eventually having the satisfaction of seeing the number of cases reduced to a fifth of those which had existed when he first took up the issue.

Many of the trades in which women were employed had practically no trade union organisation and a level of wages far below the average even for those days. Nor was there much prospect of building up a level of union membership which would make collective bargaining a possibility. Many of the employees were home workers; the rest were grouped in small scattered workshops. Dilke believed that the only possibility of attacking this problem of sweated labour was by legislation. He was himself attracted by the idea of a statutory national minimum wage, but he recognised that in practice he could hope to do no more than secure action to deal with the problem in specified trades. With this object he introduced his Wages Boards Bill in 1898. Boards comprising representatives of both sides should be set up for a limited number of trades and should have power to fix differing minimum wages in each case. It was a modest proposal, but it made no progress for a number of years, even though he continued to lay it before Parliament at the beginning of each session. In 1906 the climate of opinion changed and the outlook became far more favourable. In 1908 Dilke and the Archbishop of Canterbury jointly introduced a deputation to the Prime Minister, which led on directly to the Trade Boards Act of 1909. At first only four trades were covered by the act, but a considerable improvement was effected in these, and it was later given a wider application.

Another group with whom Dilke was particularly concerned were the shop assistants. They were a depressed and comparatively unorganised group, afflicted even more by long hours than by low wages. Dilke's association with this movement began in 1896. Thereafter he frequently addressed meetings on their behalf; he introduced into the House of Commons a bill limiting their hours of work; he inspired its introduction into the Lords; and he helped to persuade the Liberal Government of 1905 to take action in this respect which led on to an act reaching the statute book a few months after his death. When the National Union of Shop Assistants built a new London office in 1914 they called it Dilke House.

A feature characteristic of Dilke's advocacy of labour legislation, but one unusual amongst other advocates of the same cause, was the extent to which he drew for both his knowledge and his inspiration upon what was happening in other parts of the Empire, notably the white colonies. Some of these—and particularly the Australian states—were far ahead of England in the legislative protection which they gave to the working class. Dilke's habit of amassing information gave him an unsurpassed familiarity with the provisions which existed. Alfred Deakin, Prime Minister of Australia on several occasions after 1903, was one of his most fervent admirers and frequent correspondents.[§]

Dilke believed firmly that the Anglo-Saxon race was superior to any other, and that white men in general had a capacity for effective social and economic organisation which the other races were unlikely ever to equal. But he did not consider that this entitled them to exploit those whose qualities were inferior to their own. He believed in the protection of those who could not protect themselves. Indeed, J. E. B. Seely,[¶] who worked closely with him on a number of issues during these later years, reached the conclusion that "the master-key to Dilke's actions "in the post-1892 period was his determination to protect "the underdog."[10] In Seely's view this alone kept Dilke going when it had become obvious that his career could never again prosper.

A large part of Dilke's colonial activities was therefore concerned with the protection of native rights. Vestiges of slavery

---

[§] Deakin (1856–1919) had a political position closely in tune with Dilke's own. He was an advanced but undogmatic Liberal. He rejected free trade (Dilke as an Englishman did not follow him in this, but had much sympathy for the Australian protectionist viewpoint); he wanted effective imperial defence; and he returned to office as Commonwealth Prime Minister in 1905 by forming an alliance with the Australian Labour party.

[¶] 1868–1947. Secretary of State for War from 191a until Asquith replaced him at the time of the Curragh mutiny in the spring of 1914. Later Lord Mottistone.

roused him deeply, for he regarded the institution in any form as equally damaging to the white exploiters and to the coloured victims. In 1907 a long period of agitation, in which Dilke had played a central part, culminated in a Colonial Office decision against the Zanzibar practice of restoring runaway slaves to their owners. The Bishop of Uganda wrote that this result would not have been secured until many years later had it not been for the participation of Dilke.[11]

A similar but still longer extended activity of Dilke's was his work for the Congo Reform Association. The Congo Free State, under the personal suzerainty of the King of the Belgians, had been created at the Berlin Conference of 1884. England had been a party to the agreement and shared some international responsibility for what went on in the new territory, the government of which was intended to be a spearhead of civilisation in Central Africa. By the middle of the 'nineties, however, the spear looked somewhat blunted. Slave dealing persisted and the army of the Free State, it was revealed, although commanded by European officers, had been fed for long periods by means of a system of organised cannibalism. Dilke first raised these matters in the House of Commons in April, 1897. He called for the reassembly of the Berlin Conference, but the Government view, as expressed by Curzon, was hostile to this proposal and cool towards the subject as a whole. This coolness did not infect Dilke. Thereafter he pursued the issue for the remainder of his life. He initiated parliamentary debates in session after session. In 1903 these efforts mobilised House of Commons opinion to such an extent that Balfour was forced to accept a motion committing the Government to a diplomatic re-opening of the case. In 1908, when a new constitution and more direct Belgian responsibility were being evolved, the issue was forced sufficiently to the forefront of British politics that it achieved a mention in the King's Speech; and a strong memorandum was despatched to Brussels by the Foreign Office. In the spring of 1910, in one of his last House of Commons interventions, Dilke was still speaking on the issue. But great progress had been made, and in 1913, with Dilke no longer amongst them, the sponsors of the Congo Reform Association felt able to wind up the organisation. His work appeared to have been completed.

This work brought Dilke into contact with E. D. Morel, a reforming journalist of distinction and an outstanding example of the English liberal conscience in action. Thereafter Dilke co-operated freely with him on all questions touching Africa and the rights of native peoples. In 1902 Morel published his book *Affairs of West Africa*, and asked Dilke to write a preface. Dilke declined this suggestion on the characteristically precise ground that he could not agree with a statement made by Morel on page 286, but he offered to write a friendly review and to arrange for others in papers which he could influence. This refusal did not impair their good relations, and they each remained a considerable influence upon the other until the date of Dilke's death.

Dilke's interest in native rights, combined with his jingo streak, made him reserved about the South African war. It is possible that he was also influenced towards silence by the remaining traces of his friendship with Chamberlain, although by 1899 the effect of this was probably not very strong. Whatever the reasons, South Africa, like Ireland, became for Dilke a subject on which he did not see his way clearly. And just as, when the second Home Rule Bill had been before the House, he had confined his speeches to the peripheral subject of the electoral arrangements, so, in the case of the war in South Africa, he directed himself not to the merits of the struggle but to the appalling British military inefficiency which it demonstrated. He was more stirred by the damage that had been done to the reputation of the British Army than by the wrongs of the Boers. "But can any member of this House deny that the net result of these proceedings has been disastrous to the belief of the world in our ability to conduct a war?"[12] he demanded on February 1st, 1900, after the early setbacks. It was a pertinent question, but it was not one which most left-wing Liberal members would have chosen to ask.

The debate in which Dilke asked this question was on an amendment to the Address moved by Lord Edmond Fitzmaurice. It was sufficiently loose for the whole Liberal party to be able to unite behind it. This was an unusual event at the time. A more common end to a debate on the South African situation was for the party to split into two if not three factions. This occurred most signally six months later, on July 25th, when an amendment moved by Sir Wilfred Lawson led to violent "pro-Boer" speeches from Labouchere, Sir Robert Reid and Lloyd George; to an announcement from the leader of the party that he would abstain; and to a counter-announcement from Sir Edward Grey that he would vote with the Governmerit. When the division came 40 Liberals voted with the Unionists, 35 abstained with Campbell-Bannerman, and 31, including Morley and Bryce, voted for the amendment. Dilke abstained, and as his action cannot possibly be attributed to loyalty to Bannerman,** it

---

** Between Campbell-Bannerman and Dilke there existed a strong mutual antipathy. A fair indication of one aspect of it is given by a letter which Campbell-Bannerman wrote to Herbert Gladstone on January 5th, 1900, after Dilke had tabled an amendment to the Address. "I do not think

gives a clear indication of where he stood. He was not a natural compromiser, particularly when without responsibility, but he could go neither with the right of the party nor, on this issue, with the left.

Later, when the issue became one not of conquest but of reconciliation, Dilke remained cautious of giving too free a hand to the Boers in their dealings with the native population. "South Africa," he gloomily prognosticated, "is to become the home of a great proletariat, forbidden by law to rise above the present situation."[13] He fought hard against any constitutional recognition of the colour bar, against discriminatory franchise proposals, and against infringement of native rights in Basutoland, Bechuanaland and other tribal territories. In 1906 he drafted a motion incorporating these points which was accepted by the House of Commons; and in 1909 he worked in close association with W. P. Schreiner for suitable amendments to the South Africa Bill.

Dilke's other major political interest during; his second period in the House of Commons was imperial defence. His little book on *The British Army* had appeared as early as 1888. The message of this was that England was less prepared for war than any other major power. This conviction dominated an important part of Dilke's mind for the remainder of his life. He saw this military weakness as a drag on our diplomacy as well as a threat to our national security. He saw it, too, as an issue which transcended party difference, and he set himself to collaborate with

---

Citizen Dilke's amendment covers the ground," the letter ran. "It is admirably fitted as a peg on which to hang up for public admiration the intimate knowledge of the facts possessed by the originator—but that is not our sole object." (Spender, *Life of Sir Henry Campbell-Bannerman*, Vol. I, p. 369.)

any who would collaborate with him and to exercise the strongest possible pressure upon whichever government was in at the time. "I am one of those," he declared in 1898, "who are in favour of large armaments for this country, and believe in increasing the strength of our defences for the sake of peace; and one of the very reasons why I desire that is because I repudiate the idea of making our policy depend upon the policy of others."[14] Holding these views he was naturally often in conflict with the instinctive reactions of many Liberals, and sometimes expressed with some acerbity his impatience with these reactions. "Liberals should give up thinking of this question of national defence as a hateful one," he said in 1893, "and as one against which they should close their eyes and ears."[15]

In 1891 he published, jointly with Spenser Wilkinson,[††] a civilian military expert, a wider-ranging work entitled *Imperial Defence*. In the course of writing this book Dilke had been slowly converted by Wilkinson to a belief in the primacy of the navy. Britain's best means of defending her scattered imperial possessions was to possess and concentrate a naval force capable of destroying the enemy's own sea-power. Thereafter he never deviated from this view, and in the controversies of the next century he became one of the best-informed supporters of the "blue-water" school.

Imperial Defence also advocated—and here the idea was Dilke's own—a much closer co-ordination of the two services at home and of the various military resources which were scattered

---

[††] 1853–1938. Military correspondent of the *Manchester Guardian*, 1882–92, and of the *Morning Post*, 1895 1914. Chichele Professor of Military History at Oxford from 1909.

throughout the Empire. Dilke wanted a General Staff and he wanted it to operate on an imperial and not merely a United Kingdom level. "The very existence of a General Staff," he wrote, "would constitute a form of Imperial military federation." One aspect of these ideas was pressed by Dilke soon after he returned to the House of Commons. At the beginning of 1894 he organised the writing of a public letter signed by himself, General Sir George Chesney (a backbench Unionist), H. O. Arnold-Forster (later to be Secretary of State for War under Balfour) and Spenser Wilkinson. It was addressed to Gladstone as Prime Minister, to Salisbury and Balfour as the leaders of the Conservatives in the two houses, and to the Duke of Devonshire (as Hartington had become) and Chamberlain as the leaders of the Liberal Unionists. Two striking proposals were made in the letter. The first was the uniting of the two services under a single political head. Either a convention should be established by which the man who was appointed First Lord of the Admiralty should also be made Secretary of State for War, or, still more drastically, there should be a formal legislative union of the two offices. The second was that a chief of the staff should be appointed in each service, who would be the adviser of the "defence minister" and the Cabinet, and who would be responsible in the sense that he would hold office only so long as his advice was accepted.

This letter was received with uneven enthusiasm by those to whom it was addressed. It reached Gladstone when he was on the point of resignation, and it did nothing to make him wish to change his mind. He replied cryptically (for his resignation had not then been announced. ". . . I fear I ought to confine myself to assuring you that I have taken care . . . it should come to the notice of my colleagues."[16] This was the last letter which Dilke received from his former chief, and the last which was heard of his memorandum from the Liberal side.

From the Unionist leaders the response was more encouraging. It was upon Balfour that Dilke had placed his greatest reliance.

"I had sooner discuss this matter first with you," he had written to him a few weeks before, ". . . than with Chamberlain, because he is, oddly enough, a much stronger party man than you are, and would be less inclined (on account of national objects which to him are predominant) to keep party out of his mind in connection with it."[17]

Dilke's faith was not misplaced. Balfour argued against some of the details of the plan—he thought, for instance, that the concentration of naval and military advice through two individuals would weaken civilian authority but he showed an eager interest in the problems with which it sought to deal. In a debate which followed the publication of the letter he committed himself sufficiently for Dilke to withdraw the motion which had initiated the discussion. In the next period of Unionist Government a loose form of Committee of Imperial Defence was brought into existence. And in 1903, under Balfour's own premiership, the Committee was given a much more closely defined and important form. The Prime Minister became its chairman, the professional (as well as the political) chiefs of the Admiralty and War Office were made permanent members, minutes were kept and a secretariat was established.

Most of Dilke's work in the field of national defence was conducted on an equally non-party basis. Apart from Wilkinson, Arnold-Forster remained his closest civilian collaborator; and he carried on a large and friendly correspondence with a wide range of scarcely radical generals and admirals. These service chiefs often wrote in insistent terms about the quality of Dilke's knowledge and the value of his work. "I am always delighted to answer any question you may ask me," Admiral Lord Charles Beresford wrote in 1897, "as I consider that you are the only member of Cabinet rank in either party who really understands the question of Imperial Defence in all its requirements or indeed in any particular."[18] "You cannot think how grateful I am to anyone who takes an intelligent interest in the Army,"[19] came from General Sir Evelyn Wood in the following year.

From the moment of his return to Parliament Dilke acted independently of his party on defence questions. Sometimes his independence wore a radical appearance, as when, in 1893, he voted against the appointment of the Duke of Connaught to the command at Aldershot. More frequently, however, it led him into a temporary Conservative alliance. The most notable of these latter occasions was the "cordite vote "in June, 1895. This, the last occasion upon which a government was forced into resignation by defeat in the House of Commons, was a vote of censure upon Campbell-Bannerman for not having been quick enough to procure supplies of cordite for the army. There was a short debate and a small vote, but the Government was defeated by seven. Dilke made no speech, but he voted with the Opposition, and was the most prominent of the handful of Liberals who took this course. "For this vote," Dilke's official biographers baldly state, "Campbell-Bannerman never forgave him."[20] Such a judgment is necessarily something of a surmise, but it is supported, as has been already seen, by the disparaging and bitter terms in which Campbell-Bannerman wrote about Dilke in 1900; and it is in no way contradicted, as will be shown later, by the events associated with the formation of the Liberal Government of 1905.

Outside politics, Dilke's life during the 'nineties and over the turn of the century pursued a mixed course. He was popular in the Forest of Dean, respected throughout the Labour movement, and a major social figure in Paris. In English politics and society, however, he was not allowed to strike more than a minor key. By the end of the 'nineties when his friendship with Chamberlain was dead, there was no political figure of the front rank, with the doubtful exception of Morley, with whom he was on intimate terms. Lord Edmond Fitzmaurice would occasionally suggest a week-end and G. O. Trevelyan would accompany him for Sunday afternoon walks in London. This was the nearest to the centre of political power that his friendships took him. Life at Sloane Street and still less at Dockett Eddy and Pyrford was not solitary, however. Particularly at Dockett during the summer there was a stream of visitors—oarsmen, Balkan diplomats, French actors, and collaborators of Dilke's in particular enterprises like Spenser Wilkinson and D. F. Steavenson. There was a wide periphery of acquaintances but little to put in the centre. There was no core of all-purpose friends such as had existed at Sloane Street in the late 'seventies and early 'eighties.

In part this was due to the piecemeal, rather unco-ordinated pattern which Dilke's political interests had assumed. In part too it was due to the social ostracism which continued to operate against him. The Court, at least until the death of the Queen, never wavered in its hostility, despite a series of attempts by the old republican to circumnavigate the excluding barriers. In 1896 he wrote to the Prince of Wales to ask if he might recommence his attendance at levées. Knollys replied rather negatively—"You are doubtless aware that the matter is not one in which (the Prince) can officially interfere, as he only represents the Queen at Levées and co."—but saying that he had sent Dilke's letter on to the Lord Chamberlain, Lord Latham. Latham referred it to the Prime Minister, who spoke to the Queen, and then wrote to Latham for forwarding to Dilke an elliptical but firm refusal:

20 Arlington Street,
February 27

My dear Latham,

Sir C. D.'s Letter

The Queen has intimated to me that in her judgment it is not desirable that Sir C. D. should pursue in respect to the matter to which he refers a course different from that which he has followed up to this time.

Yours very truly,
Salisbury[21]

In the following year, on the occasion of the Diamond Jubilee, Dilke tried again. On June 23rd the Speaker led a procession of four hundred members to Buckingham Palace in order to convey to the Queen the congratulations of the House of Commons. Dilke, conspicuous in the levée dress of a Privy Councillor, took his place in the procession, but his presence was adversely commented on in some parts of the Press and was not welcomed, he felt, by the Queen herself. In consequence he wrote to the Prince of Wales, partly by way of self-justification and partly to ask the Prince's advice as to whether he should attend a parliamentary garden party which the Queen was giving at Windsor and to which a summons had automatically been sent to Dilke and his wife. Knollys replied more warmly on this occasion.

481

"I am desired by the Prince of Wales to thank you for your letter, and to say that he is much touched by it and that he especially appreciates the tone in which it is written.

"His Royal Highness directs me to let you know that he thinks you were quite right to accompany the Speaker to Buckingham Palace, and that though he understands the reason which prompts you and Lady Dilke to hesitate about going to Windsor to-morrow, he is at the same time of the opinion that you should both 'obey Her Majesty's commands.'"[22][‡‡]

Three and a half years later the Queen died, and the Prince of Wales, generally more tolerant and specifically more friendly, ascended the throne. The Court then ceased to be the centre of resistance to the social rehabilitation of the Dilkes. Sir Charles attended the Accession Council, and noted, perhaps attributing his own feelings to others, that relief was a more widespread reaction than sorrow. Thereafter he took his normal place, as a senior Privy Councillor, at all Court functions. In 1902 Lady Dilke was re-presented, which had not previously been possible since her second marriage, and in the

---

[‡‡] In 1916 Lord Knollys (as he had then become) wrote to Miss Gertrude Tuckwell requesting that this letter should not be published in the biography of Dilke on which she was working. "I do not think that it would be quite fair to the memory of King Edward," he argued, "that the line which he took in private in regard to Sir Charles' case should be made public when the majority of people (I imagine I am correct in saying this) adopted a totally different attitude." (D.P. 43967, 271.) It is difficult to believe that the letter would have been very damaging forty years ago, and it is clearly not so to-day.

autumn of that year there was even talk of a royal visit, very much under Dilke's auspices, to the Forest of Dean.

Lady Dilke was the moving spirit in this somewhat laborious ascent to royal favour. But even in her case the ascent was not made for its own sake. The most important purpose of her later life was to make the world recognise that it had wronged her husband. King Edward was a useful instrument for the achievement of this end. By the time that he could be used, however, the possibility of a complete recovery of Dilke's political career had disappeared. In 1892 at the age of forty-eight all things appeared still to be possible. In 1902 at the age of fifty-eight the prospect was much more limited. Given Dilke's age, his career would in any event have suffered at this stage from the long period of Unionist hegemony. Morley's did so. But Morley had been a member of the Cabinet of 1892–5 and remained one of the inner council of the Liberal party during the years of opposition. Without either of these qualifications Dilke could not hope for a central position in the next Liberal Government. The best for which he could hope was a peripheral position in the Cabinet. He would not exercise great power, but for the first time for twenty years he might again be officially recognised. Whether this comparatively modest hope would be fulfilled was the question which exercised the mind of Lady Dilke (and to a slightly lesser extent that of her husband) as the first years of Balfour's premiership marked the beginning of Unionist decline.

Chapter Nineteen

A Quiet End

Lady Dilke did not live to see her hopes for her husband put to the test. Her health had never been very good, and in the last few years of her life she was forced to reduce her activities. But at the very end she was able to round off some of her manifold interests. In the spring of 1904 she went for two months to Paris and helped to prepare an exhibition of French primitive art. After spending the summer at Dockett she travelled to Leeds in the first week of September for her sixteenth successive Trades Union Congress. From there she went to join her husband in the Forest of Dean for their regular autumn visit. Then, on Thursday, October 20th, she went to London for a meeting at the Chelsea Town Hall. Dilke, at the beginning of a campaign which he had concerted with friends and which was to be half radical propaganda and half personal rehabilitation, was to address his old constituents for the first time for many years. The meeting was a success, but later that night Lady Dilke became very ill. She insisted on travelling to Pyrford on the following morning, and once there she seemed to improve. But on the evening of the third day, after what Dilke described as "one of our happiest Sunday afternoons," she died in his arms.

The loss was a severe one for Dilke, although he was soon able to look back on his second marriage with a satisfaction which bordered on complacency. "The two people with whom I was most closely associated in my life," he wrote a year or so later, referring to his grandfather and his second wife, "both died saying that I had given them perfect happiness."[1]

As in the case of his grandfather so in the case of his second wife, Dilke sought to complete this felicity and express his sense of loss by composing a memoir and publishing it as an introduction to a selection of the subject's own writings. This tribute to Lady Dilke appeared under the title of *The Book of the Spiritual Life* in 1905. It was the last of Sir Charles's full-length publications.

Before Lady Dilke's death her hopes had fastened on the possibility of her husband becoming Secretary of State for War in the next Government. Both she and Dilke himself had informal discussions with Morley—their best contact in the Liberal Shadow Cabinet—on the point. But it is doubtful whether Morley was able to give them much encouragement. Captain Cecil Norton, a Liberal Whip and a friend of Dilke's, had advocated the appointment in a speech in his South London constituency; but the reaction, if not among the audience at least among a wider public, was unfavourable. Stead moved into action again, and, more importantly, there were letters of protest from the Bishop of Southwark, in whose diocese Norton's speech had been delivered, and from other church leaders. The way the Nonconformist wind still blew—always a matter of great importance in the Liberal party—was shown by the Lloyd George reaction to a proposal for radical collaboration which Dilke had put forward earlier in 1904. "Lloyd George was at first inclined to assent," Dilke wrote, "but on second thoughts asked for time, which I think meant to see Dr. Clifford.*[2] Dr. Clifford was never friendly to Dilke, and his influence, joined to that of a part of the Church of England, was quite enough to be decisive with Campbell-Bannerman. The Liberal leader had no wish to be brave on Dilke's behalf.

By the end of the year it had become clear to Dilke that he was most unlikely to get the War Office. On December 9th he wrote to Alfred Deakin in terms which indicated a desire to make the best of his disappointment:

> "I was in the inner ring of the Cabinet before I was either a Cabinet Minister or a Privy Councillor, 1880–1882, and I am not likely to have the offer of a place the work of which could tempt me. The W(ar) O(ffice) would kill me, but I could not refuse it. I have been told on 'authority' that it will not come to me."[3]

In fact no offer of any sort came to Dilke. He had no need to consider the problem of whether or not he should accept.

Throughout the first week of December, 1905, when Campbell-Bannerman was forming his Government, there was no communication from him to Dilke. Dilke was given no apology or direct explanation of the reasons for his exclusion.

---

* Minister at the Baptist Chapel in Praed Street, Paddington, President of the Baptist World Alliance, and at the time the recognised leader of militant Nonconformity in England.

The nearest approach to such an explanation came in a letter from John Morley which began by telling of his own appointment to the India Office, and continued:

"For yourself, of course, I well remember one at any rate of my conversations in Sloane Street, though I forget the exact date. When I opened the matter to C.-B. on his return from Marienbad the other day I found him adverse. I resumed it last Monday when things became actual. He was by that time still more adverse, and even disinclined to listen or to discuss. There was no pressure on him in the adverse direction from any quarter. I mean from either colleagues or other persons of importance. There may have been from the Noncons. or other people of that connection but he did not say so. It was a *chose jugée*, I think, from the first in his own mind. . . .

Good-bye, my dear Dilke. To nobody is your absence more truly painful than to your

John Morley"[4]

Others wrote letters which were equally distressed if less informative. "I am sick at heart at not being able to write a different account of the nominations to the War Office or Colonies,"[5] came from Reginald McKenna. And Dilke's oldest remaining political friend, Lord Edmond Fitzmaurice, who had not himself been entirely passed over, but who had been reluctantly elevated to the House of Lords and appointed to the same under-secretaryship which he had first held no less than twenty-three years previously, wrote in terms which were half apologetic and half complaining. Had his health been as good as Dilke's he would have remained a private member of the House of Commons,

"and we would have ended together where we began together."
As it was they had both been badly treated as a result of "the
wiles of the 'Lowland clans,' and very low indeed too."[6]

Dilke himself attributed the decisive role in his exclusion to
the Prime Minister's memory of the cordite vote of 1895. In a
letter to Labouchere of January 6th, 1906, he revealed at least a
part of his thoughts and expressed a high degree of philosophical
detachment:

> "I did not expect him (Campbell-Bannerman) to offer
> me any place," he wrote. "Had my wife lived that would
> have hurt her, and through her, me. As it is I prefer to be
> outside—a thing which, though often true, no one ever
> believes of others. . . .
>
> "The only pleasant thing about office would have been
> the money. I always want more than I have, and I hate to
> ride broken-down horses, and can't afford the new horses I
> want to ride. £5,000 a year for a year or two would have
> been most welcome.
>
> "But when in office—April, 1880, to June, 1885—I was
> exceptionally powerful and nearly always got my own way
> in every department. That could never have been
> repeated—a strong reason why I have all along preferred
> the pleasant front seat in the house to a less commanding
> position on the stage."[7]

The last paragraph of this letter was perhaps the most
significant. Henceforward Dilke's thoughts were to be concentrated to a growing extent upon the past. He was only
sixty-two—seven years younger than the Prime Minister—
but he had no future and his present existence was unexciting.

The great days of the 'seventies and early 'eighties therefore came increasingly to occupy his thoughts, although not to distort his values. He showed no bitterness with his current lot, he did not elevate the past, and his radicalism never wavered. But the arrangement of his old papers occupied much of his time and recollections of Gladstone or Gordon or Gambetta much of his conversation.

Nevertheless, he did not contract out of his day-to-day activities. He remained in the House of Commons; and one of his first duties after the formation of the Government was to go to the Forest of Dean and fight the "landslide" election of 1906. The result was an overwhelming majority in his favour, but the obvious disappointment of his supporters at his final exclusion from power was a source of some embarrassment to him. He remained a diligent constituency member, however. He paid no visits to the Forest while the House was sitting, except for his annual appearance at the local miners' rally in July, but he continued to spend there the greater part of a month each autumn and to pay a January visit as well. These visits, combined with his natural habits of mind, meant that he had acquired an immensely detailed knowledge of the constituency and its problems; and he was as familiar to most of its inhabitants as the statistics of their living conditions were to him.

The new Parliament, with its vast Liberal majority and its sizeable Labour party, earned Dilke's full approbation but left him with a less obvious role than that which he had previously filled. In part this was simply a function of his move to the Government side of the House. There is much more opportunity to be an effective back-bencher on the Opposition side. But in part too it was a function of the new strength of the Labour party. The election of thirty Labour members and twenty-four

489

"Lib.-Labs." gave Dilke almost unqualified satisfaction. "The triumph of the principles to which I have devoted my life are now bound up with the future of the Labour Party," he wrote. But he added: "To join it or lead it was never my thought."[8] And this being so, its emergence as a party of strength left much less place for an outside "sponsor" than had previously been the case. After 1906 the trades union members in no way cold-shouldered Dilke, but they certainly needed him less than in the preceding Parliaments. He did not allow these considerations to prejudice him against the new House of Commons. On the contrary, he wrote of its members in eulogistic terms: "I am certain that there has never met at Westminster an assembly so able and at the same time so widely different in intellectual composition from its predecessors as that which is now there gathered."[9] Furthermore, he avoided the old parliamentarians' disease of regretting the "giants" who had disappeared from the scene. He discounted heavily the view that House of Commons oratory or the stature of leading members was in decline. Campbell-Bannerman he could not admire, but for Asquith his respect was almost unqualified. Both as statesman and as parliamentarian he considered him far superior to Gladstone. He also perceived that Winston Churchill was a greater man than Lord Randolph, and, more surprisingly, believed "Lulu" Harcourt to be equally superior to Sir William.

These charitable judgments on his juniors did not prevent Dilke from expressing some suspicion about the keenness of the Government's radicalism. "The really weak point," he had written to Labouchere as early as January, 1906, "is that the Government is damned unless it fights the Lords in 1907, and that the promise of "five years in power "will prevent the hacks from fighting."[10] He therefore endeavoured to recreate the old radical group which had existed in the previous Parliament. Almost all those with whom he had then worked had been dispersed. Labouchere had retired, Stanhope had gone to the Lords, and Harcourt and Norton had taken office. Nevertheless, he assembled a new band and attempted to lay down for it a series of radical objectives. The first was given as a close working understanding with the Irish Nationalists and the Labour party. The second was adult suffrage and the single vote. Third came the payment of members of Parliament. Fourth was the problem of the House of Lords. This should be solved either by single chamber government or by a restriction of the power of the Lords, but on no account by a reform of the Upper House. Fifth was fiscal reform, to be based on a suffer graduation of death duties and the local taxation of land values. Sixth came the granting to local authorities of full power to acquire land and to indulge in all forms of "municipal socialism."

When Dilke was present at the meetings of this group he automatically presided, but he was not always very assiduous in his attendance. In part this was because he soon became deeply embroiled in the work of a Select Committee on the Income Tax. In the spring of 1906 Asquith as Chancellor pressed Dilke to accept the chairmanship of this enquiry. With some reluctance, for the field was entirely new to him, Dilke accepted, and having accepted, devoted himself to the work with characteristic thoroughness. He accumulated a vast range of evidence upon foreign and colonial practice and he launched the first powerful endeavour to make the Treasury produce statistics of the United Kingdom distribution of income. But on the whole his chairmanship was not a success. The two main practical recommendations of the commit-tee—the differentiation of earned and unearned incomes and the introduction of a super-tax—were both adopted against Dilke's opposition. It was not that he objected to the degree of progression involved in these proposals, but that their logical untidiness oppressed him. He would have preferred an entirely separate system of property taxation, as in Prussia or Holland, and he saw little point in introducing a super-tax while the possibilities of a graduated income tax were still so little exploited. But he failed to carry his colleagues with him, and there emerges unavoidably the impression that his method of thought, on a new subject at any rate, was becoming a little arid and theoretical.

Apart from this short-lived activity and from occasional radical forays against the Government, his interventions outside his specialised fields became increasingly rare. Labour legislation, defence and some aspects of foreign affairs continued to hold his attention, but the great controversies of education, licensing, the Lloyd George budget, and even the constitutional struggle itself drew forth few pronouncements from him. Soon after the first 1910 election he led a deputation of thirty advanced radicals to the Prime Minister in order to protest against a suspected tendency to mix up the reform of the House of Lords with the much more important question of the curtailment of its powers. But this was an exceptional activity.

In 1908 his health showed the first signs of serious decline. His heart was no longer strong, and he spent much of the year as a semi-invalid. But the following year showed a great improvement and he resumed his habits of fencing, riding and even sculling. He also reverted to foreign travel. From 1892 until the death of his second wife he had scarcely left England other than to pay an annual month's Christmas visit to Paris. After 1906, while he continued his Paris habit, he again began to go farther afield, principally to Italy and to Provence, travelling now not for information as in his younger days but for recollection and for pleasure. His companions were mostly his wife's niece, Miss Gertrude Tuckwell, who was later to be the principal author of his standard biography, and a friend of hers, Miss Hinton-Smith. "I hope to see you here with your two young ladies," Labouchere wrote from Florence in the autumn of 1907.

In these last years Dilke's conversation remained of outstanding quality. It was founded upon his compendious knowledge, and we catch revealing glimpses of his demonstrating it to all sorts of people in all sorts of circumstances. He amazed the gardener on the Isola Madre in Lake Maggiore by his ability to differentiate and name every tree and shrub in the collection. In a twenty-minute discourse at the end of a public meeting he taught the landlord of the Victoria Hotel at Newnham-on-Severn more facts about beer than the latter had learnt in forty years as a licensed victualler. When staying at Lyons with Miss Tuckwell he was able to recall to her the nature and position of almost every canvas in the art gallery, although he himself would not visit the collection because of the force with which it would recall memories of Lady Dilke. All points of British parliamentary procedure and almost all details of French history and culture from the structure of the Provençal language to the ramifications of the Imperial family were at his command. There was no leading European personality of the previous half century of whom he did not have a lively recollection and a store of anecdote. "His amazing knowledge," an associate wrote, "which occasionally overloaded his speeches and diverted them from their main argument, wove itself naturally into the texture of his talk and gave it a wonderful richness and depth."†¹¹

Yet Dilke was not a bore. He not only talked about a wide range of people, but a wide range of people were fascinated to listen to him doing so. Frederick Whyte, then Liberal M.P. for Perth, first met him in 1910. Dilke accosted him in a corridor of the House of Commons and congratulated him in rather unorthodox terms upon a speech. "From that first moment," Whyte wrote later, "Charles Dilke's magic and magnetism caught and held me; and such was his vitality and naturalness that I was quite unaware of the long gap of the years between us." Upon Lord Beaverbrook, too, also at that time a young member of Parliament, Dilke made an equally forceful although somewhat more venerable impression. Lord Beaverbrook remembered him as a figure of mystery who was at the same time a fountain of information upon the intricacies of parliamentary procedure. He recalled with particular vividness pacing up and down the sea-front at Nice with him while Dilke discoursed with authority upon this subject. In the same way, William Tuckwell on the one hand, an old radical parson of great scholastic distinction, and the band of young female social reformers whom Lady Dilke had left behind her on the other, were always delighted to listen to Sir Charles.

He also preserved an engaging streak of eccentricity. In these later years he much enjoyed going to plays in Paris, but however satisfying he found the performance he always left after the first act. He was not bored, but thought that one act of a play was enough. He liked to maintain exactly the pattern of life which he had built up, and whether in London or in the country nothing

---

† J. W. Hills, Conservative M.P. for Durham City.

would divert him from the most accurate and minute apportionment of his days. This gave him the gift of almost unparalleled punctuality and in the Paris fencing establishment which he patronised until the last year of his life he was remembered primarily for his habit of announcing at the end of each visit the precise date on which he would return to Paris, perhaps nearly a year ahead, and the exact hour at which he would arrive to fence; and for the fact that he could be counted upon to keep his engagement, not merely to the hour, but probably to the minute.

In 1910 his health again deteriorated. The two general elections of that year were a heavy strain upon him. His seat was still safe, but he insisted on fighting a full campaign on each occasion. During the second engagement at the beginning of December he was manifestly ill and could hardly keep going. As soon as his result was announced he left for Paris. He spent several weeks there as a semi-invalid. He then travelled on to Hyères. He had no doubt that his life was near its end, and he wished to see again the Provençal countryside in which he had spent so much time at the full tide of his success. At Hyéres he was unable to leave his bed, but he continued to read, to write book reviews, and to talk with occasional gusto.

In mid-January he returned to London. He had travelled as an invalid and he went straight from the station to his bed in Sloane Street. For nearly a week his strength held. He worked, he saw friends and he planned meetings. On the afternoon of January 25th he prepared some papers for the Women's Trade Union League. They were delivered on the following morning, but by that time he was dead. His heart had failed soon after four o'clock on the morning of January 26th, 1911.

At eight o'clock, Hudson, the secretary whom Chamberlain had found for Dilke in 1887, went out to the post office in Pont

Street and sent a telegram to the editor of the local paper in Coleford. "Sir Charles Dilke died this morning", it ran. "Please tell his friends of the Forest whom he thought of and worked for to the last." It was an appropriate epitaph on Dilke's later life, but for many the news of his death took them back, in varying ways, to Victorian Liberalism and the days of his mounting success. Bodley, walking with his small daughter at Brighton, saw "with brutal suddenness" a telegram announcing the death in a shop window. "Yet it was not quite unexpected," he wrote, "for I saw him last night just as he used to look in his room at the Local Government Board. I suppose the explanation is that in the last moments his memory took him back to those happy days, and that I was in the picture which came before his fading sight."[12] Chamberlain, a helpless invalid for the past five years and separated from Dilke not only by political bitterness but by two decades of personal indifference, received the news at 40, Princes Gardens. He wrote no letter—he would have been barely capable—but he sent his son, Austen, to the funeral.

For those whose recollection of Dilke at his zenith might have been less lively than that of Bodley or of Chamberlain, *The Times* attempted to fill the gap. It no longer wished to ignore him, and the note which it sought to strike was that of dispassionate appraisal. But a leading article was harshly disparaging towards his political talents, and the long obituary notice revived in pejorative form almost all the details of the Crawford case. Even after his death Dilke retained his enemies.

THE END

Appendix I

List of Characters Concerned with the Case

BALL, GEORGE. Butler to Mr. and Mrs. Robert Harrison.

BALLARD, MRS. MARY. Housekeeper at 9, Hill Street.

BARNETT, CANON SAMUEL. Vicar of St. Jude's, Whitechapel.

BARZETTELLI, MRS. WINIFRED. Servant at 9, Hill Street.

BIRCH, WALTER DE GRAY. Assistant in Manuscript Department of the British Museum. Called as handwriting expert in the second trial by Crawford's counsel.

BODLEY, J. E. C. Private Secretary to Dilke from 1881 to 1886.

BUTCHER, EX-INSPECTOR. Detective employed by Crawford to watch Mrs. Crawford.

BUTT, MR. JUSTICE. Judge at first trial.

CASTELL, MRS. Lodging-house keeper at 28, Earls Court Gardens.

CHATFIELD, MRS. Dilke's grandmother. She lived with him at 76, Sloane Street until her death in 1880.

CHESSON, F. W. Chairman of the committee which after the second trial continued to investigate the case on Dilke's behalf.

COLLINS, DONALD. Beadle of Trinity Church, St. Marylebone, and lodger at 65, Warren Street.

CRAWFORD, DONALD. Husband of Mrs. Crawford and petitioner at both trials. Aged about 45.

CRAWFORD, MRS. DONALD. The respondent. Born Virginia Mary Smith. Daughter of Mrs. Eustace Smith. Younger sister of Mrs. Ashton Dilke and Mrs. Harrison. Elder sister of Mrs. Priestley. Aged 23.

DALGLEISH, ELLEN. Lady's maid to Mrs. Rogerson.

DALGLEISH, ALICE. Housemaid to Mrs. Rogerson.

DESSOUSLAVY, MRS. ANNA. Sometimes known as Mrs. Davies. Former servant and pensioner of Dilke and his father. Lodger at 65, Warren Street. Aged 49.

DESSOUSLAVY, ROSALIE. Sister to Anna. Nursemaid to Dilke when he was a child. Died 1876.

DILKE, MRS. Ashton. Born Margaret Maye Smith. Sister to Mrs. Crawford. Married Ashton Dilke, younger brother of Sir Charles, in 1876. He died in the autumn of 1882. Mrs. Dilke later re-married, after the conclusion of the case, and became Mrs. Russell Cooke. Aged 29.

DILKE, LADY. Formerly Mrs. Mark Pattison. Second wife of Sir Charles Dilke, whom she married in the autumn of 1885.

DRAKE, ELLEN. Dilke's under-housemaid from april, 1880, to March, 1883.

DUNN, EDWARD JOHN. Private in Duke of Cornwall's Light Infantry Called to give evidence against Captain Forster in the second trial.

ETHERIDOE, MRS. SUSAN. Replaced Mrs. Ballard as housekeeper at 9, Hill Street.

FORSTER, CAPTAIN HENRY. Army officer who admitted to being Mrs. Crawford's lover. Aged about 35.

GIULIANO, MR. Swiss jeweller. Friend to Mrs. Dessouslavy.

GOODS, SAMUEL. Footman to Dilke from August, 1880, to August, 1882.

GOODE, WILLIAM. Brother to Samuel Goode. Footman to Dilke from August, 1882, to August, 1885.

GOUDGE, MRS. Landlady at 65, Warren Street.

GRAHAM, CAPTAIN ERNEST. Suggested lover of Mrs. Crawford.

GRANT, CHARLES. Coachman to Dilke.

GRAY, FANNY. Became Mrs. Stock in autumn of 1885. Younger sister to Sarah Gray. employed for a short time as nursery-maid in Dilke's household. Aged 21.

GRAY, MARY ANN. Niece of Sarah and Fanny Gray. Replaced Ellen Drake as under-housemaid in Dilke's house for two years from March, 1883.

GRAY, SARAH. Upper-housemaid in Dilke's household, 1873–1885. Aged, 41.

HALLET, MRS. EMILY. Temporary housekeeper at 9, Hill Street.

HANNEN, Sir JAMES. President of Probate, Divorce and

Admiralty. Division of the High Court. Judge at the second trial.

HARRISON, MRS. ROBERT. Bora Helen Smith. Elder sister to Mrs. Crawford and younger sister to Mrs. Ashton Dilke. Married Robert-Harrison, partner in the stockbroking firm of Hickens, Harrison and Co. in 1877. Aged 28.

HARVEY, WILLIAM. Private in Duke of Cornwall's Light Infantry. Witness against Captain Forster.

HILLIER, GEOROE. Tailor who lodged with his family at 65, Warren Street, from April, 1882, to July, 1884.

HILLIER, MRS. MARY. His wife.

HILLIER, EMILY. His daughter.

HUMBERT, ERNEST. Dilke's solicitor in the case.

INDERWICK, Q.C. Counsel for Crawford. He led in the first trial, but was second to Matthews in the second trial.

INGLIS, G. S. Handwriting expert called on behalf of the Queen's Proctor.

IRELAND, WILLIAM. Clerk to Bodley, Dilke's private secretary.

JAMES, Sir HENRY, Q,.C. Counsel for Dilke at both trials.

JAMIESON, ANNE. Mrs. Crawford's parlourmaid.

DE JERSEY, MR. Friend to Captain Forster.

KENNEDY, H. G. Bodley's predecessor as private secretary to Dilke.

KINGSCOTE, MR. Son-in-law to Mrs. Rogerson.

LEE, H. A. Dilke's Foreign Office private secretary.

LEWIS, GEORGE. Later Sir George. Partner in Lewis and

Lewis. Solicitor to Mrs. Crawford.

LOGKWOOD, Q,.C. Leading counsel for Mrs. Crawford in the second trial.

MCARTHUR, W. A. Member of Dilke's investigation committee.

MACCOLL, CANON. Another member of the Committee.

MARSHALL HALL, EDWARD. Junior counsel for the Queen's Proctor at the second trial.

MARTIN, CAPTAIN ERNEST. Friend of Captain Forster.

MATTHEWS, HENRY, Q.C. Leading counsel for Crawford At the second trial.

MEDLAND, MRS. JULIA. Lodging-Housekeeper at 32, Earls Court Gardens.

MEDLAND, MISS JULIA. Her Daughter.

MURPHY, Q.C. Counsel for Forster at the second trial.

PAUNCEFOTE, Sir JULIAN. Permanent under-secretary of state, Foreign Office. Witness to Dilke's morning habits.

PHILLIMORE, Sir WALTER, Q.C. Leading counsel for the Queen's Proctor at the second trial.

PRIDHAM, C. J. C. Solicitor to Dilke in investigation subsequent to the second trial.

PRIESTLEY, DR. ROBERT. Suggested lover of Mrs. Crawford. Married her younger sister. Ida, in 1884.

PRIESTLEY, MRS. ROBERT. Born Ida Smith. Sister to Mrs. Ashton Dilke, Mrs. Harrison and Mrs. Crawford. Aged 22.

ROGERSON, MRS. Born Christine Stewart. Sister to Charles Stewart, Crawford's solicitor. Friend to Dilke. Aged about 42.

RUDDIMAN, CATHERINE. Mrs. Crawford's parlourmaid.

RUFFLE, MRS. Farmer's wife in Essex with whom Fanny Gray stayed.

RUSSELL, Sir Charles, Q.C. Counsel for Dilke.

SEARLE, MR. Junior counsel for Dilke in both trials.

SHANKS, HENRY. Footman to Dilke from March, 1882, to April, 1885.

SMITH, CLARENCE. Member of Dilke's investigation committee.

SMITH, MRS. EUSTACE. Mother to Mrs. Ashton Dilke, Mrs. Harrison, Mrs. Crawford, Mrs. Priestley, etc. Aged 49.

STEAD, W. T. Editor of *Pall Mall Gazette*.

STEAVENSON, D. F. Legal Member of Dilke's investigation committee.

STEWART, CHARLES. Crawford's solicitor. Brother to Mrs. Rogerson.

STEWART, MR. Lodger at 32, Earls Court Gardens.

TALBOT, ALBERT. Mrs. Rogerson's footman.

THOMAS, HOWEL. Member of Dilke's investigation committee.

THOMAS, JOHN. Friend of Mrs. Harvey, keeper of 9, Hill Street.

THOMAS, MRS. SARAH ANNE. Wife of John Thomas.

THOMPSON, H. F. Junior counsel for Mrs. Crawford in the second trial.

THORPE, MRS. ANNE, Landlady at 14, Grafton Street, where Fanny Gray lodged for a time.

TUCKWELL, MISS GERTRUDE. Lady Dilke's niece.

WARNER, DR. FREDERICK. Suggested lover of Mrs.

Crawford.

WILLIAMS, GEORGE. Artist friend of Fanny Gray.

WILLIAMS, MR. AND MRS. Lodgers at 65, Warren Street.

WRIGHT, R. S. Junior counsel for Crawford in both trials.

Appendix II

List of Addresses in the Case

76, Shane Street, S.W.	Dilke's house.
9, Hyde Park Gate, S.W.	Mrs. Ashton Dilke's house.
40, Princes Gardens, S. W.	Chamberlain's house,
3, Sydney Place, S.W.	The Crawfords' lodgings in 1882.
27, Toung Street, Kensington, W.	The Crawfords' lodgings from February to August, 1883 and in 1884.
61, Sloane Street, S.W.	The Crawfords' lodgings in the autumn, 1884.
2, Upper George Street, Bryanston Square, W.	The Crawfords' lodgings in 1885.
73, Cromwell Road, S.W.	Mrs. Harrison's house.
52, Princes Gate, S.W.	Mrs. Eustace Smith's house.

13, Hans Place, S.W.	Mrs. Rogerson's house until April, 1885.
Albert Mansions, Victoria Street, S.W	Mrs. Rogerson's flat after April, 1885.
32, Earls Court Gardens, S.W.	House where Captain Forster lodged.
28, Earls Court Gardens, S.W.	House where Captain Forster lodged.
9, Hill Street, Knightsbridge, S.W.	House of assignation.
65, Warren Street, W.	Lodging-house where Mrs. Dessouslavy lived.
14, Grafton Street, Fitzroy Square, W.	Lodging-house where Fanny Gray stayed.

References

[D.P. is an abbreviation for Dilke Papers]

CHAPTER I

1. D.P. 43902, 18.
2. D.P. 43930, 57.
3. D.P. 43930, 59.
4. D.P. 43930, 50.
5. D.P. 43930, 50.
6. *Papers of a Critic*, a selection Mr. Dilke's essays, with a memoir by Sir Charles Dilke, p. 31.
7. D.P. 43930, 91.
8. D.P. 43930, 82.
9. Gwynn & Tuckwell, *The Life of Sir Charles W. Dilke*, I, p. 15.
10. D.P. 43930, 67.
11. D.P. 43930, 69.
12. D.P. 43930, 84.
13. D.P. 43930, 106.
14. D.P. 43900, 9.
15. D.P. 43899, 114.

16. D.P. 43899, 130.

17. D.P. 43900, 38.

18. D.P. 43930, 160.

19. D.P. 43930, 149.

20. D.P. 43930, 152.

CHAPTER II

1. C. W. Dilke, *Greater Britain*, p. 41.

2. D.P. 43930.

3. Dilke, op. cit., p. 19.

4. *Ibid.*, p. 233.

5. *Ibid.*, p. 233.

6. *Ibid.*, p. 230.

7. *Ibid.*, p. 34.

8. D.P. 43930, 186.

9. Dilke, *op. cit.*, pp. 38–9.

10. D.P. 43902, 35.

11. D.P. 43902, 216.

12. Dilke, *op. cit.*, p. 136.

13. *Ibid.*, p. 432.

14. *Ibid.*, p. 572.

15. D.P. 43897, 2.

16. D.P. 43931 13.

17. D.P. 43897, 27.

18. D.P. 43931, 1.

19. D.P. 43901, 134–5.

20. D.P. 43900, 85.

21. D.P. 43901, 216.

CHAPTER III

1. Morley, *Life of Gladstone*, II, P. 255.
2. Gwynn & Tuckwell, *The Life of Sir Charles W. Dilke*, I, p. 80.
3. *Ibid*, I, p. 84.
4. Sir Charles Dilke, *The Fall of Prince Florestan of Monaco*, p. 11.
5. D.P. 43901, 144.
6. J. L. Garvin, *Life of Joseph Chamberlain,*' I, p. 94.
7. D.P. 43890, 2.
8. Garvin, *op. cit.*, I, p. 122.
9. D.P. 43885, 10 and 15.
10. Gwynn & Tuckwell, *op. cit.*, I, p. 104.
11. D.P. 43931, 76.
12. D.P. 43931, 79–81.
13. D.P. 43931, 121.
14. D.P. 43931, 126.
15. D.P. 43931, 138.
16. D.P. 43931, 142.
17. D.P. 43931, 148–51.

CHAPTER IV

1. D.P. 43931, 194.
2. D.P. 43931, 193.
3. Philip Magnus, *Gladstone*, p. 212.
4. *Ibid.*, p. 207.
5. *The Times*, November 9th, 1871.
6. *Ibid.*
7. *Ibid.*
8. D.P. 43931, 178.
9. D.P. 43885, 24.

10. Sir Sidney Lee, *King Edward VII*, I, p. 329.

11. D.P. 43931, 184.

12. Gwynn & Tuckwell, *The Life of Sir Charles W. Dilke*, I, p. 142.

13. D.P. 43931, 185.

14. D.P. 43909, 193.

15. D.P. 43931, 185.

16. J. L. Garvin, *Life of Joseph Chamberlain*, I, p. 153.

17. D.P. 43931, 187.

18. D.P. 43931, 274.

19. D.P. 43931, 212.

20. D.P. 43931, 216.

21. D.P. 43931, 176.

22. D.P. 43931, 205–6.

23. D.P. 43931, 209.

24. D.P. 43931, 206–7.

25. D.P. 43931, 201–8.

26. D.P. 43931, 226–7.

27. D.P. 43931, 243.

28. D.P. 43909, 344.

29. Sir Charles Dilke, *The Fall of Prince Florestan of Monaco*, p. 78.

30. *Ibid.*, p. 11.

31. D.P. 43948, 50.

32. Gwynn & Tuckwell, *op. cit.*, I, p. 177.

33. D.P. 43932, 68.

34. Gwynn & Tuckwell, *op. cit.*, I, pp. 170—1.

CHAPTER V

1. D.P. 43932, 80–4.

2. D.P. 43932, 93.

3. D.P. 43932, 129–30.

4. D.P. 43890, 76.

5. Gwynn & Tuckwell, *The Life of Sir Charles W. Dilke*, II, p. 229.

6. D.P. 43932, 162–3.

7. D.P. 43933, 14–5.

8. D.P. 43933, 10.

9. D.P. 43890, 90.

10. Gwynn & Tuckwell, *op. cit.*, 1, 237.

11. D.P. 43933, 125.

12. Philip Magnus, *Gladstone*, p. 247.

13. D.P. 43933, 194.

14. D.P. 43933, 211–3.

15. D.P. 43932, 244–5.

16. Gwynn & Tuckwell, *op. cit.*, I, p. 168.

17. D.P. 43904, 12.

18. D.P. 43932, 221–2.

19. D.P. 43933, 192–3.

20. D.P. 43933, 185.

21. D.P. 43934, 88.

22. D.P. 43932, 245–6.

23. D.P, 43933, 12.

24. D.P. 43934, 91.

25. D.P. 43934, 15.

26. D.P. 43933, 181.

27. D.P. 43934, 36.

28. D.P. 43934, 32.

29. D.P. 43934, 192.

30. D.P. 43903, 265.

31. D.P. 43932, 217–8.

32. D.P. 43904, 15.

33. D.P. 43904, 92.

34. D.P. 43903, 195.

35. D.P. 49426, 47.

36. D.P. 43903, 186.

37. D.P. 43934, 27.

38. D.P. 43934, 83–6.

39. D.P. 43934, 107.

CHAPTER VI

1. D.P. 43885, 66.

2. D.P. 43934, 131.

3. D.P. 43885, 68–9.

4. J. L. Garvin, *Life of Joseph Chamberlain*, I, pp. 292–3.

5. D.P. 43934, 138.

6. D.P. 43885, 70.

7. D.P. 43885, 74–5.

8. Garvin, *op. cit.*, I, 298.

9. D.P. 43934, 149.

10. Garvin, *op. cit.*, I, p. 301.

11. Joseph Chamberlain, *A Political Memoir*, p. 3.

12. D.P. 43885, 312.

13. D.P. 43905, 63.

14. D.P. 43924, 45.

15. D.P. 43925, 34.

16. D.P. 43885, 160.

17. D.P. 43885, 283.

18. D.P. 43925, 3.

19. D.P. 43880, 167.

20. D.P. 43935, 9.

21. D.P. 43934, 198–9.

22. D.P. 43934, 182–3.

23. D.P. 43895, 156.

24. D.P. 43934, 150.

25. D.P. 43879, 172.

26. Sir Sidney Lee, *King Edward VII*, I, p. 518.

27. D.P. 43874, 40.

28. D.P. 43874, 35.

29. D.P. 43936, 273.

30. D.P. 43924, 55.

31. D.P. 43905, 241.

32. Gwynn & Tuckwell, *The Life of Sir Charles W. Dilke*, I, 414.

33. D.P. 43925, 64.

34. D.P. 43905, 123 and 138.

35. D.P. 43905, 110.

36. D.P. 43924, 77.

CHAPTER VII

1. D.P. 43904, 113.

2. D.P. 43904, 182.

3. D.P. 43924, 32.

4. D.P. 43885, 234.

5. D.P. 43936, 97.

6. D.P. 43936, 92.

7. D.P. 43936, 101.

8. D.P. 43885, 234.

9. D.P. 43885, 237.

10. D.P. 43936, 103–6.

11. D.P. 43905, 123.

12. D.P. 43894, 78.

13. D.P. 43925, 28.

14. Philip Magnus, *Gladstone*, p. 290.

15. Lord Acton, *Letters*, p. 90.

16. D.P. 43885, 295.

17. Sir Sidney Lee, *King Edward VII*, I, p . 519.

18. D.P. 43885, 297.

19. D.P. 43885, 302.

20. D.P. 43874, 52.

21. D.P. 43874, 53–4.

22. D.P. 43905, 171.

23. D.P. 43875, 122.

24. Gwynn & Tuckwell, *Life of Sir Charles W. Dilke*, I, p. 495.

CHAPTER VIII

1. D.P. 43925, 43.

2. D.P. 43937, 21.

3. D.P. 43937, 24.

4. D.P. 43886, 30.

5. D.P. 43925, 47.

6. D.P. 43925, 68.

7. D.P. 43925, 59.

8. D.P. 43942, 60.

9. D.P. 43926, 20.

10. D.P. 43939, 19.

11. D.P. 43926, 30.

12. D.P. 43925, 7.

13. D.P. 43885, 304.

14. D.P. 43925, 27.

15. D.P. 43902, 125 and 127.

16. D.P. 43902, 124 and 126.

17. D.P. 43905, 239.

18. D.P. 43938, 159.

19. *Letters of Queen Victoria;* Second Series, III, p. 452.

20. D.P. 43890, 78.

21. D.P. 43938, 144.

22. D.P. 43942, 76.

23. D.P. 43938, 61.

24. D.P. 43886, 149.

25. D.P. 43882, 119.

26. D.P. 43942, 67.

27. D.P. 43925, 78.

28. D.P. 43942, 69.

29. D.P. 43881, 150.

30. D.P. 43942, 73.

31. D.P. 43925, 82.

32. D.P. 43925, 82.

33. D.P. 43938, 78.

34. D.P. 43942, 86.

35. D.P. 43886, 190.

36. D.P. 43938, 90.

37. D.P. 43938, 76.

38. D.P. 43926, 30.

39. Philip Magnus, *Gladstone*, 321.

40. D.P. 43894, 172.

CHAPTER IX

1. Gwynn & Tuckwell, *The Life of Sir Charles W. Dilke*, II, p. 63.

2. *Letters of Queen Victoria*; Second Series, II, p . 253.

3. D.P. 43891, 264.

4. D.P. 43938, 320.

5. D.P. 43938, 325.

6. D.P. 43938, 328.

7. Philip Magnus, *Gladstone*, p. 319.

8. Gwynn & Tuckwell, *op. cit.*, II, p. 79.

9. J. L. Garvin, *Life of Joseph Chamberlain*, I, p. 483.

10. D.P. 43893, 6.

11. D.P. 43893, 25.

12. D.P. 43907, 226.

13. D.P. 43906, 23.

14. D.P. 43906, 39.

15. D.P. 43906, 87.

16. Garvin, *op, cit.*, I, p. 584.

17. D.P. 43894, 178.

18. D.P. 43942, 113.

19. D.P. 43896, 83.

20. D.P. 43907, 232.

21. D.P. 43896, 84.

22. D.P. 43939, 168–71.

23. D.P. 43906, 77.

CHAPTER X

1. Gwynn & Tuckwell, *The Life of Sir Charles W. Dilke*, II, p. 152.

2. D.P. 43894, 184.

3. D.P. 43938, 19.

4. D.P. 43940, 22.

5. D.P. 43939, 198.

6. Conor Cruise O'Brien, *Parnell and His Party*, p. 100.

7. *Ibid.*, p. 100.

8. D.P. 43906, 106.

CHAPTER XI

1. *The Times*, February 19th, 1870, also quoted by V. Cowles,

Edward VII and His Circle, p. 85.

2. D.P. 49611.

3. D.P. 43906, 109.

4. D.P. 43906, 113.

5. D.P. 43927, 5.

6. D.P. 49610.

7. D.P. 43881, 221.

8. D.P. 43881, 222.

9. D.P. 49610.

10. D.P. 49611.

11. D.P. 43874, 70.

12. D.P. 43876, 151.

13. D.P. 43875, 271.

14. D.P. 43906, 130.

15. D.P. 43906, 126.

16. D.P. 49612.

17. D.P. 43887, 207.

18. D.P. 43887, 227.

19. *The Times*, 7th October, 1885.

20. D.P. 43940, 88.

21. D.P. 43940, 101.

22. D.P. 49610.

23. D.P. 43927, 25.

24. D.P. 49610.

25. D.P. 43888, 6–7.

CHAPTER XII

1. *The Times*, February 13th, 1886.

2. J. L. Garvin, *Life of Joseph Chamberlain*, II, pp. 47–9.

3. *The Times*, February 13th, 1886.

4. D.P. 43927, 26.

5. D.P. 43940, 115.

6. J. W. Robertson Scott, *The Life and Death of a Newspaper*, p. 180.

7. *Ibid.*, p. 125n.

8. D.P. 43888, 17.

9. D.P. 43888, 18.

10. D.P. 43940, 121.

11. D.P. 43940, 123.

12. D.P. 49610.

13. D.P. 49611.

14. D.P. 43940, 144.

15. D.P. 43940, 136.

16. D.P. 49610.

17. D.P. 43940, 144.

18. 1886 55 L.T., 305.

19. D.P. 43927, 26.

20. D.P. 43888, 42.

21. D.P. 43888, 43.

22. Gwynn & Tuckwell, *The Life of Sir Charles W. Dilke*, II, p . 216.

23. D.P. 43888, 45–6.

24. Gwynn & Tuckwell, *op. cit.*, II, 219–20.

25. D.P. 43888, 50.

26. D.P. 43888, 67.

27. D.P. 43940, 151.

28. D.P. 43940, 151.

29. D.P. 43940, 154.

CHAPTER XV

1. D.P. 49610.

2. D.P. 49610.

3. D.P. 49610.

4. Gwynn & Tuckwell, *The Life of Sir Charles W. Dilke, II*, p. 244.

5. D.P. 43888, 100.

6. D.P. 49447,29.

7. D.P. 49446, 106.

8. D.P. 49447.

9. D.P. 49447.

10. D.P. 49447.

11. D.P. 49453, 122.

12. D.P. 49452, 179.

13. D.P. 49452, 185.

14. D.P. 43907, 287.

15. D.P. 49455, 254.7.

16. D.P. 49612.

17. D.P. 49446, 180.

18. D.P. 49447.

19. D.P. 46910.

20. D.P. 49454, 22.

21. D.P. 49610.

22. D.P. 49610.

23. D.P. 49610.

24. D.P. 49454, 4.

25. D.P. 49454, 4.

26. D.P. 49610.

27. D.P. 49454, 33.

28. D.P. 49612.

29. D.P. 49611.

CHAPTER XVI

1. D.P. 43907, 305.
2. D.P. 49610.
3. D.P. 43908, 186.
4. D.P. 43967, 288.
5. D.P. 43967, 231.

CHAPTER XVII

1. D.P. 43941, 135–9.
2. D.P. 43889, 34.
3. D.P. 43875, 276–8.
4. Sir Charles Dilke, *A Radical Programme*, p. 53.
5. *Ibid.*, p. 54.
6. *Ibid.*, p . 55.
7. *Gladstone Papers*, DCLXXXVIII, 218.
8. D.P. 43889, 62.
9. D.P. 43889, 82–3.
10. D.P. 43889, 52.

CHAPTER XVIII

1. D.P. 43941, 271.
2. D.P. 43927, 34.
3. D.P. 43889, 71.
4. D.P. 43889, 30.
5. D.P. 43889, 116.
6. D.P. 43889, 119.
7. D.P. 43889, 131.
8. Emrys Hughes, *Keir Hardie*, p. 66.

9. Gwynn & Tuckwell, *The Life of Sir Charles W. Dilke*, II, p. 367.

10. *Ibid.*, II, pp. 378–9.

11. D.P. 43919, 258.

12. *Hansard*, February 1st, 1900.

13. Gwynn & Tuckwell, *op. cit.*, II p. 374.

14. *Hansard*: June 10th, 1898.

15. *Hansard*: December 19th, 1893.

16. D.P. 43875, 297.

17. D.P. 43941, 277–8.

18. D.P. 43916, 14.

19. D.P. 43916, 94.

20. Gwynn & Tuckwell, *op. cit.*, II, p. 423.

21. D.P. 43915, 258.

22. D.P. 43874, 73.

CHAPTER XIX

1. D.P. 43957, 104.

2. D.P. 43941, 317.

3. Gwynn & Tuckwell, *The Life of Sir Charles W. Dilke*, II, p. 460.

4. D.P. 43895, 259–60.

5. D.P. 43918, 138.

6. D.P. 43882, 140.

7. D.P. 43892, 242–4.

8. D.P. 43941, 326.

9. Article in *Financial Review of Reviews*, April, 1906.

10. D.P. 43892, 244.

11. Gwynn & Tuckwell, *op. cit.*, II, p. 518.

12. D.P. 43967, 2.

A NOTE ON THE AUTHOR

Elected to Parliament as a Labour member in 1948, Roy Jenkins (B: 1920) served in several major posts in Harold Wilson's First Government and as Home Secretary from 1965–1967. In 1987, Jenkins was elected to succeed Harold Macmillan as Chancellor of the University of Oxford following the latter's death, a position he held until his own death in 2003. Jenkins grew to political maturity during the twilight of a great age of British parliamentary democracy. As much as Churchill, though in quite a different way, Jenkins was from the cradle a creature of the system that nurtured Palmerston and Disraeli, Gladstone, Asquith and Lloyd George.

Made in the USA
Lexington, KY
25 November 2013